Communications
in Computer and Information Science   485

T0215007

Gonzalo Hernández
Carlos Jaime Barrios Hernández
Gilberto Díaz   Carlos García Garino
Sergio Nesmachnow   Tomás Pérez-Acle
Mario Storti   Mariano Vázquez (Eds.)

High Performance Computing

First HPCLATAM - CLCAR
Latin American Joint Conference, CARLA 2014
Valparaiso, Chile, October 20-22, 2014
Proceedings

 Springer

Volume Editors

Gonzalo Hernández
Universidad Santa María, Valparaíso, Chile
E-mail: carla2014@hpclatam.org

Carlos Jaime Barrios Hernández
Universidad Industrial de Santander, Bucaramanga, Columbia
E-mail: cbarrios@uis.edu.co

Gilberto Díaz
Universidad Industrial de Santander, Bucaramanga, Colombia
E-mail: gjdiazt@uis.edu.co

Carlos García Garino
Universidad Nacional de Cuyo, Mendoza, Argentina
E-mail: cgarcia@itu.uncu.edu.ar

Sergio Nesmachnow
Universidad de la República, Montevideo, Uruguay
E-mail: sergion@fing.edu.uy

Tomás Pérez-Acle
Fundación Ciencia y Vida and Universidad de Valparaíso, Chile
E-mail: tomas@dlab.cl

Mario Storti
CIMEC, Santa Fe, Argentina
E-mail: mario.storti@gmail.com

Mariano Vázquez
Barcelona Supercomputing Center, Spain
E-mail: mariano.vazquez@bsc.es

ISSN 1865-0929   e-ISSN 1865-0937
ISBN 978-3-662-45482-4   e-ISBN 978-3-662-45483-1
DOI 10.1007/978-3-662-45483-1
Springer Heidelberg New York Dordrecht London

Library of Congress Control Number: 2014954138

Typesetting: Camera-ready by author, data conversion by Scientific Publishing Services, Chennai, India
Printed on acid-free paper
Springer is part of Springer Science+Business Media (www.springer.com)

Preface

In 2014, both major Latin American HPC Workshops (HPC Latam and CLCAR) joined to form CARLA 2014, which was held in the Universidad Santa María in Valparaíso, Chile. This conference also included the Third HPC School – ECAR 2014. Both events were organized by the following institutions:

- Valparaíso Center for Science and Technology (CCTVal), Universidad Técnica Federico Santa María
- National Laboratory for High Performance Computing (NLHPC), Universidad de Chile

The main goal of the CARLA 2014 conference was to provide a regional forum fostering the growth of the HPC community in Latin America through the exchange and dissemination of new ideas, techniques, and research in HPC. The conference featured invited talks from academy and industry, short- and full-paper sessions presenting both mature work and new ideas in research and industrial applications. The suggested topics of interest of the conference included:

- Big data management and visualizations
- GPU computing
- Grid and cloud computing
- High-performance computing applications
- Parallel algorithms and techniques
- Parallel computing architectures and technologies
- Scientific computing applications and methods
- Tools and environments for high-performance computing

I would like to thank the organizing institutions (CCTVAl and NLHPC), sponsors (Intel, NVidia, Seagate, Siasa), and everyone who helped in the organization and realization of CARLA: the co-chairs, track chairs, members of the Program Committee, keynotes, lecturers, and administrative staff.

October 2014

Gonzalo Hernández
General Chair CARLA 2014

Organization

Organizing Committee

General Chair

Gonzalo Hernández — Universidad Santa María, Chile

Co-chairs

Carlos Jaime Barrios — Universidad Industrial de Santander, Colombia
Tomás Pérez-Acle — Universidad de Chile, Chile
Claudio Torres — Universidad Técnica Federico Santa María, Chile
Mariano Vázquez — Barcelona Supercomputing Center, Spain

Track Chairs

HPC Architectures and Tools

Esteban Mocskos — Universidad de Buenos Aires, Argentina
Adrián Cristal — Barcelona Supercomputing Center, Spain

Parallel Programming

Sergio Nesmachnow — Universidad de la República, Uruguay
Gilberto Díaz — Universidad Industrial de Santander, Colombia

GPU Computing

Nicolás Wolowick — Universidad Nacional de Córdoba, Argentina
Carlos Jaime Barrios — Universidad Industrial de Santander, Colombia

Grid and Cloud Computing

Carlos García Garino — Universidad Nacional de Cuyo, Argentina
Alejandro Zunino — Universidad Nacional del Centro de Buenos Aires and CONICET, Argentina

Scientific Computing

Mario Storti — Universidad Nacional del Litoral, Argentina
Mariano Vásquez — Supercomputing Center, Spain

Technical Program Committee

Andrés Avila — Universidad de la Frontera, Chile
Lola Bautista — Universidad Industrial de Santander, Colombia

Carlos Bederián	Universidad Nacional de Córdoba, Argentina
Francisco Brazileiro	Universidade Federal de Campinha Grande, Brazil
Carlos Buil Aranda	Pontificia Universidad Católica de Chile, Chile
Leticia Cagnina	Universidad Nacional de San Luis, Argentina
Víctor Calo	King Abdullah University of Science and Technology (KAUST), Saudi Arabia
Néstor Calvo	CIMEC, Argentina
Luis Fernando Castillo	Universidad de Caldas, Colombia
Harold Castro	Universidad de los Andes, Colombia
Marcio Castro	Inria, France
Carlos Catania	Universidad Nacional de Cuyo, Argentina
Andrea Charao	Universidad Federal Santa María, Brazil
Flavio Colavecchia	Centro Atómico de Bariloche, Argentina
Daniel Cordeiro	Universidade de Sao Paulo, Brazil
Alvaro Coutinho	Universidade Federal do Rio de Janeiro, Brazil
Stefano Cozzini	Democritos, ICTP, Italy
Fernando Crespo	Universidad Bernardo O'Higgins, Chile
Marcela Cruchaga	Universidad de Santiago de Chile, Chile
Fernando Cucchietti	Barcelona Supercomputing Center, Spain
Gregoire Danoy	Universidad de Luxemburgo, Luxembourg
Claudio Delrieux	Universidad Nacional del Sur, Argentina
César Díaz	Instituto Potosino de Investigación en Ciencia y Tecnológica, Mexico
Bernabé Dorronsoro	University of Lille 1, France
Nicolás Erdody	Multicore World Conference Organiser, New Zealand
Pablo Ezzatti	Universidad de la República, Uruguay
Ruslan Gabassov	Universidad Nacional Autónoma de México, Mexico
Verónica Gil Costa	Universidad Nacional San Luis, Argentina
Isidoro Gitler	Cinvestav - IPN, Mexico
Brice Goglin	Inria Bordeaux, France
Antonio Gomes	Laboratorio Nacional de Computacional Científica, Brazil
José Luis Gordillo	Universidad Nacional Autónoma de México, Mexico
Guillaume Houzeaux	Barcelona Supercomputing Center, Spain
Roberto Isoardi	Fundación Escuela de Medicina Nuclear, Argentina
Jaime Klapp	Instituto Nacional Investigación Nucleares, Mexico
Alejandro Kolton	Centro Atómico de Bariloche, Argentina
Roberto León	Universidad Nacional Andrés Bello, Chile
Francisco Luna	Universidad Carlos III de Madrid, Spain

Luiz Angelo Steffenel	University of Reims, France
Andrei Tchernykh	Centro Investigación Científica y Educación Superior, Mexico
Fernando Tinetti	Universidad Nacional de La Plata, Argentina
Patricia Tissera	Universidad Nacional Andrés Bello, Chile
Tram Truong Huu	National University of Singapore, Singapore
Manuel Ujaldón	Universidad de Málaga, Spain
Grabiel Usera	Universidad de la República, Uruguay
Carlos A. Varela	Rensselaer Polytechnic Institute, USA
José Luis Vazquez-Poletti	Universidad Complutense de Madrid, Spain
Pedro Velho	Universidad Federal de Rio Grande do Sul, Brazil
Jesús Verduzco	Instituto Tecnológico de Colima, Colombia
Paula Villar	Universidad de Buenos Aires, Argentina
Gustavo Wolfmann	Universidad Nacional de Córdoba, Argentina

Organizing Institutions

- Valparaíso Center for Science and Technology (CCTVal), Universidad Técnica Federico Santa María
- National Laboratory for High Performance Computing (NLHPC), Universidad de Chile

Sponsors

- Intel
- NVidia
- Seagate
- Siasa

Table of Contents

Track: HPC Architectures and Tools

Track: Parallel Programming

Track: Scientific Computing

Efficient Symmetric Band Matrix-Matrix Multiplication on GPUs

Ernesto Dufrechou[2], Pablo Ezzatti[2], Enrique S. Quintana-Ortí[3],
and Alfredo Remón[1]

[1] Max Planck Institute for Dynamics of Complex Technical Systems,
Magdeburg, Germany
remon@mpi-magdeburg.mpg.de
[2] Instituto de Computación, Universidad de la República,
11.300–Montevideo, Uruguay
{edufrechou,pezzatti}@fing.edu.uy
[3] Dep. de Ingeniería y Ciencia de la Computación, Universidad Jaime I,
12.071–Castellón, Spain
quintana@icc.uji.es

Abstract. Matrix-matrix multiplication is an important linear algebra operation with a myriad of applications in scientific and engineering computing. Due to the relevance and inner parallelism of this operation, there exist many high performance implementations for a variety of hardware platforms. Exploit the structure of the matrices involved in the operation in general provides relevant time and memory savings. This is the case, e.g., when one of the matrices is a symmetric band matrix. This work presents two efficient specialized implementations of the operation when a symmetric band matrix is involved and the target architecture contains a graphics processor (GPU). In particular, both implementations exploit the structure of the matrices to leverage the vast parallelism of the underlying hardware. The experimental results show remarkable reductions in the computation time over the tuned implementations of the same operation provided by MKL and CUBLAS.

1 Introduction

The matrix product

$$C := \alpha AB + \beta C, \tag{1}$$

where $C \in \mathbb{R}^{m \times n}$, $A \in \mathbb{R}^{m \times k}$, $B \in \mathbb{R}^{k \times n}$, and both α, β are scalars is a common and well-known kernel in numerical linear algebra [6]. This operation exhibits a high level of concurrency and there exist highly tuned implementations available for most high performance computing (HPC) hardware architectures.

In this work we address the special case of the matrix-matrix product (1) when matrix A presents a symmetric band structure (and, therefore, $m = k$), meaning that all the nonzero elements of A are placed in a small set of super- and sub-diagonals adjacent to the main diagonal. Exploiting the structure of

G. Hernández et al. (Eds.): CARLA 2014, CCIS 485, pp. 1–12, 2014.

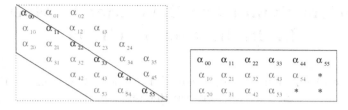

Fig. 1. 6×6 symmetric and matrix with bandwidth $k = 2$ (left); packed storage scheme used in BLAS and LAPACK (right)

A yields a large reduction in the number of computations and in memory requirements. In particular, due to the symmetry of A, only its lower/upper part needs to be stored. Additionally, due to its band structure, the null elements that lie out of the band do not need to be kept. The number of arithmetic operations may also be reduced as all the computations involving null elements are not necessary. Band matrices present also favorable differences when compared with unstructured sparse matrices. Specifically, storage formats for unstructured sparse matrices are complex, as the position of each nonzero must also be stored, but for band matrices the data layout can be simplified because the structure of the nonzeros is regular and, consequently, it is not necessary to maintain the coordinates of each element of the matrix. Additionally, the memory accesses can be performed with a regular and predictable pattern.

The positive properties of symmetric band matrices, and the availability of reordering techniques (e.g. the RCM method [3]) to transform symmetric sparse matrices, in some cases, into symmetric narrow-band matrices has motivated the exploitation of these favourable properties in several engineering applications, including real optimization, numerical solution of partial differential equations, and control theory problems; see, among others, [5,2].

The advantages of exploiting the structure of symmetric band matrices motivated the inclusion of specific routines in BLAS and LAPACK [1]. The BLAS specification defines a compact storage format for symmetric band matrices (see Figure 1) that is a trade-off between minimal storage and optimal access pattern to the matrix elements. In particular, the symmetric band storage format stores $(k+1) \times m$ elements, where k represents the number of nonzero super- and subdiagonals, and m is the number of rows and columns of the matrix. Only a few null elements are stored (marked in Figure 1 with the symbol "$*$"). However, the main feature of this storage format is that it permits a memory access pattern very convenient for today's cache-based architectures.

The support of BLAS for symmetric band matrices comprises a small set of routines that implement some key linear algebra operations. This is the case for routine SBMV, which computes a matrix-vector product where the matrix presents a symmetric band structure. Similarly, LAPACK gives support to some operations with band matrices; e.g., matrix factorizations and linear system solvers [4].

The main contribution of this paper is the introduction and evaluation of two new GPU-based routines for the symmetric band matrix multiplication (SBMM) that leverage the vast hardware parallelism of GPUs and the high data-parallelism of this operation to significantly accelerate its computation. In particular, the experimental results for the accelerator-enabled codes collected on an NVIDIA C2050 GPU and two INTEL E5520 quad-processor, demonstrate superior performance and scalability over a multithreaded CPU variant using the INTEL MKL (Math Kernel Library) and a GPU version based on CUBLAS.

The rest of the paper is structured as follows. In Section 2, we describe the routines related to band matrix multiplication available in BLAS. Then, in Section 3, we introduce a modified algorithm for the operation where most of the computations are cast in terms of BLAS-3 kernels. We describe the two new GPU-based versions that implement the aforementioned algorithm in Section 4. We present experimental results in Section 5 and, finally, we discuss some conclusions and future work in Section 6.

2 The Operation in BLAS

The BLAS specification provides support to perform computations with symmetric band matrices. In particular, it includes a specific kernel called SBMV to perform a matrix-vector product where the matrix is symmetric and banded. In contrast, BLAS does not offer the equivalent kernel for the matrix-matrix product operation when one of the matrices presents a band structure. This matrix-matrix product can be easily implemented on top of SBMV routine. Concretely, we can partition matrix B columnwise, and perform a matrix-vector product with each column of B. This procedure can be written as:

$$C_i = \alpha A B_i + \beta C_i, \tag{2}$$

where C_i, B_i stand for the i-th columns of B and C respectively, and $1 \le i \le n$.

Although this simple approach allows us the use of BLAS kernels to execute the complete operation, it is based on a level-2 BLAS routine, while the product of matrices is a level-3 BLAS operation. Thus, with this implementation the underlying architecture can not be efficiently exploited. In particular, each element of matrix A is accessed n times resulting in a suboptimal usage of the memory hierarchy.

3 Algorithm SBMM$_{BLK}$

Block-wise algorithms for linear algebra computations can efficiently leverage the memory hierarchy of current parallel computing architectures, resulting in higher performances. In this context, we propose a blocked algorithm to perform the matrix-matrix product when matrix A presents a symmetric band structure, which is presented in Figures 2 and 3. Note that it only accesses the elements in the lower triangular part of matrix A, in order to support the use of the packed

---

Algorithm: $[C] := \text{SBMM}_{BLK\_outer}(C, A, B, k)$

  Partition $\quad C \to \left(C_L \mid C_R \right), \; B \to \left(B_L \mid B_R \right)$
    where C_L, B_L have 0 columns

while $n(C_L) < n(C)$ **do**
    Determine block size c
    Repartition

$$\left(C_L \mid C_R \right) \to \left(C_0 \mid C_1 \mid C_2 \right), \; \left(B_L \mid B_R \right) \to \left(B_0 \mid B_1 \mid B_2 \right)$$
      where C_1, B_1 have c columns

$C_1 := \text{SBMM}_{BLK\_inner}(C_1, A, B_1, k)$

  Continue with

$$\left(C_L \mid C_R \right) \leftarrow \left(C_0 \mid C_1 \mid C_2 \right), \; \left(B_L \mid B_R \right) \leftarrow \left(B_0 \mid B_1 \mid B_2 \right)$$
endwhile

Fig. 2. Outer loop of Algorithm SBMM_{BLK} that computes $C := A \cdot B + C$

storage format. An analogous procedure that accesses the elements in the upper triangle or all the elements of A is straight-forward.

The algorithm consists of two loops. The outer loop (Figure 2) partitions matrices B and C into blocks of c columns; at every iteration of the loop, the elements in the active column-block of C are updated. The inner loop (Figure 3) proceeds along the main diagonal of A (top-left to down-right), updating the corresponding elements of C. Matrices B and C are partitioned row-wise, while matrix A requires a 3×3 partition. At each iteration, blocks A_{i1} and B_i with $i = 1, 2, 3$, are accessed; while block C_i where $i = 1, 2, 3$, is updated. Note that A_{11} and A_{31} are respectively, lower and upper triangular. Figure 4 details the blocks accessed and updated at a given iteration of the inner loop.

The execution of Algorithm SBMM_{BLK} can be adapted to the underlying architecture and problem by carefully choosing parameters c and b. Parameter c defines the number of columns of C computed at a given iteration of the outer loop, while b corresponds to the number of columns of A that are accessed at each iteration of the inner loop. The optimal values for c and b strongly depends on the memory organisation of the target architecture. For example, in current multicore processors, $b = 32$ is usually a convenient choice, while for GPUs larger values are recommended (e.g. $b = 128$).

4   Implementations

We next present three routines to compute the symmetric band matrix-matrix product on a CPU-GPU system. All the implementations intensively invoke kernels from CUBLAS.

Algorithm: $[E] := \text{SBMM}_{BLK\_inner}(E, A, D, k)$

Partition $E \to \left(\dfrac{E_T}{\dfrac{E_M}{E_B}}\right)$, $A \to \left(\begin{array}{c|c} A_{TL} & \\ \hline A_{ML} & A_{MR} \\ \hline & A_{BR} \end{array}\right)$, $D \to \left(\dfrac{D_T}{\dfrac{D_M}{D_B}}\right)$

    where E_T, D_T have 0 elements; A_{TL} is 0×0 and E_M, A_{ML} have k rows

while $m(E_T) < m(E)$ **do**

    Determine block size b

    Repartition

$$\left(\dfrac{E_T}{\dfrac{E_M}{E_B}}\right) \to \left(\dfrac{E_0}{\dfrac{E_1}{\dfrac{E_2}{\dfrac{E_3}{E_4}}}}\right), \left(\begin{array}{c|c} A_{TL} & \\ \hline A_{ML} & A_{MR} \\ \hline & A_{BR} \end{array}\right) \to \left(\begin{array}{c|c|c} A_{00} & & \\ \hline A_{10} & A_{11} & \\ \hline A_{20} & A_{21} & A_{22} \\ \hline & A_{31} & A_{32} \\ \hline & & A_{42} \end{array}\right), \left(\dfrac{D_T}{\dfrac{D_M}{D_B}}\right) \to \left(\dfrac{D_0}{\dfrac{D_1}{\dfrac{D_2}{\dfrac{D_3}{D_4}}}}\right)$$

    where D_1 has b rows;

               E_1 has b rows;

               E_3 has 0 rows if $m(D_0) > (n(A) - k - 1)$ and has b rows otherwise;

               A_{11} is $b \times b$;

               A_{31} is empty if $m(D_0) > (n(A) - k - 1)$ and is $b \times b$ otherwise

---

    $E_1 := E_1 + A_{11} \cdot D_1$

    $E_1 := E_1 + A_{21}^T \cdot D_2$

    $E_1 := E_1 + A_{31}^T \cdot D_3$

    $E_2 := E_2 + A_{21} \cdot D_1$

    $E_3 := E_3 + A_{31} \cdot D_1$

    Continue with

$$\left(\dfrac{E_T}{\dfrac{E_M}{E_B}}\right) \leftarrow \left(\dfrac{E_0}{\dfrac{E_1}{\dfrac{E_2}{\dfrac{E_3}{E_4}}}}\right), \left(\begin{array}{c|c} A_{TL} & \\ \hline A_{ML} & A_{MR} \\ \hline & A_{BR} \end{array}\right) \leftarrow \left(\begin{array}{c|c|c} A_{00} & & \\ \hline A_{10} & A_{11} & \\ \hline A_{20} & A_{21} & A_{22} \\ \hline & A_{31} & A_{32} \\ \hline & & A_{42} \end{array}\right), \left(\dfrac{D_T}{\dfrac{D_M}{D_B}}\right) \leftarrow \left(\dfrac{D_0}{\dfrac{D_1}{\dfrac{D_2}{\dfrac{D_3}{D_4}}}}\right)$$

endwhile

Fig. 3. Inner loop of Algorithm SBMM_{BLK} that computes $C := A \cdot B + C$

4.1 Implementation SBMM_{blk}

Routine SBMM_{blk} is an implementation of Algorithm SBMM_{BLK} with all the computations performed via the appropriate CUBLAS kernel. Initially, all the matrices are sent to the GPU. Then, βC is computed via the corresponding CUBLAS routine. This is not a BLAS-3 operation, but it presents a relatively small computational cost and can be efficiently computed on the accelerator. Next, the operations in SBMM_{BLK} are executed; and finally C is transferred back to the CPU. The update of C_1 requires three matrix-matrix products: one involving a symmetric matrix (block A_{11}), a second with an upper triangular matrix (block A_{31}); and the last one with two general matrices. CUBLAS provides specific routines for all these operations. Blocks C_2 and C_3 are updated via a product of two general matrices and a product of an upper triangular matrix times a general matrix, respectively.

The use of CUBLAS routines also presents a drawback, as the kernel that implements the product of a triangular matrix times a general matrix (routine TRMM) indeed computes

$$C = \alpha\ op(A)\ B, \tag{3}$$

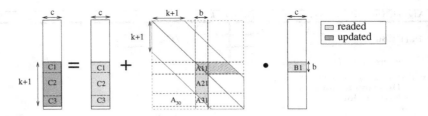

Fig. 4. Elements read and updated during a step of the inner loop of the SBMM$_{BLK}$ algorithm

where A is an upper or lower triangular matrix and $op(A)$ denotes A or A^T hereafter. In contrast, the updates of C_1 and C_3 require an operation of the type

$$C = C + \alpha \; op(A) \; B, \qquad (4)$$

To overcome this problem, routine SBMM$_{blk}$ performs the following sequence of operations in order to update C_1:

$$\text{(TRMM) } W = A_{31}^T B_1,$$
$$\text{(GEAM) } C_1 = C_1 + W.$$

(Next to each operation, we indicate the CUBLAS kernel that implements it.) The update of C_3 is analogous. This procedure requires an auxiliary workspace ($W \in R^{b \times c}$).

High performance can be expected of this implementation due to the use of tuned CUBLAS routines.

4.2   Implementation SBMM$_{blk+ms}$

The SBMM$_{blk}$ implementation presents some drawbacks that reduce its performance. In particular, it requires up to 6 operations per iteration. Besides, two of the operations involve a triangular matrix and are computed in two steps (as discussed in the previous subsection). Thus, up to 8 kernels are invoked at each iteration and some of them require a low computational effort (as do the two invocations to GEAM). The SBMM$_{blk+ms}$ implementation aims to reduce the number of routine invocations, specifically by removing those with a lower computational cost. To make this possible, we perform some changes in the matrix storage. Assume A presents a symmetric band structure and its lower part is stored following the BLAS specific format. Then, in order to accelerate algorithm SBMM$_{BLK}$ we add b additional rows to the bottom of A. Correspondingly, when the upper part of A is stored, then the new rows should be added at the top of A. Additionally, in a GPU environment, we suggest that this number is chosen to enable a coalesced access to the elements of A.

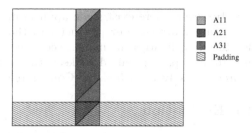

Fig. 5. Modified storage scheme for symmetric band matrices and how it is accessed in the inner loop from SBMM$_{BLK}$

Figure 5 shows the modified storage scheme and how it is accessed during an inner loop iteration in SBMM$_{BLK}$. The strictly lower triangular part of A_{31} is now conveniently placed in the added rows. Consequently, blocks A_{21} and A_{31} can be merged, and so can the operations they are involved in. Thus, the updates performed at each step of the inner loop can be reformulated as:

$$E_1 := E_1 + A_{11} \cdot D_1,$$
$$E_1 := E_1 + \begin{bmatrix} A_{21}^T & A_{31}^T \end{bmatrix} \cdot D_1$$
$$\begin{bmatrix} E_2 \\ E_3 \end{bmatrix} := \begin{bmatrix} E_2 \\ E_3 \end{bmatrix} + \begin{bmatrix} A_{21} \\ A_{31} \end{bmatrix} \cdot \begin{bmatrix} D_2 \\ D_3 \end{bmatrix}.$$

This approach presents two main advantages:

- The number of invocations to CUBLAS kernels is reduced from 8 to 3 per step and, consequently, the overhead introduced by the kernels invocations is also reduced.
- It eliminates the invocations to kernels with a moderate to low cost, which can not exploit the massively parallel architecture of the GPU. Concretely, the operations that dissapear involve triangular matrices and present load-balancing problems.

There are also some drawbacks related to this implementation. First of all, the memory requirements are enlarged. In addition, the number of arithmetic operations is also increased, as it operates with the null elements in A_{11} and A_{31}.

4.3 Implementation SBMV$_{ms}$

Additionally, we implemented a symmetric banded matrix-vector product variant based on the modified storage scheme. Due to the different storage scheme, this variant may be slightly faster than the implementation from CUBLAS. The overhead introduced by transforming A to the modified storage can be relatively high, in principle higher than the gain that SBMV$_{ms}$ introduces with respect to the CUBLAS routine. However, there exist some applications where the same matrix is involved in several matrix-vector products. In those applications, it may pay off to accelerate (even slightly) the matrix-vector products at the price of an increase in the storage space required to keep the matrix. This is, for example, the case for iterative solvers such as the Conjugate-Gradient method.

5   Experimental Evaluation

We evaluate the performance of the band matrix multiplication implementations presented in the previous section, namely the SBMM$_{blk}$ routine built upon the BLAS packed storage format, and SBMM$_{blk+ms}$ that supports the modified storage. Additionally we include in the evaluation three implementations based on the band matrix-vector product: two based on the routines provided by MKL (SBMM$_{mkl}$) and CUBLAS (SBMM$_{cublas}$), and one more based on routine SBMV$_{ms}$ (SBMM$_{ms}$).

We computed the products where the dimension of A varies from $m = 12,800$ to $m = 64,000$. Three bandwidths were tested for each dimension, $k = 0.5, 1,$ and 2% of m. Matrices B, C featured a reduced number of columns: $n = 1, 10, 20$. The first one corresponds in fact to a matrix-vector product.

The evaluation was performed in a platform eqquiped with an NVIDIA C2050 and two INTEL Xeon E5520 quad-core processors. The implementations perform a heavy use of routines from libraries INTEL MKL v9.293 and NVIDIA CUBLAS v5.5. They were compiled with gcc v4.1.2. Finally, all the experiments were performed using IEEE double-precision real arithmetic.

Table 1 shows the execution time for all the routines evaluated. All the results include the time required to transfer data between the CPU and the GPU memories. If matrices B and C present a single column, meaning that we are computing a matrix-vector product, then SBMM$_{mkl}$ obtains the best performance. The reason is that the computational cost of the operation is too low, and the larger parallelism of the GPU can not compensate for the communication time. The fastest routine in the device is SBMM$_{cublas}$ when the dimension of A is medium to small. For larger products, e.g. when $m > 38,400$ and $k \geq 2\%$, SBMV$_{ms}$ outperforms SBMM$_{cublas}$.

As soon as n becomes larger, the blocked variants become more efficient. In particular, with $n = 10$, SBMM$_{blk}$ attains the best execution times. Only the performance of SBMM$_{blk+ms}$ is comparable but always lower to that of SBMM$_{blk}$. This is due to the extra memory required to store A using the modified storage scheme and the subsequent overhead when the matrix is transferred to the GPU. Note that in most of the cases, SBMM$_{ms}$ outperforms the SBMM$_{cublas}$ implementation. Only for the smallest values of m and when the bandwidth $k < 2\%$, the CUBLAS routine outperforms SBMM$_{ms}$. This is because the matrix-vector kernel in SBMM$_{ms}$ is more efficient than its counterpart in CUBLAS, and it can compensate the overhead introduced by the extra data transfers required by the modified storage.

This behaviour is reinforced when $n = 20$. The blocked variants deliver the best performances even for the smallest test-cases evaluated. Additionally, with the

Table 1. Execution time (in seconds) for the symmetric band matrix-matrix product routines when $n = 1, 10, 20$. The bandwidth is expressed as a percentage of the matrix dimension.

Matrix Dimension	Bandwidth	SBMM$_{mkl}$	SBMM$_{cublas}$	SBMM$_{blk}$	SBMM$_{ms}$	SBMM$_{blk+ms}$
			$n = 1$			
12800	0.5%	0.002	0.004	0.011	0.009	0.013
	1.0%	0.005	0.006	0.012	0.011	0.017
	2.0%	0.006	0.011	0.016	0.014	0.024
25600	0.5%	0.006	0.012	0.022	0.022	0.032
	1.0%	0.011	0.024	0.030	0.032	0.048
	2.0%	0.020	0.042	0.064	0.047	0.078
38400	0.5%	0.014	0.028	0.040	0.040	0.062
	1.0%	0.022	0.054	0.071	0.063	0.099
	2.0%	0.039	0.101	0.133	0.096	0.157
51200	0.5%	0.023	0.049	0.060	0.063	0.096
	1.0%	0.039	0.092	0.126	0.094	0.156
	2.0%	0.070	0.159	0.227	0.147	0.254
64000	0.5%	0.035	0.076	0.106	0.090	0.140
	1.0%	0.056	0.130	0.175	0.124	0.200
	2.0%	0.103	0.252	0.320	0.231	0.354
			$n = 10$			
12800	0.5%	0.011	0.016	0.014	0.034	0.015
	1.0%	0.029	0.029	0.014	0.039	0.019
	2.0%	0.054	0.052	0.019	0.048	0.027
25600	0.5%	0.059	0.058	0.027	0.076	0.038
	1.0%	0.115	0.105	0.036	0.094	0.053
	2.0%	0.193	0.180	0.070	0.113	0.083
38400	0.5%	0.129	0.124	0.046	0.127	0.068
	1.0%	0.224	0.228	0.080	0.173	0.106
	2.0%	0.392	0.379	0.132	0.199	0.150
51200	0.5%	0.231	0.211	0.070	0.186	0.099
	1.0%	0.388	0.358	0.137	0.226	0.165
	2.0%	0.704	0.631	0.237	0.338	0.263
64000	0.5%	0.350	0.317	0.113	0.250	0.150
	1.0%	0.624	0.557	0.205	0.319	0.241
	2.0%	1.031	0.989	0.357	0.505	0.391
			$n = 20$			
12800	0.5%	0.020	0.029	0.016	0.057	0.018
	1.0%	0.057	0.053	0.017	0.064	0.020
	2.0%	0.116	0.097	0.022	0.079	0.029
25600	0.5%	0.117	0.106	0.033	0.127	0.042
	1.0%	0.230	0.195	0.042	0.157	0.058
	2.0%	0.417	0.328	0.077	0.180	0.089
38400	0.5%	0.258	0.227	0.051	0.203	0.081
	1.0%	0.643	0.425	0.092	0.302	0.115
	2.0%	0.867	0.706	0.153	0.329	0.171
51200	0.5%	0.461	0.399	0.084	0.310	0.114
	1.0%	0.757	0.661	0.144	0.346	0.164
	2.0%	1.409	1.138	0.253	0.523	0.273
64000	0.5%	0.699	0.592	0.138	0.434	0.176
	1.0%	1.429	1.019	0.225	0.501	0.255
	2.0%	2.069	1.840	0.379	0.783	0.407

Table 2. Execution time (in seconds) for the symmetric band matrix-vector product routines. The CPU-GPU communication times are not reported in this table. The bandwidth is expressed as a percentage of the matrix dimension.

Matrix Dimension	Bandwidth	SBMV$_{mkl}$	SBMV$_{cublas}$	SBMV$_{ms}$
12800	0.5%	0.002	0.001	0.002
	1.0%	0.004	0.002	0.003
	2.0%	0.009	0.004	0.003
25600	0.5%	0.006	0.005	0.005
	1.0%	0.012	0.008	0.006
	2.0%	0.019	0.015	0.007
38400	0.5%	0.013	0.010	0.009
	1.0%	0.023	0.019	0.011
	2.0%	0.039	0.031	0.012
51200	0.5%	0.023	0.018	0.012
	1.0%	0.055	0.030	0.013
	2.0%	0.071	0.050	0.018
64000	0.5%	0.035	0.027	0.017
	1.0%	0.056	0.045	0.018
	2.0%	0.103	0.081	0.027

blocked variants, the cases with $n = 10$ and $n = 20$ present a similar execution time. On the contrary, as could be expected, SBMM$_{mkl}$ requires 2× more time, while SBMM$_{cublas}$ and SBMM$_{ms}$ require approximately between 1.75 and 2× more time. This is because in the GPU-based variants, although the computing time is doubled, the data transfer time is similar. Thus, the total time is increased by a factor lower but near to 2×.

As stated above, the SBMV$_{ms}$ routine is more efficient than the corresponding kernel from CUBLAS. However the gains reported do not compensate the overhead introduced by the higher volume of data transfer, and the mandatory transform of A to the modified storage scheme. There are some applications where several matrix-vector products have to be computed using the same matrix. This is the case of iterative solvers of systems of linear equations such as the Conjugate-Gradient method. In such applications, the matrix can be transformed and transferred to the device once, and can be then successively re-used at each iteration of the algorithm. Thus, the overhead introduced by data transfers can be easily compensated after several steps iterations if the matrix-vector routine is more efficient.

Table 2 shows the execution time required by the matrix-vector implementations without taking into account the time dedicated to the data transfers. The SBMV$_{mkl}$ kernel is outperformed by both GPU-based routines and the SBMV$_{ms}$ variant in particular obtains remarkable speed-ups. These results show that the speed-up is higher for larger matrices. In this experimental evaluation, SBMV$_{ms}$ reports an acceleration factor of up to 4× when compared with its MKL counterpart, and up to 3× when compared with the CUBLAS routine.

6 Concluding Remarks

We have addressed the computation of the symmetric band matrix-matrix multiplication on CPU-GPU platforms. Exploiting the structure of the matrix yields relevant savings in both memory and computational cost. Two specific implementations, SBMM$_{blk}$ and SBMM$_{blk+ms}$, are presented and evaluated. Both routines leverage the parallelism of the target architecture to deliver remarkable performance. Routine SBMM$_{blk}$ adopts the packed storage scheme defined in BLAS and, consequently, presents some drawbacks that limit its performance in parallel hardware architectures. Routine SBMM$_{blk+ms}$ partially overcomes these problems by relying on a modified packed storage scheme which is more suitable for the underlying architecture, at the cost of a minor increase in the memory requirements. The experimental evaluation shows remarkable gains of both routines over the naive implementations based on the kernels in MKL and CUBLAS for this operation.

Additionally, we have developed a symmetric band matrix-vector routine, SBMV$_{ms}$, that exploits the benefits from the modified storage scheme revealed by SBMM$_{blk+ms}$. Specifically, this new routine renders higher performance than its counterpart from CUBLAS. Although our solution requires an additional effort to transform the matrix to the modified storage scheme, we believe it may be useful in methods that perform several symmetric band matrix-vector products involving the same matrix such as, e.g., iterative Krylov subspace-based solvers for symmetric band linear systems.

Acknowledgements. Ernesto Dufrechou and Pablo Ezzatti acknowledge support from Programa de Desarrollo de las Ciencias Básicas, and Agencia Nacional de Investigación e Innovación, Uruguay. Enrique S. Quintana-Ortí was supported by project TIN2011-23283 of the Ministry of Science and Competitiveness (MINECO) and EU FEDER, and project P1-1B2013-20 of the Fundació Caixa Castelló-Bancaixa and UJI.

References

1. Anderson, E., Bai, Z., Demmel, J., Dongarra, J.E., DuCroz, J., Greenbaum, A., Hammarling, S., McKenney, A.E., Ostrouchov, S., Sorensen, D.: LAPACK Users' Guide. SIAM, Philadelphia (1992)
2. Benner, P., Dufrechou, E., Ezzatti, P., Igounet, P., Quintana-Ortí, E.S., Remón, A.: Accelerating band linear algebra operations on gPUs with application in model reduction. In: Murgante, B., Misra, S., Rocha, A.M.A.C., Torre, C., Rocha, J.G., Falcão, M.I., Taniar, D., Apduhan, B.O., Gervasi, O. (eds.) ICCSA 2014, Part VI. LNCS, vol. 8584, pp. 386–400. Springer, Heidelberg (2014)
3. Cuthill, E., McKee, J.: Reducing the bandwidth of sparse symmetric matrices. In: Proceedings of the 1969 24th National Conference, ACM 1969, pp. 157–172. ACM, New York (1969)

4. Du Croz, J., Mayes, P., Radicati, G.: Factorization of band matrices using level 3 BLAS. LAPACK Working Note 21, Technical Report CS-90-109, University of Tennessee (July 1990)
5. Dufrechou, E., Ezzatti, P., Quintana-Ortí, E.S., Remón, A.: Accelerating the LYAPACK library using GPUs. J. Supercomput. 65(3), 1114–1124 (2013)
6. Golub, G., Loan, C.V.: Matrix Computations, 3rd edn. The Johns Hopkins University Press, Baltimore (1996)

Adaptive Spot-Instances Aware Autoscaling for Scientific Workflows on the Cloud

David A. Monge[1,2] and Carlos García Garino[1,3]

[1] ITIC Research Institute, National University of Cuyo (UNCuyo), Argentina
[2] Faculty of Exact and Natural Sciences, UNCuyo, Argentina
[3] Faculty of Engineering, UNCuyo, Argentina
{dmonge,cgarcia}@itu.uncu.edu.ar

Abstract. This paper deals with the problem of autoscaling for cloud computing scientific workflows. Autoscaling is a process in which the infrastructure scaling (i.e. determining the number and type of instances to acquire for executing an application) interleaves with the scheduling of tasks for reducing time and monetary cost of executions. This work proposes a novel strategy called Spots Instances Aware Autoscaling (SIAA) designed for the optimized execution of scientific workflow applications. SIAA takes advantage of the better prices of Amazon's EC2-like spot instances to achieve better performance and cost savings. To deal with execution efficiency, SIAA uses a novel heuristic scheduling algorithm to optimize workflow makespan and reduce the effect of tasks failures that may occur by the use of spot instances. Experiments were carried out using several types of real-world scientific workflows. Results demonstrated that SIAA is able to greatly overcome the performance of state-of-the-art autoscaling mechanisms in terms of makespan (up to 88.0%) and cost of execution (up to 43.6%).

Keywords: Scientific workflows, Cloud Computing, Autoscaling, Scheduling, Spot instances.

1 Introduction

Many scientific areas have turn to in silico experimentation giving birth to the so-called discipline *e-Science*. In this sense, workflow technology plays a central role and has been widely adopted for guiding the design and execution of complex scientific experiments [13]. Workflow applications comprise a set of computation tasks and a set of dependencies between them, which determine constraints for the execution order of tasks arranged in a directed acyclic graph (see figure 1). To meet the computational requirements, which are usually high and efficiently execute the applications, cloud computing technologies are being extensively used [17,11].

Public cloud providers permit a transparent, on-demand and inexpensive access to computational resources relying on virtualization strategies [4]. Infrastructure as a Service (IaaS) providers permit the *on-demand* acquisition of Virtual Machine (VM) *instances* under a pay-per-use fashion with a fixed

G. Hernández et al. (Eds.): CARLA 2014, CCIS 485, pp. 13–27, 2014.
© Springer-Verlag Berlin Heidelberg 2014

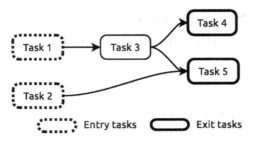

Fig. 1. Directed acyclic graph (DAG) workflow example with 5 tasks. Edges represent control-flow dependencies.

price. Providers offer several types of instances, which present different cost-performances (i.e. computing power/price).

Some providers also permit the acquisition of instances under a different scheme in which prices change over time. Amazon's Elastic Compute Cloud (EC2) spot instances [3] are a strategy for selling idle computing capacity using a dynamic market-driven pricing scheme, in other words based on the law of supply and demand. These dynamically changing prices are generally significantly lower than the fixed price of on-demand instances.

To acquire a set of spot instances, the user must bid for the price that is willing to pay. If the user's bid is greater than the current spot price, the requested instances are provided. If in any moment the spot price overcomes the user's bid, the instances are terminated without previous notice. This situation is called an out-of-bid error. As can be perceived, this scheme of computation supposes a trade-off between the cost of each instance and its reliability. To face such issue many strategies to select the proper bid have been proposed. Most of them rely on the use of historical spot prices [1,15]. These kind of strategies for price prediction has been applied in many contexts [14,16].

When running a scientific workflow application, deciding the number and type of instances to acquire becomes a particularly complex problem. In first place, because the unbalance of task durations and the existent dependencies generate *variable computation requirements* during the execution of the application [7]. In second place, because it may be difficult to *accurately predict the performance* of tasks. On the one hand because experimental applications usually explore different sets of data and parameters, which may hinder the proper performance modeling of tasks. On the other hand because performance variability in the cloud is inevitable [12,6].

These two factors make very hard to know in advance the necessary amount of instances. For such reason, *autoscaling* mechanisms [9] emerged to (*i*) automatically determine the number and type of instances to acquire, while (*ii*) scheduling the workflow tasks onto the acquired instances. As autoscaling is a two-fold problem with circular dependencies, the mechanisms operate during the entire execution of an application dynamically resizing the computing infrastructure, scheduling and executing the tasks.

Current autoscaling techniques present some limitations that deteriorate the performance of applications. Some techniques [17,11] lack on adaptivity because they assume a fixed infrastructure and schedule the tasks in a best effort manner. Other techniques [2] are constructed upon very simple ad-hoc rules that must be defined by the user. Finally some techniques do not take advantage of the better cost-performances offered by spot instances [9]. This work proposes a novel adaptive autoscaling strategy that overcomes the mentioned limitations exploiting the advantages of using spot instances and dealing with task failures intelligently to reduce the time and cost of execution for scientific workflows.

This paper is organized as follows. Next section provides a discussion of the current advances on managing cloud workflows. Section 3 presents a novel autoscaling strategy for scientific workflows. Section 4 discusses the experiments carried out and analyzes the obtained results. Finally, section 5 concludes this work and provides future research directions.

2   Related Work

The problem of executing workflows in the cloud has been extensively addressed over the last years. Several techniques and strategies have been proposed to cope with the objective of achieving fast and cheap executions. We grouped these approaches in 3 categories: *scheduling on fixed-size infrastructures*, *rule-based* scaling methods, and *autoscaling* mechanisms.

Scheduling on fixed-size infrastructures: these strategies rely on heuristic and metaheuristic methods for a best-effort scheduling considering a predefined cloud infrastructure [17,11]. Their main limitation is that the infrastructure is kept unchanged during the entire execution. The **lack of adaptability** to the variable workload inherent of workflow applications precludes from taking advantage of time and cost optimization possibilities.

Rule-based scaling: for addressing the problem of load variability on web applications (e.g. facebook, vimeo, etc), cloud providers suggest using ad-hoc rule-based methods to adapt the size of the infrastructure [2]; e.g. "if CPU load overcomes a certain percentage then acquire x new instances". However, this type of rules depend on the characteristics of the application running and might be **unsuitable for experimental applications** like scientific workflows.

Autoscaling: these are techniques specially designed for workflow applications to cope with the problems of scaling and scheduling simultaneously [9]. Under this category, two strategies denominated *Scheduling First* and *Scaling First* have been proposed. As their names indicate the strategies differ in which of the phases (scaling or scheduling) are accomplished first. On both cases, the strategies operate continuously while the applications are running. The mentioned strategies use on-demand instances disregarding the use of spot instances **missing important time and cost saving opportunities**. As both strategies present a considerable complexity they are not further discussed due to space limitations. To obtain a better understanding of the strategies, please refer to the existing literature [9].

Our contribution: to the best of our knowledge, this is the first paper dealing with the problem of cloud infrastructure autoscaling using spot instances in the context of scientific workflows. Next section describes a novel autoscaling strategy designed for achieving superior cost-performance on the execution of scientific workflows. The strategy proposed in this work differentiates from others on the following features:

1. it exploits spot instances for achieving an overall better cost-performance aiming the reduction of time and/or cost of scientific workflow executions, and
2. it uses an heuristic method for workflow makespan optimization, which schedules critical tasks intelligently minimizing the effect of failures in the overall running time.

3   Spot Instances Aware Autoscaling

The aim of the Spot Instances Aware Autoscaling (SIAA) strategy proposed in this work is to achieve a better cost-performance of scientific workflows on the cloud. This is attained, first, by acquiring an infrastructure comprising on-demand and spot instances according to the computation requirements for the next hour. And, second, by minimizing the overall makespan and reducing the probability of task failures due to out-of-bid errors.

The strategy performs the autoscaling process on an hourly basis through a sequence of 4 phases, namely: (i) information update, (ii) infrastructure scaling (iii) heuristic tasks scheduling, and (iv) shutdown idle instances. The purpose of each of these phases is explained through the following subsections. The execution interval SIAA was set to 1 hour as in alternative autoscaling strategies [9].

3.1   Phase 1: Information Update

Every time SIAA is invoked it updates the workflow execution information. This phase of the algorithm is fundamental because (i) it permits a dynamic adaptation of the strategy to changes in the infrastructure, and (ii) it reduces the adverse effects of errors in performance and bid price prediction methods. In other words, having updated information allows a more accurate decision making process on the following phases of autoscaling.

When SIAA is invoked it updates the state of the instances and predicts the remaining execution time for **already running** tasks. For **waiting tasks** it updates *duration, (earliest and late) start times*, and identifies which of those tasks are *critical* for executing the workflow in minimum time.

Task durations the duration d_t of a task t can be estimated in practice using some of the existent performance prediction mechanism [10]. For the purpose of our experiments, task durations are estimated using a linear model relating the task's size and the instance's performance, plus the addition of an uniformly distributed error. Durations are estimated considering the *preferred instance type* for each task. The preferred instance type for a *waiting* task is such that provides the **best cost-performance ratio** (i.e. the minimum cost/time value). In the case of a *running* task, the preferred instance type is the type of the instance where the task is executing. For running tasks, the remaining execution time is estimated by subtracting the time that the task has been running. Task durations are the basis information to compute earliest and late start times.

Earliest start time (EST) is the minimum time at which a task can start its execution considering its predecessors. The EST of a waiting task t is computed as $EST(t) = \max_{1 \leq k \leq p} \{EST(t_k) + d_k\}$, where t is a waiting task, t_k is one of the p parent tasks of t and d_k is the estimated running time of t_k. For tasks which are *ready* to execute, the EST is set to the current time.

Late start time (LST) is the maximum start time at which a task can start without delaying any of its successor tasks. The LST of a task t is computed as $LST(t) = \min_{1 \leq k \leq c} \{LST(t_k) - d_k\}$, where t_k is one of the c child tasks of t and d_k is the estimated running time of t_k. For each of the n *exit* tasks the LST is computed as $LST(t) = FT - d_t$, where FT is finish time of the workflow computed as $FT = \max_{1 \leq k \leq n} \{EST(t_k) + d_k\}$.

Critical tasks are tasks that if delayed, will produce an increment of the overall application execution time (makespan). The *slack* time of a task permits identifying which of the tasks are critical. The slack time of a task t is computed as $slack(t) = LST(t) - EST(t)$. Tasks with a slack time of 0 are critical tasks and should not be delayed.

3.2 Phase 2: Infrastructure Scaling

SIAA relies on the exploitation of spot instances for achieving an overall better cost-performance. But, as spot instances also introduce the possibility of task failures derived from out-of-bid situations, SIAA generates a scaling plan comprising on-demand and spot instances. A scaling plan generated by SIAA can be formally defined as $plan_{scaling} = \{\langle VMType, scheme \rangle \rightarrow \mathbb{N}\}$ which maps the amount of instances to acquire for each combination of instance type $VMType$ and pricing *scheme* (on-demand/spot).

On-demand instances provide a stable computing platform very suitable for critical tasks but at expenses of a higher cost. Conversely, spot instances extend such infrastructure with unreliable instances of better cost-efficiency ideal for short duration or non-critical tasks. The balance between both types of instances is governed by the *spots ratio* parameter ($\alpha \in [0,1]$) as follows.

The parameter α determines which proportion of a given budget B available for acquiring instances is assigned to spot or on-demand instances. The algorithm assigns a portion of B for *on-demand* instances as $B_{od} = B * (1 - \alpha)$; and the remaining portion for *spot* instances, i.e. $B_s = B * \alpha$. These two budgets conform constraints that prevent from acquiring a number of instances whose monetary cost exceeds the maximum permitted budget (B).

According to the budget constraints the algorithm constructs a scaling plan that best fit the workflow computation requirements for the next hour. Algorithm 1 presents the process of infrastructure scaling.

Algorithm 1. Infrastructure scaling algorithm

```
 1: procedure SCALEINFRASTRUCTURE:
 2:     tasks ← GETTASKSINTHEPERIOD()          ▷ tasks running during the next hour
 3:     C_unbound ← ESTIMATECONSUMPTION(tasks) ▷ get unconstrained consumption
 4:     C_od ← SCALE(C_unbound, B_od/cost_unbound)    ▷ determine on-demand instances
 5:     C_unbound ← C_unbound − C_od
 6:     bidPrices ← PREDICTBIDPRICES()         ▷ invokes a bid price prediction method
 7:     C_s ← SCALE(C_s, B_s/cost_s)                   ▷ determine spot instances
 8:     C_od = C_od − R
 9:     C_s = C_s − (R − C_od)
10:     for all VMType_i in VMTypes do:                        ▷ request instances
11:         REQUESTINSTANCE(C_od[VMType_i])
12:         REQUESTSPOTINSTANCE(C_s[VMType_i], bidPrices[VMType_i])
```

To generate the scaling plan, the algorithm starts by estimating the computation load for the next hour (lines 2 and 3). A consumption vector $C_{unbound} = \{c_1, c_2, \ldots, c_n\}$ represents the amount of instances necessary for each type for the next hour with **unconstrained budget**. Each component c_i represents the amount of instances of type $VMType_i$.

Each c_i value is estimated summing the computation hour portions for all the tasks which prefer and instance of type $VMType_i$. In the case of **running tasks**, the computation load is set to the type of the instance where such task is executing.

To generate the scaling plan, the algorithm computes two consumption vectors, C_{od} and C_s (for on-demand and spot instances respectively) derived from the unconstrained consumption vector $C_{unbound}$. This process is carried out in two steps:

1. The consumption vector of **on-demand** instances C_{od} is determined fitting the number of instances according to the available budget B_{od}. The C_{od} vector is obtained scaling the unconstrained consumption vector $C_{unbound}$ by the factor $B_{od}/cost_{od}$, where $cost_{od}$ is the total cost of acquiring all the instances in $C_{unbound}$ using the on-demand instance prices (line 4). A consumption vector C is scaled by a factor $r > 0$ as $scale(C, r) = \begin{cases} round(C \cdot r) & r < 1 \\ round(C) & r \geq 1 \end{cases}$, where $C \cdot r$ is the product of a vector and a scalar and the ROUND function is applied to each element of the resulting vector.

2. In analogous manner, the consumption vector of **spot** instances C_s is determined by scaling the remaining unconstrained instances: $C_{unbound} - C_{od}$ (line 5). This new consumption vector is then scaled by the factor $B_s/cost_s$

using the same criteria as before. Note that $cost_s$ is the total cost of acquiring all the instances in C_S according to a *bid price prediction method* (lines 6 and 7). Next paragraphs detail the strategy used for spot prices bidding used in this work.

Both consumption vectors (C_{od} and C_s) represent the scaling plan generated by SIAA. The algorithm then acquires the necessary instances considering the number of instances already running (lines 10 to 12).

Spot Prices and Bidding. Many strategies for bidding the spot prices have been proposed relying on the use of historical data prices [1]. The performance of bid price prediction methods have impact on the These prediction methods present estimation errors that may affect the overall behavior of the autoscaling strategy. If the method tends to underestimate the minimal bid price, instances may fail earlier augmenting the number of interrupted tasks and reducing the size of the infrastructure. Overestimation of the optimal bid price reduces the chances of failure but may unnecessary increase the cost of execution if idle instances are not terminated wisely. Because the aim of this work is not evaluating the performance of bidding strategies, we simulate bid prediction methods as follows. The bid is computed by sampling from a uniform distribution centered on the optimal price for the next hour with bounds determined by a specified error percentage of such optimal price. Prices used correspond to an existent databases [16]. This bidding schema permits modeling a non-perfect bid-price estimation method by just specifying the desired prediction error.

3.3 Phase 3: Heuristic Tasks Scheduling

At this point of the process, the infrastructure has been fitted to the needs for the next hour of computation for an application. The scheduling algorithm is now in charge of efficiently execute the workflow application considering the available instances. SIAA uses an heuristic scheduling algorithm which optimizes the workflow makespan, i.e. the total running time of the workflow.

The objective of makespan minimization is accomplished keeping in mind two premises: (i) execute the tasks as fast as possible, and (ii) minimize the negative effects of instance failures. For such purpose, knowing which are the critical tasks (slack times) plays a central role in the optimization process. Algorithm 2 describes the pseudocode of the scheduling strategy in SIAA.

The algorithm undertakes the minimization of workflow makespan reducing the execution time of critical tasks. Tasks ready to execute are sorted prioritizing those with the smaller slack times (line 3). Then, one by one, the tasks are scheduled to the instance that offers the earliest completion time (ECT). This process (lines 5 to 9) is repeated until there are no more ready tasks to schedule or available instances (line 4). Please note that in all cases only waiting tasks and available instances are considered. Tasks currently running continue their execution on the instances they were previously assigned.

Although, the bid price prediction method (used during the scaling phase) aims to reduce the number of task failures, out-of-bid errors are likely to occur.

Algorithm 2. Tasks scheduling algorithm

1: **procedure** SCHEDULETASKS($instances_{od}, instances_s$):   ▷ input:lists of available
   on-demand and spot instances
2:      $readyTasks \leftarrow$ GETREADYTASKS()   ▷ tasks ready to run
3:      $queue \leftarrow$ SORTBYPRIORITY($readyTasks$)
4:      **while** there are instances available **and** SIZE($queue$) > 0 **do**:
5:          $task \leftarrow queue$.POP()
6:          $instance \leftarrow$ FASTEST($task, instances_{od}$)   ▷ ETC on-demand instance
7:          **if** $instance ==$ **null then**:   ▷ no on-demand instances available
8:              $instance \leftarrow$ FASTEST($task, instances_s$)   ▷ ETC spot instance
9:          SCHEDULE($task, instance$)   ▷ submit for execution

---

For such reason, the algorithm addresses the minimization of the negative effects of such failures on the workflow makespan. This second objective is achieved by reducing the number of failures that may affect critical tasks. The algorithm prioritizes the execution of the tasks (sorted by slack time), first on on-demand instances and then on spot instances (lines 6 to 8). In this way, most of the critical tasks are executed safely on on-demand instances.

This scheme is highly convenient because non-critical tasks can fail and be re-launched for execution without handicapping the overall makespan as they have a wider margin for delays (larger slack times). When a task is terminated due to an out-of-bid failure, the task is re-inserted in the execution queue. Then, the workflow information is updated and the scheduling algorithm is invoked to initiate the execution of more tasks or the re-submission of failed tasks.

3.4   Phase 4: Shutdown Idle Instances

For avoiding the use of unnecessary instances (and therefore reducing monetary costs), SIAA shuts down all the idle instances that are close to an hour of computation. This step can be seen as a scale down process complementary to the infrastructure scaling (phase 2).

4   Experiments and Results

The evaluation of SIAA was carried out by two main experiments. The first one evaluates the performance of SIAA with some state-of-the-art autoscaling strategies. The second one analyzes the performance of SIAA on different scenarios varying the portion of spot instances used and the error affecting the bid price prediction method. The following paragraphs describe the workflow applications and the instances used in the experiments. Then, sections 4.1 and 4.2 discuss both experiments.

Workflow Applications. Several scientific workflow applications from Geo Sciences, Astronomy and Bioinformatics were used for both experiments [7]. These applications are CyberShake (seismic hazard simulation), LIGO's Inspiral (detection of gravitational waves), Montage (generation of mosaics from the sky) and SIPTH (search for small untranslated RNAs). Figure 2 shows the duration in minutes for each task type of the 4 mentioned applications. Each application comprises about 1000 tasks each one.

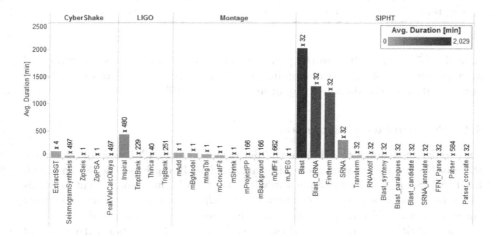

Fig. 2. Scientific workflows tasks profile. Bars represent the average duration in minutes of each task type. The label on the top of each bar represents the total number of tasks of each type.

From the figure can be seen that the applications present very different workload patterns. For example, CyberShake and LIGO have just 5 and 4 types of tasks respectively while Montage and SIPHT are constructed using 9 and 13 different types of tasks respectively. Other difference to note is that the duration of tasks greatly vary between applications ranging from a few seconds to tasks of very long duration (e.g. 430 minutes for Inspiral tasks in LIGO and 2029 minutes for Blast tasks in SIPHT). Such differences are convenient because they serve to evaluate the performance of the algorithms under very dissimilar conditions.

VM Instances. The experiments were conducted considering 5 different types of instances. Table 1 presents the characteristics for each type of the on-demand instances considered. *Price* denotes the cost of an hour of computation. The relative performance of the instances is measured in *EC2 Compute Units (ECU)* [1]. *Cost-performance* represents is the ratio *ECU/Price* and represents the effectiveness of each instance type. *Lag time*, represents the mean initialization time for each instance type [8].

Spot instances have the same characteristics presented on the above table except that their prices vary over time. Time series of spot price observations are

---

[1] One ECU is equivalent to a CPU capacity of a 1.0-1.2 GHz 2007 Opteron.

Table 1. Characteristics of the on-demand instances

Attribute	t1.micro	m3.medium	c3.2xlarge	r3.xlarge	m3.2xlarge
Price [$]	0.02	0.07	0.42	0.35	0.56
Performance [ECU]	1	2	28	13	26
Cost-perf. [ECU/$]	50.0	28.6	66.7	37.1	46.4
Lag time [s]	60	80	90	90	120

spaced by 5 minutes. It is worth pointing out that the spot prices are expressed as a percentage of the corresponding on-demand prices. The data used is a normalization of the data used by other colleagues [16].

4.1   Performance Comparison

This experiment aims to evaluate the performance of SIAA in comparison with state-of-the-art autoscaling methods, namely: Scheduling First (SchF) and Scaling First (ScaF) [9]. The comparison with other workflow management methods like *ad-hoc rules* or *fixed-infrastructure scheduling* are omitted from this study since Mao et al. [9] already proved the advantages of SchF and ScaF.

The algorithms were executed on several simulated scenarios with different settings. Each scenario is defined by the workflow application executed (Cyber-Shake, LIGO, Montage, SIPHT), and the budget available ($10, $20 or $30 per hour in concordance with other works [9]). Each experimental scenario was simulated 4 times using the CloudSim simulator [5]. In all cases, tasks running times and instance lag times were affected by a 20% error to increase the uncertainty during the simulations and to provide a more realistic environment according to the performance variability of the cloud. For SIAA the bid price predictions were affected by errors of 0%, 10% and 20% to model bid estimations methods of different quality.

Figure 3 presents the performance comparison of the studied autoscaling algorithms for each of the 4 selected applications. Performance comparison comprises three different metrics namely *speedup*, *cost* and instances *percentage of use*.

The first row presents the average **speedup** with respect to the linear execution time of the applications on an instance of the type «c3.2xlarge», which provides the best cost-performance. Formally the speedup is computed as $S_x = \frac{T_{seq}}{T_x}$, where x indicates an autoscaling strategy, T_{seq} is the sequential time of the application and T_x is the workflow makespan using the autoscaling strategy x. In all cases SIAA outperformed its competitors with a wide margin (from 14.1% to 88.0%). As SIAA takes advantage of instances of better cost-performance, it is able to acquire more computing power (more instances) with the same budget. This leads to an increase of tasks executed in parallel and therefore to a reduction of the overall makespan.

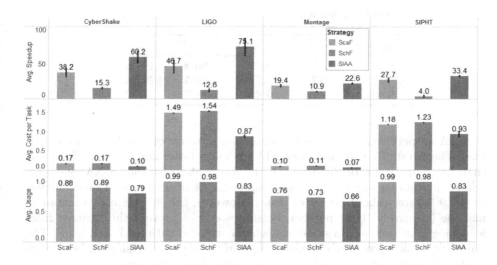

Fig. 3. Performance comparison for each type of workflow. Three autoscaling algorithms are analyzed: (a) Scaling First (ScaF), and (b) Scheduling First (SchF) and (c) SIAA. Algorithms are compared considering speedup, average execution cost per task and efficiency.

The worst performing method is SchF because the algorithm purchases instances in decreasing cost (and performance) until the hourly budget is consumed. In practice happens that some tasks are scheduled to very slow instances increasing the overall makespan.

With respect to the **cost of execution** (second row), the graphics show that SIAA obtains the lowest cost of execution per task (reductions are in the range 21.5%-43.6%). Again, these results respond to the fact that SIAA is able to acquire instances with better cost-performance relation. Hence, for the same levels of performance instances of lower price can be acquired. For SchF and ScaF the average cost per task is similar. It is noticeable that in general, tasks for the LIGO and SIPHT workflows are considerably more expensive (about one order of magnitude). The reason is that such applications comprise tasks of very long duration (see figure 2).

The third row of graphics present the average **instance percentage of use** for each algorithm. It can be seen that SIAA presents the lowest usage of instances (6.6%-16.6% of use below its competitors). The reason for such behavior is that SIAA acquires a higher number of instances increasing the total *lag time* and *unused partial hours* of computation. However, it is worth mentioning that the majority of this *wasted* instance time corresponds to (cheap) spot instance hours (in average, SIAA acquired 5.49 spot instances per each on-demand instance).

As a summary, table 2 presents the results of the three strategies considered. The best results per analyzed aspect (column) are highlighted in bold font.

Table 2. Summary of results averaged by strategy

Strategy	Speedup	Cost/task	Usage [%]	Failures
ScaF	33.0	0.73	**90.4**	**N/A**
SchF	10.7	0.75	89.5	**N/A**
SIAA	**47.9**	**0.48**	77.7	100.9

SIAA outperforms the remaining strategies in terms of speedup and cost per task. These results corroborate that SIAA permits faster and cheaper executions than its competitors. In the downside, it can be also seen that SIAA evidences a lower percentage of instances usage (up to 22.3% of time wasted) and number of 100.9 failures (about 10.1% of tasks). However, the inferior use of instances and the (relatively) large number of failures do not prevent the strategy from achieving high time and cost savings when compared with ScaF and SchF. The following section provides a deeper insight in the aspect of task failures by analyzing the robustness of SIAA in several uncertainty scenarios.

4.2   Robustness Analysis

The previous experiment evidenced the advantages of using SIAA by comparing its performance with other autoscaling strategies. This section analyzes the robustness of SIAA in terms of the number of failures and speedup for a wide number of settings involving different balances of on-demand/spot instances and different errors affecting the bid price prediction methods.

Although for this second experiment the same type of workflows were used we focused on applications around 100 tasks to limit the size of the experiment. All the simulations were carried out using a 20% error for tasks running time and instances lag time. In all cases the budget was set to $30. Figure 4 presents the number of task failures and speedups according to scenarios defined by:

1. The *spotsRatio* parameter (percentage of the total budget assigned to spot instances) varying from $0, 20, \ldots, 100\%$ (horizontal axis), and
2. The *bidError* parameter (error affecting the bid price prediction methods) (vertical axis). Errors vary from 0 (an hypothetical perfect predictor) and a 48.5% predictor error.

Task Failures. From the top figure it can be seen that as the *spotsRatio* parameter increases, the number of failures augments. This is because having a smaller proportion of on-demand instances makes the critical tasks more prone to run on spot instances and therefore are more likely to fail. By looking on the other axis, as the prediction error increases the number of failures also increases. Larger errors on the prediction of the optimal bid price increment the probability of failure contributing to an increase of the total number of failures.

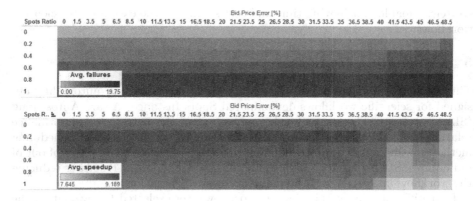

Fig. 4. Heat-maps of the **number of task failures** (on top) and the **speedup** (bottom). Results are presented for different combinations of (*i*) the percentage of budget assigned to spot instances (horizontal axis), and (*ii*) the error on the prediction of the optimal bid price for the next computation hour (vertical axis).

The largest number of failures (top figure) is circumscribed to scenarios where the *spotsRatio* parameter (percent of the budget is used for acquiring spot instances) varies from 40% to 100% and the *bidError* parameter (bid price prediction error) ranges from 41.5% to 48.5%. We call this set of scenarios the max-failures region.

Speedups. Comparing the top and bottom heat-maps a common pattern is evidenced. The speedups achieved in the *max-failures* region are the lowest (bottom figure). This correlation indicates that the number of failures directly affects the speedup achieved by SIAA. A larger number of failures not only reduces the number of instances running but also forces the restart of the tasks affected by the failure incrementing the workflow makespan.

The best speedups are achieved using a 20%-40% of budget assigned to spot instances. Within this range, the highest speedup levels correspond to scenarios where the bid prediction error is below 5%. From the analysis arises that for achieving the maximum speedup in practice it could be convenient to properly select the *spotsRatio* parameter considering the quality of the bid price prediction method.

It is also worth to point out that using an infrastructure entirely composed of on-demand instances (*spotsRatio* = 0) permits the achievement of better speedups than those corresponding to the max-failures region indicating that for some *bad quality* bid price predictors it is very important to select the proper value of *spotsRatio*.

From the results of both experiments, we can conclude that the use of spot instances plays a fundamental role on the reduction of execution times and costs of scientific workflows on the cloud. Moreover, SIAA has proved that is a robust strategy capable of achieving time and cost savings in the execution of scientific workflows.

5 Concluding Remarks

This paper presented a novel strategy for cloud infrastructure autoscaling designed for scientific workflows denominated Spots Instances Aware Autoscaling (SIAA) strategy. The strategy takes advantage of the better cost-performance relation provided by spot instances in combination with a heuristic scheduling method for makespan optimization and reduction of the negative effect of out of bid failures. SIAA permits a highly efficient use of cloud infrastructures reducing the workflow makespan and the monetary cost of execution.

Four different real-world scientific workflows were selected for evaluating the performance of SIAA. Results evidenced that assigning a half of the budget to spot instances permits SIAA to overcome the state-of-the-art autoscaling methods in a 14.1%-88.0% of makespan. Results also demonstrated that SIAA conduced to cost reductions of 21.5% to 43.6%. From the experiments is also evidenced that SIAA is capable of providing good performance levels regardless of the number of failures occurring. Results highlighted the importance of (*i*) determining the adequate proportion of the budget assigned to spot instances as well as (*ii*) having access to bid price prediction methods with good accuracy, to improve the workflow makespan.

As part of our future work we plan to study checkpointing techniques for reducing the time and and money loses derived from failures of large duration tasks. Checkpointing would also permit a more extensive use of spot instances without compromising the workflow makespan. A second aspect to investigate in the future is a method for determining the proper value of the *spotsRatio* parameter considering the characteristics of the application and the quality of the available bid price prediction method. Finally it is interesting to study the repercussion of data transfer times and cost during the autoscaling process. These features are crucial for studying new autoscaling techniques designed for big data applications like, for example, MapReduce workflows.

Acknowledgements. The first author wants to thank National Scientific and Technical Research Council (CONICET), for the postdoctoral fellowship granted. This research is supported by ANPCyT through project No. PICT-2012-2731. Also, the financial support provided by SeCTyP-UNCuyo through project No. M004 is gratefully acknowledged. Finally we want to thank the anonymous reviewers who helped improving the quality of this paper.

References

1. Agmon Ben-Yehuda, O., Ben-Yehuda, M., Schuster, A., Tsafrir, D.: Deconstructing amazon EC2 spot instance pricing. ACM T. Econ. Comput. 1(3), 16 (2013)
2. Amazon: Amazon Auto Scaling, http://aws.amazon.com/autoscaling/ (June 2014) (Online accessed June 24, 2014)

3. Amazon: EC2 spot instances (June 2014), http://aws.amazon.com/ec2/purchasing-options/spot-instances/ (Online accessed June 24, 2014)
4. Buyya, R., Yeo, C., Venugopal, S., Broberg, J., Brandic, I.: Cloud computing and emerging IT platforms: Vision, hype, and reality for delivering computing as the 5th utility. Future Gener. Comp. Sy. 25(6), 599–616 (2009)
5. Calheiros, R.N., Ranjan, R., Beloglazov, A., De Rose, C.A., Buyya, R.: Cloudsim: a toolkit for modeling and simulation of cloud computing environments and evaluation of resource provisioning algorithms. Software Pract. Exper. 41(1), 23–50 (2011)
6. Iosup, A., Yigitbasi, N., Epema, D.: On the performance variability of production cloud services, pp. 104–113 (May 2011)
7. Juve, G., Chervenak, A., Deelman, E., Bharathi, S., Mehta, G., Vahi, K.: Characterizing and profiling scientific workflows. Future Gener. Comp. Sy. 29(3), 682–692 (2013)
8. Mao, M., Humphrey, M.: A performance study on the vm startup time in the cloud. In: 2012 IEEE 5th International Conference on Cloud Computing (CLOUD), pp. 423–430. IEEE (2012)
9. Mao, M., Humphrey, M.: Scaling and scheduling to maximize application performance within budget constraints in cloud workflows. In: 2013 IEEE 27th International Symposium on Parallel & Distributed Processing (IPDPS), pp. 67–78. IEEE (2013)
10. Pllana, S., Brandic, I., Benkner, S.: A survey of the state of the art in performance modeling and prediction of parallel and distributed computing systems. Int. J. Comput. Int. Sys. Res. 4(1), 279–284 (2008), http://eprints.cs.univie.ac.at/326/
11. Rahman, M., Hassan, R., Ranjan, R., Buyya, R.: Adaptive workflow scheduling for dynamic grid and cloud computing environment. Concurr. Comp. Pract. E 25(13), 1816–1842 (2013)
12. Schad, J., Dittrich, J., Quiané-Ruiz, J.A.: Runtime measurements in the cloud: Observing, analyzing, and reducing variance. Proc. VLDB Endow. 3(1-2), 460–471 (2010), http://dx.doi.org/10.14778/1920841.1920902
13. Taylor, I., Deelman, E., Gannon, D., Shields, M.: Workflows for e-Science: Scientific Workflows for Grids, 1st edn. Springer, London (2007)
14. Voorsluys, W., Buyya, R.: Reliable provisioning of spot instances for compute-intensive applications. In: 2012 IEEE 26th International Conference on Advanced Information Networking and Applications (AINA), pp. 542–549. IEEE (2012)
15. Wallace, R., Turchenko, V., Sheikhalishahi, M., Turchenko, I., Shults, V., Vazquez-Poletti, J., Grandinetti, L.: Applications of neural-based spot market prediction for cloud computing. In: 2013 IEEE 7th International Conference on Intelligent Data Acquisition and Advanced Computing Systems (IDAACS), vol. 2, pp. 710–716 (September 2013)
16. Yi, S., Andrzejak, A., Kondo, D.: Monetary cost-aware checkpointing and migration on amazon cloud spot instances. IEEE Transactions on Services Computing 5(4), 512–524 (2012)
17. Zhu, M., Wu, Q., Zhao, Y.: A cost-effective scheduling algorithm for scientific workflows in clouds. In: 2012 IEEE 31st International Performance Computing and Communications Conference (IPCCC), pp. 256–265 (2012)

SI-Based Scheduling of Parameter Sweep Experiments on Federated Clouds

Elina Pacini[1,3], Cristian Mateos[2,3], and Carlos García Garino[1]

[1] ITIC - UNCuyo University, Mendoza, Mendoza, Argentina
{epacini,cgarcia}@itu.uncu.edu.ar
[2] ISISTAN - UNICEN University, Tandil, Buenos Aires, Argentina
cmateos@conicet.gov.ar
[3] Consejo Nacional de Investigaciones Científicas y Técnicas (CONICET)

Abstract. Scientists and engineers often require huge amounts of computing power to execute their experiments. This work focuses on the federated Cloud model, where custom virtual machines (VM) are launched in appropriate hosts belonging to different providers to execute scientific experiments and minimize response time. Here, scheduling is performed at three levels. First, at the *broker level*, datacenters are selected by their network latencies via three policies –Lowest-Latency-Time-First, First-Latency-Time-First, and Latency-Time-In-Round–. Second, at the *infrastructure level*, two Cloud VM schedulers based on Ant Colony Optimization (ACO) and Particle Swarm Optimization (PSO) for mapping VMs to appropriate datacenter hosts are implemented. Finally, at the *VM level*, jobs are assigned for execution into the preallocated VMs. Simulated experiments show that the combination of policies at the broker level with ACO and PSO succeed in reducing the response time compared to using the broker level policies combined with Genetic Algorithms.

1 Introduction

Scientific computing is a field that applies Computer Science to solve typical scientific problems. A representative example of scientific experiments is parameter sweep experiments (PSEs) [13]. Running PSEs involves managing many independent jobs, since the experiments are executed under multiple initial configurations a large number of times, to locate a particular point in the parameter space that satisfies certain user criteria. Indeed, users relying on PSEs need a computing environment that delivers large amounts of computational power over a long period of time. A kind of parallel environment that has gained momentum is represented by Clouds [14].

Executing PSEs on Clouds is not free from the well-known scheduling problem, i.e., it is necessary to develop efficient scheduling strategies to appropriately allocate the jobs and reduce the associated computation time. Moreover, in federated Clouds [3] it is necessary to properly manage physical resources, when they are part of geographically distributed datacenters. Therefore, for the efficient execution of jobs in federated Clouds, scheduling should be performed at three levels. Firstly, at the broker level, scheduling strategies are used for selecting datacenters taking into account issues such as network interconnections or monetary cost of allocating VMs on hosts that compose

G. Hernández et al. (Eds.): CARLA 2014, CCIS 485, pp. 28–42, 2014.

them. Secondly, at the infrastructure level, by using a VM scheduler, the VMs are allocated on the available hosts belonging to the previously selected datacenters. Lastly, at the VM level, by using job scheduling techniques, jobs are assigned for execution into allocated virtual resources. However, scheduling is in general an NP-Complete [21] problem and therefore it is not trivial from an algorithmic standpoint. Besides, in this context, the necessity of scheduling algorithms spans the three levels.

In the last ten years, Swarm Intelligence (SI) has received increasing attention among researchers. SI refers to the collective behavior that emerges from a swarm of social insects [9]. Inspired by these capabilities, researchers have proposed algorithms or theories for combinatorial optimization problems, where the most popular SI-based strategies are Ant Colony Optimization (ACO) and Particle Swarm Optimization (PSO). Moreover, job scheduling in Clouds is also a combinatorial optimization problem, and schedulers in this line that exploit SI have been proposed.

Existing efforts which address SI have not being studied in the context of federated Clouds. In this paper, unlike previous works of our own [16,18] where we proposed a two-level scheduler for Clouds composed of a single datacenter, in this work we extend the scheduler for operating in federated Clouds. To this end, the scheduler operates at three levels. Firstly, by means of a policy that operates at the broker level, datacenters are selected according to their network interconnections and latencies. Indeed, the network latencies among datacenters can contribute to negatively affect the response time delivered to the user. We consider three policies, Lowest-Latency-Time-First (LLTF), First-Latency-Time-First (FLTF), and Latency-Time-In-Round (LTIR). Then, at the infrastructure level, we have explored ACO and PSO for allocating the VMs into the physical resources of a datacenter. To allocate the VMs into hosts, each scheduler must make a different number of "queries" to hosts to determine their availability upon each VM allocation attempt. These queries are actually messages sent to hosts over the network to obtain information regarding their availability. The number of queries to be performed by each algorithm and the latencies of datacenters also influence the response time to the user. Finally, at the VM level, PSE-jobs are assigned to the preallocated VMs by using FIFO, as in [18]. Briefly, in this paper we include the broker level and evaluate how decisions taken both at the broker level and infrastructure level influence the response time.

Simulated experiments performed with job data extracted from a real-world PSE [6] involving a viscoplastic problem suggest that the SI schedulers at the infrastructure level, in combination with these policies at the broker level and FIFO at the VM level, deliver competitive performance with respect to the response time. Experiments were performed by using the CloudSim [2] simulator. To set the basis for comparison, and since VM scheduling is highly challenging and heavily contributes to the overall performance in Cloud scheduling [20], we used the same three policies at the broker level and FIFO at the VM level in combination with a scheduler based on Genetic Algorithms (GA) [1].

The rest of the paper is as follows. Section 2 gives some background necessary to understand the concepts underpinning our scheduler. Section 3 surveys relevant related works. Section 4 presents our proposal. Section 5 presents the experimental evaluation. Section 6 concludes the paper and discusses future prospective extensions.

2 Background

Clouds [14] are the current emerging trend in delivering IT services, and offer to end-users a variety of services covering the entire computing stack. Scientists in general and PSEs users in particular can completely customize their execution environment, thus deploying the most appropriate setup for their experiments. Another related important feature is the ability to scale up and down the computing infrastructure according to PSEs resource requirements.

In the next subsections we describe the federated Cloud basics (Subsection 2.1), and introduce the classical SI-based algorithms (Subsection 2.2), the core optimization techniques of the schedulers implemented in this work at the infrastructure level.

2.1 Federated Clouds

Federated Clouds [15] consist of infrastructures with physical resources belonging to different Cloud providers. A federated Cloud could involve different architectures and levels of coupling among federated datacenters. Federated Clouds also make use of *brokers* to meet the needs of their participating organizations. A broker is an entity which keeps a queue of requests from a particular user that need to be provisioned by a datacenter. In the context of this work, where a user runs PSEs, only one broker is associated with that user.

Clouds allow the dynamic scaling of users applications by the provisioning of computing resources via *machine images*, or VMs. In order to achieve good performance, VMs have to fully utilize its services and resources by adapting to the Cloud dynamically. Proper allocation of resources must be guaranteed so as to improve resource usefulness [15].

For running applications in a Cloud, resources are scheduled at three levels (Figure 1): Broker level, Infrastructure level, and VM level. At the broker level, different policies can be implemented in order to serve users. Some examples are policies considering the influence of network interconnections among Cloud datacenters or monetary cost of hosts that compose them [1]. Furthermore, the scheduler at this level can decide to deploy the VMs in a remote Cloud when there are insufficient physical resources in the datacenter where the VM creation was issued. Secondly, once a datacenter/provider has been selected by a broker, at the infrastructure level, the VMs are allocated into real hardware through a VM scheduler. Finally, at the VM level, by using job scheduling techniques, jobs are assigned for execution into virtual resources (the allocated VMs). Figure 1 illustrates a Cloud where one or more users are connected via a network and require the creation of a number of VMs for executing their experiments, i.e., a set of jobs. As can be seen in the Figure 1, a broker is created for each user that connects to the Cloud. Each broker knows who are the providers that are part of the federation through network interconnections –the relation of each broker is colored with green and blue dotted lines–. In addition, the Figure 1 illustrates how jobs sent by *User N* are executed in the datacenter of *Cloud Provider 2*. At the right of this provider –inside the dotted Cloud– the intra-datacenter scheduling activities are depicted, i.e., at the infrastructure level and the VM level.

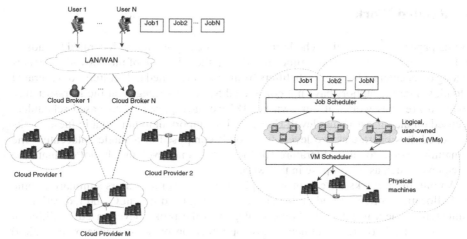

Fig. 1. High-level view of a federated Cloud

2.2   SI Techniques for Cloud Scheduling

Broadly, SI techniques [9] have shown to be useful in optimization problems. The advantage of these techniques derives from their ability to explore solutions in large search spaces in a very efficient way. The most popular SI-based techniques are ACO and PSO. ACO [9] arises from the way real ants behave in nature, i.e., from the observation of ant colonies when they search the shortest paths to reach a food source from their nest. In nature, real ants move randomly from one place to another to search for food, and upon finding food and returning to their nest each ant leaves a *pheromone* that lures other working ants to the same course. When more and more ants choose the same path, the pheromone trail is reinforced and even more ants will further choose it. Over time the shortest paths will be intensified by the pheromone faster since the ants will both reach the food source and travel back to their nest at a faster rate.

On the other hand, PSO [9] is a population-based technique that finds solution to a problem in a search space by modeling and predicting insect social behavior in the presence of objectives. In the algorithm the general term "particle" is used to represent birds, bees or any other individuals who exhibit social behavior as group and interact with each other. An example based on nature to illustrate the algorithm is as follows: a group of bees flies over the countryside looking for flowers. Their goal is to find as many flowers as possible. At the beginning, bees do not have knowledge of the field and fly to random locations with random velocities looking for flowers. Each bee has the capability of remember the places where it saw the most flowers, and moreover, somehow knows the places where other bees have found a high density of flowers. These two pieces of information –*nostalgia* and *social knowledge*– are used by the bees to continually modify their trajectory, i.e., each bee alters its path between the two directions to fly somewhere between the two points and find a greater density of flowers. Occasionally, a bee may fly over a place with more flowers than any other place found previously by other bees in the swarm. If this happens the whole swarm is attracted towards this new direction.

3   Related Work

In this paper we address the scheduling of scientific application in federated Clouds in order to minimize the response time considering the influence of the network latencies among datacenters. Our approach differs from those presented in literature for federated Cloud, where the authors have not considered SI-based strategies at the infrastructure level. In previous works of our own [16,18] we have presented SI-based schedulers focused on the infrastructure level. However, it is important to note that in these works the schedulers operate at two levels for Clouds composed of a single datacenter. The remaining works found in literature are focused on one level and do not evaluate the three levels such as we propose in this work.

Among these works we can mention [5,10,20]. In [5] the authors summarize some VM allocation policies based on linear programming for different Cloud federation architectures. Then, in [10] scheduling strategies at the broker level based on different optimization criteria (e.g., monetary cost optimization or performance optimization) and different user constraints (e.g., budget, performance, VMs types) were proposed. Moreover, in [20], the scheduler restricts the deployment of VMs according to some placement constraints (e.g., Clouds to deploy the VMs) defined by the user.

Two works that deserve special attention are [1,4]. In [1], the authors used at the broker level, a Dijkstra algorithm to select the datacenter with lower monetary cost, and a GA for allocating the VMs at the infrastructure level. Although in this work the authors target the broker and the infrastructure levels, the goal was to reduce the monetary costs without considering the response time. For scientific applications in general, the response time is very important [18]. Moreover, in [4] the authors proposed an ACO scheduler based on load balancing to perform efficient distribution of jobs by finding the best VM to execute jobs. The aim of this work was minimizing the makespan and improve load balancing in the VMs. Makespan is the maximum execution time of a set of jobs. To the best of our knowledge, this is the only work in literature in which the authors have considered the use of SI for federated Clouds. However, it is important to note that ACO was implemented at the VM level and not at the infrastructure level.

With respect to works which address the scheduling problem at the infrastructure level –intra-datacenter– using SI-based strategies as we propose in this work, few efforts have been found [17]. However, in these related works, it is important to note that SI techniques are used to solve the job scheduling problem, i.e., determining how the jobs are assigned to pre-allocated VMs, and few efforts have aimed to solve VM scheduling problems to date [17]. It is worth noting that, from the related works found, most of them have been proposed for Clouds taking into account only one of the scheduling levels without considering SI for allocating VMs, or Clouds composed by a single datacenter where only scheduling of jobs (and not VMs) is addressed. The next Section explains our approach, which considers the three levels described in Subsection 2.1.

4   Proposed Scheduler

The goal of our scheduler is to minimize the response time of a set of PSE jobs. Response time is the period of time between a user makes a request to the Cloud and gets the answer, i.e., the period of time in which a user requests a number of VMs to execute its PSE, and the time in which all the entire PSE-jobs finish their execution. Conceptually, the scheduling problem to tackle down can be formulated as follows. A PSE is formally defined as a set of $N = 1, 2, ..., n$ independent jobs, where each job corresponds to a particular value for a variable of the model being studied by the PSE. The jobs are distributed and executed on the v VMs issued by the user. With the goal of minimizing the response time, the need to implement strategies to select the appropriate datacenters in which to place the VMs arises. For example, the most suitable datacenter might be the one that provides the lowest communication latency to a broker when this latter asks about the availability of physical resources. Latency is due to delays by packets moving over the various networks between the end user computer and the geographically distributed Cloud datacenters. One way to mitigate the effects of such latencies is to choose a datacenter which operates with a fast and efficient internal network and plenty of capacity.

The proposed scheduler proceeds as follows. Firstly, at the broker level, a datacenter is selected by a policy that takes into account network interconnections and/or network latencies. Secondly, at the infrastructure level, by means of a VM scheduler, user VMs are allocated in the physical resources (i.e., hosts) belonging to the selected datacenter at the broker level. When there are no available hosts in the datacenter to allocate the VMs, a new datacenter is selected at the broker level. Finally, at the VM level, a policy for assigning user jobs to allocated VMs is also used (currently we use FIFO).

4.1 Scheduler at the Broker Level

The scheduler at the broker level is executed both to select the first datacenter to allocate the VMs, which are managed by the scheduler implemented at the infrastructure level, as well as each time such datacenter is not able to perform the allocation of VMs anymore. At present, the policies implemented at this level are:

- Lowest-Latency-Time-First (LLTF), maintains a list of all network interconnected datacenters sorted by their latencies. Each time a user requires a number the VMs to execute their PSE, this policy is responsible for selecting first the datacenter with the lowest latency in the list. Then, whenever a datacenter has no more physical resources to allocate VMs, then the algorithm selects the next datacenter in the list.
- First-Latency-Time-First (FLTF) selects the first datacenter from a list sorted randomly, containing all network interconnected datacenters to which a user can access and allocate his VMs. When the selected datacenter has no more available physical resources to allocate VMs, the algorithm selects the next datacenter in the list.
- Latency-Time-In-Round (LTIR) maintains a list of all network interconnected datacenters that make up the Cloud, sorted by increasing latency, and assigns each VM required by the user to a datacenter from the list in a circular order.

4.2 Scheduler at the Infrastructure Level

To implement the Infrastructure level policy, the SI algorithms proposed in [18] are used. Below we describe these algorithms.

Scheduler Based on Ant Colony Optimization. In this algorithm, each ant works independently and represents a VM "looking" for the best host to which it can be allocated. When a VM is created in a datacenter, an ant is initialized and starts to work. A master table containing information on the load of each host in the selected datacenter is initialized. Subsequently, if an ant associated to the VM that is executing the algorithm already exists, the ant is obtained from a pool of ants. If the VM does not exist in the ant pool, then a new ant is created. To do this, first, a list of all suitable hosts belonging to the selected datacenter in which can be allocated the VM is obtained.

Algorithm 1. ACO-based Cloud scheduler: Core logic

```
Procedure AntAlgorithm()
Begin
  step=1
  initialize()
  While (step < maxSteps) do
    currentLoad=getHostLoadInformation()
    AntHistory.add(currentLoad)
    localLoadTable.update()
    if(currentLoad = 0.0)
      break
    else if (random() < mutationRate) then
      nextHost=randomlyChooseNextStep()
    else
      nextHost=chooseNextStep()
    end if
    mutationRate=mutationRate-decayRate
    step=step+1
    moveTo(nextHost)
  end while
  deliverVMtoHost()
End
```

Then, the working ant and its associated VM is added to the ant pool and the ACO-specific logic starts to operate (see Algorithm 1). In each iteration, the ant collects the load information of the host that is visiting and adds this information to its private load history. The ant then updates a load information table of visited hosts (`localLoadTable.update()`), which is maintained in each host. This table contains information of the own load of an ant, as well as load information of other hosts of the datacenter, which were added to the table when other ants visited the host. Here, load refers to the total CPU utilization within a host and is calculated taking into account the number of VMs that are executing at a given time in each physical host.

When an ant moves from one host to another it has two choices: moving to a random host using a constant probability or *mutation rate*, or using the load table information of the current host (`chooseNextStep()`). The mutation rate decreases with a *decay rate* factor as time passes, thus, the ant will be more dependent on load information than to random choice. When an ant reads the information from a load table in a host, the ant chooses the lightest loaded host in the table, i.e., each entry of the load information table is evaluated and compared with the current load of the visited host. If the load of the visited host is smaller than any other host provided in the load information table, the ant chooses the host with the smallest load. This process is repeated until the finishing criterion is met. The completion criterion is equal to a predefined number of steps (*maxSteps*). Finally, the ant delivers its VM to the current host and finishes its task. Since each step performed by an ant involves moving through the intra-datacenter network, we have added a control to minimize the number of steps that an ant performs: every time an ant visits a host that has not allocated VMs yet, the ant allocates its associated VM to it directly without performing further steps. Every time an ant sends a message through the intra-datacenter network to obtain information regarding the availability of the hosts from the selected datacenter latencies are produced. The smaller the number messages sent to the hosts through the network, the smaller the impact of the latencies in the response time given to the user.

Every time an ant visits a host, it updates the host load information table with the information of other hosts in the datacenter, but at the same time the ant collects the information already provided by the table of that host, if any. The load information table acts as a pheromone trail that an ant leaves while it is moving, to guide other ants to choose better paths rather than wandering randomly in the Cloud. Entries of each local table are the hosts that ants have visited on their way to deliver their VMs together with their load information.

Scheduler Based on Particle Swarm Optimization. In this algorithm, each particle works independently and represents a VM looking for the best host –in the selected datacenter at the broker level– to which it can be allocated. Following the analogy from the example of bees in Subsection 2.2, each VM is considered a bee and each host represent locations in the field with different density of flowers. When a VM is created, a particle is initialized in a random host, i.e., in a random place in the field. The density of flowers of each host is determined by its load.

This definition helps to search in the load search space –in the field of flowers– and try to minimize the load. The smaller the load on a host, the better the flower concentration. This means that the host has more available resources to allocate a VM. In the algorithm (see Algorithm 2), every time a user requires a VM, a particle is initialized in a random host of the selected datacenter (`getInitialHost()`). Each particle in the search space takes a position according to the load of the host in which is initialized through the `calculateTotalLoad(hostId)` method. Load refers to the total CPU utilization within a host and is calculated as well as ACO. The neighborhood of each particle is composed by the remaining hosts in a datacenter excluding the one in which the particle is initialized. The neighborhood of that particle is obtained through `getNeighbors(hostId,neighborSize)`. Each one of the neighbors –hosts– that compose the neighborhood are selected randomly. Moreover, the size of the particle neighborhood is a parameter defined by the user.

In each iteration of the algorithm, the particle moves to the neighbors of its current host in search of a host with a lower load. The velocity of each particle is defined by the load difference between the host to which the particle has been previously assigned with respect to its other neighboring hosts. If any of the hosts in the neighborhood has a lower load than the original host, then the particle is moved to the neighbor host with a greater velocity. Taking into account that the particles move through hosts of their neighborhood into a datacenter in search of a host with the lower load, the algorithm reaches a local optimum quickly. Thus, each particle makes a move from their associated host to one of its neighbors, which has the minimum load among all. If all its neighbors are busier than the associated host itself, the particle is not moved from the current host. Finally, the particle delivers its associated VM to the host with the lower load among their neighbors and finishes its task.

Algorithm 2. PSO-based Cloud scheduler: Core logic

```
Procedure PSOallocationPolicy (vm, hostList)
Begin
  particle = new Particle (vm, hostList)
  initialHostId = particle.getInitialHost ()
  currentPositionLoad = particle.calculateTotalLoad (initialHostId)
  neighbours = particle.getNeighbours (initialHostId, neighbourSize)
  While (i < neighbours.size()) do
    neighbourId = neighbours.get(i)
    destPositionLoad = particle.calculateTotalLoad (neighbourId)
    if (destPositionLoad == 0)
      currentPositionLoad = destPositionLoad
      destHostId = neighbours.get(i)
      i=neighbours.size ()
    end if
    if (currentPositionLoad - destPositionLoad > velocity)
      velocity = currentPositionLoad - destPositionLoad
      currentPositionLoad = destPositionLoad
      destHostId = neighbours.get(i)
    end if
  i=i+1
  end while
  allocatedHost=hostList.get(destHostId)
  if (! allocatedHost.allocateVM (vm)
    PSOallocationPolicy (vm, hostList)
End
```

Since each move a particle performs involves traveling through the intra-datacenter network, similarly to ACO, a control to minimize the number of moves that a particle performs have been added: every time a particle moves from the associated host to a neighbor host that has not allocated VMs yet, the particle allocates its associated VM to it immediately. The smaller the number messages sent to the hosts through the network by a particle, the smaller the impact of the latency in the response time given to the user.

4.3   Scheduler at the VM Level

Once the VMs have been allocated to physical resources at the Infrastructure level, the job scheduler proceeds to assign the jobs to these VMs. This sub-algorithm uses two lists, one containing the jobs that have been sent by the user, i.e., a PSE, and the other list contains all user VMs that are already allocated to a physical resource and hence are ready to execute jobs. The algorithm iterates the list of all jobs, and then retrieves jobs by a FIFO policy. Each time a job is obtained from the list, it is submitted to be executed in a VM in a round robin fashion. Internally, the algorithm maintains a queue for each VM that contains its list of jobs to be executed. The procedure is repeated until all jobs have been submitted for execution. Due to their high CPU requirements, and the fact that each VM requires only one PE, we assumed a 1-1 job-VM execution model, i.e., jobs within a VM waiting queue are executed one at a time by competing for CPU time with other jobs from other VMs in the same hosts. This is, a time-shared CPU scheduling policy was used, since it is a good alternative for executing CPU-intensive jobs in terms of fairness.

5   Evaluation

To assess the effectiveness of our proposal, we processed a real case study for solving a well-known benchmark problem [6]. Details on the experimental methodology are provided in Section 5.1. After that, we compared our proposal with a GA in terms of the metric of interest in this paper, i.e., response time. The results are explained in Subsection 5.2.

5.1   Experimental Methodology

A plane strain plate with a central circular hole, see reference [6] and therein is studied. The dimensions of the plate were 18 x 10 m, with $R = 5$ m. The 3D finite element mesh used had 1,152 elements. To generate the PSE jobs, a material parameter –viscosity η– was selected as the variation parameter. Then, 25 different viscosity values for the η parameter were considered, namely $x.10^y$ Mpa, with $x = 1, 2, 3, 4, 5, 7$ and $y = 4, 5, 6, 7$, plus 1.10^8 Mpa. Introductory details on viscoplastic theory and numerical implementation can be found in [6].

After establishing the problem parameters, we employed a single machine to run the parameter sweep experiment by varying the viscosity parameter η as indicated and measuring the execution time for the 25 different experiments, which resulted in 25 input files with different input configurations and 25 output files. The tests were solved using the SOGDE finite element solver software [7]. Once the execution times were obtained from the real machine, we approximated for each experiment the number of executed instructions by the following formula $NI_i = mipsCPU * T_i$, where NI_i is the number of million instructions to be executed by or associated to a job i, $mipsCPU$ is the processing power of the CPU of our real machine measured in MIPS, and T_i is the time that took to run the job i on the real machine. For example, for a job taking 539 seconds to execute, the approximated number of instructions was 2,160,657 MI (Million Instructions). By means of the generated job data, we instantiated the CloudSim toolkit [2].

The experimental scenario consists of a Cloud composed of 5 datacenters. The network topology is defined in the Boston university Representative Internet Topology gEnerator (BRITE) [8] format. BRITE is a file used by CloudSim which defines the different nodes that compose a commonly-found federation (e.g., datacenters, brokers) and the network connections among them. This file is then used to calculate latencies in network traffic. Then, each datacenter is composed of 10 physical resources –or "host" in CloudSim terminology–. The characteristics of hosts are 4,008 MIPS (processing power), 4 GBytes (RAM), 400 GBytes (storage), 100 Mbps (bandwidth), and 4 CPUs.

Furthermore, each datacenter has an associated latency of 0.8, 1.5, 0.5, 0.15, 2.8 seconds, respectively. These latencies have been assigned taking into account other works proposed in the literature [12,19].

Moreover, a user requests 100 VMs to execute its PSE. Each VM has one virtual CPU of 4,008 MIPS, 512 Mbyte of RAM, a machine image size of 100 Gbytes and a bandwidth of 25 Mbps. For further details about the job data gathering and the CloudSim instantiation process, please refer to [13,18].

In this work, we evaluated the performance of the user PSE-jobs as we increased the number of jobs to be performed from 1,000 to 10,000. This is, the base job set comprising 25 jobs that was obtained by varying the value of η was cloned to obtain larger sets. Each job was determined by a length parameter or the number of instructions to be executed by the job, which varied between 1,362,938 and 2,160,657 MI. Moreover, another parameter was PEs, or the number of processing elements (cores) required to perform each individual job. Each job required one PE since jobs are sequential (not multi-threaded). Finally, the experiments had input files of 291,738 bytes and output files of 5,662,310 bytes.

5.2   Performed Experiments

In this subsection we report results obtained through our proposed three level scheduler. Particularly, at the infrastructure level we compare to another alternative scheduler based on GA proposed in [1], which has been previously evaluated via CloudSim as well. The population structure is represented as the set of physical resources that compose a datacenter and each chromosome is an individual in the population that represents a part of the searching space. Each gene (field in a chromosome) is a physical resource in a datacenter, and the last field in this structure is the *fitness* field, which indicate the suitability of the hosts in each chromosome.

In our experiments, the GA-specific parameters were set to the following values: *chromosome size = 8, population size = 10* and *number of iterations = 10*. Moreover, we have set the ACO-specific parameters to values within the range of values studied in [11]: *mutation rate = 0.6, decay rate = 0.1* and *maximum steps = 8*, and the PSO-specific parameter *neighbourhood size = 8*. Since the number of hosts that compose each datacenter is equal to 10, a specific parameter values (i.e., maxSteps in ACO, neighborhood in PSO and chromosome size in GA) equal to 8, means exploring a percentage of the 80% of the number of hosts for each datacenter.

Figure 2 compares the obtained results for all the considered scheduling algorithms (ACO, PSO, GA) and each one the policies at the broker level (LLTF, FLTF, LTIR) in subfigures a), b) and c), respectively. Graphically, it can be seen that the response time presents a linear tendency in all cases. As shown in the subfigures included in Figure 2, regardless of the policy used at the broker level, GA is the algorithm that produces the greatest response time to the user with respect to ACO and PSO.

Since the GA algorithm contains a population size of 10 and chromosome sizes of 8, for each datacenter in which it tries to create the VMs, to calculate the fitness function, the algorithm sends one message for each host of the chromosome to know its availability and obtain the chromosome containing the best fitness value. The number of messages sent is equals to the number of host within each chromosome multiplied by

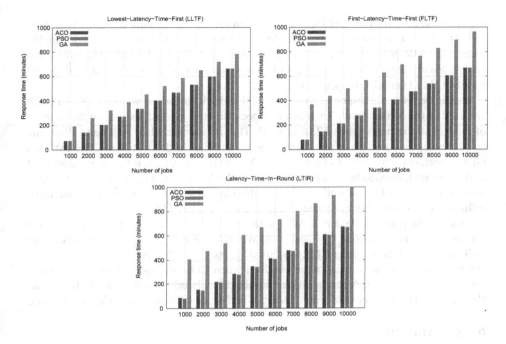

Fig. 2. Response time as the number of jobs increases

the population size. The number of messages to send through the network for each algorithm directly impacts the response time to the user. This is because for each message sent to query about hosts availability, latencies from datacenters affect the answers.

The proposed ACO and PSO, however, make less use of network resources than GA, being in some cases PSO the one which sends less network messages. The number of messages to send by ACO depends of the maximum number of steps that an ant carries out to allocate its associated VM. For example, when the maximum number of steps is equals to 8, ACO sends a maximum of 8 messages per VM allocation. Moreover, when ACO finds an idle host, it allocates the current VM and does not perform any further step. This reduces the total number of network messages sent. On the other hand, the number of network messages to send by PSO depends of the neighborhood size, which is also equals to 8, i.e., PSO sends a maximum of 8 messages per VM allocation. Furthermore, like ACO, when PSO finds an idle host, it allocates the current VM and does not make any further move. This also reduces the total number of network messages sent, and therefore, the total latency that influences the user response time.

Another observations from the subfigures included in Figure 2 are that when the LLTF policy is used combined with PSO, ACO and GA, the response time decreases with respect to FLTF and LTIR policies. This happens because most VMs are created in datacenters with lower latencies. For example, when the LLTF policy is used and the number of jobs to be executed is increased from 1,000 to 10,000, the response time varied between (71–661), (72–661), and (191–780) minutes, for PSO, ACO and GA, respectively. On the other hand, when the FLTF policy is used at the broker level, the response time for PSO, ACO, and GA, when the number of jobs was increased from 1,000 to 10,000, varied between (79–668), (79–668), and (367–962) minutes. Finally, when the LTIR policy is used, the response time rose from (79– 668), (84–673), and (409–996) minutes, when the number of jobs was increased from 1,000 to 10,000, and for PSO, ACO and GA, respectively.

As can be seen, the response times for ACO and PSO are close when FLTF and LTIR are used at the broker level. The reason is because both algorithms reduce the number of queries to the hosts when LTIR is used. This is because when ACO and PSO find an idle host, they not make any further move, and due to the fact that LTIR explores all datacenters (in a circular order for each VM to be allocated), it has more chance of finding an underloaded hosts where to allocate the VMs. However, if the user requests the execution of a larger number of VMs, the latencies of datacenters will have more influence in the response time when LTIR is used instead of FLTF.

Finally, the gains of PSO and ACO with respect to GA, when LLTF is used at the broker level varied between 15% and 62%. When FLTF was used, gains varied between 30% and 78%. Lastly, when LTIR was used, gains varied between 32% and 80%. As can be seen, the greatest gains were obtained when LTIR was used at the broker level. The is because, since GA sent a greater number of network messages to the hosts than PSO and ACO, the inter-datacenter latencies had more influence on the response time.

6   Conclusions

One popular kind of scientific experiments are PSEs, which involve running many CPU-intensive independent jobs. These jobs must be efficiently processed –i.e., scheduled– in the different computing resources of a distributed environment such as the ones provided by Cloud. The growing popularity of Cloud environments has increased the attention in the research of resource allocation mechanisms across datacenters. Federated Clouds potentially provide plenty of resources to users, specially when the number of VMs required by a user exceeds the maximum that can be provided by a single provider or datacenter. Then, job/VM scheduling plays a fundamental role.

Recently, SI-inspired algorithms have received increasing attention in the Cloud research community for dealing with VM and job scheduling. In this work, we described two schedulers –based on ACO and PSO– for the efficient allocation of VMs in a datacenter combined with three strategies –LLTF, FLTF and LTIR– that consider network information for selecting datacenters. Simulated experiments performed with CloudSim and real PSE job data suggest that our PSO and ACO schedulers provide better response times to the user than GA. In addition, when PSO, ACO and GA are combined with LLTF, the response time is the lowest for all of them w.r.t. FLTF and LTIR, being LTIR the most influential on the response time.

We are extending this work in several directions. We will explore the ideas exposed in this paper in the context of other bio-inspired techniques such as Artificial Bee Colony (ABC), which is also extensively used to solve combinatorial optimization problems. Another issue which deserves attention is to consider other Cloud scenarios [15] with heterogeneous physical resources belonging to different Cloud providers.

Due to multi-tenancy, in Clouds it is necessary to provide distributed scheduling mechanisms for allocating resources to a number of independent users' VMs/jobs along with time constraints. For this, we plan to implement a Cloud scheduler based on SI techniques in order to *fairly* schedule users' VMs/jobs based on different optimization criteria (e.g., cost, execution times, etc.).

Finally, another interesting issue consists of providing more elaborated dynamic optimization capabilities, enabling the dynamic reallocation (migration) of VMs from one physical machine to another to meet a specific optimization criteria such as improving the response time, reducing the number of physical resources in use for minimizing energy consumption, or balancing the workload of all resources to avoid resources saturation and performance slowdown. In addition, the user could also specify constraints for the scheduler decisions such as hardware (amount of CPU, memory, bandwidth, etc.), platform (type of hypervisor, operating system, etc.), location (geographical restrictions), among others.

Acknowledgments. We acknowledge the financial support provided by ANPCyT through grants PICT-2012-0045 and PICT-2012-2731, and National University of Cuyo project 06B/308. The first author acknowledges her Ph.D. fellowship granted by the National Scientific and Technological Research Council (CONICET).

References

1. Agostinho, L., Feliciano, G., Olivi, L., Cardozo, E., Guimaraes, E.: A Bio-inspired approach to provisioning of virtual resources in federated Clouds. In: Ninth International Conference on Dependable, Autonomic and Secure Computing (DASC), DASC 2011, December 12-14, pp. 598–604. IEEE (2011)
2. Calheiros, R., Ranjan, R., Beloglazov, A., De Rose, C., Buyya, R.: Cloudsim: A toolkit for modeling and simulation of Cloud Computing environments and evaluation of resource provisioning algorithms. Software: Practice & Experience 41(1), 23–50 (2011)
3. Celesti, A., Fazio, M., Villari, M., Puliafito, A.: Virtual machine provisioning through satellite communications in federated Cloud environments. Future Generation Computer Systems 28(1), 85–93 (2012)
4. de Oliveira, G., Ribeiro, E., Ferreira, D., Araújo, A., Holanda, M., Walter, M.: ACOsched: a scheduling algorithm in a federated Cloud infrastructure for bioinformatics applications. In: International Conference on Bioinformatics and Biomedicine, pp. 8–14. IEEE (2013)
5. Gahlawat, M., Sharma, P.: Survey of virtual machine placement in federated Clouds. In: International Advance Computing Conference (IACC), pp. 735–738. IEEE (2014)
6. García Garino, C., Ribero Vairo, M., Andía Fagés, S., Mirasso, A., Ponthot, J.P.: Numerical simulation of finite strain viscoplastic problems. Journal of Computational and Applied Mathematics 246, 174–184 (2013)
7. García Garino, C., Gabaldón, F., Goicolea, J.M.: Finite element simulation of the simple tension test in metals. Finite Elements in Analysis and Design 42(13), 1187–1197 (2006)
8. Jung, J., Jung, S., Kim, T., Chung, T.: A study on the Cloud simulation with a network topology generator. World Academy of Science, Engineering & Technology 6, 303–306 (2012)
9. Kennedy, J.: Swarm Intelligence. In: Zomaya, A. (ed.) Handbook of Nature-Inspired and Innovative Computing, pp. 187–219. Springer, US (2006)
10. Lucas-Simarro, J., Moreno-Vozmediano, R., Montero, R., Llorente, I.: Scheduling strategies for optimal service deployment across multiple clouds. Future Generation Computer Systems 29(6), 1431–1441 (2013)

11. Ludwig, S., Moallem, A.: Swarm Intelligence approaches for Grid load balancing. Journal of Grid Computing 9(3), 279–301 (2011)
12. Malik, S., Huet, F., Caromel, D.: Latency based group discovery algorithm for network aware Cloud scheduling. Future Generation Computer Systems 31, 28–39 (2014)
13. Mateos, C., Pacini, E., García Garino, C.: An ACO-inspired algorithm for minimizing weighted flowtime in Cloud-based parameter sweep experiments. Advances in Engineering Software 56, 38–50 (2013)
14. Mauch, V., Kunze, M., Hillenbrand, M.: High performance cloud computing. Future Generation Computer Systems 29(6), 1408–1416 (2013)
15. Moreno Vozmediano, R., Montero, R., Llorente, I.: IaaS Cloud architecture: FromvVirtualized datacenters to federated Cloud infrastructures. IEEE Computer 45(12), 65–72 (2012)
16. Pacini, E., Mateos, C., García Garino, C.: Dynamic scheduling of scientific experiments on Clouds using Ant Colony Optimization. In: Topping, B.H.V., Iványi, P. (eds.) Proceedings of the Third International Conference on Parallel, Distributed, Grid and Cloud Computing for Engineering, paper 33. Civil-Comp Press, Stirlingshire (2013)
17. Pacini, E., Mateos, C., García Garino, C.: Distributed job scheduling based on Swarm Intelligence: A survey. Computers & Electrical Engineering 40(1), 252–269 (2014), 40th-year commemorative issue
18. Pacini, E., Mateos, C., García Garino, C.: Multi-objective Swarm Intelligence schedulers for online scientific Clouds. Computing. Special Issue on Cloud Computing, 1–28 (2014)
19. Somasundaram, T., Govindarajan, K.: CLOUDRB: A framework for scheduling and managing High-Performance Computing (HPC) applications in science Cloud. Future Generation Computer Systems 34, 47–65 (2014)
20. Tordsson, J., Montero, R., Moreno Vozmediano, R., Llorente, I.: Cloud brokering mechanisms for optimized placement of virtual machines across multiple providers. Future Generation Computer Systems 28(2), 358–367 (2012)
21. Woeginger, G.: Exact Algorithms for NP-Hard Problems: A Survey. In: Jünger, M., Reinelt, G., Rinaldi, G. (eds.) Combinatorial Optimization - Eureka, You Shrink! LNCS, vol. 2570, pp. 185–207. Springer, Heidelberg (2003)

Distributed Cache Strategies for Machine Learning Classification Tasks over Cluster Computing Resources

John Edilson Arévalo Ovalle[1], Raúl Ramos-Pollan[2],
and Fabio A. González[1]

[1] Universidad Nacional de Colombia
{jearevaloo,fagonzalezo}@unal.edu.co
[2] Unidad de Supercómputo y Cálculo Científico,
Universidad Industrial de Santander Colombia
rramosp@uis.edu.co

Abstract. Scaling machine learning (ML) methods to learn from large datasets requires devising distributed data architectures and algorithms to support their iterative nature where the same data records are processed several times. Data caching becomes key to minimize data transmission through iterations at each node and, thus, contribute to the overall scalability. In this work we propose a two level caching architecture (disk and memory) and benchmark different caching strategies in a distributed machine learning setup over a cluster with no shared RAM memory. Our results strongly favour strategies where (1) datasets are partitioned and preloaded throughout the distributed memory of the cluster nodes and (2) algorithms use data locality information to synchronize computations at each iteration. This supports the convergence towards models where "computing goes to data" as observed in other Big Data contexts, and allows us to align strategies for parallelizing ML algorithms and configure appropriately computing infrastructures.

1 Introduction

Data caching strategies have become a key issue in scaling machine learning methods that typically iterate several times over a given dataset aiming at reducing some error measure on their predictions. It is known that as dataset sizes increase we need to adapt or even redesign the algorithms and devise the appropriate software and hardware architectures to support them. This is especially true if we want to endow our systems with horizontal scalability, where increased performance is to be achieved not by upgrading the existing computing resources (faster machines with more memory) but by adding more computing resources of a similar (commodity) kind.

In this sense, machine learning methods are particularly sensible to below-optimal architectures as they typically need to iterate or process large amounts of data which necessarily lives on distributed storage. Despite the fact there is a rich variety of machine learning methods, many of them follow a common pattern:

G. Hernández et al. (Eds.): CARLA 2014, CCIS 485, pp. 43–53, 2014.

iterative optimization of a loss function which is evaluated (several times) on a training data set. For this, machine learning algorithms need to be redesigned to efficiently access and reuse data in a synchronized manner to preserve their behavior (i.e. improving the prediction accuracy) whilst scaling horizontally to analyze larger datasets.

Different complementary approaches exist today to deal with this problem, such as using the map-reduce computing model [11], engineering stochastic or online versions of existing algorithms [1,5], reformulating the algorithms in a distributed manner [3,4], etc. Furthermore, several software frameworks have emerged in the last years to support these processes in a scalable manner to different extents [12,13,6]. Notably, Spark proposes a memory-only caching architecture which is recently gaining popularity.

This work complements this architecture by combining disk and memory caches and enabling a finer grained configuration for deciding what portions of data reside on the caches of each computing node. We focus on ML algorithms that fit the Statistical Query Model [2] (see section 2.1) which represents a vast majority of the algorithms. This way, we obtain parallel versions with relatively low effort and combine them with distributed cache strategies [8] to understand their behavior and settle for suitable strategies for scalable machine learning methods. Our experiments are based on BIGS (Big Image Data Analysis Toolkit), a framework which enables programming such algorithms in a distributed and opportunistic manner; and were run over a virtualized computing cluster using the OpenNebula stack at the computing facilities in our universities. BIGS was extended by implementing the cache strategies described and benchmarked in this work.

Our results strongly favour strategies where (1) datasets are partitioned and pre loaded throughout the distributed memory of the different cluster nodes and (2) algorithms use data locality information to maximize data reuse and synchronize computations at each iteration through the data. This supports the convergence towards models where "computing goes to data" as observed in other Big Data related contexts.

The rest of this paper is structured as follows. Section 2 describes our implementation of a parallel machine learning classification algorithms with distributed cache. Section 3 describes our experimental setup. Section 4 discuss the experiments results and, finally, in Section 5 we expose our concluding remarks.

2   Distributed Machine Learning

A majority of ML algorithms adhere to the Statistical Query Model [2], through which algorithms trying to learn a function $f(x,y)$ of the data (such as to measure the prediction or classification errors) are required to return an estimate of the expectation of $f(x,y)$ using test and train data. Algorithms falling in this class approach this problem through mathematical optimization (such as to minimize prediction error) and use gradients or sufficient statistics for this. These computations are typically expressible as a sum over data points and therefore are partitionable and distributable. If we have m data points, a sum of a gradient function over all data points can be split into partial sums and then the results can be aggregated:

$$\sum_{i=1}^{m} g_\theta(x_i, y_i) = \sum_{i=1}^{1000} g_\theta(x_i, y_i) + \sum_{i=1001}^{2000} g_\theta(x_i, y_i) + \ldots + \sum_{i=m-999}^{m} g_\theta(x_i, y_i).$$

Each partial sum can then be executed over a different computing node and a designated node performs the final aggregation of partial sums. However, this poses additional problems as each partition of the data has to be made available to the computing node that is going to perform each partial sum. Furthermore, each iteration over the data requires the global sum to be recomputed. At each iteration each computing node will have to access the partition of the data it is commanded to sum upon which might not necessarily be the same for all iterations. This may generate huge amounts of network traffic within the computing cluster, specially if there is a central storage system shared by all computing nodes as it is typically the case.

In this context is where caching come to be valuable. However, as shown in this work, caching alone might only solve partially the problem, and we need to devise caching strategies to encourage computing nodes to reuse as much as possible cached data throughout all iterations.

2.1 BIGS

The Big Image Data Analysis Toolkit (BIGS) was developed by our research group to enables distributed image processing workflows over heterogeneous computing infrastructures including computer clusters and cloud resources but also desktop computers in our lab or seldom servers available in an unplanned manner. BIGS promotes opportunistic, data locality aware computing through

1. a data partition iterative programming model supporting the parallelization scheme described in the previous section,
2. users assembling image processing jobs by pipelining machine learning algorithms over streams of data,
3. BIGS workers are software agents deployed over the actual distributed computing resources in charge of resolving the computing load,
4. a NoSQL storage model with a reference NoSQL central database,
5. removing the need of a central control node so that workers contain the logic to coordinate their work through the reference NoSQL database,
6. simple and opportunistic deployment model for workers, requiring only connectivity to the reference NoSQL database,
7. redundant data replication throughout workers,
8. a two level data caching in workers in memory and disk,
9. a set of strategies for workers for data access so that users can enforce data locality aware computing or only-in- memory computing,
10. a set of APIs through which BIGS can be extended with new algorithms, storage and data import modules. More information can be found at http://www.3igs.org. Prototype releases of BIGS are described in [10,9].

BIGS endorses a data partition iterative computing model (such as described in Section 2.1) through which workers can exploit locality aware computation if so desired by the user. Through this model, distributed data analysis jobs are structured into a repeatable sequence of INIT-STATE, MAP and AGGREGATE-STATE operations as shown in Figure 1.

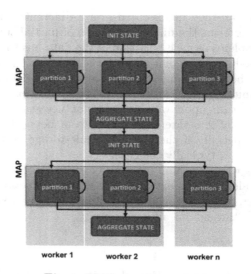

Fig. 1. BIGS algorithm model

All operations receive a State Object as input and they may produce another State Object as output. Any operation cannot start until the preceding ones have finished according to the job dependency graph in Figure 1, which is stored in the reference NoSQL database. Input datasets to be processed are split into a user definable number of partitions, and there is one MAP operation per partition. Each MAP operation can loop over the elements of the partition it is processing and may produce elements for an output dataset. For instance, an image feature extraction MAP operation would produce one or more feature vectors for each input image. Workers take over operations by inspecting the job dependency graph stored in the reference database. Developers program their algorithms by providing implementations for the Java Process API methods. When a BIGS worker takes over an operation, it creates the appropriate programming context and makes the corresponding data available (through data caches) to the implementation being invoked. As it can be seen in Figure 2, AGGREGATE-STATE operations use all output states of the preceding MAP operations to create the resulting state of iteration or the whole process.

2.2   Data Access and Caching Strategies

BIGS takes advantage of data parallelism approach. Given a large amount of data that can be processed independently, BIGS can distribute them in data partitions across workers in order to process them separately and then aggregate their results. A critical step in this parallelization strategy is the way that each worker accesses to the data partitions. The most conventional way to deal with this issue is by implementing caching systems.

BIGS implements two levels of caching, both of them implemented using the Java Caching System library. The memory cache stores Java objects in the main memory of the Java Virtual Machine indexed by an unique ID. The local cache stores information in a raw database in the local hard drive of the worker. Both caching systems allows faster access than performing a request from the worker directly to the HBASE server. Notice that the memory cache allows the fastest access because avoids reading hard drive as well as the parsing from the raw data to the Java object. On the other hand, the local cache allows greater storage capacity. This allowed us to implemented 2 strategies for deciding what partition a worker takes: **any-partition** and **only-local-partitions**. This combination of a two level caching architecture (disk and memory) together with these caching strategies constitutes the main contribution of this work.

In the **any-partition** strategy the worker reads the next execution unit in the schedule, if the data partition required by such execution unit is in the memory cache, then the worker processes it at once, otherwise the worker requests the data partition to the HBASE server, stores it in the memory cache and processes it.

The **only-local-partitions** strategy requires that one or more copies of the dataset be distributed through data partitions over all the active workers before the job be submitted. Those partitions are stored in the local cache. A worker will process **only** execution units for which it has their data partitions previously loaded in its local cache. The worker will also keep its memory cache enable.

2.3 Multiclass Logistic Regression

Logistic regression (LR) is a popular supervised machine learning algorithm and, despite its name, it is really applied to learn classification models, not to regression models. LR is probabilistic in nature, it learns a model which estimates the class posterior probability, $P(C|\mathbf{x})$, where $\mathbf{x}$ is a vector of input features and C is a random variable representing the class to be predicted. If C is assumed to have a multinomial distribution the posterior probability is calculated as:

$$y_i = \hat{P}(C_i|\mathbf{x}) = \frac{exp[\mathbf{w}_i^T\mathbf{x} + w_{i0}]}{\sum_{j=1}^{K} exp[\mathbf{w}_j^T\mathbf{x} + w_{j0}]}, \quad i=1..K,$$

where K is the number of classes, $\mathbf{x} \in \mathbb{R}^n$ is a vector with the input features and $W \in \mathbb{R}^{K\times(n+1)}$ is the set of parameters to be learned. Observe that W is a matrix and for each class i contains a row vector $\mathbf{w}_i \in \mathbb{R}^n$ and a bias parameter w_{i0}. The learning algorithm works by finding the set of parameters, W, that minimizes a loss function $L(W, X)$, equivalent to the negative likelihood over the training data set (X). This is usually done by using a gradient descent strategy which iteratively updates W by adding a vector, $\triangle W$, which points in the opposite as the gradient of the loss function, $\nabla L(W, X)$

$$W^{t+1} = W^t - \eta \nabla L(W^t, X).$$

This update is performed iteratively until some convergence criterion is met. An interesting characteristic of the gradient of the LR loss function is that the evaluation of it over the whole dataset is equivalent to the sum of the individual evaluations over each data samples, i.e.:

$$\nabla L(W^t, X) = \sum_{i=1}^{m} \nabla L(W^t, x_i).$$

Giving rise to a form in the sense described in Section 2 above for the gradient function that can be calculated in a distributed fashion, by separating the training dataset in several groups, independently calculating the gradient for each group, and then summing them up to find the overall gradient.

3 Experimental Setup

3.1 Dataset

The goal of our experiments was to measure the parallelization capabilities of a gradient descent based method over a fixed number of computing resources as the dataset size and number of iterations over the data increased using three different caching strategies (1) no cache, (2) default caching, (3) local only caching. For this, we used the MNIST dataset [7] containing about 60,000 images with handwritten digits (from 0 to 9), which is typically used as a benchmark for computer vision algorithms. Each digit is contained within a 28x28 gray scale image and represented by a vector of 784 components with the gray intensities of each pixel. Given any digit image, the machine learning task is to classify each image as the digit it represents. Figure 2 shows a sample of the dataset.

Fig. 2. MNIST dataset sample

3.2 Experimental Runs

We perform the evaluation on three dataset versions: 30000, 60000 and 120000. To build the 120k dataset the original dataset was duplicated. Conversely, the 30k was built by subsampling at 50% the original dataset. From each dataset, 80% was taken as training set and the remainder 20% as the test set. Each dataset was partitioned on 10 data partitions and loaded in the HBASE database to be processed by the BIGS workers. The gradient descent algorithm hyperparameters were fixed for all runs. Each run used 5 workers. We evaluated the experiment for 25, 40 and 100 iterations. Each configuration was executed twice and their average is reported. Table 1 shows the list of evaluated configurations.

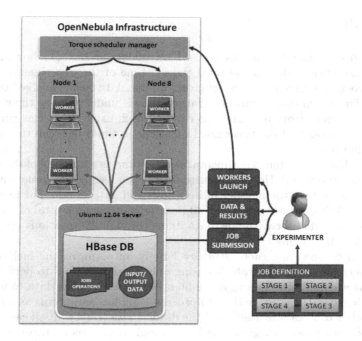

Fig. 3. Computing resources for experimentation

Table 1. List of evaluated configurations. Note that each one was executed twice and the average is reported. Each configuration was evaluated using 3 strategies: no cache, any partition and only local partitions.

# of iterations	Dataset size	# of processed samples
25	30K	750K
25	60K	1500K
40	30K	1200K
40	60K	2400K
40	120K	4800K
100	60K	6000K

3.3 Computing Infrastructure

HBASE version 0.94 run in Ubuntu 10.04 server with Intel® Xeon®. The workers process were scheduled in TORQUE, a distributed resource manager that provides control over batch jobs over five virtualized compute nodes managed by OpenNebula (http://opennebula.org/). All nodes and the HBASE server run the Java Virtual Machine 1.6 version, each node with dual quad core processor and 64 GB of RAM. This is shown in Figure 3

4   Results

Metrics collected in experiments focused on understanding (1) how different
cache configurations affected the total elapsed time of the experiments and (2)
how the processing time per data item (or 1 million data items) evolved throughout the different run configurations. Elapsed time is understood as the wall time
of each experiment from beginning to end. As each experiment was run twice,
results show averages of the two runs. Deviations in times between the two runs
were insignificant.

Figure 4 (left) shows the experimental elapsed time as a function of the number
of data items processed. Here we averaged runs processing the same number of
data items, regardless the number of iterations and dataset size. For instance, a
dataset with 30K data items through 40 iterations processes a total of 1.2M data
items, whereas a dataset with 60K data items through 25 iterations processes a
total of 1.5M data items.

As it can be seen any cache strategy largely outperforms the lack of cache
and, furthermore, caching strategies using only local data tend to perform even
better that caching strategies that use no criteria to select the data to work on.

Figure 5 shows the average time to process 1 million data items as a function
of the number of iterations (left) and the dataset size (right). In all cases, as the
amount of data processed grows (either through iterations or through dataset
size) the time to processes 1 million data items tends to decrease, probably as
the first data items loads in other low level caches (processor, OS, Java virtual
machine, etc.). Anyhow, again we see that exploiting local data outperforms all
other strategies.

When coming to compare the two caching strategies used we can observe in
Figure 6, as expected, that using only local data results in a reduced number of
writes (PUTs) to the cache whereas the number of reads is similar. This signals
data reuse within each cache and we interpret this as the root cause of the
observed improvement of caching strategies using data locality information.

Figure 4 (right) shows the number of cache HITs per PUT with respect to
dataset size where one can observe some indication of the degree of data reuse in
each configuration. In general each data item is re-used about 5 times more often

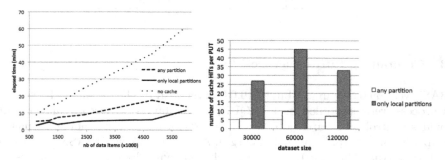

Fig. 4. Total elapsed time of experiments (left) and data reuse (right)

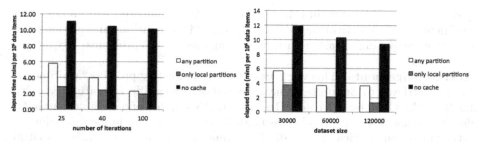

Fig. 5. Time to process 1 million data points vs the dataset size and the number of iterations

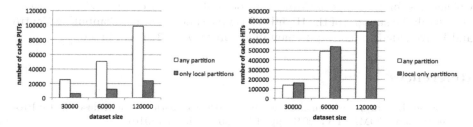

Fig. 6. Number of cache PUTS (writes) and HITS (reads) per dataset size

using cache with local only partitions but, interestingly enough, as we increase dataset size, this reuse drops, probably to due to RAM memory exhaustion on each computing node. This behavior is a subject for further experimentation and understanding.

Finally, it is worthwhile mentioning that our experiments produced an average train accuracy of 86.77% of successful digit recognition (with 0.59 standard deviation), and an average 86.91% accuracy on the test data (with 0.76 standard deviation). This figures fall within the expected accuracy of similar methods reported for the MNIST dataset, including the method stability (very low standard deviation, under 1%) and generalization capabilities (very low difference between train and test data), and guarantees the well behavior of the algorithms throughout all experiments.

5   Conclusions

Caching strategies are key to enable scaling machine learning methods of iterative nature. This work shows that even different strategies yield to different scalability properties and, thus, caching arquitectures for distributed data must be taken into account when devising scalable algorithms. Our results evidence that strategies favoring cache reuse throughout the different iterations over the data outperform simpler strategies, but this requires the algorithms (or the frameworks used) to keep track and exploit data locality, combining different levels of caching (disk and memory). This supports the convergence towards models where "computing goes to data" as observed in other Big Data related contexts, and allows us to confidently envision strategies for parallelizing ML algorithms and aligning the design of computing infrastructures to solving specific ML problems.

Acknowledgements. This work was partially funded by projects "Multimodal Image Retrieval to Support Medical Case-Based Scientific Literature Search", ID R1212LAC006 by Microsoft Research LACCIR, "Diseño e implementación de un sistema de cómputo sobre recursos heterogéneos para la identificación de estructuras atmosféricas en predicción climatológica" number 1225-569-34920 through Colciencias contract number 0213-2013 and "Proyecto Centro de Super-computación de la Universidad Nacional de Colombia". John Arevalo also thanks Colciencias for its support through a doctoral grant in call 617 2013. Authors also thank the support of the High Performance and Scientific Computing Centre and Universidad Industrial de Santander (http://sc3.uis.edu.co).

References

1. Bottou, L.: Large-scale machine learning with stochastic gradient descent. In: Proceedings of COMPSTAT 2010, pp. 177–186. Springer (2010)
2. Chu, C., Kim, S.K., Lin, Y.-A., Yu, Y., Bradski, G., Ng, A.Y., Olukotun, K.: Map-reduce for machine learning on multicore. Advances in neural information processing systems 19, 281 (2007)
3. Coates, A., Huval, B., Wang, T., Wu, D., Catanzaro, B., Andrew, N.: Deep learning with cots hpc systems. In: Proceedings of the 30th International Conference on Machine Learning, pp. 1337–1345 (2013)
4. Dean, J., Corrado, G., Monga, R., Chen, K., Devin, M., Mao, M., Senior, A., Tucker, P., Yang, K., Le, Q.V., et al.: Large scale distributed deep networks. In: Advances in Neural Information Processing Systems, pp. 1223–1231 (2012)
5. Hsu, D., Karampatziakis, N., Langford, J., Smola, A.J.: Parallel online learning. CoRR, abs/1103.4204 (2011)
6. Kraska, T., Talwalkar, A., Duchi, J.C., Griffith, R., Franklin, M.J., Jordan, M.I.: Mlbase: A distributed machine-learning system. In: CIDR (2013)
7. LeCun, Y., Bottou, L., Bengio, Y., Haffner, P.: Gradient-based learning applied to document recognition. Proceedings of the IEEE 86(11), 2278–2324 (1998)
8. Navruzyan, A.: Online machine learning with distributed in-memory clusters (2013)
9. Ramos-Pollan, R., Cruz-Roa, A., Gonzalez, F.A.: A framework for high performance image analysis pipelines. In: 2012 7th Colombian Computing Congress (CCC), pp. 1–6 (October 2012)
10. Ramos-Pollan, R., Gonzalez, F.A., Caicedo, J.C., Cruz-Roa, A., Camargo, J.E., Vanegas, J.A., Perez, S.A., Bermeo, J.D., Otalora, J.S., Rozo, P.K., Arevalo, J.: Bigs: A framework for large-scale image processing and analysis over distributed and heterogeneous computing resources. In: 2012 IEEE 8th International Conference on E-Science (e-Science), pp. 1–8 (October 2012)
11. Rosen, J., Polyzotis, N., Borkar, V., Bu, Y., Carey, M.J., Weimer, M., Condie, T., Ramakrishnan, R.: Iterative mapreduce for large scale machine learning. arXiv preprint arXiv:1303.3517 (2013)

12. Shvachko, K., Kuang, H., Radia, S., Chansler, R.: The hadoop distributed file system. In: 2010 IEEE 26th Symposium on Mass Storage Systems and Technologies (MSST), pp. 1–10. IEEE (2010)
13. Zaharia, M., Chowdhury, M., Franklin, M.J., Shenker, S., Stoica, I.: Spark: cluster computing with working sets. In: Proceedings of the 2nd USENIX Conference on Hot Topics in Cloud Computing, p. 10 (2010)

A Flexible Strategy for Distributed and Parallel Execution of a Monolithic Large-Scale Sequential Application

Felipe Navarro[1], Carlos González[1], Óscar Peredo[1], Gerson Morales[1],
Álvaro Egaña[1], and Julián M. Ortiz[1,2]

[1] ALGES Laboratory, Advanced Mining Technology Center (AMTC),
University of Chile, Chile
[2] Department of Mining Engineering, University of Chile, Chile

Abstract. A wide range of scientific computing applications still use algorithms provided by large old code or libraries, that rarely make profit from multiple cores architectures and hardly ever are distributed. In this paper we propose a flexible strategy for execution of those legacy codes, identifying main modules involved in the process. Key technologies involved and a tentative implementation are provided allowing to understand challenges and limitations that surround this problem. Finally a case study is presented for a large-scale, single threaded, stochastic geostatistical simulation, in the context of mining and geological modeling applications. A successful execution, running time and speedup results are shown using a workstation cluster up to eleven nodes.

Keywords: HPC, parallel computing, distributed system, workload modeling, gslib.

1 Introduction

The development of scientific computing applications has been benefited by new hardware technologies and software frameworks, allowing new applications to reach faster execution times, using better programming practices. Despite these advances, many fields in science and engineering still use algorithms and methods implemented in large monolithic applications, in the sense that they have single-tiered and self-contained software designs, contrary to current trends of modular and flexible designs. From those monolithic applications, only a portion were designed to efficiently use multi-core architectures and even less can be executed in distributed environments. Nowadays, many monolithic sequential applications are still actively used, taking several minutes, hours or days to compute.

Many scientists are not parallel computing users and *−in some cases−* have basic programming skills. Most of the time they use large old code or libraries designed for single-core workstations, mostly because their research priority is

G. Hernández et al. (Eds.): CARLA 2014, CCIS 485, pp. 54–67, 2014.

to explore new methods, techniques or just to have a simple proof of concept. In mining, projects require uncertainty quantification for risk analysis, which is done through the construction of multiple simulated scenarios. These scenarios often are represented by a numerical model that discretizes the volume of the ore deposit into small cells, each one requiring a prediction of its properties, such as grades or geological attributes. The construction of these models is costly in computing time, and currently done using legacy code.

Many attempts to parallelize these algorithms have been made, but most of them have been aimed at specific codes rather than providing a global solution that can be implemented to all algorithms. The focus has been put into optimizing interpolation methods [4,6,24], sequential simulation code [19,18,27], multiple point geostatistical methods [14,15,20,21,22,25]. In many of these cases, the use of a GPU based approach has been central, however, we aim at providing a more general solution to use many computers with different hardware characteristics.

Our goal is to solve these problems by enabling the use of multiple computers connected in a local network, making them to work seamlessly. This would allow scientists run many types of legacy code for large-scale applications and to have a simple scheduler for easy and efficient execution of tasks.

In a recent work of Bergen et al. [5], they successfully transformed existing monolithic C applications into a distributed semi-automatic system, making that legacy code relevant again, through the use of remote procedure calls by an approach similar to *map-reduce* — doing small modifications to their legacy code. Later, Lunacek et al. [17] have proved through a scaling study that Python is an excellent option to execute many-tasks on a compute cluster. There are others solutions based on software as a service [3] or cloud technologies [1,2], but we pursuit a different goal: develop an in-house tool, not running any extra configuration on our machines nor installing an enterprise solution. Based on these experiences, our contribution is to give a simple strategy for distributed and parallel execution of tasks, using an existing heterogeneous computer local network, in a clean an efficient way. We choose Python because it is easy to learn, provides a wide range of scientific tools, it is supported by a strong community and it is multi-platform.

This document is organized as follows: a description of the proposed strategy and implementation topics are presented in sections 2 and 3 respectively. In section 4, a case study using a sequential indicator simulation (`sisim` in GSLIB[7]) is developed and section 5 shows some discussion on the results and some ideas for future work.

2 Strategy Design

2.1 System Requirements

For the reasons explained above, we have defined the following requirements for our distributed and parallel execution strategy:

- **Polyglot model.** Should be able to perform native executions of existing code and binary executables. Here, the bottom line is to execute applications written in Fortran, C, C++ and Python. This cannot be done using Remote Object Call (ROC) or Remote Procedure Call (RPC), because the source code is not always available.
- **Data handling.** Must use different scientific data types as multidimensional arrays, hashed tables, time tables, among others. Continuous and categorical variables are represented in different formats and ranges — integer, float or strings.
- **Input/output.** There is the need to simplify the parametrization of the processes and the input files required for each of them. The output from each execution could be numerical data, (probably several) big binary files and large images.
- **Distributed computing.** Computation must be easily and seamlessly distributed. Message Passing Interface (MPI) is discarded because, on the one hand, it requires to make big changes to the legacy code and, on the other hand, our workstation cluster is extremely heterogeneous.
- **Hardware availability.** The available resources on each workstation (computation node) must be transparently visible and highly configurable in order to allow managing the limited resources, taking advantage of as much computing power as possible (multicore CPUs, multiple GPUs or SSD units) without interfering with user common tasks — optimizing idle computing capacity.
- **System heterogeneity.** Should be able to deploy in a multi-platform system.
- **Multi-master topology.** Every computation node should be set up as a master, configuring in this way a decentralized system.

2.2   Architecture Overview

The architecture is composed of two main components: *a)* a distributed task scheduler and *b)* a shared data storage. The task scheduler is necessary to assign workload to different workstation nodes. The shared data storage is required to save and retrieve input and output files, session variables and corresponding metadata.

Distributed Task Scheduler. A *Task* represents an abstract definition of the target (actual legacy) code that is needed to be executed. Every node in the cluster must run some component in background in order to accept and generate remote (task) execution calls. That component is called the *Distributed Task Scheduler*. In order to provide a strategy as general as possible, the scheduler modules were grouped in three categories: front-end, broker and back-end. Details are shown in Figure 1.

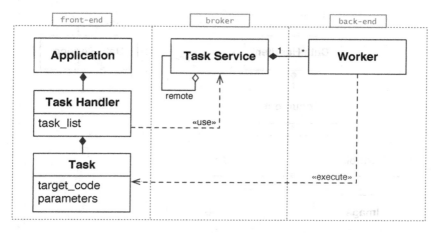

Fig. 1. Distributed task scheduler architecture

a. **Front-end.** It is composed of *Task Handlers* and *Applications*. The former is
   a module designed to provide a high level API for task creation, task control
   (run, stop, pause, cancel, delete) and to handle notifications. Every Task
   Handler controls a task list and uses a messaging system to connect them
   with the rest of the components. An Application uses the Task Handler API
   to orchestrate the tasks execution flow which has the logic related to every
   specific problem.
b. **Broker.** Encapsulates all services related with task distribution, load balancing, remote communications requirements and response messages routing. It
   is called *Task Service*. Each node must have a single instance of the latter
   running. Task distribution can be either dynamic or static. Dynamic scheduling may include different load balancing methods, fault tolerant strategies
   and automatic network discovery functionalities. On the other hand, static
   scheduling can use simple selection methods like a static weighted round-robin
   scheme.
c. **Back-end.** Its main components are the *Workers*. Their responsibility is
   to actually execute tasks. They are highly configurable: number of them,
   resources allowed to be used and permissions.

Shared Data Storage. Analogously to the *task*-related architecture, it is necessary to define an architecture for data handling which provides functionalities
for CRUD [1] operations on atomic data and every other required actions on data
sets — like searching or listing. The atomic data will be handled as a *Document*
that represents different kind of data: variables, files, images or tasks; could be
extended to any other datatype. The categories in this case are front-end and
back-end showed in Figure 2.

---

[1] Create, Read, Update, Delete.

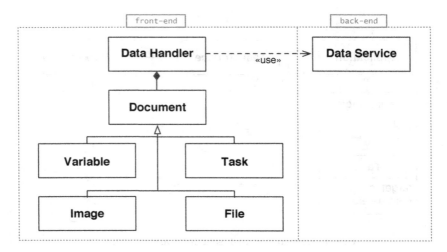

Fig. 2. Shared storage system schema

a. **Front-end.** A *Document Handler* is defined to provide a general API for document operations. It acts as a proxy which allows to handle different data types seamlessly and independently of the back-end implementation.
b. **Back-end.** It is composed of a *Document Service* and runs in background on a defined node or can be splitted using sharding when available, allowing splitting the data volume and computational load over multiple servers.

3   Implementation Topics

The strategy presented so far is quite straightforward because it is based on standard design patterns [10]. However, it is worth to mention four critical implementation aspects. Deployment details are shown in Figure 3.

a. **Messaging system.** A JSON based message specification that includes both internal and external events was defined. This satisfies the requirement to have heterogeneous interoperability. A simple protocol was defined which, despite it is lightweight, it is flexible enough to contain a rich message set — ranging from low level messages (system calls, synchronization messages or callbacks) to user defined commands. ZeroMQ [8,12] was chosen for message transport, that implements IPC socket for internal messaging and TCP sockets for node communications. It also provides fault tolerance functionalities, to deal with issues like *slow joined* or sockets disconnections.
b. **Parallel and distributed processing.** Each node contributes with a number of Workers (running as separated processes) and an implementation of a Task Service (running as background server). They are all synchronized using message passing through the messaging system, avoiding classic approaches with low level structures such as semaphores or mutex [13]. Every node can

be configured independently to optimize the usage of node specific resources. Task Services keep a known remote node list (multi-master topology) and load balancing is implemented using static round-robin.

c. **Shared storage system.** The Data model is extremely simple, using just one entity (Document). Thus the natural choice was using MongoDB [23], a Document-oriented database — which has great performance, scalability and flexibility with low level of complexity [26,16]. Furthermore, MongoDB has a specification called *GridFS* for storing and retrieving files, making easier working with large input/output distributed data files.

d. **Programming language.** The glue language is Python. It is multi-platform and has stable bindings to ZeroMQ, MongoDB and direct JSON handling functions. Additionally, C was used to provide GridFS functionality for Fortran as required by the case study (section 4).

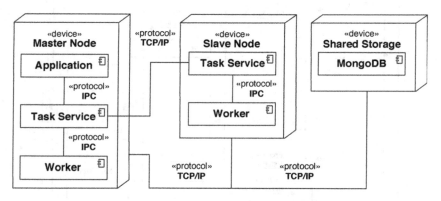

Fig. 3. Deployment diagram of the presented strategy

3.1   Execution Flow

The proposed strategy is fulfilled by the described architecture allowing to run several distributed instances of a Task using a simple schema, shown as a UML sequence diagram in Figure 4. The execution flow starts with the initial set up of the workstation cluster: on each node a Task Service and a set of Workers are created and configured. At least one node running a Document Service instance is required. A node is chosen as the current master (CM) and runs the Application that controls the Task execution flow.

The Application `main` uses a Task Handler instance to create a new Task, containing all necessary information to execute the target code — executable, number of executions, parameters, input/output data or environment variables. This application starts a Task execution using the Task Handler interface, which communicates using message passing to the Task Service. The later distributes all Task instances over the available local or remote Workers. After each Worker runs the target code or command, results are notified back to the CM, which routes messages to the corresponding Task Handler instance using the Task Service.

To finally get the results of the parallel (distributed) execution, application main waits for all Task instances to finish. Again, Task Handler provides proper methods for this purpose.

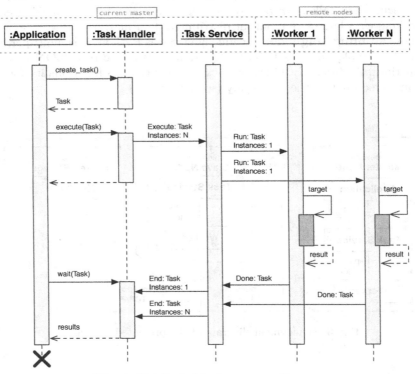

Fig. 4. Distributed task sequence diagram

The target code needs to be available in every remote node. This requirement can be accomplished in two ways:

1. Using external remote node configuration software to maintain desired target code updated across the network, then the Task just has to execute a shell command.
2. Using the shared storage system to upload desired code, then the Task is configured to download and execute it.

A combination of those options can be used to run complex tasks –commonly found in legacy applications– that may require to run multiple commands, difficult parameter settings and processing partial results.

4   Case Study

The strategy was tested using a well-known geostatistical simulation program, named sisim, which delivers 3D stochastic simulations of either integer-coded categorical variables, or continuous variables with indicator data defined from a cumulative density function. The sisim algorithm is part of a legacy library of geostatistical tools called GSLIB [7], which was implemented in Fortran 77/90 and uses a single thread of execution.

A sketch of sisim execution can be viewed in Algorithm 9. For each simulation, a regular lattice is defined over which a random path $\mathcal{P}$ of points in the domain Ω are visited and simulated. At every node, a local search of neighboring data or previously simulated nodes is performed, and for each category (categorical case) or each threshold value (continuous case) a local interpolation is done by simple or ordinary kriging, using the corresponding structural variographic model that provides a measure of the spatial continuity of the indicator variables. With these results a conditional cumulative distribution function is built of the random variable at the simulation location, from which a simulated value is drawn using Monte-Carlo simulation. The routine create_random_path creates the random path $\mathcal{P}$ based in the seed τ and simulate modifies the index-th value of the array $\mathbf{V}^{tmp}$ storing in it the result of a local interpolation using the parameters γ, κ and τ. None of these routines have side effects, so each iteration of the outer loop, corresponding to simulations, can be executed independently. This kind of application can be easily parallelized, distributing the iterations through local threads and/or distributed processes (embarrassingly parallel application [28]).

Input: $(\mathbf{V}, \Omega)$: sample data base values defined in a 3D domain; γ: structural variographic models; κ: local interpolation parameters; τ: seed for pseudo-random number generator; N: number of generated simulations; output.txt: output file

1 **for** $isim \in \{1, \ldots, N\}$ **do**
2      $\mathcal{P} \leftarrow$ create_random_path(Ω, τ);
3      $\mathbf{V}^{tmp} \leftarrow$ zeros$(\mathbf{V})$;
4   **for** $ixyz \in \{1, \ldots, |\Omega|\}$ **do**
5   index $\leftarrow \mathcal{P}_{ixyz}$;
6          $\mathbf{V}^{tmp}_{index} \leftarrow$ simulate$(index, \gamma, \kappa, \tau)$;
7   **end**
8   write(output.txt, $\mathbf{V}^{tmp}$);
9 **end**

Output: N stochastic simulations stored in file output.txt

Algorithm 1. SISIM geostatistical simulation program, sequential algorithm

4.1   Tests Setup

Two types of test configurations were used: homogeneous and heterogeneous machines. The homogeneous setting uses a cluster of eight workstations, each node having the following features: CPU Intel Xeon E3 1225 3.10GHz (four cores), 16GB of RAM, 1TB HDD running different GNU/Linux distributions (openSUSE 12.3, Ubuntu 13.04/13.10/14.04, Kubuntu 14.04) with Python 3.3/3.4 installed. Similarly, the heterogeneous settings uses up to eleven nodes: nine four cores nodes, one eight core node, all using a wider range of Intel Xeon CPUs and an iMac with Intel Core i5 2.7 GHz. All nodes are connected to campus facilities local network.

For all test a dedicated local server Intel Dual Core CPU, 2GB RAM and 1TB HDD was configured with the shared storage system using MongoDB and GridFS.

A manager for configuring all remote nodes was used. We chose Ansible [11] because its syntax is easy to read-and-learn and does not require specific agents on every node. The configuration steps are as follows:

- Compile and install the standard GSLIB 90 with `sisim` v3.0
- Optional: compile and install the implemented C API with MongoDB and GridFS drivers (section 4.3)
- Optional: compile and install an improved GSLIB `sisim` routine with GridFS, named `sisim-gfs` to avoid ambiguities (section 4.3)
- Run Task Service with four Workers in each node with remote support:
  `$ taskservice.py --workers 4 --hosts nodes.txt`
- Create the script who encapsulate the task to execute, to manage I/O and required parameters (See Listing 1.1)
- On the master node, run the Application `main` which controls the task execution flow (Figure 4) with 96 realizations using 16 distributed workers:
  `$ main_app.py --script sisim_script.py -n 96 --workers 16`

The creation, configuration and execution of the sisim script is straightforward and no more requirements are needed. A simple measure, the average development time for several programmers, has shown that it takes less than 25 minutes

Listing 1.1. Code snippet of sisim script

```
import subprocess
from strategy.prototype import StrategyScript
from strategy.prototype import GridFS as fs


class SisimScript(StrategyScript):
    def main(self):
        input = "/path/to/input/file"
        output = "/path/to/output/file"
        cmd = "sisim {0} {1}".format(input, output)
        exit_status = subprocess.call(cmd, shell=True)
        fs.save(output_file)
```

to fully understand all the required steps to deploy a script using different underlying applications. More complex scripts can be extended using standard Python programming techniques.

4.2 Standard SISIM Scalability Test

In the first test the simulation workload was distributed using our strategy, without any code modifications to the existing sisim program. We implemented a Python script that set the parameters and data files pointing to sisim executable. Also a simple main application was developed. This main application creates a Task that will configure the target code input parameters, uploads the target code and corresponding input data to the shared storage system and finally send the Task for execution. The code was instrumented to report partial and overall execution times.

This case study includes a comparison between the base execution of standard sisim routine and the distributed version up to 32 cores using the homogeneous cluster. Timing and speedup results can be viewed in Table 1. Base case denotes an execution of sisim with $N = 96$ (number of simulations) and a domain Ω of 2880000 points. Single node tests use the strategy to distribute simulations in one machine as independent native system processes, namely, up to four parallel workers running 24 simulations each one. Distributed tests use four workers in each node, using the implemented round-robin scheduler to assign workload. Under this configuration, sisim was parallelized up to 32 instances, each Worker running 3 simulations.

Table 1. Standard algorithm parallelized and distributed

case	processes	time[s]	speedup	efficiency
base	1	9124.64	1.00	
sisim single node	1	9240.11	0.99	99%
	2	4748.68	1.91	95%
	3	3240.30	2.82	94%
	4	2518.77	3.62	91%
sisim distributed	4	2890.09	3.16	79%
	8	1515.58	6.02	75%
	12	1101.01	8.29	69%
	16	909.53	10.03	63%
	24	712.66	12.80	53%
	32	627.36	14.54	45%

Table 1 shows that using the proposed strategy it is possible to increase the speedup in single node, having an efficiency of 91% when using all available resources on a local workstation. Distributed tests results also demonstrate scalability reducing overall computation time progressively. However, it shows that we lose efficiency when more nodes were added. This phenomenon is explained by the increase of overhead produced by nodes interactions, the time used to write output files to hard disk, and their uploading time into the shared storage system.

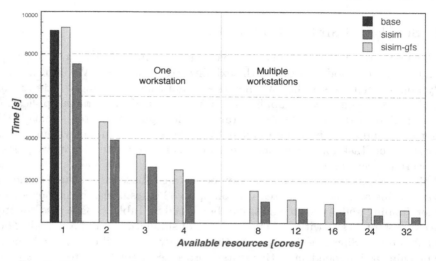

Fig. 5. Time comparison of sisim and sisim-gfs with available resources

4.3 Improved SISIM Scalability Test

To avoid the bottleneck generated by multiple processes writing result files to hard disk and the overhead of uploading those files to the shared storage system, we use the C API to make a simple wrapper from Fortran, allowing us to write each simulation result directly to GridFS. Doing a simple modification to the sisim code, we replaced line 8 on the Algorithm 9 by our own write_to_gfs function which saves the final V^{tmp} array directly to the shared storage system.

We perform the same tests detailed in section 4.2 and the results can be viewed in Table 2. Furthermore, Figures 5 and 6 show a comparison between standard sisim and improved sisim-gfs tests.

Speedup results are based on standard sisim single core execution time. Both, single node and distributed tests results show a clear overall computation time reduction. The sisim-gfs results shows a reduction on overhead by using GridFS. Figures 5 and 6 shows that sisim-gfs perform better than the standard sisim and when using more workstations, the former tend to outperform twice the standard.

4.4 Heterogeneous Cluster Distribution Test

Finally, in order to run a larger test using all computational resources available in our laboratory, a cluster of eleven heterogeneous nodes with a total of 46 cores was used, as specified in section 4.1. Initially was needed close to 2 hours 32 minutes to run 96 simulations in a single thread execution (base case, Tables

Table 2. Improved algorithm parallelized and distributed

case	processes	time[s]	speedup	efficiency
sisim single node	1	9240.11	1.00	
sisim-gfs single node	1	7522.86	1.23	123%
	2	3909.90	2.36	118%
	3	2636.28	3.50	117%
	4	2051.63	4.50	113%
sisim-gfs distributed	4	1994.82	4.63	116%
	8	1005.58	9.19	115%
	12	674.75	13.69	114%
	16	516.15	17.90	112%
	24	388.29	23.80	99%
	32	307.39	30.06	94%

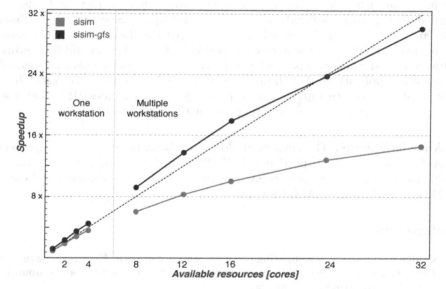

Fig. 6. Speedup test of sisim and sisim-gfs with available resources

1 and 2). Using the described strategy is possible to run the same number of simulations in less than 6 minutes.

5   Conclusions and Future Work

The proposed strategy has successfully fulfilled the requirements presented in section 2.1 and has been flexible enough to fit many embarrassingly parallel algorithms. Results show that using the proposed software architecture and available computational resources (local computer network, clusters or cloud services), the overall execution time can be considerably reduced —*up to 24 times*— and can be applied on monolithic legacy code used in geological modeling applications (like `sisim`) within real scenarios, making it practical to be used in industrial workflows. It is worth to mention that this strategy is general enough to be used in other analogous domains.

The entire system implementation exercise presented different challenges related to distributed systems that were solved using cutting edges approaches. For example, multiple processes synchronization and node communication were implemented with message passing; data handling, via a distributed Document-oriented NoSQL database; and, cluster management, with a remote configuration management tool.

The presented work was focused on a particular algorithm, but this (general) strategy can be applied to a wide range of applications. In geosciences only, there are many other algorithms that have the same characteristics, like being embarrassingly parallelizable or having heavy task workflows (Sequential Gaussian Simulation [7], Turning Bands Methods [9], Multi-point Statistics Algorithms [14], among others). This point is a motivation to replicate this architecture many times. Thus, an efficient way to do this, is to build a general framework software to easily generate parallel and distributed executions, specially focused in scientific applications. This framework could be a helpful tool for researchers that need to generate rapid software prototypes that includes HPC features, allowing to integrate new and existing code with a small effort.

Acknowledgments. The authors would like to thank the industrial supporters of ALGES laboratory, in particular BHP Billiton, Codelco Chile and Yamana Gold, as well as the support from the Advanced Mining Technology Center (AMTC) and the whole ALGES team.

References

1. Gridgain = in-memory computing platform computing, http://www.gridgain.com
2. Proactive: Open source solution for parallel, distributed, multi-core computing, http://proactive.activeeon.com
3. Remics: Reuse and migration of legacy applications to interoperable cloud services, http://www.remics.eu
4. Armstrong, M.P., Marciano, R.J.: Massively parallel strategies for local spatial interpolation. Computers & Geosciences 23(8), 859–867 (1997)
5. Bergen, A., Yazir, Y.O., Muller, H.A., Coady, Y.: RPC automation: Making legacy code relevant. In: 2013 ICSE Workshop on Software Engineering for Adaptive and Self-Managing Systems (SEAMS), pp. 175–180 (2013)
6. Cheng, T.: Accelerating universal Kriging interpolation algorithm using CUDA-enabled GPU. Computers & Geosciences 54, 178–183 (2013)
7. Deutsch, C., Journel, A.: GSLIB: Geostatistical software library and users guide. Oxford University Press, New York (1998)
8. Dworak, A., Charrue, P., Ehm, F., Sliwinski, W., Sobczak, M.: Middleware Trends and Market Leaders 2011. In: 13th International Conference on Accelerator and Large Experimental Physics Control Systems, p. 1334 (2011)

9. Emery, X., Lantuéjoul, C.: Tbsim: A computer program for conditional simulation of three-dimensional gaussian random fields via the turning bands method. Computers & Geosciences 32(10), 1615–1628 (2006), http://www.sciencedirect.com/science/article/pii/S0098300406000549

10. Gamma, E., Helm, R., Johnson, R., Vlissides, J.: Design Patterns: Elements of Reusable Object-oriented Software. Addison-Wesley Longman Publishing Co., Inc., Boston (1995)

11. Hall, D.: Ansible Configuration Management. Packt Publishing (2013)

12. Hintjens, P.: ZeroMQ: Messaging for Many Applications. O'Reilly Media (2013)

13. Hintjens, P., Sustrik, M.: Zeromq: Multithreading magic (2010), http://www.zeromq.org/whitepapers:multithreading-magic

14. Huang, T., Li, X., Zhang, T., Lu, D.T.: GPU-accelerated Direct Sampling method for multiple-point statistical simulation. Computers & Geosciences 57, 13–23 (2013)

15. Huang, T., Lu, D.T., Li, X., Wang, L.: GPU-based SNESIM implementation for multiple-point statistical simulation. Computers & Geosciences 54, 75–87 (2013)

16. Lith, A., Mattsson, J.: Investigating storage solutions for large data: A comparison of well performing and scalable data storage solutions for real time extraction and batch insertion of data (2010)

17. Lunacek, M., Braden, J., Hauser, T.: The scaling of many-task computing approaches in python on cluster supercomputers. In: 2013 IEEE International Conference on Cluster Computing (CLUSTER), pp. 1–8 (2013)

18. Mariethoz, G.: A general parallelization strategy for random path based geostatistical simulation methods. Computers & Geosciences 36(7), 953–958 (2010)

19. Nunes, R., Almeida, J.A.: Parallelization of sequential Gaussian, indicator and direct simulation algorithms. Computers & Geosciences 36(8), 1042–1052 (2010)

20. Peredo, O., Ortiz, J.M.: Parallel implementation of simulated annealing to reproduce multiple-point statistics. Computers & Geosciences (2011)

21. Peredo, O., Ortiz, J.M.: Multiple-Point Geostatistical Simulation Based on Genetic Algorithms Implemented in a Shared-Memory Supercomputer. In: Geostatistics Oslo 2012, pp. 103–114. Springer, Netherlands (2012)

22. Peredo, O., Ortiz, J.M., Herrero, J.R., Samaniego, C.: Tuning and hybrid parallelization of a genetic-based multi-point statistics simulation code. Parallel Computing 40(5-6), 144–158 (2014)

23. Plugge, E., Hawkins, T., Membrey, P.: The Definitive Guide to MongoDB: The NoSQL Database for Cloud and Desktop Computing, 1st edn. Apress, Berkely (2010)

24. Gutiérrez de Ravé, E., Jiménez-Hornero, F.J., Ariza-Villaverde, A.B., Gómez-López, J.M.: Using general-purpose computing on graphics processing units (GPGPU) to accelerate the ordinary kriging algorithm. Computers & Geosciences 64, 1–6 (2014)

25. Straubhaar, J., Renard, P., Mariethoz, G., Froidevaux, R., Besson, O.: An Improved Parallel Multiple-point Algorithm Using a List Approach. Mathematical Geosciences 43(3), 305–328 (2011)

26. Strauch, C., Sites, U., Kriha, W.: NoSQL databases. Lecture Notes (2011)

27. Tahmasebi, P., Sahimi, M., Mariethoz, G.G.: Accelerating geostatistical simulations using graphics processing units (GPU). Computers & Geosciences 46(0), 51–59 (2012)

28. Wilkinson, B., Allen, M.: Parallel Programming: Techniques and Applications Using Networked Workstations and Parallel Computers, 2nd edn. Prentice-Hall, Inc., Upper Saddle River (2004)

A Model to Calculate Amazon EC2 Instance Performance in Frost Prediction Applications

Lucas Iacono[1,2], José Luis Vázquez-Poletti[3], Carlos García Garino[1,4],
and Ignacio Martín Llorente[3]

[1] ITIC, Universidad Nacional de Cuyo. Mendoza, Argentina
[2] Instituto de Microelectrónica. Facultad de Ingeniería, Universidad de Mendoza
Mendoza, Argentina
lucas.iacono@um.edu.ar
[3] Departamento de Arquitectura de Computadores y Automática, Facultad de
Informática, Universidad Complutense de Madrid, Madrid, Spain
jlvazquez@fdi.ucm.es,
llorente@dacya.ucm.es
[4] Facultad de Ingeniería, Universidad Nacional de Cuyo. Mendoza, Argentina
cgarcia@itu.uncu.edu.ar

Abstract. Frosts are one of the main causes of economic losses in the
Province of Mendoza, Argentina. Although it is a phenomenon that happens every year, frosts can be predicted using Agricultural Monitoring
Systems (AMS). AMS provide information to start and stop frosts defense systems and thus reduce economic losses. In recent years, the emergence of infrastructures called Sensor Clouds improved AMS in several
aspects such as scalability, reliability, fault tolerance, etc. Sensor Clouds
use Wireless Sensor Networks (WSN) to collect data in the field and
Cloud Computing to store and process these data. Currently, Cloud
providers like Amazon offer different instances to store and process data
in a profitable way. Moreover, due to the variety of offered instances
arises the need for tools to determine which is the most appropriate instance type, in terms of execution time and economic costs, for running
agro-meteorological applications. In this paper we present a model targeted to estimate the execution time and economic cost of Amazon EC2
instances for frosts prediction applications.

1 Introduction

Frost is an agro-meteorological event which causes both damage in crops and
important economic losses. The impact of frost damages in the Province of Mendoza, region of Cuyo, Argentina (which affected up to 80% of crops in 2013)
resulted in economic emergency in all the region. Due to frosts happen every
year, there are different defense methods (such as surface irrigation, heaters and
others) that can be used to minimize damage.

Defense systems should be activated based on information provided by Agricultural Monitoring Systems (AMS). AMS perform in-field data acquisition and
data management. Moreover, AMS ensure production quality and guarantee
crops traceability.

G. Hernández et al. (Eds.): CARLA 2014, CCIS 485, pp. 68–82, 2014.

On the one hand, in-field data acquisition process can be performed by measuring instruments, weather stations and Wireless Sensor Networks (WSN) [1,2]. Compared to traditional measurement instruments and weather stations, WSNs have the advantage that they can cover extensive areas with low cost devices called sensor nodes. Moreover, sensor nodes low-power consumption and long lifetime (over 2 years) allow long-term monitoring with low maintenance.

On the other hand, the WSNs data management include data remote access, storage and data processing. This management process can be reliably and easily performed using Cloud Computing technologies [3,4,5,6,7]. The use of Cloud Computing for data management allow to incorporate the benefits of this technology (data replication, fault tolerance, resources scalability, etc.) to AMS.

There are two main reason for using public Clouds in order to process and store WSN data. The first one is the large volume of data generated by WSNs. As an example, in the region of Cuyo there are up to 170000 hectares of crops which can be instrumented with one sensor node per hectare. For this reason, there are 170000 potential sensors that generate data, which must be processed and stored in a proper infrastructure. The second one is the traffic bottle neck from the WSNs to an isolated private data center. Several Cloud providers offer different types of public infrastructure resources which can be used to store and process data in a profitable way. Today one of the leading providers is Amazon. The Elastic Compute Cloud (EC2) toolkit service provides different types of virtual machines (instances) for both processing and data storage. In addition, due to the wide range of instances offered by Amazon, arises the need to identify which of them has better performance, in terms of execution time and economic cost, for processing frost prediction applications.

In this paper we propose a set of models, constructed from empirical data, that can be used to estimate the performance and economic costs of Amazon EC2 instances applied to frost prevention applications processing. Although there are other costs associated with the use of Amazon EC2 instances (like the ones for data transfer), the target of our study are the economic costs for WSN data processing. These ones are more relevant compared with the ones for data transfer.

This paper is structured as follows. Section 2 introduces Agricultural Monitoring Systems based in WSN. Next, Section 3 surveys relevant related works. Section 4 describes the application developed for frost prediction. Then, Section 5 presents our proposal of models for each Amazon EC2 instance and the methodology used to construct them. Finally Section 6 concludes this paper and discusses future prospective extensions.

2   Agricultural Monitoring Systems Based in WSNs

In this section we provide an introduction to the technologies used to perform both the data acquisition and data management in WSN's based AMS.

2.1   Data Acquisition with WSN

Sensor nodes, a technology appeared in the late 90s, are composed of a micro-controller, memory, different sensors, battery and a radio module. Sensor nodes can be interconnected into special networks called WSNs and interact among them. Such WSN networks are used to study the environment and for acquiring different variables related to weather (temperature, humidity, pressure, and others).

Within a WSN, data are acquired by source nodes and sent via radio frequency to a special node (known as sink) connected to the base station. The base station coordinates all operations of the WSN and can be a personal computer (PC) or embedded system. Furthermore, the base station can store or transmit via the Internet all the information collected by sensor nodes.

WSNs nodes must meet requirements such as autonomy, low power consumption, low cost, robustness and reliability. Unlike traditional wireless networks, WSNs nodes use communications protocols specifically designed for working with scarce energy sources and hardware resources. In addition, these protocols are not compatible with TCP/IP networks.

2.2   Data Management

Data collected by AMS through WSNs, can be used to provide a solution to many scientific and commercial problems (e.g., frost prevention, fire detection, etc.). The data management process starts when WSN data are sent to remote machines. Next, data are stored and processed in order to extract useful information. Next subsections detail different technologies used to WSN data management.

Traditional Technologies. Generally, the use of isolated machines such as computers and mainframes is adequate to process low volumes of non-critical WSN data. A typical use case of isolated machines is when low volumes of data (in the order of Kbytes) are sent from the base station deployed in-field to a remote server. The external server stores the data and then proceeds to run the processing application.

Although this technology is easy to use, it presents some problems for (i) processing large volume of data, (ii) scaling to a large number of WSN nodes and (iii) ensuring availability 24 hours a day - 365 days a year. A possible solution to solve these issues is by using powerful servers, mainframes and clusters in appropriate datacenter infrastructures. However, this solution generates prohibitive economic costs, at least for agro-meteorological applications.

As the use of traditional technologies is not always suitable, different authors proposed the use of Cloud Computing infrastructures for processing WSN data [3,4,5,6,7].

Cloud Computing. Cloud Computing is a computing paradigm for application development and the use of computing and storage resources [8]. Through the use of virtualization techniques and web services, hardware resources and applications can be dynamically provided to the user.

Foster et. al. [9] define Cloud Computing as *"A large-scale distributed computing paradigm that is driven by economies of scale, in which a pool of abstracted, virtualized, dynamically-scalable, managed computing power, storage, platforms, and services are delivered on demand to external customers over the Internet"*.

One of the main advantages of Clouds is resources scalability. In this way Clouds can solve the computational and storage requirements of the applications. Another advantage is that the users can easily to access to development frameworks of applications that use Cloud services in order to allow the scaling of resources. Cloud services are deployed in terms of certain business models. Clouds providers offer their services according to three fundamental models which are described below.

Infrastructure as a Service (IaaS), where "service" means resource. Through infrastructure services users can access to virtualized high performance computing (HPC) resources (CPUs, storage devices, etc.). The service provider delivers resources to a client in accordance to the specific requirements such as CPU type and power, memory, storage, operating system, etc. Among others IaaS, Amazon EC2 [10] can be cited. Amazon EC2 is a set of Cloud services which allow to run applications on custom virtual machines (VM) deployed on servers of Amazon datacenters. Amazon offers various types of VMs (also called *Instances*) with different processing power and memory capabilities.

Platform as a Service (PaaS), where "service" means platform-level functionality. These services provide Application Programming Interfaces (APIs) and standard development kits (SDKs) in order to allow users to develop and implement their own applications for Clouds. Some examples of these platforms are Google App Engine [11] and Windows Azure [12].

Software as a Service (SaaS), where "service" means application. The SaaS Cloud providers deliver applications that can be accessed by an end user through a Internet connection and a standard web browser. Furthermore, the applications can be developed with Platform Services and executed with Infrastructure Services. As an example of SaaS is Google Drive [13].

3   Related Works

Recently, different authors have proposed the use of Cloud technologies for managing the WSN's resources. In Lee et. al. [14] the authors describe concepts of Cloud like: virtualized resources, SaaS, pay-per-use price model, and applied them to create a Cloud infrastructure capable of integrate devices with sensing capabilities. The authors also implement a new infrastructure called Tangible Cloud which use Amazon EC2 instances to process data from sensor nodes [3].

In the paper the authors show that the platform solves (through resources scalability) the computational power requirements of environmental monitoring and modeling applications.

Another work proposed by Ahmed and Gregory [4] presents an integration framework between WSN and Cloud Computing. The main objective of the proposed framework is to *"facilitate the shift of data from WSN to the Cloud Computing environment"*. In addition, the authors suggest that the linkage of Cloud Computing and WSNs allows the possibility of storage the WSNs data in publics domains. Then, different users and applications can access to the information of the sensors and these results in a better data usage.

Another platform to integrate WSN into Clouds is Aneka [5]. This platform uses resources of private and public Clouds in order to provide support to applications of smart environments including health-care, transportation, urban monitoring and others.

Regarding to the use of Clouds in agricultural environments, Hirafuji et. al. [6] developed a Ambient Sensor Cloud System for High-throughput Phenotyping. This platform allows the storage and access to data collected by sensor nodes using Twitter Cloud services. The main goal of the system is to provide a simple and economical solution to solve the access and storage of large datasets from various sensor nodes. Hori et. al. [7] present a commercial solution to storage and process WSNs data. The platform allows the integration with business management, production history, traceability and good agricultural practice systems provided as a SaaS model.

Based on the works studied in this section, it can be concluded that Cloud is a promising technology for solving the management and processing of data in WSN's based AMS. Although most of the studied works use Amazon EC2, to the best of our knowledge there are no works oriented to model the performance and economic cost of EC2 instances in Agricultural Monitoring Systems.

4   Frost Prediction Application

In this Section we present the application for frost prediction. The main objective of this application is to compute the minimum temperature that happen in the night. Then, this temperature value is useful to predict if a frost may occur on the farm. The Section is organized as follow: in subsection 4.1, we present the method for frost prediction used in our application. Next, in subsection 4.2 the application implementation is detailed.

4.1   Frost Prediction Method

The frost prediction application was developed using the frost prediction method (FPM) of Snyder and de Melo-Abreu [15], which is based on Allen's equation [16]. The FPM predicts the minimum temperature that will occur in nights without both clouds and cold fronts. Therefore, it is only suitable to predict radiation frosts. The data used to calculate the minimum temperature are extracted from an historical dataset of ten years. The FPM uses a sample of fifty days from the historical dataset (of the month to which belongs the day of the prediction) in which radiation frosts occurred.

Formally, the minimum temperature is calculated by the following linear regression (LR) equation:

$$T_p = s_T * T_o + s_D * D_0 + i \,, \tag{1}$$

where T_p is the minimum temperature to be predicted, T_o represents the minimum temperature and D_0 the dew point. The parameters T_o and D_0 have to be acquired the same day of the prediction, two hours after sunset. Finally, i is the LR intercept, s_T temperature slope and s_D dew point slope.

The values of s_T and i are calculated from the equations (2) and (3), respectively.

$$s_T = \frac{\sum (T_{h0} - \bar{T}_{h0})(T_m - \bar{T}_m)}{\sum (T_{h0} - \bar{T}_{h0})^2} \,, \tag{2}$$

$$i = \frac{\sum T_m - s_T \sum T_{h0}}{n} \,, \tag{3}$$

where T_{h0} are historical temperatures registered two hours after sunset, T_m minimum temperatures that succeed in the night, and n is the number of historical data. Finally, $\bar{T}_{h0}$ and $\bar{T}_m$ account for the average data temperatures.

The slope s_D is calculated by using the equation (4).

$$s_D = \frac{\sum (D_{h0} - \bar{D}_{h0})(R - \bar{R})}{\sum (D_{h0} - \bar{D}_{h0})^2} \,, \tag{4}$$

where D_{h0} are historical dew points two hour after sunset and R the residuals. The parameters $\bar{D}_{h0}$ and $\bar{R}$ are the average of D_{h0} and R, respectively. Finally, the residual is calculated with the expression: $R = T_m - s_T * T_o + i$.

4.2   Application Implementation

In order to develop the frost prediction application we implement the Snyder and de Melo-Abreu [15] FPM, using Java and MySQL. MySQL was used to store the data from the sensor nodes and the results obtained after running the FPM. The application was executed using Amazon EC2 instances.

The integration of WSN data with Cloud infrastructures was performed with a WSN - Cloud integration platform called Sensor Cirrus [17,18,19]. Sensor Cirrus manages the WSN data using Cloud services and includes the developed frost prediction application for data processing.

Figure 1 illustrates a scheme of the frost prediction module. The information collected by WSN sensors in the field is stored in a proper database, as it seen in process (1). Next, in process (2), the application performs a query to catch the sample of fifty days. This sample includes all the collected data (temperature, humidity, solar radiation, wind speed, etc.) by the WSNs. Then, in process (3) the application retrieves from the sample of fifty days only the FPM input data (T_o ,D_o , etc.). Finally, in (4) the FPM is executed, resulting in the minimum temperature that occurs next night through process (5).

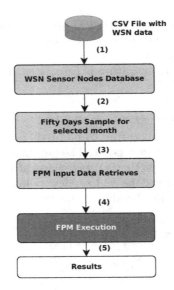

Fig. 1. Frost Detection Module

5   Performance Estimation Models

In the present Section we present our models to estimate the performance of EC2 instances for processing frost prediction applications. The methodology used to construct the models is the following: first, we execute the frost prediction application in each instance to obtain empirical results of performance indicators (execution time and economic cost). Then, we use polynomial expressions and empirical results to generate the performance models. Next, we extract conclusions about the accuracy of the proposed models. Finally we select the most suitable instance for frost prediction through a comparison in a typical use case.

5.1   Frost Prediction Application Execution

The execution consists of running the frost prediction application and measure the execution time. In order to extract the average value of the execution time, the procedure is repeated four times for different number of sensor nodes (from 10 to 1000) in each instance. Finally we use the average execution time and the pricing list of Amazon to calculate the economic cost required to execute the application.

We have considered five test scenarios, one for each instance types to model (see Table 1). Each row in the Table 1 represents the different instance types, i.e., t1.micro, m1.small, m1.large, m1.xlarge and c3.xlarge, and each column indicates the instance characteristics, i.e., number of virtual CPUs (vCPUs), Amazon EC2 Compute Unit (ECU), Memory (expressed in GBytes) and Instance Pricing. Regarding the Amazon's pricing model used in our work, we use the *"on demand"* pricing model. It is noteworthy that in this paper we do not make an analysis of the accuracy of the minimum temperature predicted by the frost detection application. However (and based in our experience with agronomists) we can affirm that an error of +/- 1.5 celsius degrees is an acceptable error value to predict frosts, and the used FPM meets this requirement.

Table 1. Test Scenarios

Amazon EC2 Instance	vCPUs	ECU	Memory (GBytes)	Pricing on demand (U$S)
t1.micro	1	variable	0.615	0.020
m1.small	1	1	1.7	0.047
m1.large	2	4	7.5	0.190
m1.xlarge	4	8	15	0.379
c3.xlarge	4	14	7.5	0.239

The application execution allows to obtain empirical performance results in each EC2 instance. Figure 2a shows the execution time versus the number of processed sensor nodes for the scenarios considered. Figure 2b details the economic cost versus the number of processed sensor nodes.

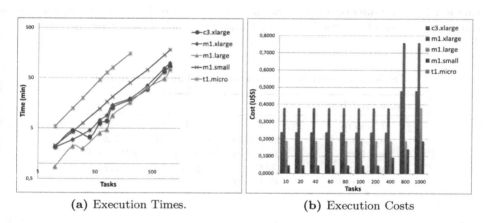

(a) Execution Times.   (b) Execution Costs

Fig. 2. Empirical Results.

From the Figure 2a can be observed that m1.large is the instance which have achieved the shorter execution times for the frost prediction application. In addition, it can be seen that up to 200 sensor nodes processed, the performance of m1.large is notable. Next, the performance of m1.large becomes similar to the m1.xlarge and c3.xlarge.

Furthermore, results show that for multiprocessor machines as m1.large and c3.xlarge, the processing times decrease for 30 and 40 sensor nodes, respectively. Regarding the observed decrease, the decrease in m1.large instance is lower (about 9% over the previous calculation) than the c3.xlarge instance (20% compared to the previous point).

The analysis of hardware features of such instances (ng"m1.large and c3.xlarge) shows that they have: (i) two and four vCPUs respectively and (ii) the same RAM memory (7.5 GBytes). Then it can be concluded that the decrease of processing times could be due to the load balancing between processors and the access to shared resources such as memory, buses, etc.

Figure 2b shows the empirical economic costs. Is noted that economic costs are the same from 10 to 400 nodes. The cause of this behavior is because Amazon set the pricing of instances per hour of use. Reason why, the pricing is the same if the processing time is less or equal than one hour. Similarly, if processing time is longer than one hour (for example 800 to 1000 nodes), it doubles the cost and so on.

5.2   Perfomance Estimation Proposed Models

In this subsection we introduce the proposed models in order to estimate the performance for each instance considered. These models were obtained through polynomials up to second degree of the form:

$$t = ax^2 + bx + c \, ,$$

where, x is the number of sensor nodes processed and t is the estimated execution time. The values of the coefficients a, b and c for each scenario are detailed in Table 2).

Table 2. Coefficients of Each Scenario Theoretical Model

Amazon EC2 Instance	a	b	c
t1.micro	0	$7.85E-01$	-1.44
m1.small	$1.84E-06$	$1.78E-01$	1.80
m1.large	$6.02E-06$	$6.50E-02$	$9.98E-01$
m1.xlarge	$1.40E-05$	$8.24E-02$	2.25
c3.xlarge	$1.66E-05$	$6.73E-02$	2.59

In order to evaluate the proposed models we calculate the execution time and economic cost for each scenario. In addition, the execution of the application has been conducted for more than 1000 nodes (up to 5000).

Finally, with the aim of determining the accuracy of the proposed models, Figure 3 and Figure 4 show a comparison between the results of empirical experiments and our performance models for each scenario.

Specifically, Figure 3 shows that execution times calculated through the proposed model differ seconds or few minutes (depending on the instance) with respect to those obtained through the execution of the frost prediction application. Then the proposed models can predict the results with a reasonable good accuracy.

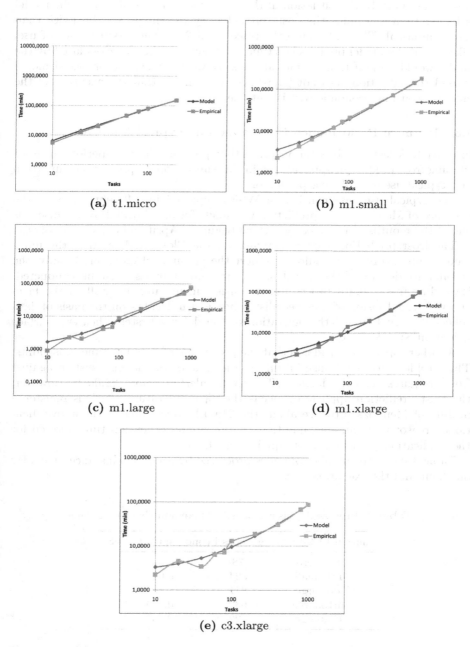

(a) t1.micro

(b) m1.small

(c) m1.large

(d) m1.xlarge

(e) c3.xlarge

Fig. 3. Proposed Model versus Empirical Execution Times

Regarding economics costs, a particular case is when the execution times are close to an hour. In this situation, if the execution time calculated by the model is longer than one hour, the costs predicted by the model will be twice than those empirical. This is because the price of EC2 instances is per hour of use. Likewise, if the model predicts less time than one our, the cost calculated by the model would be half than empirical costs. However, when the proposed model is used this situation does not happen, so we can say that the accuracy of the models regarding economic cost is suitable.

5.3   Instance Performance Comparison in Typical Use Case

In order to select which is the instance that presents the best performance for running frost prediction applications, in this subsection we present a comparison in a typical use case of frost prediction.

The typical use case consists of WSNs deployed in different farms in the Province of Mendoza. The prediction was made for one day of July because it is one of the months of frost season, which begins in April and ends in October.

The frost prediction application runs on the Cloud and predicts the minimum temperature, which allows to alert the agronomist engineer. Finally, the agronomist decides if the guard procedure against frosts must be conducted. Regarding frosts guard procedure, it consists in moving the staff to the farm and wait the decision of the specialist, who in turn decide - on the basis of data collected in real time - the activation of the defense system (heaters, surface irrigation, sprinklers, etc.).

Another aspect to consider is that the processing of data has time constraints. This problem arises because in July the logistic of the defense system against frosts requires that the farm staff must be alerted before 22:00 h. However, the frost prediction application needs the T_0 temperature which is registered in July of Mendoza province about the 21:00 h. According to the above mentioned reasons we can conclude that the maximum execution time allowed for the application must be less or equal to one hour.

Table 3 shows the number of nodes processed by each EC2 instance model for one hour and the execution cost.

Table 3. Processed Sensor Nodes in Maximum Execution Time

Amazon EC2 Instance	Nodes	Economic Cost (U$S)
t1.micro	78	0.020
m1.small	324	0.047
m1.large	841	0.190
m1.xlarge	632	0.379
c3.xlarge	722	0.239

Results showed that the most suitable machine for this application type is the instance m1.large. The reason is because the m1.large is the machine that can

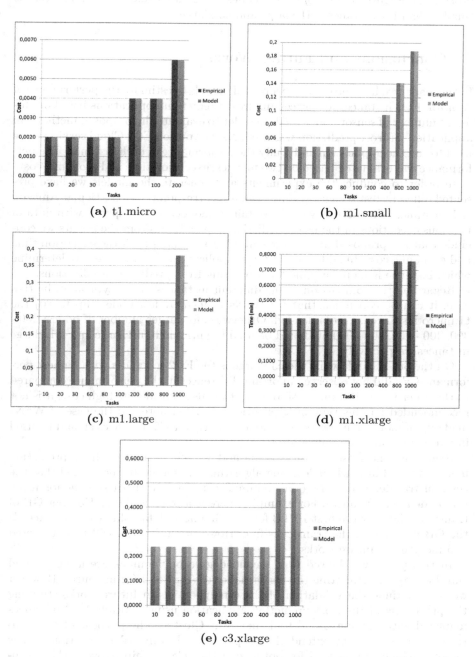

Fig. 4. Model versus Empirical Economic Costs

process the largest number of sensor nodes in one hour and its economic cost is smaller than the instances m1.xlarge and c3.xlarge.

6   Conclusions and Future Works

In this paper we have proposed theoretical models to estimate the performance of Amazon EC2 instances for processing frost prediction applications based on different number of sensor nodes used. In order to evaluate the proposed method, an application for frost prediction was used. Next, Amazon EC2 Cloud services were used to run the application and study the performance of each instance. The performance was evaluated based on two metrics, execution time and economic cost.

In order to conduct the experiments and generate the models we have presented different test scenarios. Each scenario corresponds to a particular Amazon EC2 instance. The accuracy of the obtained models was compared with data of previous executions of the frost prediction application. From the results we conclude that the proposed models are suitable to estimate both the execution time and economic cost. In addition, a typical application case was used to determine which instance is more suitable for processing frost prediction applications.

Regarding the comparison of the different instances in the typical evaluation case, it can be concluded that for WSNs formed by few nodes (up to 80) the t1.micro instance is recommended. Otherwise, for larger number of nodes: 200 - 300, 400 - 700, 800 - 900; it should be used the m1.small, m1.large and m1.xlarge instances, respectively.

On the other hand, while the c3.xlarge is the EC2 instances with highest performance, we did not observe important differences in the performance compared to the other tested instances. Moreover, if we also consider its high cost, it is not recommended for this type of applications. Furthermore, for the case of WSNs made up of more than 1000 sensor nodes, multiple EC2 instances should be used in parallel to run the application.

Regarding the frosts prediction method we will test other frost prediction methods based in machine learning algorithms. It should be mentioned that the costs of transfer and storage are minimal compared with these ones for using the on demand instances. For example, there is a pricing of 0.12 U$S per GB of transfered data for the first 10 TB for month, and if data volume do not exceeds the GB per month, the transfer is free. However, such costs will be considered and included in future works.

In this paper we showed that second degree polynomials are a simple and suitable way for estimating the performance of Amazon EC2 instances. However we will continue the validation of these polynomials in future works studying the processing of the frost prediction application using multiple EC2 instances managed with specific Cloud tools like Star Cluster. The purpose of these future experiments is to extend the proposed models in order to estimate how many machines are needed for optimizing the relationship between the execution time and economic cost for frost prediction applications and how they must be managed.

Acknowledgements. The authors acknowledge the financial support provided by the Argentinean Agency for R&D activities (ANPCyT) through the projects PAE-PID 146 and PICT-2012-2731, and to the Spanish National Plan for Research, Development and Innovation for financial support provided by the project TIN2012-31518 (ServiceCloud). Also the authors thank Dr. Elina Pacini, Dr. David Monge and Ing. Pablo Godoy for their constructive comments to improve the paper. The first author acknowledges his type II doctoral scholarship provided by CONICET, to Norberto Faraz for the source code provided for the frost prediction application, and finally to the Bec.AR program.

References

1. Oliveira, L., Rodrigues, J.: Wireless Sensor Networks: A Survey on Environmental Monitoring. Journal of Communications 6(2), 143–151 (2011)
2. Abbasi, A., Islam, N., Shaikh, Z.A., et al.: A Review of Wireless Sensors and Networks Applications in Agriculture. Computer Standards & Interfaces 36(2), 263–270 (2014)
3. Lee, K., Murray, D., Hughes, D., Joosen, W.: Extending Sensor Networks Into the Cloud Using Amazon Web Services. In: 2010 IEEE International Conference on Networked Embedded Systems for Enterprise Applications (NESEA), pp. 1–7. IEEE (2010)
4. Ahmed, K., Gregory, M.: Integrating Wireless Sensor Networks with Cloud Computing. In: Seventh International Conference on Mobile Ad-hoc and Sensor Networks (2011 MSN), pp. 364–366. IEEE (2011)
5. Gubbi, J., Buyya, R., Marusic, S., Palaniswami, M.: Internet of Things (IoT): A Vision, Architectural Elements, and Future Directions. Future Generation Computer Systems 29(7), 1645–1660 (2013)
6. Hirafuji, M., Yoichi, H., Kiura, T., Matsumoto, K., Fukatsu, T., et al.: Creating High-performance/Low-cost Ambient Sensor Cloud System using OpenFS (Open Field Server) for High-throughput Phenotyping. In: Proceedings of 2011 SICE Annual Conference (2011 SICE), pp. 2090–2092. IEEE (2011)
7. Hori, M., Kawashima, E., Yamazaki, T.: Application of cloud computing to agriculture and prospects in other fields. Fujitsu Scientific & Technical Journal 46(4), 446–454 (2010)
8. Buyya, R., Yeo, C., Venugopal, S., Broberg, J., Brandic, I.: Cloud Computing and Emerging IT Platforms: Vision, Hype, and Reality for Delivering Computing as the 5th Utility. Future Generation Computer Systems 25(6), 599–616 (2009)
9. Foster, I., Zhao, Y., Raicu, I., Lu, S.: Cloud Computing and Grid Computing 360-Degree Compared. In: Grid Computing Environments Workshop 2008 (GCE 2008), pp. 1–10. IEEE(2008)
10. Amazon EC2, Amazon Web Services (June 2014),
    http://aws.amazon.com/es/ec2/
11. Google, Google App Engine (June 2014),
    https://developers.google.com/appengine/
12. Microsoft, Windows Azure (June 2014), http://www.windowsazure.com/es-es/
13. Google, Google Docs (June 2014), https://drive.google.com/
14. Lee, K., Hughes, D.: System Architecture Directions for Tangible Cloud Computing. In: International Workshop on Information Security and Applications (IWISA 2010), Qinhuangdao, China, vol. 25 (2010)

15. Snyder, R.L., de Melo-Abreu, J.P.: Frost protection: Fundamentals, Practice and Economics, vol. 1. Food and Agriculture Organization of the United Nations, FAO (2005)
16. Allen, C.C.: A Simplified Equation for Minimum Temperature Prediction. Monthly Weather Review 85, 119–120 (1957)
17. Iacono, L.: Acceso Remoto a Redes de Sensores Inalámbricas Mediante Tecnologías de Computación Distribuida, Thesis Proposal, Facultad de Ingeniería, Universidad de Mendoza (2013)
18. Iacono, L., García Garino, C., Marianetti, O., Párraga, C.: Wireless Sensor Networks: A Software as a Service Approach. In: García Garino, C., Printista, M. (eds.) Prospective and Ongoing Projects, VI Latin American Symposium on High Performance Computing (HPCLatAm 2013), Mendoza, Argentina, pp. 184–195 (2013)
19. Sensor Cirrus (June 2014), https://sites.google.com/site/sensorcirrus/

Ensemble Learning of Run-Time Prediction Models for Data-Intensive Scientific Workflows

David A. Monge[1,2], Matěj Holec[3], Filip Železný[3], and Carlos García Garino[1,4]

[1] ITIC Research Institute, National University of Cuyo (UNCuyo), Argentina
[2] Faculty of Exact and Natural Sciences, UNCuyo, Argentina
[3] IDA Research Group, Czech Technical University, Czech Republic
[4] Faculty of Engineering, UNCuyo, Argentina
{dmonge,cgarcia}@itu.uncu.edu.ar,
{holecmat,zelezny}@fel.cvut.cz

Abstract. Workflow applications for in-silico experimentation involve the processing of large amounts of data. One of the core issues for the efficient management of such applications is the prediction of tasks performance. This paper proposes a novel approach that enables the construction models for predicting task's running-times of data-intensive scientific workflows. Ensemble Machine Learning techniques are used to produce robust combined models with high predictive accuracy. Information derived from workflow systems and the characteristics and *provenance* of the data are exploited to guarantee the accuracy of the models. The proposed approach has been tested on Bioinformatics workflows for Gene Expressions Analysis over homogeneous and heterogeneous computing environments. Obtained results highlight the convenience of using ensemble models in comparison with single/standalone prediction models. Ensemble learning techniques permitted reductions of the prediction error up to 24.9% in comparison with single-model strategies.

Keywords: Performance prediction, Scientific workflows, Ensemble Learning, Data Provenance, Data-intensive computing.

1 Introduction

Workflow technology is intended to ease the development of applications through the combination of reusable software components. This approach facilitates the development of large-scale applications by people with low or even null experience on programming languages. For such reason, workflow technology has been widely accepted on many scientific areas [13].

Scientific data-intensive computing is in vogue nowadays [6]. In this sense, workflows are used to describe large-scale applications, whose execution is delegated to Workflow Management Systems (WMSs) that take in the details of the underlying computing infrastructure. This aspect is very important for executing large-scale applications because the users can take advantage of a huge computing power (i.e. clusters, grids or clouds) abstracting them from the particularities of the underlying infrastructure.

G. Hernández et al. (Eds.): CARLA 2014, CCIS 485, pp. 83–97, 2014.

For managing the applications efficiently, WMSs rely on run-time estimates of tasks. This information is the basis for several processes like for example: tasks scheduling, fulfillment of Quality of Service (QoS) requirements, autoscaling cloud infrastructures among others [3,5,9].

Most of the prediction methods used by WMSs were crafted for characterizing parallel applications. Although such techniques provide accurate predictions, they require the supervision of an expert for constructing and tuning the prediction models. Such requirements lure one of the main advantages of workflow technology: *simplicity for the user*.

To cope with such limitation many authors applied Machine Learning strategies to generate the prediction models (semi-)automatically. Following this line of thought, we propose a novel method for the autonomous generation of multiple **combined** run-time prediction **models** derived using *Ensemble Learning* methods. The final objective of our approach is the minimization of the human effort when generating the models without handicapping the accuracy of predictions. For accomplishing such objective this work utilizes the performance information available in WMSs and workflow provenance information to learn robust combined models.

The rest of this paper is organized as follows. In section 2 we provide a review of performance prediction strategies based on Machine Learning methods. Section 3 presents the proposed approach for learning run-time prediction models. Section 4 describes a set of Bioinformatic workflows and the methodology used for validating our proposal. Section 5 presents and discusses the results obtained. Finally, conclusions and future work are given in section 6.

2   Related Works

The prediction of application's performance has been studied since the genesis of parallel and distributed computing [1]. Many of such strategies use historical data to carry out the predictions instead of constructing the models by hand. Statistical and Machine Learning techniques permit the derivation of models based on the available historical data (examples). This approach supposes an important advantage for workflow applications executing on Grid or Cloud environments because models can be refined over time and the user does not need to be supervising the construction of the models or performing tedious tasks such as benchmarking resources, profiling applications, etc.

Some of these strategies address the prediction issue using the k-Nearest Neighbors strategy [8,11]. Predictions are performed by first looking execution *examples* with similar settings to the prediction query (e.g. examples with similar task parameters, processor speed, etc.). Then, the execution times corresponding to the selected examples are averaged and returned as the prediction. Other authors use methods such as regression trees for predicting the performance of applications [12]. More recently, Artificial Neural Networks have been applied to estimate the price of market-based computing resources [15].

Mentioned strategies apply statistical or machine-learning methods to predict several aspects of the execution of applications in the context of distributed computing environments. Like so, surveyed techniques have been developed having in mind compute-intensive applications disregarding important information sources such the size or the structure of data, to say nothing of *data provenance* [4] (i.e. the origin and transformations suffered by the data during the execution of an application). In the context of scientific workflows (where data is becoming the first-class citizen [6,10]) this information is fundamental for achieving accurate performance predictions.

A second aspect to remark is that these strategies rely on the use of a single model for performing the predictions. It is known that combining multiple models usually permits achieving a higher performance than using a unique model [17]. The following list describes the main limitations of the reviewed techniques in the light of scientific data-intensive workflows:

- *Disregard of data provenance information.* Attributes of the data are a central source of information for achieving high quality task's performance predictions.
- *Use of standalone models.* Techniques reviewed in this section rely on a single model for predicting the running time of tasks.

Our contribution this paper proposes a novel method for minimizing the intervention of a human expert to model the performance of tasks in the context of scientific workflows. The proposed method relies on **ensemble** Machine Learning methods for generating models in a automatic fashion. The proposed strategy incorporates several sources of information provided by the underlying WMS, such as task parameters, hardware information, **data characteristics and provenance** information to maximize the accuracy of the models.

3   Learning Performance Models

This section describes a novel generic strategy for the autonomous generation of performance models (AGPM) for the prediction of workflow tasks run-time. Unlike other strategies, AGPM relies only on the information that can be accessible from the underlying workflow system. The user only needs to define the *meta-data* of tasks that might be important for modeling their performance. In this way, the process of performance modeling is focused on the parameters and data that affect the performance (user's empirical knowledge) and not in the particular process implemented by the tasks. This is one of the main advantages of AGPM because it considers tasks as *black boxes*, which permits the modeling of legacy applications or web/grid services (i.e. software components whose code is unavailable or inaccessible).

AGPM uses machine learning (ML) techniques to model task's running time using information of workflow tasks parameters, data and dependencies as well as resource benchmark metrics. ML methods permit the construction of the models and their readjustment as new performance data becomes available. In this manner, the required human effort to maintain the models is greatly reduced maintaining a high predictive accuracy. AGPM uses ensemble Machine Learning methods to construct a meta-model comprising several sub-models to achieve higher quality predictions.

3.1 AGPM Learning Process

AGPM drives an adaptive learning process that comprises 4 stages (see figure 1): (*i*) execution of workflow tasks, (*ii*) performance data gathering, (*iii*) model learning, and (*iv*) tasks run-time prediction. In the following paragraphs we briefly discuss each of them.

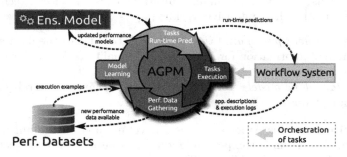

Fig. 1. Learning process carried out by AGPM

Stage 1: Workflow tasks execution. This stage involves the execution and monitoring of tasks as well as the generation of the corresponding *execution logs*, which are later used in the following stages. This stage is carried out entirely by the WMS.

Stage 2: Performance-data Gathering. Consists in the harvesting of the necessary information for the further learning/refinement of the performance models. Execution logs are used to extract valuable information of tasks performance such as the parameters and the data used, provenance information and the characteristics of the resources where the tasks executed. The appliance of AGPM is not restricted to applications for grid and cloud but also to web services. AGPM compiles all the information that can be gathered from the running workflow management system. The collected data is stored in separate databases for each type of runnable task.

Stage 3: Model Learning. At this point of the process, the databases contain updated information of the last task execution. AGPM then learns a new model for each type of task following a two-step procedure consisting on (*i*) data preprocessing, and (*ii*) ensemble model learning. AGPM pre-processes the databases in order to prepare the data for the ensemble learning strategy. As a second step, multiple models are learned from the data and combined in order to perform future running-time predictions. Sections 3.2 and 3.3 provide a deeper insight on the described process which is the central contribution of this paper.

Stage 4: Tasks Run-time Prediction. Consists in the generation of running time estimates for tasks using the models constructed on the previous stage. Run-time estimates are obtained considering the inputs of workflow tasks (i.e. parameters and data) and the characteristics of the resources which will eventually execute such tasks.

This sequence of stages is repeated continuously throughout the execution of several applications. Each one of these cycles permits the improvement of the predictive accuracy of the models. This strategy allows the adaptation of the models to new (unseen) execution examples. The important aspect to note is that this *adaptive learning* process improves the accuracy of the prediction models without requiring human intervention more than the initial setup of the performance data to collect. Ensemble learning plays a central role in such objective because enables the strategy with very robust models autonomously.

3.2   Performance-Data Representation

Performance data is stored separately for each type of task. The performance dataset for a task can be formally defined as a set $\mathcal{D} = \{x^{(i)}, y^{(i)}\}_m^{i=1}$, where $x^{(i)}$ represents a column vector of features for the ith (out of m) recorded *execution example* of a task, and $y^{(i)}$ is the measured *running time* for such execution, also known as *target*.

Each feature vector $x = [x_1, x_2, \cdots, x_n]$ comprises three types of elements: (*i*)   *task features*, which represent the inputs of the task, e.g. parameter values, data size, etc.; (*ii*) *provenance features*, describe previous processes that generated or modified the input data; and (*iii*) *resource features*, which model characteristics of the resource used on the execution of the task.

Task features. This kind of features describe the task's inputs. This information includes the values taken by input parameters and characteristics of the data such as size, number of lines, registers or columns, etc.

Provenance features. This type of features capture information of the data origin and the transformations produced by other tasks during the execution of the workflow. Such information can be easily extracted from the description of the workflow. The incorporation of such information permits the obtainment of more accurate performance models. As said before, to the extent of our knowledge, there is no other strategy in the state of the art using such information for producing run-time predictions.

Resource features. This kind of features describe the computing resources used in the tasks execution. These features can be obtained from the WMS. Features used for modeling the performance of an application are those which measure the performance of the resources (i.e. those that impact directly on the performance of tasks). Such information is mainly provided by resource benchmarks. In general, most part of the WMSs provide such metrics and update them regularly. Note that in the case of web services, this type of features will be inaccessible.

3.3 Learning Prediction Models

Machine Learning (ML) methods are the core of our approach. This section briefly describes some of the traditional Machine Learning techniques used in state-of-the-art works to produce (standalone) prediction models. This section also discusses an ensemble learning strategy denominated Bootstrap Aggregating used to validate our hypothesis.

Standalone Models. Our implementation of AGPM includes some well established Machine Learning strategies used in some of the papers dealing with performance prediction. The following paragraphs describe the essential concepts behind such strategies. Please note that the implementations of the algorithms used in this work are provided by the Weka library [14].

Artificial Neural Networks (ANNs). These kind of Networks belong to a family of models that emulate the operation of biological neural networks [17]. The models comprise a set of neurons (units) arranged in multiple layers. Units in one layer are connected to units in the following layer throughout the net reaching an output neuron that predicts the target value y. Networks used in this study comprise one hidden layer with $n/2$ hidden units, where n is the number of features in the input vector. The parameters of the network are two matrices $\Theta^{(1)}$ and $\Theta^{(2)}$ of size $(n+1) \times (n/2)$ and $(n/2+1) \times 1$ that model the interactions between the units in different layers. Figure 2 shows an example neural network.

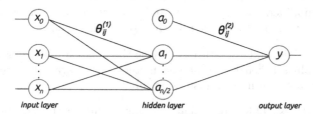

Fig. 2. Artificial Neural Network example. The network comprises one hidden layer and a single output unit y that provides the run-time prediction.

The activation (outputs) of the hidden units are computed as $a = \sigma(\bar{x} \cdot \Theta^{(1)})$, where $\bar{x}$ is an input vector x extended with a first component $x_0 = 1$ (bias unit), and $\sigma(z) = 1/(1 + e^{-z})$, which is the sigmoid function. Activation of the hidden units are forward propagated to the next layer to produce the predicted value of the running time $y = \bar{a} \cdot \Theta^{(2)}$, where $\bar{a}$ is the activation vector a of the hidden layer extended with a bias unit $a_0 = 1$. Learning the model consists on learning the weights in the network, i.e. the values of matrices $\Theta^{(1)}$ and $\Theta^{(2)}$. To such end the back-propagation algorithm [17] is used, which for space limitations is not discussed in this paper.

k-Nearest Neighbors (k-NN). In this strategy, training examples are stored verbatim. A distance function is used to determine which are the k examples of the training set that are closest to an unknown test example [17]. The output of the method is the average of the target values (i.e. running time) corresponding to those k nearest examples. In this study we use the Euclidean distance. Given two examples $x^{(1)}$ and $x^{(2)}$ with components $x_1^{(1)}, x_2^{(1)}, \ldots, x_n^{(1)}$ and $x_1^{(2)}, x_2^{(2)}, \ldots, x_n^{(2)}$ respectively, the Euclidean distance between them is: $\sqrt{\sum_1^n (x_i^{(1)} - x_i^{(2)})^2}$.

Support Vector Regression (SVR). SVR [17] is an adaptation of the Support Vector Machines (SVM) to deal with the prediction of numeric classes. Produced models can be expressed in terms of a few support vectors that best describe the prediction surface. The SVR model has the form $f(x) = \sum_{i \in SV} \alpha_i K(x^{(i)}, x) + b$, where SV is the set of support vectors and $K(x^{(i)}, x)$ is a kernel function that maps an example into a feature space of higher dimensions. α_i and b are model parameters determined by solving the following optimization problem:

$$\min_{\alpha, b, \xi_i, \xi_i^*} \frac{1}{2} \alpha^T \alpha + C \sum_{i=1}^l (\xi_i + \xi_i^*) \quad subject\,to: \quad \begin{aligned} y - f(x_i) &\leq \varepsilon + \xi_i \\ f(x_i) - y &\leq \varepsilon + \xi_i^* \\ \xi_i, \xi_i^* &> 0 \end{aligned}$$

where C is the model complexity parameter which penalizes the loss of training errors, ξ_i and ξ_i^* are slack variables that specify upper and lower bound training errors subject to an error tolerance ε. To model non-linear functions of the running time we use a radial basis function (RBF) kernel $k(x^{(i)}, x^{(j)}) = exp(-\gamma \left\| x^{(i)} - x^{(j)} \right\|^2)$ with $\gamma = 0.01$. The values parameters of SVR were set to $C = 1$ and $\varepsilon = 0.001$, which are the default values in Weka.

M5P Regression trees. The M5 Prime (M5P) algorithm [17] permits the induction of decision trees whose leaves are associated to regression models. M5P trees are a combination of decision trees and linear models in the tree leaves. The model is constructed in three phases as follows. First, a decision tree is constructed minimizing the variability the output variable (i.e. examples with very similar running time are grouped). Then, the tree is pruned starting from the leaf nodes. If an inner node is pruned, it is converted into a leaf node and a regression plane is associated. Finally, a smoothing function is applied to avoid sharp discontinuities between the hyperplanes. An example of M5P regression tree is given in Figure 3b.

Preprocessing. Before constructing the models, the available performance data is normalized to avoid the dominance of some features of higher orders of magnitude in the construction of the models. To such end, each feature x_i is transformed into a new feature $\hat{x}_i$ according to the equation $\hat{x}_i = \frac{x_i - \mu}{\sigma}$, where μ and σ are the mean and the standard deviation of all the values for the feature x_i. In this work we only focused on data normalization but much more can be done to improve the quality of the models [2].

Learning Ensemble Models. One of the main advantages of ensemble learning methods is that they permit achieving predictions of better quality than those obtained by standalone models. For generating the models we use the Bootstrap Aggregating (Bagging) technique [17]. This technique reduces the *variance*, i.e. the expected error derived from all the possible training sets for the problem.

The Bagging technique works as follows. For a given training dataset $\mathcal{D}$, n new training datasets $(\mathcal{D}_i)$ of size m' are obtained by sampling the set $\mathcal{D}$ randomly with replacement (some examples are removed and some are repeated). Each of the n bootstrap samples are used to generate n different (base) models. The outputs of the n models are combined by averaging them. This procedure generates a combined model that usually outperforms the single models and is never considerably worse. As base models we use M5P regression trees, which were discussed in the previous paragraphs. The entire process is illustrated in Figure 3a.

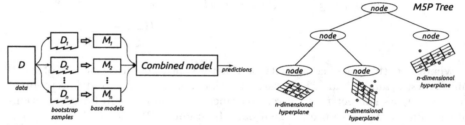

(a) Bagging process. The n bootstrap samples (D_i) are used to construct the base models (M_i). The base models are M5P regression trees.

(b) Example of an M5P tree constructed for one of the D_i bootstrap samples.

Fig. 3. Process for Bagging M5P regression trees

4   Experiment Settings

To analyze the performance of the ensemble models we evaluated the predictive accuracy of standalone models generated using the reviewed methods and ensemble models learned with the Bagging strategy. Following sections describe a bioinformatics application used as case of study, and details the methodology used for the validation of our proposal.

4.1   Gene Expression Analysis Workflows

For the purposes of this work we evaluated our approach on bioinformatics data-mining workflows, which perform a large-scale gene expression analysis experiment (GEAE). The goal of the experiment is to compare a novel classification algorithm (GELF) and the state-of-the-art approach (baseline) [7] on their respective ability to classify unseen data.

The experiment comprises the execution of several workflows. Each of them processes one of the 20 microarray datasets used for the experiment using a 10-fold cross-validation scheme. Figure 4a represents one GEAE example workflow. Sub-experiments, cover a set of several parameters in order to consider various aspects of methods intended to compare. As can be seen on Figure 4b each sub-experiment involves 3 types of tasks:

There are two *ranker tasks* that perform a selection of genes in order to reduce the number of features for learning the classifier. The first one uses recursive feature elimination using support vector machines (called **SVM-RFE**), and the second one returns a random order of features (**RandomR**). The third task consists on consists on *learning and evaluating* the performance of the (**GELF**) classifier. GELF is a feature construction algorithm based on iterative improvement of the best solution obtained by the state-of-the-art approach [7].

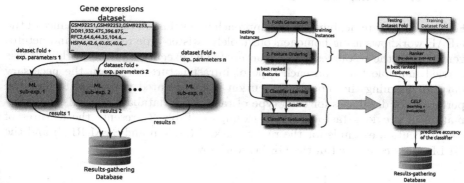

(a) Scheme of one of the GEAE workflows. (b) Abstract and concrete views of a ML sub-experiment.

Fig. 4. GEAE workflows. Overview of one of the GEAE workflows (a) and decomposition of for one sub-experiment (b).

Each workflow comprises 20 sub-experiments: both combinations of the GELF task with the rankers (Random and SVM-RFE) applied on the 10 dataset folds. As can be seen each workflow application consists of 40 tasks (i.e. 10 Random ranker executions, 10 SVM-RFE ranker executions and 20 GELF executions). Considering that we executed the workflows over 20 different datasets. This gives 800 task executions. To generate a wide spectrum of performance-data examples, each workflow was executed 10 times on resources of different type. Table 1 describes the characteristic of the resources used for executing the GEAE workflows. JavaMFlops, KFlops and MIPS are performance values provided by the SciMark2 [1], Linpack [2] and Dhrystone [16] benchmarks respectively.

---

[1] SciMark2 benchmark. http://math.nist.gov/scimark2
[2] Linpack benchmark. http://www.netlib.org/linpack

Table 1. Computing infrastructure summary

Characteristics	Resource type		
	Twister	Reloaded	Opteron
Processor type	Intel Core2 Duo	Intel P4 HT	AMD Opteron 242
Processor frequency	3.0 GHz	3.0 GHz	1.6 GHz
Memory	4 GB	1 GB	2 GB
Average JavaMFlops	962.23	281.05	400.76
Average KFlops	17.54E5	4.99E5	6.63E5
Average MIPS	4983.80	1465.42	2057.00
No. of resources	10	12	4

4.2   Performance Datasets

For testing the applicability of our approach we evaluated the performance of the GEAE workflows using homogeneous (solely twister-type resources) and heterogeneous (all the resources) infrastructures. The execution of the workflows was carried multiple times on each type of infrastructure to obtain the necessary data for learning the models. Execution logs generated were used to feed the performance databases for each type of task. Each database contains the information of previous task execution examples. Table 2 presents the features of each execution example for the ranker tasks (Random and SVM-RFE) and the GELF tasks comprised in the GEAE workflows.

Table 2. Features of the performance datasets for the tasks in GEAE workflows

Feature	Type	Description
dataset-id	provenance	identification of the used dataset {1,2,...,20}
ranker *	provenance	feature ranking task {RandomR, SVM-RFE}
tr-size	task	size in bytes of the training dataset folds
tr-rows	task	number of rows in the training dataset folds
tr-columns	task	number of columns in the training dataset folds
tt-size *	task	size in bytes of the training testing folds
tt-rows *	task	number of rows in the testing dataset folds
tt-columns *	task	number of columns in the testing dataset folds
java-mflops	resource	SciMark2 benchmark for the resource used
kflops	resource	Linpack benchmark for the resource used
mips	resource	Dhrystone benchmark for the resource used
execution-time	target	measured running time for the task execution example

* features that pertain only to GELF (not applicable to rankers).

According to this configuration, six different datasets were generated. One of each combination of task type (RandomR, SVM-RFE or GELF) and type of infrastructure (homogeneous or heterogeneous)

5   Results and Analysis

In this section we present the results obtained during the experimental process. Six different scenarios were analyzed: the three types of GEAE tasks on **homogeneous** and **heterogeneous** infrastructures.

For measuring the performance of each model we use the Relative Absolute Error (RAE), which is computed as $error = \frac{|p_1 - a_1| + ... + |p_m - a_m|}{|a_1 - \bar{a}| + ... + |a_m - \bar{a}|} \cdot 100\%$, where, p_i and a_i represent the predicted and actual values respectively for i^{th} example. $\bar{a}$ represents the mean value of the actual values and m is the number of testing examples. This metric measures the deviation of predictions with respect to the actual values. Following sections present the results obtained for the homogeneous and heterogeneous environments respectively, and an overall analysis of results.

Homogeneous Environment.   Table 3 presents the errors for the homogeneous environments. Highlighted values represent the minimum errors for each type of task. For the RANDOMR task, ANN achieves the minimum error (34.1%), but all the methods present very similar performances (except for SVR whose error ascends to 43.1%). It is worth to point out that regardless that high errors are evidenced, in practice these errors do not imply very negative effects because the mean duration of tasks is very small (7.7 s).

SVM-RFE is a much more simple task to model as can be evidenced by lower errors on the table. Once again ANN achieves the best results. The impact of these errors is depreciable because SVM-RFE tasks have an average duration of 16.3 s.

For GELF tasks, it can be seen that the Bagging strategy presents the minimum error. This error is about 20.7%, which represents a reduction of the error ranging from 10.5% to 21.2% in comparison with the rest of the competitors. In contraposition to the ranker tasks, large errors on the prediction of GELF task's duration have much more undesirable consequences because the duration of the tasks are much larger (2183.6 s).

As a general note, it can be seen that the highest errors are obtained for RANDOMR, because of two reasons. First, its performance is not determined by any parameter or characteristic of the data (the task randomly sorts the genes without any particular input than the data). Second, its short duration is very likely to be disturbed by other factors (i.e. background load, workflow system overhead, etc.).

Another result to note, the ensemble method evidenced errors in the same range than the best of the methods (ANN) with only a 1%-2% increase of the error. In addition, for the case of GELF, the performance of ANN drops dramatically becoming the worst performing method. In contrast, the ensemble method

Table 3. Relative Absolute Errors for the Homogeneous environment

Strategy	RandomR	SVM-RFE	GELF
M5P	34.7%	22.0%	31.2%
ANN	**34.1%**	**20.8%**	41.9%
k-NN	35.1%	21.2%	32.0%
SVR	43.1%	24.8%	40.9%
Ensemble model	36.0%	21.1%	**20.7%**

(that had an average performance for the rankers) achieved the lowest error for GELF. This behavior evidences an important characteristic of the ensemble method, i.e. its robustness. The method can be applied to different scenarios resulting always in a good performance.

Heterogeneous Environment. Table 4 shows the errors for the heterogeneous environment. Highlighted values represent the minimum errors for each type of task. For the RANDOMR task, the best performing methods are k-NN and Bagging-M5P with a 19.8% error. The predictions for this (heterogeneous) environment are much more accurate than in the previous case. For the SVM-RFE task, the best performance is achieved by the ensemble method which evidences a 10.1% error. This is also the case with GELF for which an error of 15.7% is manifested. In the case of GELF, the improvements range from 8.0% to 24.9% compared to all other methods.

Table 4. Relative Absolute Errors for the Heterogeneous environment

Strategy	RandomR	SVM-RFE	GELF
M5P	22.1%	14.7%	23.7%
ANN	23.7%	11.0%	40.6%
k-NN	**19.8%**	10.3%	24.3%
SVR	32.6%	25.5%	32.3%
Ensemble model	**19.8%**	**10.1%**	**15.7%**

From the table, similar observations to the homogeneous case are derived. Higher errors are obtained for the RANDOMR task and there is a wide margin between the ensemble model and the remaining ones while modeling the performance of GELF tasks.

Overall Comparison. Figure 5 presents the average error for each of the strategies considering the six scenarios. It can be seen that the ensemble strategy presents the minimum average error (20.6%). These results highlight the robustness of the ensemble model. It is important to note that the standalone M5P achieves an average performance among the learning methods. But, a combined model of M5P trees permits achieving much more accurate predictions. The ensemble method lead to error reductions ranging between 3% and 13% considering the six scenarios. The robustness of the ensemble method makes it very suitable for real world settings where effort and intervention of experts in performance modeling must be minimized.

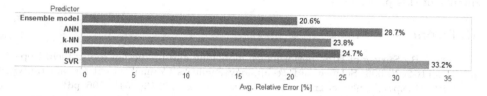

Fig. 5. Relative Absolute Error for each model

6 Concluding Remarks

In this paper we proposed an adaptive scheme for the construction of performance models for workflow-tasks run-time prediction suitable for Grids and Clouds. This scheme uses Machine Learning methods to construct *ensemble models* using *data-provenance* information and other sources of data available from the workflow systems.

Conducted experiments were designed for evaluating the performance of an ensemble model in comparison with other single-model machine learning techniques. Experiments focused on predicting the running time of tasks comprised in real-world bioinformatic workflows. The performance of the studied strategies was measured on both computing environments.

Results evidenced that the ensemble method outperforms its competitors except for two of the six analyzed scenarios. For those two cases, the ensemble method achieved a prediction errors only 1%-2% higher than the best strategy. For the remaining 4 scenarios, the ensemble method outperformed their competitors. The best results present wide margins of improvement with respect to their competitors. In the best case the ensemble method presented error reductions in the range of 10.5% to 21.2% on the homogeneous environment, and 8.0% to 24.9% for the heterogeneous case.

Undoubtedly, there is much more that can be investigated in relation with complex models for predicting the performance of data-intensive scientific workflows. This paper is an initial step towards such objective. As future work we plan to evaluate other ensemble learning strategies to gain more insights on the importance of utilizing combined models for predicting the performance of applications. Also, studying new techniques for improving the quality of features may help to increase the accuracy of the models [2]. Another idea to explore in this direction is to study the applicability of these ensemble models into applications for the processing of massive amounts of data, i.e. Big Data applications.

Acknowledgements. This research is supported by the ANPCyT through project No. PICT-2012-2731. This study is also founded by the Argentine Ministry of Science (MINCyT) and the Czech Ministry of Education, Youth and Sports (MEYS) through projects Nos. RC0904 and MEB111005. The financial support from SeCTyP-UNCuyo through project No. M004 is gratefully acknowledged. The first author wants to thank CONICET for the granted fellowship. Finally we want to thank the anonymous reviewers who helped improving the quality of this paper.

References

1. Allan, R.: Survey of HPC performance modelling and prediction tools. Tech. Rep. DL-TR-2010-006, Science and Technology Facilities Council, Great Britain (July 2010), http://epubs.cclrc.ac.uk/bitstream/5264/DLTR-2010-006.pdf
2. Bengio, Y., Courville, A.C., Vincent, P.: Representation Learning: A Review and New Perspectives. Computing Reseach Repository-arXiv abs/1206.5538, 1–30 (April 2014), http://arxiv.org/abs/1206.5538
3. Chen, W., Deelman, E.: Partitioning and scheduling workflows across multiple sites with storage constraints. In: Wyrzykowski, R., Dongarra, J., Karczewski, K., Waśniewski, J. (eds.) PPAM 2011, Part II. LNCS, vol. 7204, pp. 11–20. Springer, Heidelberg (2012)
4. da Cruz, S., Campos, M., Mattoso, M.: Towards a taxonomy of provenance in scientific workflow management systems. In: 2009 World Conference on Services - I, pp. 259–266 (2009)
5. Genez, T., Bittencourt, L., Madeira, E.R.M.: Workflow scheduling for SaaS / PaaS cloud providers considering two SLA levels. In: 2012 IEEE Network Operations and Management Symposium (NOMS), pp. 906–912 (2012)
6. Hey, T., Tansley, S., Tolle, K. (eds.): The Fourth Paradigm: Data-Intensive Scientific Discovery. Microsoft Research, Redmond, Washington (October 2009)
7. Holec, M., Klema, J., Železný, F., Tolar, J.: Comparative evaluation of set-level techniques in predictive classification of gene expression samples. BMC Bioinformatics 13(Suppl. 10, S15), 1–15 (2012)
8. Iverson, M., Ozguner, F., Potter, L.: Statistical prediction of task execution times through analytic benchmarking for scheduling in a heterogeneous environment. In: Heterogeneous Computing Workshop (HCW 1999) Proceedings of the Eighth, vol. 8, pp. 99–111. IEEE Computer Society, San Juan (1999)
9. Mao, M., Humphrey, M.: Scaling and scheduling to maximize application performance within budget constraints in cloud workflows. In: 2013 IEEE 27th International Symposium on Parallel & Distributed Processing (IPDPS), pp. 67–78. IEEE (2013)
10. Marx, V.: Biology: The big challenges of big data. Nature 498(7453), 255–260 (2013)
11. Monge, D.A., Bělohradský, J., García Garino, C., Železný, F.: A Performance Prediction Module for Workflow Scheduling. In: 4th Symposium on High-Performance Computing in Latin America (HPCLatAm 2011), vol. 4, pp. 130–144. SADIO, Córdoba (2011)
12. Ould-Ahmed-Vall, E., Woodlee, J., Yount, C., Doshi, K., Abraham, S.: Using model trees for computer architecture performance analysis of software applications. In: IEEE International Symposium on Performance Analysis of Systems Software, ISPASS 2007, pp. 116–125. IEEE Computer Society (April 2007)

13. Taylor, I., Deelman, E., Gannon, D., Shields, M.: Workflows for e-Science: Scientific Workflows for Grids. 1st edn. Springer, London(December 2007)
14. M.L.G. at the University of Waikato, Weka 3: Data mining software in java. (September 2013), http://www.cs.waikato.ac.nz/ml/weka
15. Wallace, R., Turchenko, V., Sheikhalishahi, M., Turchenko, I., Shults, V., Vazquez-Poletti, J., Grandinetti, L.: Applications of neural-based spot market prediction for cloud computing. In: 2013 IEEE 7th International Conference on Intelligent Data Acquisition and Advanced Computing Systems (IDAACS), vol. 2, pp. 710–716 (September 2013)
16. Weicker, R.P.: Dhrystone: a synthetic systems programming benchmark. Communications of the ACM 27(10), 1013–1030 (1984)
17. Witten, I.H., Frank, E., Hall, M.A.: Data Mining: Practical Machine Learning Tools and Techniques, 3rd edn. Morgan Kaufman (January 2011)

Implications of CPU Dynamic Performance and Energy-Efficient Technologies on the Intrusiveness Generated by Desktop Grids Based on Virtualization

Germán Sotelo, Eduardo Rosales, and Harold Castro

Universidad de los Andes, Systems and Computing Engineering Department,
School of Engineering, Colombia
{ga.sotelo69,ee.rosales24,hcastro}@uniandes.edu.co

Abstract. We evaluate how dynamic performance and energy-efficient technologies, as features introduced in modern processor architectures, affect the intrusiveness that Desktop Grids based on virtualization generate on desktops. Such intrusiveness is defined as degradation in the performance perceived by an end-user that is using a desktop while it is opportunistically utilized by Desktop Grid systems. To achieve this, we deploy virtual machines on a selection of desktops representing recent processor architectures. We then benchmark CPU intensive workloads simultaneously executed on both the virtual and the physical environment. The results show that dynamic performance and energy-efficient technologies, when incorporated on the supporting desktops, directly affect the level of intrusiveness an end-user perceives. Furthermore, depending on the processor architecture the intrusiveness percentage varies in a range from 3% to 100%. Finally, we propose policies aimed to minimize such intrusiveness according to the supporting processor architectures to be utilized and end-user profiles.

Keywords: Desktop Grid, Grid Computing, Volunteer Computing, Benchmarking, Virtualization, Intrusiveness, Performance.

1   Introduction

Desktop Grid Computing benefits from idle computing resources available in volunteer computers around the world (known as Public, Global, Peer-to-Peer, Public-Resource, or Internet-based Desktop Grids) or desktops deployed at an institution (known as Local, Private, or Enterprise Desktop Grids) [13]. These efforts mostly aim to support e-Science projects by integrating non-dedicated, distributed, and heterogeneous computing resources that usually belong to different administrative domains in order to provide large-scale computational capacities at low-cost. Since desktops tend to be underutilized during significant periods, there is usually a large amount of idle computing resources available (processing, networking and storage). Therefore, Desktop Grids are an economically attractive solution to deploy large-scale computing infrastructures, avoiding not only underutilization, but also financial investments in new and dedicated hardware.

G. Hernández et al. (Eds.): CARLA 2014, CCIS 485, pp. 98–112, 2014.

In this context, several scientific projects have been leveraging the potential of Desktop Grids. Initiatives such as Distributed.net [4], XtremWeb [17], SETI@home [12], BOINC [2], SZTAKI [14], and OurGrid [10], among others, have shown foremost research results by exploiting opportunistic infrastructures mainly composed of desktop computers. These Desktop Grid systems are based on software agents that are installed directly on the operating system in order to manage the usage of idle computing resources.

More recently, initiatives such as VMware@Home [16], LHC@Home [8], and UnaCloud [11], among others, are pioneers in the use of virtualization technologies to build Desktop Grid Computing. Indeed, virtualization has appeared as an innovative technology to enable running complete guest operating systems on top of a single hypervisor (hypervisor type I) or a hypervisor on top of a host operating system (hypervisor type II). This latter feature allows the deployment of single or a number of virtual machines on off-the-shelf desktops, thus facilitating the deployment of large-scale virtual environments aimed to support Desktop Grids. Above all, virtualization enables the deployment of customized operating systems along with the full software stack required by scientific applications across a set of desktops that may considerably differ in terms of hardware and/or software.

Nonetheless, when the execution of Desktop Grid systems (based on agents, virtualization or hybrids) occur in parallel to tasks performed by end-users, a level of intrusiveness is caused. Such intrusiveness is defined as the degradation in the performance perceived by an end-user that is using a desktop while a Desktop Grid is concurrently leveraging its idle computing resources. Since most of such desktops are non-dedicated and temporally donated resources, the level of intrusiveness becomes a key factor either to encourage or to dissuade the donation of idle computing resources to support Desktop Grids for e-Science projects.

In this paper, we study how intrusiveness of Desktop Grids based on virtualization is directly related to hardware specifications of the supporting desktops. We analyze how technologies incorporated on several generations of modern processor architectures have been consistently altering such intrusiveness. Specifically, we evaluate how dynamic performance and energy-efficient technologies, when incorporated on the processor of the supporting desktop, directly affect the level of intrusiveness an end-user is able to perceive when using Desktop Grid systems based on virtualization.

The remainder of this paper is organized as follows: section 2 summarizes the related work. Section 3 presents the methodology used to conduct this research. Section 4 presents the results and discussion. Section 5 presents a set of recommendations based on our research findings. Finally, in section 6 are presented the conclusions and future work.

2   Related Work

In the context of benchmarking virtualization for Desktop Grids, there are two main groups of existing work related to the research presented in this paper.

The first group is concerned with measuring the performance degradation (overhead) of using virtual machines over desktops for the execution of applications in comparison with the direct use of the physical environment, so called native. In [15] the authors compare the floating-point performance of VMware Player virtual machines by using Windows and Linux as host and guest operating systems on the AMD Dual-Core architecture. They conclude that both operating systems used as guests induced performance penalties compared to a native execution, but as a guest operating system Linux delivers better performance than Windows. Since VMware Player emulates only the kernel-mode instructions, the authors hypothesize that incidence of such instructions in Linux is lower than in Windows.

In [7] the authors compare the performance of executions on native versus virtualized environments by using benchmarks based on CPU intensive tasks. They found that overhead induced by virtualization is less than 10%. The experiments are set on architectures based on the Intel Dual Pentium III processor by using VMware Workstation as hypervisor and RedHat as host and guest operating system.

A second group, which is more related to our research, is concerned with evaluating the intrusiveness of virtual machines executed as low-priority processes on a desktop in relation to the performance perceived by an end-user that is simultaneously using its environment. In [5] the authors evaluate the performance of virtual environments based on the hypervisors VMware Player, QEMU, VirtualPC, and VirtualBox on Intel Dual-Core processors by using Windows as host and Linux as guest operating systems. The results show marginal performance impact in the presence of a single virtual machine as long as only single-threaded applications run at the host operating system. In contrast, multi-threaded applications running at the host operating system suffer a considerable performance drop which ranges from 10% to 35% compared with the same execution on the native environment. On the other hand, for the applications executed on the virtual environment they found that performance depends on the application type and the virtualization software used. Indeed, for CPU intensive tasks the overhead revolves around 15% to 30% which is considered acceptable. However, disk IO and network IO performances are severely penalized, and thus the authors suggest not using virtual environments for such execution scenarios.

In [3] the authors evaluate the intrusiveness of a Desktop Grid system named UnaGrid. For this purpose, they execute the hypervisor type 2 VMware Workstation over an Intel Core 2 Duo processor. They simultaneously execute CPU intensive tasks on two operating systems, Linux as guest and Windows as host. Each virtual machine is executed as a low-priority process in background and it is assigned with one and two cores subsequently. In such tests, the results show performance degradation of less than 1%. The authors conclude that priority set to the virtual environment at the operating system level allows an exclusive harvesting of idle CPU resources that guarantees very low impact on the performance perceived by end-users.

This research complements and extends the work presented above by benchmarking a Desktop Grid based on virtualization over several generations of modern processor architectures in order to evaluate variations in the intrusiveness caused to end-users. As a result, we demonstrate that intrusiveness caused by Desktop Grids based on virtualization varies according to dynamic performance and energy-efficient technologies enabled on the supporting processor. To the best of our knowledge, our work is the first to evaluate how dynamic performance and energy-efficient technologies, as features introduced in modern processor architectures, affect the intrusiveness that Desktop Grids based on virtualization generate on desktops. Furthermore, a first set of strategies are recommended to implementations of Desktop Grid systems in order to reduce degradation on the performance perceived by end-users when donating their resources to Desktop Grid Computing.

3   Methodology

The aim of this research is to show implications of technologies incorporated on recent processor architectures in relation to intrusiveness produced by Desktop Grids. Specifically, our hypothesis is that dynamic performance and energy-efficient technologies directly affect the intrusiveness that Desktop Grids supported by virtualization generate when running over desktops. We clarify that our research findings may not be limited to Desktop Grids based on virtualization, but they may be generalized to every type of Desktop Grid; however, such generalization cannot be confirmed from the limited data obtained in this research. In addition, our research outcomes are not limited to the generations of processors studied, but they can be obtained in similar processor architectures, including servers. Nevertheless, the scope of this paper considers a specific selection of processors and a unique Desktop Grid system supported by virtualization technologies. In consequence, a set of test scenarios based on virtualization are proposed and performed over a variety of desktops. Finally, we clarify the test scenarios were designed in order to exclusively evaluate intrusiveness in terms of the performance delivered by the processor. To validate our hypotheses, the following methodology was developed.

3.1   Experimental Setup

The tests were executed over different generations of off-the-shelf desktop computers from laboratories open to employees, professors, and students on our university campus. Moreover, such computers have been opportunistically exploited in order to execute virtual machines for multiple e-Science projects [11]. The variety of such desktops was constrained by the inventory of hardware on our campus. This inventory is updated annually, hence limiting the amount of processor architectures to be studied. All of these desktops had Windows 7 as host operating system. This selection is justified by the fact that Windows is the dominating operating system for Desktop Grids [1]. The hardware configurations used in the experiments are shown in Table 1.

Table 1. Configurations of the hardware tested

CPU	RAM	Cores	Threads	Cache
Intel Core i7-4770	16 GB DDR3	4	8	8 MB
Intel Core i7-2600	16 GB DDR3	4	8	8 MB
Intel Core i5-660	8 GB DDR3	2	4	4 MB
Intel Core 2 Duo e7600	4 GB DDR3	2	2	3 MB
Intel Core 2 Duo e6300	4 GB DDR2	2	2	2 MB
AMD Athlon 64 X2 5000+	8 GB DDR2	2	2	1 MB

In order to avoid bias, the tests were conducted on separate virtual environments supported by two different hypervisors type II, VMware Workstation 10 (using .vmx files) and VirtualBox 4.3 (using .vdi files). Consequently, the simultaneous execution of both hypervisors on the same desktop is not within the scope of this research.

Each virtual machine had a new and default Debian 7 installation with the Oracle Java Virtual Machine (JVM) version 7.0.15. The hardware specifications for each virtual machine consisted of the use of 1 CPU core and 1 GB of RAM. Additionally, each virtual machine had the VMware Tools or the VBox Guest Additions installed (according to the hypervisor) in order to facilitate its management and deployment.

3.2 Test Deployment

Desktop Grid System: The tests were assisted by UnaCloud [11], our local opportunistic Cloud Computing Infrastructure as a Service (IaaS) implementation. Similarly to a Local Desktop Grid solution, UnaCloud is able to opportunistically execute single instances and/or clusters of virtual machines. It is important to emphasize that such execution is mostly supported by off-the-shelf, non-dedicated, distributed, and heterogeneous computing resources (such as desktops) that may belong to a variety of administrative domains. Furthermore, UnaCloud uses virtualization technologies as a strategy to enable on-demand deployments of customized execution environments that meet complex computing requirements from e-Science projects. UnaCloud executes each virtual machine as a low-priority process that remains running in background. Such deployment features enable harvesting idle computing resources opportunistically, that is, virtual machines are executed while an end-user is simultaneously utilizing the desktop or when it is fully available. In consequence, UnaCloud design specifications strongly consider intrusiveness, since it runs over computer laboratories mainly used by students to perform their daily work. In such a context, the management and utilization of idle computing resources must be as least intrusive as possible.

Virtual environment: The test scenarios differed in the amount of virtual machines concurrently executed on the physical machine. This number was in a range from no virtual machines to a number equivalent to the amount of physical CPU cores. In addition, all the virtual machines used were rebooted before and after each test scenario in order to avoid bias produced by incidental or cumulative consumption of computing resources.

3.3   Benchmark Selection

In order to represent and assess the intrusiveness in the execution of virtual environments for Desktop Grids, two benchmarks were set and performed over the selection of processors. Both benchmarks were exclusively based on CPU intensive workloads generated through the execution of a program able to calculate prime numbers by using the sieve of Eratosthenes [9]. This integer arithmetic algorithm was selected in order to avoid potential bias caused by improvements on the architectures tested to perform floating-point operations. Moreover, the execution of this program had negligible demands of RAM memory and no network activity was required.

The first benchmark was designed to test the virtual environment. For this purpose, the program was set to run on the virtual machine for approximately 10 hours thus loading permanently it with CPU intensive tasks. As explained formerly, according to the test scenario, the number of virtual machines varied from zero to the number of physical CPU cores.

The second benchmark was designed to test the physical environment. For this end, a number of concurrent processes were executed simulating an end-user without root privileges. According to the test scenario, this number ranged from 1 to the number of CPU threads. The concurrent processes were the same CPU intensive workloads used in the virtual environment. However, in this case the program was set to run for only 60 seconds on average.

Each test scenario consisted of the simultaneous execution of both benchmarks. The measurements were obtained only from the second benchmark. While the first benchmark was executed once to permanently load the virtual machine, the second was executed 24 separate times to obtain averaged results. This number allowed discarding the two measurements that were most distant from the median in order to avoid biases mainly produced by periodical processes running at the host operating system level.

3.4   Intrusiveness Definition

In the context of this research, intrusiveness is defined as degradation in the performance perceived by an end-user that is using a desktop while it is opportunistically utilized by a Desktop Grid system based on virtualization. Such intrusiveness is exclusively measured in terms of the performance delivered by the processor thus discarding intensive operations related to RAM memory, storage, network or any other computing resource. It is calculated as a percentage, named intrusiveness percentage ($\%intr$), and its formula is explained as follows:

$$\%intr = 100 * \frac{t_{real} - t_{free}}{t_{free}} \tag{1}$$

Where, t_{free} represents the average time a physical machine requires to finalize a CPU intensive workload in the absent of virtual machines and processes unrelated to those normally executed by the host operating system. On the other hand, t_{real} represents the average time the same physical machine requires to conclude the same CPU intensive workload in presence of as many virtual machines as set in the test scenario.

4   Results and Discussion

The figures presented in this section summarize the results for the aforementioned tests scenarios. To ease interpretations, the Y-axis shows the intrusiveness percentage, while the X-axis shows the amount of processes being executed by the end-user during the test. It is important to note that the intrusiveness percentage is calculated as presented in (1). Besides, each line represents the number of virtual machines simultaneously executed on the same desktop. Finally, acronyms are used to shorten words as follows: Virtual Machines – VMs, VMware Workstation - VMware, and Virtual-Box – Vbox.

First of all, as shown in Figure 1, the intrusiveness percentage measured over a desktop based on the Intel Core 2 Duo Legacy architecture is below 4%. Similar results were obtained on the AMD Athlon architecture as depicted on Figure 2. Since virtual machines are executed as low-priority processes, the host operating system penalizes release and allocation of computing resources to perform them in presence of processes executed in normal or any higher priority. Indeed, processes executed by end-users by default are set with normal priority thus guarantying negligible intrusiveness. Such research findings corroborate the results presented in [3] and [5]. Furthermore, these outcomes reveal that the opportunistic use of desktops based on Intel Core 2 Duo Legacy and AMD Athlon processors can be considered as nonintrusive. This is probably a consequence of the absent of dynamic performance and energy-efficient technologies on both processor architectures.

Secondly, Figure 3 shows the measurements obtained on desktops which processor architectures range from 1st, 2nd, and 4th generations of Intel Core processor. The line which marker symbol is a square represents a scenario where simultaneous CPU intensive workloads are executed on the same physical processor in the absent of virtual machines. The results show that individual completion time of a task executed by an end-user increases proportionally to the number of simultaneous tasks executed on the same desktop, even when it is less than or equal to the number of CPU threads. Such findings can be explained by the introduction of a selection of technologies aimed to increase performance and energy-efficiency on recent processor architectures. As detailed thereafter, one of these features is Intel Turbo Boost Technology [6]. This technology automatically allows CPU cores to run faster than the base operating frequency when the processor is working below rated power, temperature, and current specification limits [6]. Therefore, Turbo Boost dynamically controls the CPU clock frequency to be increased in presence of CPU lightweight workloads (single-threaded or multi-threaded) and to be nominal in presence of CPU intensive workloads.

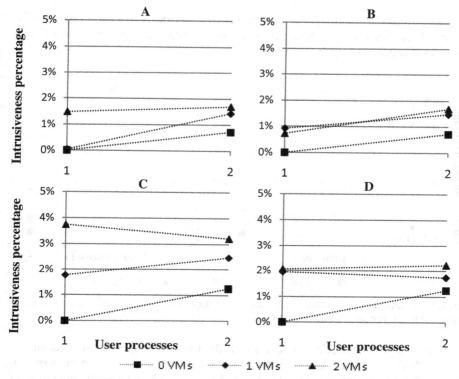

Fig. 1. Measurements obtained on Intel Core 2 Duo processors. A and B were obtained on Intel Core 2 Duo e7600 and C and D on Intel Core 2 Duo e6300. The results shown in the first column (to the left) were obtained by using VBox. The results shown in the second column were obtained with VMware.

Under certain configurations and workloads, Turbo Boost technology can be used to enable higher performance through the availability of increased core frequency [6]. Despite this fact, it also can affect the intrusiveness that end-users are able to perceive when using Desktop Grids based on virtualization that run simultaneously to their tasks. That is, when the processor is being opportunistically used by a Desktop Grid (e.g. low-priority processes), it thermally behaves likewise being executing processes of an end-user in normal priority. Under such circumstances, Turbo Boost technology dynamically decreases the clock frequency thus affecting the overall performance of the processor. As a result, this feature and other similar technologies severely impact on the performance perceived by end-users that are donating their idle computing resources to Desktop Grids. In fact, as can been seen on Figure 3 A and B measurements show that according to the number of virtual machines opportunistically executed on a desktop equipped with a processor Intel Core i7-4770, the intrusiveness percentage varies up to 60%. Furthermore, Figure 3 E and F show the intrusiveness percentage measured over a desktop equipped with a processor Intel Core i5-660. In this test, intrusiveness percentage is approximately 100% in the worst case. That is, when an end-user is executing 3 or 4 processes simultaneously to a pair of opportunistic virtual machines on a single desktop, the individual completion time of such processes is approximately duplicated.

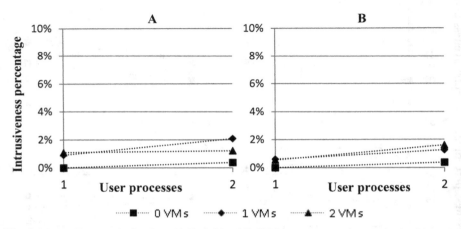

Fig. 2. Measurements obtained on AMD Athlon X2 5000+ processors. A was obtained by using VBox and B was obtained by using VMware.

These results show that intrusiveness directly depends on specific implementation of technologies aimed to deliver performance and energy-efficiency on modern processors. The results can be attributed to the fact that each subsequent generation of processor architectures incorporates improvements on the performance and optimizations on thermal-controls. In particular, it is worthwhile to note that processors Intel Core i7-4770 and Core i7-2600 incorporate Turbo Boost technology in version 2.0 whereas processor Intel Core i5-660 incorporates such technology in version 1.0.

Thirdly, Figure 4 shows the intrusiveness percentage measured over a desktop based on the Intel Core i7-4770 architecture. In such tests, Turbo Boost technology was deactivated from the BIOS. As a result, intrusiveness percentage decreased 4.3% on average; however, similarly to the results previously presented, it can be increased up to 60% in the worst case.

In such scenario centered on Intel processors and based on the limited data collected, we hypothesize that variations not attributed to Turbo Boost technology may be produced by other dynamic performance and energy-efficient technologies able to modify power consumption, temperature, and CPU rate, among others features of the processor. They include but may not be limited to: SpeedStep, Hyper-Threading, and Thermal Monitoring technologies. They were designed to optimize energy consumption and increase performance under particular circumstances. Therefore, reducing intrusiveness through deactivation of such technologies is actually a counterproductive arrangement. In such case, the overall performance would be reduced dramatically thus meaning permanent intrusiveness to end-users.

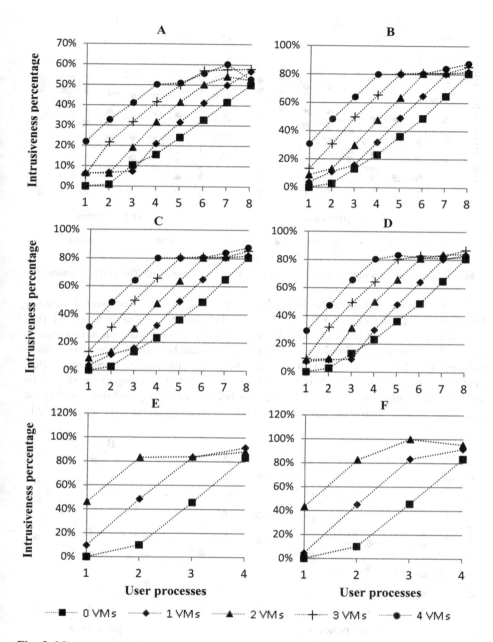

Fig. 3. Measurements obtained on modern Intel processors. A and B were obtained on Intel Core i7-4770, C and D on Intel Core i7-2600, and E and F on Intel Core i5-660. The results shown in the first column (to the left) were obtained by using VBox. The results shown in the second column were obtained with VMware.

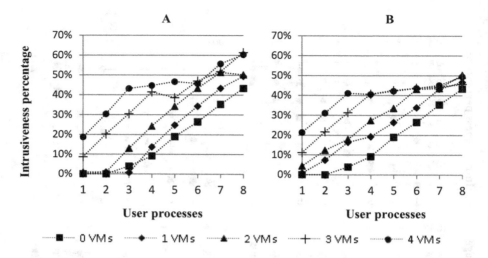

Fig. 4. Measurements obtained on Intel Core i7-4770 processors with Turbo Boost disabled

Finally, Figure 5 shows the intrusiveness percentage measured over a desktop based on the Intel Core i7-4770 architecture. In these tests, Turbo Boost, Hyper-Threading, and Speed Step technologies were disabled. In comparison with Figure 1 A and B, where such technologies were enabled, it can be seen that intrusiveness is reduced from 50% to 14% in the worst case. Moreover, on average intrusiveness percentage reduces up to 14%. It is important to note that such comparison should be considered to only a maximum of 4 processes being executed by end-users during the test, since CPU threads were halved when Hyper-Threading technology was disabled.

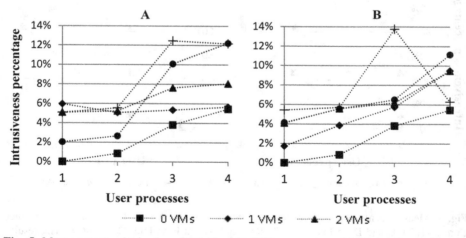

Fig. 5. Measurements obtained on Intel Core i7-4770 processors with Turbo Boost, Hyper-Threading, and Speed Step technologies disabled. This graph shows a range from 1 to 4 user processes because processor threads were reduced when Hyper-Threading was disabled.

5   Recommendations

The experimental results presented on this paper lead to a comprehensive understanding on the implications of the supporting infrastructure utilized by Desktop Grids in relation to its intrusiveness. Since intrusiveness plays a key role in promoting or discouraging the donation of idle computing resources to support Desktop Grids, we propose a set of general recommendations to minimize it based on our research findings. Such recommendations consider that dynamic performance and energy-efficient technologies, when incorporated on the supporting processor of desktops, directly affect the intrusiveness generated by Desktop Grids. Therefore, opportunistic strategies aimed to harvest as many idle computing resources as available should be considered as intrusive. Indeed, new strategies should be considered in order to minimize the degradation on the performance that end-users are able to perceive while donating their idle computing resources to Desktop Grids.

The set of recommendations are focused, but not necessarily limited to, Desktop Grids based on virtualization to be executed on desktops based on processors ranging from 1st, 2nd, and 4th generations of Intel Core. Since intrusiveness caused by Desktop Grids affects the performance perceived by an end-user when simultaneously executing CPU intensive workloads, we propose that new execution policies should be considered for this particular scenario. Such policies are based on end-user profiles and can be divided into two types: pessimistic and optimistic.

Firstly, in the context of pessimistic policies, it is stated that the end-user permanently requires the maximum performance the processor is able to deliver. In such a scenario, any opportunistic activity generated by a Desktop Grid system must be halted as soon as an end-user starts using the physical machine. In consequence, as soon as no end-user is using the physical machine, opportunistic activity should continue its normal execution. Precisely, the opportunistic harvesting of idle computing resources must exclusively occur when the physical machine is fully available.

Secondly, in terms of optimistic policies, it is supposed that the end-user tolerates a level of degradation on the performance delivered by the processor. However, such level must be in a range of acceptance, that is, at least, discontinuous intrusiveness. In order to implement optimistic policies, continuous monitoring is required in terms of computing resources usage. Hence, in the absent of CPU intensive workloads executed by end-users, idle computing resources should be dynamically assigned to the Desktop Grid system. It is important to emphasize that specific implementations of such policies depend on the supporting processor architectures to be used.

5.1   A Case Study

In order to briefly illustrate a specific implementation of the proposed policies, a basic case study is developed. Figure 6 depicts relative intrusiveness percentage measured over a desktop computer based on the Intel Core i7-4770 architecture. It is important to note that relative intrusiveness in considered in terms of the performance an end-user is expecting from the physical machine and its formula is explained as follows:

$$\%relative Intr = 100 \times \frac{t_{real} - t_{expected}}{t_{expected}} \qquad (2)$$

Where, t_{real} represents the average time a physical machine requires to finalize a CPU intensive workload in the execution conditions set for the test. On the other hand, $t_{expected}$ represents the average time the same physical machine requires to conclude the same CPU intensive workload in the absent of virtual machines (the amount of processes being executed by the end-user during the test is constant).

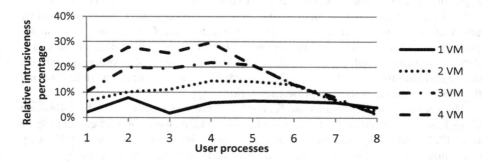

Fig. 6. Intrusiveness of a Desktop Grid system in relation to the performance expected by an end-user using an Intel Core i7-4770 processor

In Figure 6, the solid line at bottom represents the intrusiveness caused by the execution of a virtual machine assigned with a single CPU core. Indeed, its execution can be categorized as non-intrusive since the degradation an end-user perceives on the performance delivered by the processor remains below 10%. These conclusions can be extended to scenarios with two virtual machines only when the end-user is not executing CPU intensive workloads (i.e. by using 1 or 2 CPU cores). Similarly, when the end-user is executing CPU intensive workloads (i.e. by using 7 to 8 CPU cores) the results show that intrusiveness generated by Desktop Grids is below 10%. However, in the latter case, all the virtual machines in execution are not assigned with processor resources thus severely decreasing its performance.

According to the results presented above, the following policy is proposed for the non-intrusive opportunistic use of desktops based on the Intel Core i7-4770 architecture:

1. In the absent of an end-user: opportunistically harvest all the computing resources.
2. In presence of an end-user that is not executing CPU intensive workloads (i.e. by using 1 or 2 CPU cores on average): opportunistically harvest up to 2 CPU cores.
3. In presence of an end-user that is executing CPU intensive workloads (i.e. by using 2 to 6 CPU cores on average): opportunistically harvest 1 CPU core to diminish intrusiveness up to 10% or to exploit 2 CPU cores in order to decrease intrusiveness up to 15%.
4. In presence of an end-user that is using the entire processing resources (i.e. by using 7 to 8 CPU cores on average): opportunistically harvest as many idle resources as available (even though they will be very limited to low-priority processes).

6   Conclusions and Future Work

We evaluated the implications of dynamic performance and energy-efficient, as technologies incorporated in modern processor architectures in relation to intrusiveness generated by Desktop Grids based on virtualization. Such intrusiveness is defined as degradation in the performance perceived by an end-user that is using a desktop while at the same time it is opportunistically utilized by a Desktop Grid system.

The tests were performed on off-the-shelf desktops with Windows 7 installed as host operating system. These desktops were equipped with a variety of processors, including: Intel Core i7-4770, Intel Core i7-2600, Intel Core i5-660, Intel Core 2 Duo e7600, Intel Core 2 Duo e6300, and AMD Athlon 64 X2 5000+.

All the test scenarios varied in the number of virtual machines executed in each psychical machine, ranging from zero to the number of physical CPU cores. To avoid bias, such virtualization was supported by two independent hypervisors type II: VMware Workstation and VirtualBox. Each virtual machine was installed with a Debian 7 installation from scratch and the Oracle JVM. The hardware specifications for each virtual machine were set to 1 CPU core and 1 GB of RAM.

In order to produce intrusiveness, two benchmarks were set and performed over the selection of desktops. Both benchmarks were based on CPU intensive workloads generated through a program able to calculate prime numbers by using the sieve of Eratosthenes [9]. The benchmarks were simultaneously executed on both, the virtual and the physical environment. In the first benchmark, the program was set to run over 10 hours on each virtual machine initiated. In the second benchmark, the program was set to run on average 60 seconds on the physical machine. This latter benchmark was executed a number varying from 1 to the number of CPU threads, thus simulating CPU intensive tasks executed by an end-user without root privileges.

The experimental outline pursued herein has several implications for Desktop Grids. The results obtained demonstrate that intrusiveness caused by Desktop Grids based on virtualization varies according to the use of desktops which processor architectures incorporate dynamic performance and energy-efficient technologies. The results show that depending on the processor architecture the intrusiveness percentage varies in a range from 3% up to 100%. For instance, on Intel Core i7-2600 the intrusiveness percentage varies from 10% up to 80% as the number of virtual machines varied from 1 to 4. In consequence, we propose that specific policies should be implemented in Desktop Grids in order to reduce its intrusiveness to end-users that donate their idle computing resources to e-Science. Such policies were classified according to end-user profiles as pessimistic and optimistic. The specific implementations of such policies directly depend on the supporting processor architectures to be used by Desktop Grids. Therefore a case study was developed to illustrate such implementation for the non-intrusive opportunistic use of desktops based on the Intel Core i7-4770 architecture.

New challenges will have to be faced in order to exhaustively analyze the implications of the supporting infrastructure used by Desktop Grids in relation to its intrusiveness. In the future we will analyze the incidence that each dynamic performance and energy-efficient technology has in terms of intrusiveness to end-users. We plan to enhance the experimental setup by extending the statistical test sample, including additional processor architectures, increasing the number of repetitions of each test scenario, using other host and guest operating systems, using a variety of hardware configurations for the virtual environment, using additional hypervisors type 2, and using other Desktop Grid systems (e.g. based on agents). In addition, we plan to evaluate the degradation in the performance obtained on opportunistic virtual environments in relation to CPU-intensive workloads executed by end-users. Such research efforts will be aimed but not limited to extend the scope of our conclusions, particularly, in order to improve and generalize the policies presented on this paper and test its implementation in a Desktop Grid system.

References

1. Anderson, D.P., Fedak, G.: The Computational and Storage Potential of Volunteer Computing. In: IEEE International Symposium on Cluster Computing and the Grid, pp. 73–80. IEEE Press, Singapore (2006)
2. BOINC, http://boinc.berkeley.edu/
3. Castro, H., Rosales, E., Villamizar, M., Jiménez, A.: UnaGrid: On Demand Opportunistic Desktop Grid. In: Proceedings of the 10th IEEE/ACM International Conference on Cluster, Cloud and Grid Computing, pp. 661–666. IEEE Press, Melbourne (2010)
4. Distributed.Net, http://www.distributed.net/
5. Domingues, P., Araujo, F., Silva, L.: Evaluating the Performance and Intrusiveness of Virtual Machines for Desktop Grid Computing. In: Proceedings of the IEEE International Symposium on Parallel & Distributed Processing, pp. 1–8. IEEE Press, Rome (2009)
6. Intel Turbo Boost Technology in Intel Core Microarchitecture (Nehalem) Based Processors, http://files.shareholder.com/downloads/INTC/0x0x348508/C9259E98-BE06-42C8-A433-E28F64CB8EF2/TurboBoostWhitePaper.pdf
7. Langer, S.G., French, T.: Virtual Machine Performance Benchmarking. Journal of Digital Imaging 24, 883–889 (2011)
8. LHC@Home, http://lhcathomeclassic.cern.ch/
9. O'Neill, M.E.: The Genuine Sieve of Eratosthenes. Journal of Functional Programming 19, 95–106 (2008)
10. OurGrid, http://www.ourgrid.org/
11. Rosales, E., Castro, H., Villamizar, M.: UnaCloud: Opportunistic Cloud Computing Infrastructure as a Service. In: Proceedings of the Second International Conference on Cloud Computing, GRIDs, and Virtualization, pp. 187–194. XPS, Rome (2011)
12. SETI@Home, http://setiathome.ssl.berkeley.edu/
13. Choi, S., Buyya, R., et al.: A Taxonomy of Desktop Grids and its Mapping to State-of-the-Art Systems. Technical Report, GRIDS-TR-2008-2013, the University of Melbourne, Australia (2008)
14. SZTAKI, http://szdg.lpds.sztaki.hu/szdg/
15. Tanaka, K., Uehara, M., Mori, H.: A case study of a Linux Grid on Windows Using Virtual Machines. In: Proceedings of the 22nd International Conference on Advanced Information Networking and Applications, pp. 195–200. IEEE Press, Okinawa (2008)
16. VMware@Home, https://twiki.cern.ch/twiki/bin/view/EGEE/VMwareAtHome
17. XtremWeb, http://www.xtremweb.net/

Efficient Fluorescence Microscopy Analysis over a Volunteer Grid/Cloud Infrastructure

Miguel Da Silva[1], Sergio Nesmachnow[1], Maximiliano Geier[2],
Esteban Mocskos[2], Juan Angiolini[3], Valeria Levi[3], and Alfredo Cristobal[4]

[1] Universidad de la República, Uruguay
[2] Departamento de Computación, Facultad de Ciencias Exactas y Naturales
Universidad de Buenos Aires, Argentina
[3] Departamento de Química Biológica-IQUIBICEN, Facultad de Ciencias Exactas y
Naturales, Universidad de Buenos Aires
[4] Universidad Veracruzana, México

Abstract. This work presents a distributed computing algorithm over volunteer grid/cloud computing systems for Fluorescence Correlation Spectroscopy, a computational biology technique for obtaining quantitative information about the motion of molecules in living cells. High performance computing is needed to cope with large computing times when performing complex simulations, and volunteer grid/cloud computing emerges as a powerful paradigm to solve this kind of problems by coordinately using many computing resources distributed around the world. The proposed algorithm applies a domain decomposition technique for performing many simulations using different cell models at the same time. The experimental evaluation performed on a volunteer distributing computing infrastructure demonstrates that efficient execution times are obtained when using OurGrid middleware.

Keywords: fluorescence analysis, grid/cloud computing, volunteer computing.

1 Introduction

Nowadays, fluorescence microscopy is considered a routine technique in biomedical research. It was originally devised as a tool to observe the localization of fluorescent labels, but has significantly evolved with time. A fluorescence microscope is capable of providing extremely relevant dynamical information of the biological specimen under study with very high temporal and spatial resolution (for example see [12,13])

Among the new tools designed to obtain such dynamical information, Fluorescence Correlation Spectroscopy (FCS) and related methods [9] are considered key techniques to obtain quantitative information regarding the motion of molecules in living cells. Briefly, FCS is based on the analysis of intensity fluctuations caused by fluorescence-labeled molecules moving through the small detection volume of a confocal or two-photon excitation microscope (see a detailed description of the technique in Section 2).

G. Hernández et al. (Eds.): CARLA 2014, CCIS 485, pp. 113–127, 2014.
© Springer-Verlag Berlin Heidelberg 2014

FCS captures fluctuations of the fluorescence due to the motion of single molecules. Thus, it is necessary to process a large number of data points to obtain a statistically sound simulation of the underlying dynamical process. These numerical experiments are computing demanding: the motion of each molecule (data point) must be followed, and the interaction with other molecules (i.e. reactions) must be solved in every simulated time step.

High Performance Computing (HPC) techniques come to play a key role to process the needed amount of data points during sufficient time steps to capture the biological process. Using HPC for treating reaction diffusion systems is presented in previous works like [14,15,16], but the implementation of a specific application for fluorescence fluctuation analysis based on a volunteer computing platform is novel at the best of our knowledge. Moreover, the techniques described in this paper allows the simultaneous analysis of several experiments, considerably increasing the capability of generation and validation of the proposed models for complex biological phenomena.

In this line of work, the main contribution of the research reported in this article is the use of a volunteer computing system to support the efficient execution of the cases to perform FCS measurements analysis in a realistic scenario.

The article is organized as follows. Section 2 describes the numerical techniques and computing tools to simulate the biological processes. Section 3 introduces the main concepts about distributed computing on volunteer grid/cloud infrastructures.

The approach using HPC techniques for solving the problem is presented in Section 4, just before reporting the experimental analysis in Section 5. Section 6 summarizes the main conclusions and lines for future work.

2   Fluorescence Correlation Spectroscopy and Tools

This section describes FCS techniques and the computing tools used to simulate the underlying biological processes.

2.1   Fluorescence Correlation Spectroscopy

FCS is a well-known technique applied to obtain quantitative information regarding the motion of molecules in living cells. It is based on the analysis of intensity fluctuations caused by fluorescence-labeled molecules moving through the small detection volume of a confocal or two-photon excitation microscope.

Fig. 1 shows a schema of an experiment: some molecules emit photons when they are under the observation volume defined by the laser beam. The photon emission is a stochastic process, its probability is related to the relative position of the molecule and the beam center, which is the most probable position, while the probability diminishes when moving out (see Eq. 1), ω_{xy} and ω_z are the radial and axial waists of the point spread function. Standard values are: $\omega_{xy} = 0.2\mu m$ and $\omega_z = 1\mu m$.

$$g(x,y,z) = \exp\left(\frac{-2(x^2 + y^2)}{\omega_{xy}^2} + \frac{-2z^2}{\omega_z^2}\right) \qquad (1)$$

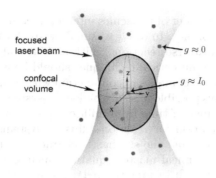

Fig. 1. Fluorescent molecules diffuse through the small observation volume. The probability of emitting a photon depends on the relative position of the molecule respect to the center of the observation volume.

FCS has been applied to study diffusion, transport, binding, etc. [7]. In the case of simple scenarios such as molecules passively moving in a homogeneous media, the FCS analysis yields analytical functions that can be fitted to the experimental data to recover the phenomenological rate parameters (e.g. diffusion coefficients, chemical rate constants, etc.). However, many dynamical processes in cells do not follow these simple models and, in many instances, it is not possible to obtain an analytical function through the theoretical analysis of a more complex model [7].

In those cases, the experimental analysis can be combined with Monte Carlo simulations to help with the interpretation of the experimental data recovered in FCS experiments (see for example, [6]). The comparison between the expectations for a reduced, simulated model and the experimental data could provide important clues of the dynamical processes hidden in the FCS data. Despite of being useful, most Monte Carlo tools used to simulate FCS experiments are developed as sequential ad-hoc programs designed only for specific scenarios.

The procedure for FCS measurements is presented in Fig. 2: (a) shows a cartoon of the experimental setup required in these experiments. The sample (e.g. cells expressing a fluorescent protein) is placed on top of the microscope stage of a confocal or two-photon excitation microscope. The excitation laser is focused in a diffraction-limited spot on the sample and fluorescence photons produced in the small observation volume (near 1 fl.) as presented in (b); (c) shows a representative fluorescence intensity trace obtained in an FCS experiment. This trace shows fluctuations due to fluorescent molecules moving in and out of the observation volume. The amplitude of the fluctuations are inversely related to the number of molecules in the observation volume while their duration is given by the dynamics of these molecules. This information can be recovered calculating the autocorrelation function, such as the example presented in (d).

2.2 Tool Description

At cellular scales, a finite number of molecules interact in complex spaces defined by cell and organelle membranes. In order to simulate stochastic cellular events (movements, interactions, diverse reactions) with spatial realism at reasonable computational cost, specific numerical techniques should be employed [3,18].

Using these optimization techniques in conjunction with Monte Carlo reaction probabilities, it is nowadays possible to study biological systems considering their evolution during a wide range of time from milliseconds to minutes [11].

The standard approximation for reaction-diffusion systems ignores the discrete nature of the reactants and the stochastic character of their interactions. Techniques based on the chemical master equation, such as the Gillespie algorithm [20], assume that at each instant the particles are uniformly distributed in space.

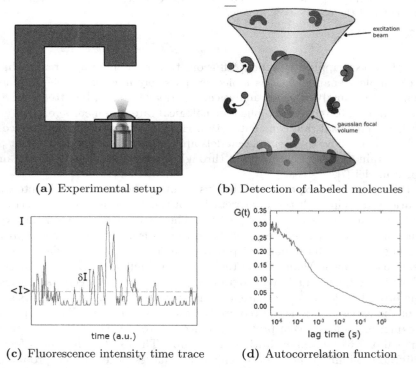

(a) Experimental setup

(b) Detection of labeled molecules

(c) Fluorescence intensity time trace

(d) Autocorrelation function

Fig. 2. Representation of a confocal or two photon microscope Fluorescence Correlation Spectroscopy measurements

In order to take into account both the full spatial distribution of the components and the stochastic character of their interactions, a technique based on Brownian dynamics is used. The MCell simulation package [11,19,18] is based on an event-driven algorithm, named Green's function reaction dynamics, which uses Green's functions to combine in one step the propagation of the particles in space with the reactions between them. In this algorithm, the particles move diffusively; it is assumed that if a reaction exists, it follows a Poisson process and it happens instantaneously. This means that the reaction event can be decoupled from the diffusive motion of the particle. The time step of the algorithm is determined such that only single particles or pairs of particles have to be considered, avoiding complex reaction rules.

MCell is used as the simulation engine; one of its outputs consists in the position of each molecule in the system every time step. These positions are used as the input for FERNet (Fluorescence Emission Routine Network), which generates the fluorescent trace for each sample time. This data is then compared against the experimental data and can support the validation of the proposed model.

3 Volunteer Grid/Cloud Computing

This section describes the paradigms of grid and cloud computing, and the OurGrid middleware for developing applications over volunteer grid/cloud platforms.

3.1 Grid and Cloud Computing

Grid computing is a paradigm for parallel/distributed information processing that allows the integration of many computer resources to provide a powerful computing platform that allows solving applications with high computing demands. This paradigm has been increasingly employed to solve complex problems (i.e. e-Science, optimization, simulation, etc.) in the last twenty years [10].

Grid infrastructures are conceived as a large loosely-coupled virtual supercomputer formed by many heterogeneous platforms of different characteristics, usually working with non-interactive workloads with a large number of files. Grid infrastructures have made it feasible to provide pervasive and cost-effective access to distributed computing resources for solving hard problems [5]. Starting from small grids in the earlier 2000's, nowadays grid computing is a consolidated field of research in Computer Science and many grid infrastructures are widely available. As of 2012, more than 12 PFLOPS are available in the current more powerful grid system, from the Folding@home project.

In the last years, cloud computing [4,8] emerged as one of the main existing computing paradigms, mainly due to several very interesting features it provides, including elasticity, flexibility, or large computational power, among many others. Cloud computing has raised the interest of both academic and industrial research communities, by providing a computing model which is able to cope efficiently with complex problems involving hard computing functions and handling very large volumes of data.

Cloud computing provides a stack with different kinds of services to users, including: Infrastructure as a Service (IaaS), dealing with resources as servers, storage, or networks; Platform as a Service (PaaS), providing an operating system as well as a set of tools and services to the user; or Software as a Service (SaaS) that allows providers to grant customers with access to licensed software.

3.2   The OurGrid Middleware

OurGrid is an open source middleware for grid and cloud computing based on a peer-to-peer architecture, developed by researchers at Universidade Federal do Campina Grande, Brazil [5]. This middleware enables the creation of peer-to-peer computational grids, and it is intended to speed up the execution of Bag-of-Tasks (BoT) applications.

The OurGrid architecture is built by aggregating several participants in a grid environment, allowing them to use remote and local resources to run their applications. OurGrid uses the eXtensible Messaging and Presence Protocol (XMPP), an open technology for real-time communication which powers a wide range of applications, including instant messaging, presence, multi-party chat, voice and video calls, collaboration, lightweight middleware, content syndication, and generalized routing of XML data. XMPP allows federation, it is Internet-friendly, and efficient, since several services can use the same XMPP server.

The main components of the OurGrid architecture are:

— *Broker*: implements the user interface to the grid. By using the broker, the users can submit jobs to the grid and also track their execution. All the interaction between the user and the grid infrastructure is performed through the broker.
— *Workers*: used for processing the jobs submitted to the grid. Each worker represents a real computing resource. OurGrid workers support virtualization, and so they offer an isolated platform for executing jobs comprising no risks to the local system running the component.
— *Peers*: have a twofold role; from the point-of-view of the user, they search and allocate corresponding computing resources for the execution of his jobs. From the point-of-view of the infrastructure (implicitly, for the site administrator) each peer is responsible for determining which workers can be used to execute an application, and also how they will be used. Normally, it is enough to have one peer per site. Communication between peers makes possible to execute jobs remotely; in case that the local resources are not enough for satisfying the requirements of a job, the peer seeks for additional resources available in remote sites.
— *Discovery Service*: keeps updated information about the system composition. It finds out the end points that peers should use to communicate with.

All these components are integrated in a transparent way to the user, allowing the system to provide a single-image of an infrastructure with a large computing power. A description of the OurGrid architecture is shown in Fig. 3.

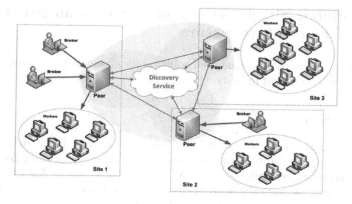

Fig. 3. Description of the OurGrid architecture

3.3 Volunteer Computing

The OurGrid middleware provides support for implementing the volunteer computing paradigm[2,17]. Volunteer computing is based on individual users making available their computing resources to execute applications and projects. The first volunteer computing projects were proposed in the mid-1990s. In 1999, the well-known SETI@home and Folding@home distributed projects were launched. Both became pioneering projects to demonstrate the power of gathering volunteer computing resources to solve very large scale scientific problems.

The main features of volunteer computing are:

i) often unaccountable and potentially anonymous users voluntarily provide their resources for computation;
ii) users can join and leave the volunteer computing platform at any time;
iii) users "credits" are accounted in order to know how much computing time h in the systems been used and provided by every user;
iv) replication is usually applied for fault-tolerance, in order to cope with incorrect results or anomalous events that occur when volunteers unexpectedly leave the system.

The middleware for volunteer computing is a software layer that provides support for creating, managing, and using the volunteer distributed computing infrastructure, independently from the scientific computing applications to execute. The Berkeley Open Infrastructure for Network Computing (BOINC) [1] is the most widely used middleware system for volunteer computing. The general architecture of a middleware for volunteer computing is like the one presented for OurGrid: a client program runs on the volunteer side, which periodically contacts servers over the Internet, requesting jobs and reporting the results of completed jobs. In OurGrid, the standard volunteer computing model is extended to support a full P2P architecture. This feature allows OurGrid to be used in cloud infrastructures too.

4 Distributed Fluorescence Analysis over an Ad-Hoc Grid/Cloud Infrastructure

This section presents the implemented solution for efficient fluorescence analysis over an ad-hoc grid/cloud infrastructure.

4.1 Motivation

The final objective of our research is to bring the user of Biomedical or Biology fields an easy-to-use tool to complement the analysis of the experimental data obtained using real microscopes. A cloud-oriented portal for Fluorescence Microscopy Analysis and related applications will provide an integrated way for accessing and displaying information to the end user.

Grid/cloud technologies allow to take full advantage of powerful simulation tools, as the one describing using FCS, without having to follow a complex installation procedure. This technology will also allow users to access and browse the obtained data from any mobile device (e.g. smart phone, tablet, etc.).

Furthermore, cloud computing will also provide immediate benefits for executing highly computing-demanding fluorescence microscopy simulations in reasonable execution times, by applying HPC techniques over a highly robust computing infrastructure composed of geographically distributed resources. OurGrid middleware is chosen for it is able to provide a stable infrastructure for executing BoT applications and is suitable for this article.

4.2 Design and Parallel Model

MCell and FERNet were conceived as sequential applications. MCell produces the data that is later consumed/processed by FERNet to finally generate the output (i.e. fluorescence trace) that can be used to analyze the biological process.

The *domain distribution* technique is used as the parallel model for the application to be deployed in a distributed environment. No further modifications are necessary to MCell or FERNet applications. Any UNIX-like computational platform can execute MCell+FERNet properly. The domain distribution is implemented by partitioning the set of models in a given workload and distributing them to the available computational resources.

4.3 Implementation in OurGrid

An OurGrid site will provide the environment to execute MCell and FERNet. The site is composed by a peer, a set of worker nodes and, potentially many broker/client nodes. The local peer can associate to a community and connect to other peers. Then, it will be able to share local resources and consume remote ones.

As described in section 4.2, different subsets containing various instances of cellular models, possibly from different users, can be created and submitted for execution. In OurGrid, the *job description files* (JDF) is used to specify these subsets. This file is interpreted by the middleware, which then performs the actions needed to execute each instance.

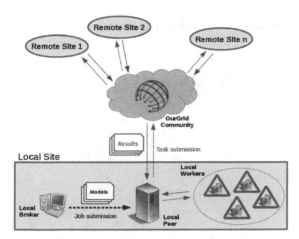

Fig. 4. Job submission and execution scheme in OurGrid

Figure 4 shows the proposed approach using OurGrid. Considering a *job* as a subset of instances and a *task* as one of these instances, various jobs and tasks can be specified and submitted for execution. The middleware is in charge of finding available resources (local or remote) and sending the jobs for execution. Once the job execution is finished, the results are retrieved automatically and stored in the broker that submitted it.

```
job   :
label : mcell-fernet-scenario-1
task:
init :
put job.mcell.sh job.mcell.sh
put mcell.fernet.tar.bz2 mcell.fernet.tar.bz2

remote: sh job.mcell.sh
final :
get out_point.txt out_point.txt
```

Listing 1.1. JDF file example

The listing 1.1 shows an example of a JDF file used in the simulations. The tags `job` and `label` declare a new job for execution and give it a name for control purposes. `put` and `get` are used to indicate the files to be uploaded and downloaded, and `remote` determines the commands to be executed in the worker nodes.

5   Experimental Analysis

This subsection reports the experimental analysis of the proposed parallel algorithm for distributed fluorescence analysis.

5.1   Development and Execution Platform

Fig. 5. OurGrid platform is used to create a federation of volunteer computing nodes. Nodes from Argentina, Brazil, Mexico, and Uruguay were assembled to support the execution of the distributed version of MCell+Fernet.

The experimental evaluation was performed on a volunteer infrastructure with computing resources from four Latin America research institutions: Universidad de Buenos Aires (UBA) in Argentina, Universidade Federal de Campina Grande (UFCG) in Brazil, Universidad Veracruzana (UV) in Mexico, and Universidad de la República (UdelaR), in Uruguay, as it is shown in Fig. 5.

The volunteer computing infrastructure gathers a heterogeneous collection of computing resources, including:

- UBA, Argentina: IBM Express x3650 M4, Xeon E5-2620 12 cores, (2.0GHz), 128GB RAM, Gigabit Ethernet.
- UFCG, Brazil: : Intel i5-3470S, 4 cores (2.9 GHz) and i7-2600, 8 cores (3.40GHz), 8 GB RAM, Gigabit Ethernet.
- UV, Mexico: Intel i5-3470S, 4 cores (2.3 GHz), 48 GB RAM, Ethernet.
- UdelaR, Uruguay: AMD Opteron 6172, 24 cores (2.1 GHz), 24 GB RAM, Gigabit Ethernet, from Cluster FING.

5.2   Problem Instances

The problem instances are inspired in the study of the dynamics of the binding of a special molecule called *transcription factor* to a specific site (i.e. *binding site*). Thus, three types of molecules exists in the system: *i*) TF: transcription factor (most of molecules correspond to this type); *ii*) B (Binding site); and *iii*) [TF-B] (binded molecule).

The interactions between these molecules are described by the chemical equation (Eq. 2), where k_{on} and k_{off} corresponds to the parameters that control the binding and unbinding between TF and B. TF molecules can diffuse through the specified domain, while the binding sites maintain their initial position during the simulation (i.e. diffusion constant is 0).

$$\text{TF} + \text{B} \underset{k_{off}}{\overset{k_{on}}{\rightleftharpoons}} [\text{TF}-\text{B}] \tag{2}$$

In the case of FCS analysis, some of the parameters that should be specified include the size of the volume, the initial number of molecules and the type of reactions that may occur in the system.

Table 1 shows the three different configured scenarios. The simulation domain is a cube of 3μm per side for all the cases. The main difference lays in the amount of initial TF molecules. There are [TF-B] molecules since the simulation starting to set the system at equilibrium. It can be configured to be initially 0, but in this case, it should be waited until stabilization is reached. 8 instances were created for each scenario, and in each instance a different value for a chosen group of parameters is used (i.e. parameter sweeping).

Table 1. Parameters used for the three configured scenarios

parameter	description	small	medium	large
$\#TF$	Number of initial TF molecules	415	1660	4150
$\#B$	Number of initial B molecules		10000	
$\#[TF-B]$	Number of initial $[TF-B]$ molecules	85	340	850
D_{TF}	Diffusion coefficient for TF		55×10^{-08} cm^2/s	
D_B	Diffusion coefficient for B		0	
$D_{[TF-B]}$	Diffusion coefficient for $[TF-B]$		0	
k_{on}	Constant controlling binding of TF and B		1.7×10^6 M^{-1}s^{-1}	
k_{off}	Constant controlling the unbinding of TF and B		5 s^{-1}	
TIME_STEP	Preferred time step for the numerical integration		1×10^{-5}	

5.3   Results and Discussion

The computational resources of the volunteer platform form a single federation of OurGrid sites and the execution of each task can, eventually, take place in any of these resources. The sequential executions used as a reference baseline to compare the execution times were performed only in the local resources at UdelaR. Due to characteristics of the infrastructure, the hardware available in UdelaR is able to provide better performance for sequential executions.

Table 2 summarizes the parameter settings defining each instance and reports the processing times of sequential executions. Edge size and step size are parameters correspond to the dimensions of the volume containing the molecules and the area of coverage that is analyzed by the microscope.

The problem instances are split in groups of tasks for submission in the volunteer computing infrastructure. This method emulates the work of a grid/cloud

Table 2. Details of the instances and sequential processing times

scenario	edge size	instance id	step size	execution time (s)
1	1.5	1	0.05	210
		2	0.10	177
		3	0.20	217
		4	0.50	1030
	3.0	5	0.05	318
		6	0.10	214
		7	0.20	198
		8	0.50	362
2	1.5	9	0.05	765
		10	0.10	672
		11	0.20	809
		12	0.50	4068
	3.0	13	0.05	1160
		14	0.10	780
		15	0.20	712
		16	0.50	1500
3	1.5	17	0.05	2044
		18	0.10	1715
		19	0.20	2002
		20	0.50	9796
	3.0	21	0.05	2271
		22	0.10	2002
		23	0.20	1596
		24	0.50	3798

Workload Management System that arranges several requests submitted by different users from an (application-oriented) back-end portal.

Groups of 4 and 6 tasks were created, and each group is executed as a single job. This way a total of 4 and 6 jobs will be launched. The main reasons for grouping tasks in different jobs are to apply the paradigm of domain decomposition and also to avoid job failures due to a single task failure. OurGrid allows setting the number of times a certain task will be rescheduled if it fails; the default value is 3 and it was not changed for experimentation. The groups comprise instances of different scenarios, selected using uniform distributions of integer numbers in the range $[1, 24]$ for instance selection, and in the ranges $[1, 6]$ and $[1, 4]$ for group selection (depending on the number of groups created).

OurGrid allocates resources according to the number of tasks included in a job. If a job is composed of a large number of tasks, a site with insufficient resources could be ignored by the allocation algorithm. As we are dealing with volunteer infrastructures, 4 and 6 tasks per job is a suitable number. It has to be remarked that MCell is a computing demanding application and launching many tasks in a single job could overload a single site.

The groups for 4 and 6 tasks are shown in Table 3, along with the execution times for the parallel executions.

Table 3. Parallel execution times

using 4 tasks/job			using 6 tasks/job		
group ID	instances	time (s)	group ID	instances	time (s)
1	4,5,10,21	2891	1	3,7,10,12,17,22	4212
2	1,8,22,23	2045	2	4,8,13,14,20,23	10124
3	24,9,11,7	3450	3	1,5,6,9,11,15	914
4	2,20,15,13	9976	4	2,16,18,19,22,24	3977
5	6,12,14,17	4500			
6	3,16,18,19	2240			

Based on data generated by MCell, FERNet creates a single plain text containing the amount of photons collected every time step. For each instance, a different file is generated and approximately 300 KB of storage space is needed. Once the task is finished, the output is transfered to the broker/client that submitted the corresponding job.

The output generated by MCell consists in the positions of each molecule every time step. The size of this file depends on the amount of molecules configured in the simulation, resulting in files between 8 and 15 GB. These files are discarded once the task is finished.

Figure 6 shows the processing times for each group of tasks. Each group of tasks corresponds to a job that is launched in the grid/cloud infrastructure. A JDF file defining the job and the corresponding tasks is created for each job. The total processing time for sequential execution of the 24 instances is approximately 10.81 hours. The parallel execution time is approximately 2.78 hours. Figure 6 shows that both grouping methods require approximately the same time to complete all the considered instances. As MCell is designed as a

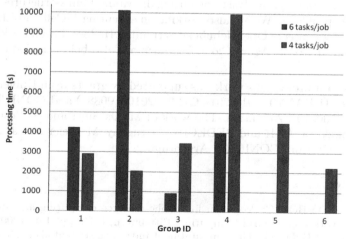

Fig. 6. Processing times for parallel execution

sequential application, the processing times are conditioned by the time required to complete the most CPU demanding task.

No optimization is applied for grouping tasks as the processing times for each task is unknown before hand. As mentioned earlier in this section, groups are created using uniform distributions and random selection. This method of selection explains why a group of 6 tasks (group #3) is processed faster than all groups of 4 tasks. Even though a subset of results is obtained earlier, the total processing time still remains comparable.

As the main goal of this work is to reduce the time needed to process the whole set of instances, the results obtained using groups of different sizes are valid. The speedup factor obtained is approximately 4.

6   Conclusions and Future Work

This article presented an experimental analysis of applying a grid/cloud approach for the execution of different scenarios for fluorescence analysis. Results for sequential and parallel execution of MCell and FERNet were reported.

The experimental evaluation of the proposed distributed computing approach was carried out using a volunteer federation of OurGrid sites distributed in four countries in Latin America. The efficiency analysis demonstrates that the use of a volunteer grid/cloud infrastructure is an effective method for reducing the overall execution time of simulations. Overall, execution time reductions up to about **70-75%** were obtained when solving different scenarios for the considered problem. These results suggest that the volunteer computing paradigm suits well for executing simulations of complex biological phenomena.

The main lines for future work include increasing the number of models and scenarios to be simulated and performing more realistic experiments including more biologically-relevant parameters of the models. Additional studies regarding the composition of groups of tasks should also be performed, as well as further extending the scalability analysis when using distributed infrastructures for solve very complex problems. We are also working on executing MCell and FERnet on federations of volunteers OpenNebula sites running Hadoop Framework. Besides that, tests on Microsoft Azure Cloud Platform are also being carried out.

Acknowledgements. This work was supported by grants from Universidad de Buenos Aires (UBACYT 2011-2014 GC 20020100100889) and CONICET (PIP GI 11220110100379), Argentina. The work of M. Da Silva and S. Nesmachnow is partly funded by ANII and PEDECIBA, Uruguay. M. Geier and J. Angiolini have scholarship from CONICET, Argentina.

References

1. Anderson, D.: BOINC: A system for public-resource computing and storage. In: 5th Int. Workshop on Grid Computing, Pittsburgh, USA, pp. 4–10 (2004)
2. Anderson, D., Fedak, G.: The computational and storage potential of volunteer computing. In: 6th Int. Symp. on Cluster Computing and the Grid, pp. 73–80 (2006)

3. Bartol, T., Land, B., Salpeter, E., Salpeter, M.: Monte carlo simulation of miniature endplate current generation in the vertebrate neuromuscular junction. Biophys J. 59(6), 1290–1307 (1991)
4. Buyya, R., Broberg, J., Goscinski, A.M.: Cloud Computing Principles and Paradigms. Wiley Publishing (2011)
5. Cirne, W., Brasileiro, F., Andrade, N., Costa, L., Andrade, A., Novaes, R., Mowbray, M.: Labs of the world, unite! Journal of Grid Computing 4(3), 225–246 (2006)
6. Dix, J., Hom, E., Verkman, A.: Fluorescence Correlation Spectroscopy Simulations of Photophysical Phenomena and Molecular Interactions: A Molecular Dynamics-Monte Carlo Approach. J. Phys. Chem. B 110(4), 1896–1906 (2006)
7. Elson, E.L.: Fluorescence correlation spectroscopy: Past, present, future. Biophys J. 101(12), 2855–2870 (2011)
8. Foster, I., Zhao, Y., Raicu, I., Lu, S.: Cloud Computing and Grid Computing 360-Degree Compared. In: Grid Computing Environments Workshop, pp. 1–10 (2008)
9. Haustein, E., Schwille, P.: Ultrasensitive investigations of biological systems by fluorescence correlation spectroscopy. Methods 29(2), 153–166 (2003)
10. Joseph, J., Fellenstein, C.: Grid Computing. Prentice Hall PTR, Upper Saddle River (2003)
11. Kerr, R., Bartol, T., Kaminsky, B., Dittrich, M., Chang, J., Baden, S., Sejnowski, T., Stiles, J.: Fast Monte Carlo simulation methods for biological reaction-diffusion systems in solution and on surfaces. SIAM Journal on Scientific Computing 30(6), 3126–3149 (2008)
12. Lidke, D.S., Wilson, B.S.: Caught in the act: quantifying protein behaviour in living cells. Trends in Cell Biology 19(11), 566–574 (2009)
13. Lippincott, J., Altan, N., Patterson, G.: Photobleaching and photoactivation: following protein dynamics in living cells. Nat. Cell Biol. Suppl. (2003)
14. Martínez, E., Marian, J., Kalos, M., Perlado, J.: Synchronous parallel kinetic Monte Carlo for continuum diffusion-reaction systems. J. Comp. Phys. 227(8), 3804–3823 (2008)
15. Meriney, S., Dittrich, M.: Organization and function of transmitter release sites at the neuromuscular junction. The Journal of Physiology 591(13), 3159–3165 (2013)
16. Molnár Jr., F., Izsák, F., Mészáros, R., Lagzi, I.: Simulation of reaction-diffusion processes in three dimensions using CUDA. Chemometrics and Intelligent Laboratory Systems 108(1), 76–85 (2011)
17. Nov, O., Anderson, D., Arazy, O.: Volunteer computing: A model of the factors determining contribution to community-based scientific research. In: 19th Int. Conf. on World Wide Web, pp. 741–750 (2010)
18. Stiles, J.R., Bartol, T.M.: Monte Carlo methods for simulating realistic synaptic microphysiology using MCell, ch. 4, pp. 87–127. CRC Press (2001)
19. Stiles, J.R., Van Helden, D., Bartol, T.M., Salpeter, E.E., Salpeter, M.M.: Miniature endplate current rise times less than 100 microseconds from improved dual recordings can be modeled with passive acetylcholine diffusion from a synaptic vesicle. Proc. Natl. Acad. Sci. USA 93(12), 5747–5752 (1996)
20. van Zon, J., ten Wolde, P.: Simulating biochemical networks at the particle level and in time and space: Green's function reaction dynamics. Phys. Rev. Lett. 94(12), 128103 (2005)

Multiobjective Energy-Aware Datacenter Planning Accounting for Power Consumption Profiles

Sergio Nesmachnow[1], Cristian Perfumo[2], and Íñigo Goiri[3]

[1] Universidad de la República, Montevideo, Uruguay
sergion@fing.edu.uy
[2] CSIRO Energy, Newcastle, Australia
cristian.perfumo@csiro.au
[3] Rutgers University, New Jersey, USA
goiri@cs.rutgers.edu

Abstract. Energy efficiency is one of the major concerns when operating datacenters nowadays, as the large amount of energy used by parallel computing infrastructures impacts on both the energy cost and the electricity grid. Power consumption can be lowered by dynamically adjusting the power demand of datacenters, but conflicting objectives such as temperature and quality of service must be taken into account. This paper proposes a multiobjective evolutionary approach to solve the energy-aware scheduling problem in datacenters, regarding power consumption, temperature, and quality of service when controlling servers and cooling infrastructures. Accurate results are reported for both best solutions regarding each of the problem objectives and best trade-off solutions.

1 Introduction

Nowadays, cluster/grid/cloud computing datacenters host powerful high performance computing (HPC) resources having large and increasing energy demands [28]. Energy efficiency is a major concern in datacenter operation, as recent surveys point out that datacenters account for about 1.5% of the total energy usage in the world [14]. Thus, power consumption in datacenters raises many important environmental and economic issues. Owners and operators are highly interested in energy-efficient datacenters that applies intelligent planning to reduce and adjust power consumption, and integrate renewable generation [8].

Within the research community, there is growing interest in energy-aware planning of HPC infrastructures, including dynamic operation control [8][21][27], and energy-aware scheduling and planning [28][1].

Dynamic control approaches are especially useful when considering the cost reductions that the operator can achieve by shifting operation to periods of cheaper energy prices, and the possible utilization of (intermittent) renewable solar and wind energy. Energy-aware datacenters can also participate as providers of ancillary services in the electricity market. Ancillary services are used to compensate

G. Hernández et al. (Eds.): CARLA 2014, CCIS 485, pp. 128–142, 2014.

for short-term variability in the grid as well as for contingency purposes, such as recovering after faults in transmission lines or generators.

Many different techniques have been proposed to reduce the energy consumption of data-centers [1], from low-level hardware solutions to high-level software methods. Sustainable energy-aware techniques are in conflict with system performance metrics that accounts for the QoS perceived by the user, because increasing performance usually leads to increase the energy consumption. Thus, multiobjective approaches are required to model the reality of current datacenters operation when taking into account the energy efficiency.

This paper presents a multiobjective approach for datacenter planning that accounts for both server (IT) and cooling infrastructures: free cooling and air conditioning (AC) in order to provide appropriate levels of quality of service (QoS) and temperature when following a specific power consumption profile.

We propose a two-phase approach for control and scheduling. In the upper level, a multiobjective evolutionary algorithm (MOEA) is applied for power control according to a reference power profile and temperature, providing multiple trade-off solutions to the problem. In the lower level, specific energy-aware scheduling heuristics are applied to provide appropriate QoS according to Server Level Agreements (SLA) between provider and user. The multiobjective approach helps the datacenter planner to explore different options for controlling the system performance and energy consumption.

The experimental evaluation, performed considering a set of realistic workloads and hardware scenarios, indicate that the proposed approach is a useful option for power management in datacenters. When compared against a business-as-usual (BAU) strategy, the proposed MOEA is able to compute solutions with up to **78%** improvement on power tracking and **86%** on the temperature values, with very low degradation in QoS-related metrics.

The paper is organized as follows. Section 2 reviews the related work about power control and energy-aware scheduling in datacenters. The problem model and the proposed control and planning strategies for energy-aware datacenters is described in Section 3. The proposed MOEA for energy-aware datacenter control and planning is described in Section 4. The experimental evaluation is reported and discussed in Section 5. Finally, Section 6 presents the conclusions and formulates the main lines for future work.

2   Related Work

This section reviews the main related work in literature in the areas of control and energy-aware scheduling in datacenters.

Control and energy aware datacenters. GreenSlot [9] considers job allocation for HPC applications in a datacenter powered by solar panels, using job information (nodes per job, deadline, estimated runtime) for scheduling when solar energy is available. GreenHadoop [10] considers green generation and energy prices to allocate MapReduce jobs using heuristics to predict the energy requirements. GreenSwitch [8] also considers energy storage (batteries and net metering), managing energy sources and workloads to minimize electricity costs. This approach is evaluated on Parasol, a solar-powered micro-datacenter [8].

An alternative to shifting load is to trade-off energy and QoS. The scheduler by Kriukov et al. [15] follows wind generation, using less power by delaying requests with slack. Aikema et al. [2] presented simulation results for a datacenter in the New York ancillary service market. A selective approach is applied in [7], where participation as an ancillary services provider is determined by expected profits (the compensation is weighed against the SLA penalties).

Ghamkhari and Mohsenian-Rad [21] schedule non-critical jobs based on predicted power output and datacenter load. This is to the best of our knowledge the only other existing approach for energy-aware scheduling in data centres that considers air conditioning power. The main differences with our control approach are: (a) we look at fine time granularity (minutes), broadening the applications of datacenter energy management, e.g. by enabling ancillary services; (b) we apply a multiobjective approach to the problem, thus considering a range of trade-off solutions between power, temperature, and QoS; and (c) different schedulers are studied in order to provide diverse power/QoS trade-offs.

Energy aware scheduling. A simple optimization approach for energy-aware scheduling assumes energy and performance as independent. A more comprehensive one is to optimize performance and energy at the same time, modeling the problem as a multiobjective optimization. Algorithms are oriented to find Pareto optimal schedules; *i.e.*, no scheduling decision can strictly dominate the others with better performance and lower energy consumption at the same time.

Khan and Ahmad [12] applied game theory for scheduling independent jobs, simultaneously minimizing makespan and energy on a Dynamic Voltage Scaling (DVS)-enabled grid system. Lee and Zomaya [17] studied several heuristics to minimize the weighted sum of makespan and energy using a makespan conservative local search to slightly modify scheduling decisions when they do not increase energy consumption, in order to escape from local optima. Later, Mezmaz et al. [22] proposed a parallel bi-objective hybrid genetic algorithm (GA) for the same problem. significantly reducing the scheduler execution time.

Kim et al. [13] studied the deadline constrained scheduling problem in ad-hoc grids with limited-charge batteries, proposing a resource manager to exploit the task heterogeneity while managing energy. Li et al. [19] introduced an online dynamic strategy with multiple power-saving states to reduce energy consumption of scheduling algorithms. Pinel et al. [26] proposed a double minimization approach for scheduling independent tasks on grids, using an heuristic to optimize makespan, and then a local search to minimize energy consumption. Lindberg et al. [20] proposed six greedy algorithms and two GAs to solve the makespan-energy scheduling problem subject to deadline and memory requirements.

Le et al. [16] proposed a scheduler for deciding the datacenter to run virtual machine requests and job migration, taking into account electricity price and temperature, which can trigger AC activation, increasing power consumption.

Our previous work [24] introduced an energy consumption model for multi-core computing systems based on the energy the system requires to operate at full capacity, the energy when not all the available cores of the machine are used, and the energy that each machine consumes in idle state (*MIN-MAX* mode). Iturriaga *et al.* [11] showed that a parallel multiobjective local search based on Pareto dominance outperforms deterministic heuristics based on the traditional Min-Min strategy. We also apply the MIN-MAX mode in this present article.

Dorronsoro *et al.* [6] presented a two-level strategy for scheduling large parallel applications in multicore distributed systems, minimizing the total computation time and the energy consumption. The approach combines a higher-level (between distributed datacenters) and a lower-level (within each datacenter) scheduler. Accurate schedules were computed by using heuristics accounting for both problem objectives in the higher level, and ad-hoc schedulers to take advantage of multicore infrastructures in the lower level. We adapt three low-level schedulers from that previous article for the problem we consider in this work.

We initially explored the application of multiobjective control planning for datacenters in [25]. We introduced the problem model and initial results about controlling datacenter power consumption while maintaining temperature and QoS levels. The present work extends the previous study, focusing on further analyzing the multiobjective approach and studying different scheduling strategies for reducing power consumption and increasing QoS.

3   Control and Scheduling Approach for Energy-Aware Datacenters

This section describes the approach for control and energy-aware scheduling in datacenters, according to reference power consumption profiles.

3.1   Datacenter Model

Fig. 1 shows the datacenter model applied in this work. We follow the power management approach applied to the Parasol datacenter [8], considering two systems: heating-ventilation-air conditioning (HVAC) and computing infrastructure (IT).

The *control signals* are variables that alter the behavior of the datacenter:

1. HVAC control (c_k): we consider a datacenter equipped with free and AC cooling infrastructure. c_k comprises a set of signals: AC compressor state (binary), free cooling fan speed (%), and free cooling damper state (binary).
2. Schedule (s_k): shape the IT power consumption, considering the number of servers running, load constraints, and specific user requirements.

The *controllable variables* are handled via manipulation of the control signals:

1. Quality of service (QoS_k): depends on user and system related metrics, which are computed using a specific scheduling strategy applied in the datacenter.
2. Internal temperature (T_k): thermostat reading of the datacenter (^oC).
3. Cooling power (C_k): the sum of AC power and free cooling fan power (kW).
4. IT power (I_k): the power of the servers, switches and all IT equipment in the datacenter (kW).
5. Total power (P_k): the total power used by the datacenter ($P_k = C_k + I_k$).

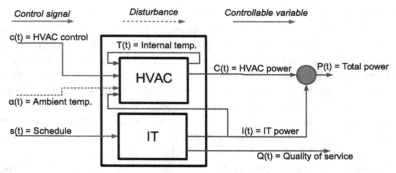

Fig. 1. Diagram of the datacenter model

The *disturbances* are variables that affect the datacenter behavior but we have no control over, in our case the external temperature α_k ($^\circ C$).

3.2 Scheduling Model

The scheduling model considers a set of tasks to be executed in the datacenter. Each task is defined by its arrival time, the estimated execution time, and a deadline, which represents the time by which the user wants the task to finish.

We assume that tasks arrive following a Poisson distribution (parameter $\lambda=$ instance size/simulation time). Tasks durations follow a normal distribution, with average and standard deviations following a typical cluster, according to traces from Cluster FING [23] and the Parallel Workload Archive repository. Three levels are used for deadlines, modeling different SLA between the provider and the users, according to three slack factors (*sf*): *tight* (*sf*<10%), *medium* (10%<*sf*<30%), and *loose* (*sf*>30%), which represent the time the user admits the tasks end (over the task duration and since the arrival time).

We apply a dynamic scheduling strategy applying specific QoS and energy-aware scheduling heuristics, which are described in the following section.

3.3 The Optimization Problem

We want to control the datacenter so that its total power demand P_k and temperature T_k follow as closely as possible a desired reference demand and temperature profiles R_k and T_{ref}, while minimizing the impact on QoS.

The datacenter executes n tasks in the simulation period (K steps). Each user submission requests execution before a deadline $D(i)$ for task i, and the scheduler executes the task according to the availability of computing resources and energy consumption. Each task i finishes at time $FT(i)$, and QoS is evaluated according the deadline satisfaction. Formally, we want to *minimize* the deviation regarding the reference power profile (1) and regarding the temperature (2), and the total time of deadline violations (3) during the simulating period.

$$\sum_{k=1}^{K} \frac{|P_k - R_k|}{\max(R_k)} \quad (1) \qquad \sum_{k=1}^{K} |T_{ref} - T_k| \quad (2) \qquad \sum_{i=1}^{K} \max(0, FT(i) - D(i)) \quad (3)$$

The total IT power is $I_k = S_k^{max} + S_k^{idle} + S_k^{sleep}$ where S_k^{max}, S_k^{idle} and S_k^{sleep} are the total power of servers executing, idle, and sleep at time k.

AC is used to keep temperature within a specified hysteresis band. In free cooling mode, outside air is blown into the datacenter using a fan. The cooling power C_k takes the values C_{PWR} in AC mode, compressor ON; 0 in AC mode, compressor OFF; and FAN_{PWR} in free cooling mode. Based on two months of operation data from Parasol, we identified an Auto-Regressive eXogenous [18] model for temperature: $A(q)T_k = B(q)u_k + e_k$.

4   A Multiobjective Evolutionary Approach for Energy-Aware Datacenter Planning

This section presents the proposed MOEA for energy-aware datacenter planning.

4.1   Evolutionary Algorithms and NSGA-II

Evolutionary algorithms (EAs) are non-deterministic methods that emulate the natural evolution to solve optimization problems [3]. In the last thirty years, EAs have been successfully applied for solving many optimization problems.

MOEAs [5] have been applied to solve hard optimization problems, obtaining accurate results when solving real-life problems in many research areas. Unlike many traditional methods for multiobjective optimization, MOEAs are able to find a set with several solutions in a single execution, since they work with a population of tentative solutions.

MOEAs must be designed aiming at two goals at the same time: *i*) approximating the Pareto front, by applying a Pareto-based search, and *ii*) maintaining diversity instead of converging to a reduced section of the Pareto front, by using specific techniques from multimodal optimization (sharing, crowding, etc.).

In this work, we apply the *Non-dominated Sorting Genetic Algorithm, version II* (NSGA-II) [5], a popular MOEA that has been successfully applied in many application areas. NSGA-II includes features to deal with specific issues of the search: *i*) a non-dominated elitist ordering that diminishes the complexity of the dominance check; *ii*) a crowding technique for diversity preservation; and *iii*) a fitness assignment method considering the crowding distance values.

4.2   The Proposed Resolution Approach

Solution encoding: Each solution represents the power (cooling and IT) to be used at each time step k. A solution is encoded as an integer vector of $2K$ elements, representing the cooling (positions 1 to K) and server power (positions $K+1$ to $2K$). The server power is encoded directly as Watts, whereas the cooling power is encoded as an integer value representing three states: (a) *1–100*: free cooling mode is applied, and the value represents the fan speed as a percentage of its maximum; (b) *101–200*: the air conditioning unit is assumed to be operating, and (c) *201–300*: neither air conditioning nor free cooling are in operation.

Evolutionary operators: We apply a three-point crossover (using cross points p_1, p_2, and p_3); p_1 is selected randomly in $(1,K)$, p_2 is K and p_3 is $K + p_1$. This approach assures that portions representing the same time interval for both cooling and server power move together from parents to offspring.

Mutation is applied to each gene with probability p_M. For a cooling power gene (position 1 to K) its value v is replaced with $mod(v + rand() \times$ MAX_HVAC, MAX_HVAC)). For the other genes, they are redefined with a random value between 0 and the maximum server power, *i.e.* representing all servers on.

4.3   Energy and QoS-aware Scheduling

In order to model a realistic task planning in the simulated datacenter, we apply three heuristic energy-aware QoS schedulers. They are based on the ones defined from our previous work [6], but adapted to deal with the specific features of the problem addressed in this article.

The schedulers apply different backfilling-oriented techniques to work with computing resources that are available in certain periods of time (we call these periods slack-times or simply *holes*) and unavailable in other moments (e.g. due to sleeping and/or switching off servers). The heuristics differ in the way they fill holes/slack-times that are left after a given policy for sleeping/shutting down holes is applied to reduce the energy consumption:

1. *Best Fit Hole* (BFH): Tasks are first sorted according to their arrival times, and then assigned to computing resources to fill their existing holes/slack-times. If a task fits into more than one hole, the one that "best fits" the task (i.e., the hole that minimizes the difference between the hole duration and task execution time) is selected. Holes within each machine are processed according to their finishing times. A specific logic is included to deal with deferrable tasks. When no hole is available to execute a task, BFH assigns it to the machine that provides the minimum finishing time for that task. The rationale behind this strategy is to use available holes and spare unoccupied large holes and empty machines for upcoming tasks with potential larger execution times.

2. *Best Deadline* (BD): This scheduler applies a greedy approach to select the slack to execute each incoming task, improving the QoS of the resulting schedule. As in BFH, a specific logic is included to deal with deferrable tasks, which can be scheduled in any available hole within the simulation period. When no hole is available to execute a task, BD also assigns it to the machine that provides the minimum finishing time for that task.

3. *Earliest Finishing Time Hole* (EFTH): In this strategy, holes/slack-times are selected to minimize the tasks' finishing times. That is, instead of finding the hole that best fits a given task (as in BFH), a hole that can finish it earlier is selected regardless of its length. As a result, EFTH should lead to fewer

deadline violations. If no hole is available to execute a task, EFTH selects the machine that provides the minimum finishing time to the task.

5   Experimental Analysis

This section reports the experimental analysis of the proposed MOEA for energy-aware datacenter control and scheduling for a simulated data center with the characteristics described above. Both the MOEA and the datacenter simulator were implemented in MATLAB.

5.1   Problem Instances

Instances are defined by a *workload*, a *scenario*, and a *reference power profile*.

Workloads are sets of tasks. We consider *non-deferrable workloads* and *deferrable workloads*, where 25% of the tasks are allowed to end after the deadline without having a negative impact in the QoS perceived by the user. We study three different workload dimensions: *low operation* (50 tasks in 150 time steps), *normal* (75 tasks in 150 time steps), and *full steam* (100 tasks in 150 time steps).

The hardware scenarios assume 64 Atom-based servers in the datacenter, as in Parasol [8]. The power consumption of each server is 30W(max), 22W(idle), 3W(asleep). We consider a time horizon of 75 minutes (150 30-second time steps) in the simulation, and an average utilization of 50%, to allow for a reasonable task planning (utilization values as low as 15–20% have been reported [27]).

We consider three reference power profiles to follow (see Fig. 2, percentages represent a fraction of the maximum datacenter power):

- *Profile A:* 20% during 25 time steps, 80% during 25 time steps and 20% during 25 time steps. This scenario studies how the system responds to step changes (both up and down) in power profile.
- *Profile B:* 50% during 15 time steps, 80 % during 10 time steps, 20% during 20 time steps, 80% during 10 time steps and 50% during 20 time steps. In this situation, it is known in advance that demand will have to be dropped in the near future (*e.g.* forecast indicates that renewable generation will drop) and we decide increasing power demand before and after the drop.
- *Profile C:* 80% during 25 time steps, then a linear ramp decreasing to 20% during the course of 25 time steps, and then 20% during 25 time steps. This scenario tests how the control responds to ramp changes, a very common type of power change in the electricity market.

5.2   Multiobjective Optimization Metrics

In this work, we apply several relevant metrics to evaluate the results obtained by the studied MOEAs, regarding the goals of converging to and correctly sampling the set of non-dominated solutions of the problem [5][4]:

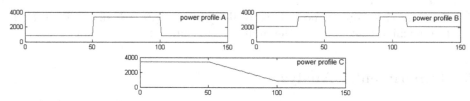

Fig. 2. Power profiles considered in the study

- The number of (different) non-dominated solutions (ND).
- Generational Distance (GD): the sum of the distances between the non-dominated solutions in the computed Pareto front and a set of uniformly distributed points in the true Pareto front (Eq. 4). Smaller values of GD mean a better approximation to the Pareto front.
- Spread (s): evaluates the dispersion of non-dominated solutions in the computed Pareto front, including the distance from the extreme points of the true Pareto front (Eq. 5); d_i is the distance between solution i in the computed Pareto front and its nearest neighbor, $\bar{d}$ is the average of all d_i and d_h^e is the distance between the extreme of the h-th objective in the true Pareto front and the closest point in the computed Pareto front [5]. Smaller values of spread mean a better distribution of non-dominated solutions.

$$GD = \frac{\sum\limits_{v \in P^*} d(v, P)}{|P^*|} \quad (4) \qquad s = \frac{\sum\limits_{h=1}^{k} d_h^e + \sum\limits_{i=1}^{ND} |\bar{d} - d_i|}{\sum\limits_{h=1}^{k} d_h^e + ND \times \bar{d}} \quad (5)$$

- Relative hypervolume (RHV): the ratio of the volume (in the objective functions space) covered by the computed Pareto front and the one covered by the true Pareto front. The ideal RHV value is 1.

The true Pareto front—unknown for the problem instances studied—was approximated by gathering the non-dominated solutions found for each instance, in each execution performed for the three variants of the proposed MOEA.

5.3 Results and Discussion

All the reported results were computed in 15 independent executions of the proposed MOEA for each problem instance dimension solved.

Parameter setting. The proposed MOEA was executed using the best parameter values from a previous analysis that studied: population size (#P, candidate values {50,75,100}), and the probabilities for crossover (p_C, candidate values {0.6,0.75,0.9}) and mutation (p_M, candidate values {0.01,0.05,0.1}). The best results were obtained using the parameter setting #P = 75, p_C = 0.9, and p_M = 0.01. The stopping criterion is 500 generations, providing a reasonable trade-off between results quality and execution time.

Multiobjective analysis. Table 1 reports the average results for the multiobjective metrics studied for each algorithm, workload dimension, and power profile. The results shows that all the studied MOEAs are able to compute a large number of non-dominated solutions (between 35 and 55, *i.e.* more than 50% of the population) for all problem instances.

Table 1. Multiobjective optimization metrics results

		ND			GD			spread			RHV		
profile	n	BFH	BD	EFT	BFH	BD	EFT	BFH	BD	EFT	BFH	BD	EFT
						non-deferrable workloads							
A	50	**44.9**	40.9	40.6	1899.4	1198.9	**926.1**	0.74	1.09	**0.71**	0.90	**0.95**	0.93
	75	**44.1**	36.1	37.9	4975.5	5982.7	**433.4**	0.70	0.88	0.74	0.85	0.92	**0.98**
	100	39.9	38.6	**50.6**	3104.8	5102.9	**760.4**	0.73	0.80	0.85	0.89	0.91	**0.98**
B	50	40.3	**42.7**	39.0	3896.8	820.2	**361.7**	**0.86**	0.95	0.95	0.91	0.76	**0.97**
	75	39.0	41.8	**44.9**	1113.4	4710.3	**462.6**	0.83	0.96	0.92	0.91	0.91	**0.98**
	100	39.3	42.4	**53.4**	**2142.3**	2596.5	5764.7	0.78	0.86	0.96	0.92	0.88	**0.96**
C	50	**42.0**	38.6	40.6	1459.9	1146.6	**742.2**	0.71	0.80	0.78	0.95	**0.97**	0.93
	75	35.7	**39.9**	37.9	**1948.1**	5150.8	2084.9	**0.64**	0.82	0.72	0.88	**0.95**	0.91
	100	36.9	39.5	**44.7**	2904.8	2145.7	**612.7**	0.74	0.90	0.75	0.88	**0.93**	0.88
						deferrable workloads							
A	50	41.1	40.9	37.9	1449.9	7267.1	**554.4**	0.75	0.89	0.80	0.94	0.88	**0.94**
	75	41.3	38.5	**41.5**	1302.3	3559.9	**1239.3**	0.79	0.81	**0.76**	0.91	**0.94**	0.92
	100	41.7	36.5	**53.5**	2703.3	5870.8	**1180.9**	0.74	0.83	0.79	0.89	0.93	**0.95**
B	50	**47.6**	44.4	42.5	708.8	1344.6	**562.2**	0.75	0.88	0.78	**0.94**	0.90	0.93
	75	38.1	39.6	**43.3**	813.0	2022.0	**740.8**	0.79	0.95	0.89	**0.94**	0.93	0.91
	100	38.1	39.5	**44.2**	850.6	2128.9	**793.7**	0.85	0.87	0.85	0.96	0.95	**0.96**
C	50	36.8	**40.8**	39.3	**735.7**	2591.9	931.5	0.66	0.76	0.70	**0.94**	**0.94**	0.93
	75	37.3	**44.3**	39.1	2083.1	8176.6	**1025.3**	0.71	0.76	0.78	0.88	**0.93**	**0.93**
	100	38.1	40.5	39.7	**1103.0**	8043.6	1733.9	0.72	0.76	**0.68**	**0.95**	0.89	**0.95**

Regarding the GD metric, NSGA-II+EFT computed the closest solutions to the Pareto front for most of the problem instances. However, NSGA-II+BFH achieves a better distribution of non-dominated solutions, as the spread results indicate. Mixed results are obtained for the RHV metric: NSGA-II+EFT and NSGA-II+BD work better for non-deferrable workloads, as they take into account the deadlines for the task-to-processor assignment, and all NSGA variants compute competitive results for deferrable workloads. The previous results suggest that NSGA-II+EFT is the most promising alternative to solve the problem.

Best and trade-off results. Table 2 reports the average improvements on power and temperature when comparing with a business-as-usual (BAU) strategy, and the QoS metrics—time (dv_T) and number (dv_n) of deadline violations—for non-deferrable/deferrable workloads and the power profiles studied. The BAU strategy represents a conventional datacenter operation. It does not apply an energy-aware control, assumes that all the servers are on, AC is used to maintain the temperature within 1.5 C around the desired level, and applies a FIFO scheduler. All improvements are averaged by problem dimension and SLA type. The best improvements obtained for each problem class and dimension are in bold.

We analyze the best results computed for each objective (*best power*, *best temperature*, and *best QoS* solutions). This analysis is useful in case the datacenter planner is mainly interested in prioritizing a specific objective. We also

Table 2. Average improvements and QoS results over the BAU strategy

		power	temp.	dv_T	dv_n	power	temp.	dv_T	dv_n	power	temp.	dv_T	dv_n	power	temp.	dv_T	dv_n
A	50	**77.8%**	-75.1%	239.2	17.5	23.6%	76.3%	133.6	16.0	48.5%	4.9%	3.8	1.8	57.8%	30.2%	127.0	13.5
	75	**75.3%**	-60.6%	464.4	29.5	26.1%	73.2%	477.6	29.3	38.6%	27.8%	13.0	10.5	55.5%	27.4%	158.2	27.4
	100	**76.1%**	-89.3%	879.2	36.7	28.2%	74.6%	351.2	34.3	44.3%	4.3%	40.4	16.9	56.6%	34.4%	162.4	32.2
B	50	51.1%	-6.0%	184.8	40.0	10.9%	75.1%	28.8	43.0	34.8%	-24.3%	39.0	1.4	40.9%	35.4%	118.6	26.0
	75	53.5%	-80.6%	525.8	39.0	13.6%	76.6%	138.6	43.0	32.8%	0.8%	11.0	19.0	46.2%	25.7%	114.6	34.0
	100	56.1%	-8.5%	552.2	46.0	14.1%	75.7%	163.4	45.0	37.3%	2.5%	31.6	17.0	43.3%	41.9%	216.4	50.0
C	50	58.7%	-226.0%	355.4	40.0	5.8%	75.3%	221.2	14.0	36.1%	-137.9%	34.0	3.6	38.6%	-15.4%	107.8	38.0
	75	58.0%	-272.5%	190.6	14.0	15.2%	78.2%	139.4	34.0	23.6%	9.8%	40.0	13.0	40.7%	-11.3%	75.6	52.0
	100	55.1%	-293.5%	637.0	48.0	11.2%	76.1%	587.4	45.0	30.0%	-60.8%	27.0	16.0	40.4%	-26.9%	153.4	48.0

NSGA-II using BD

P	n	best power solution				best temperature solution				best QoS solution				best trade-off solution			
		power	temp.	dv_T	dv_n	power	temp.	dv_T	dv_n	power	temp.	dv_T	dv_n	power	temp.	dv_T	dv_n
A	50	70.5%	-52.5%	465.8	8.5	22.5%	**81.8%**	541.4	8.6	53.2%	-15.8%	**0.0**	**0.0**	52.1%	38.5%	134.4	6.2
	75	71.7%	-63.6%	766.1	14.7	19.2%	**82.5%**	1303.9	15.4	54.3%	-95.8%	**0.0**	**0.0**	56.8%	16.1%	275.7	10.1
	100	74.9%	-78.0%	863.8	15.2	21.1%	**82.3%**	1626.3	21.7	55.7%	-41.2%	**0.3**	**0.2**	54.9%	28.1%	243.3	10.3
B	50	52.4%	2.9%	587.0	8.1	18.2%	**81.8%**	532.8	10.2	41.2%	34.9%	2.0	0.6	38.3%	58.4%	104.0	4.1
	75	54.6%	-24.0%	1292.0	19.8	13.1%	**82.6%**	1134.2	15.4	32.3%	29.2%	**0.0**	**0.0**	44.8%	43.5%	259.2	12.0
	100	53.2%	-38.6%	1784.0	23.8	11.3%	**81.9%**	881.9	15.5	24.0%	8.2%	**2.7**	**0.5**	40.5%	29.8%	300.2	11.9
C	50	57.5%	-144.8%	259.7	4.6	11.3%	**81.9%**	583.7	8.3	36.1%	-29.2%	**0.0**	**0.0**	41.0%	21.6%	61.3	3.5
	75	56.1%	-140.3%	269.5	6.1	11.0%	**82.1%**	723.3	9.3	40.8%	-98.9%	**0.0**	**0.0**	39.6%	24.1%	136.9	4.4
	100	**58.6%**	-153.3%	227.8	7.0	18.7%	**82.9%**	1030.4	11.0	36.9%	-44.2%	0.8	0.4	45.2%	4.8%	193.4	8.6

NSGA-II using EFT

P	n	best power solution				best temperature solution				best QoS solution				best trade-off solution			
		power	temp.	dv_T	dv_n	power	temp.	dv_T	dv_n	power	temp.	dv_T	dv_n	power	temp.	dv_T	dv_n
A	50	74.7%	-61.1%	166.6	5.0	24.7%	**85.8%**	409.2	7.2	62.2%	-88.7%	2.6	0.1	60.4%	20.2%	92.0	2.0
	75	73.6%	-73.6%	291.6	6.2	25.6%	**84.5%**	414.4	6.9	47.4%	10.8%	5.2	2.2	60.5%	16.9%	97.4	3.4
	100	77.0%	-73.8%	398.0	7.1	27.2%	**85.6%**	491.0	8.4	60.0%	-51.8%	9.8	0.7	61.0%	24.5%	102.2	5.3
B	50	**53.1%**	-66.6%	251.8	12.5	11.2%	75.4%	72.4	20.0	34.7%	33.6%	**0.0**	**0.0**	45.3%	36.9%	21.4	4.7
	75	**56.1%**	-18.5%	673.2	18.0	13.9%	76.2%	209.2	36.0	33.2%	-20.0%	0.4	0.1	48.0%	39.9%	90.8	8.4
	100	**57.1%**	-50.5%	751.8	22.8	13.6%	75.4%	81.4	29.7	38.9%	20.8%	6.9	3.6	49.0%	31.3%	171.6	14.2
C	50	54.5%	-296.0%	25.2	13.3	11.4%	76.9%	152.6	9.3	26.8%	-48.4%	0.0	1.4	37.6%	-24.6%	26.8	11.1
	75	57.4%	-276.3%	212.8	12.1	13.4%	77.1%	315.8	19.5	50.2%	-253.4%	0.4	0.8	42.6%	-40.1%	58.2	11.1
	100	58.5%	-279.1%	139.2	27.5	19.8%	76.7%	221.8	25.7	30.0%	-66.0%	**0.6**	**0.1**	43.8%	-24.0%	102.0	16.1

deferrable workloads

NSGA-II using BFH

P	n	best power solution				best temperature solution				best QoS solution				best trade-off solution			
		power	temp.	dv_T	dv_n	power	temp.	dv_T	dv_n	power	temp.	dv_T	dv_n	power	temp.	dv_T	dv_n
A	50	**77.5%**	-95.1%	138.2	17.3	28.9%	76.5%	231.0	15.0	58.4%	-20.6%	12.0	2.8	61.7%	17.2%	42.6	15.3
	75	**76.6%**	-79.8%	394.0	12.0	21.7%	76.2%	313.2	14.0	55.8%	-33.6%	12.4	6.0	58.5%	25.0%	91.0	13.3
	100	**77.4%**	-65.9%	478.0	19.0	25.6%	74.2%	544.8	7.0	60.3%	-70.8%	15.4	5.0	61.4%	15.5%	148.2	14.3
B	50	57.8%	-40.7%	405.2	36.0	10.7%	75.5%	419.2	40.0	36.8%	28.6%	20.0	4.8	46.2%	35.0%	59.8	43.0
	75	**53.8%**	-62.2%	152.2	36.0	9.7%	78.0%	159.0	50.0	36.1%	29.8%	20.0	5.4	44.4%	32.9%	91.0	45.0
	100	**57.5%**	-37.6%	328.4	26.0	12.1%	75.7%	220.0	34.0	34.8%	-13.5%	16.8	7.0	44.7%	34.5%	125.4	33.0
C	50	**58.7%**	-221.4%	94.6	47.0	15.2%	76.9%	163.4	12.0	29.4%	-45.4%	29.0	3.8	40.2%	-10.3%	48.0	32.0
	75	**57.5%**	-247.1%	389.4	29.0	10.3%	76.6%	261.0	47.0	22.6%	2.9%	12.4	8.0	36.1%	-16.9%	59.2	33.0
	100	**58.6%**	-294.1%	301.8	24.0	8.2%	76.9%	273.8	19.0	34.2%	-95.7%	32.6	6.0	44.4%	-23.7%	152.2	12.0

NSGA-II using BD

P	n	best power solution				best temperature solution				best QoS solution				best trade-off solution			
		power	temp.	dv_T	dv_n	power	temp.	dv_T	dv_n	power	temp.	dv_T	dv_n	power	temp.	dv_T	dv_n
A	50	70.8%	-64.3%	485.6	8.9	20.0%	**83.1%**	833.0	11.7	41.3%	-17.1%	7.5	0.4	55.1%	28.4%	119.1	5.9
	75	71.8%	-82.9%	619.9	15.3	23.3%	**82.3%**	1010.7	17.7	47.2%	-45.7%	5.3	0.5	56.7%	23.0%	268.1	11.6
	100	74.2%	-81.2%	765.0	17.7	19.9%	**82.5%**	1103.9	17.1	53.8%	-60.7%	**0.2**	**0.1**	58.0%	9.5%	218.9	11.1
B	50	50.7%	-22.1%	594.2	10.1	10.3%	**82.1%**	383.1	6.3	27.6%	18.4%	1.4	0.1	38.2%	49.1%	142.5	4.9
	75	52.6%	-18.0%	1674.2	21.6	10.9%	**81.6%**	873.0	15.4	15.4%	36.0%	**0.0**	**0.0**	40.1%	46.8%	297.4	11.4
	100	52.6%	-33.8%	1418.1	20.5	10.8%	**82.6%**	977.7	18.7	33.3%	-20.2%	6.3	0.9	39.3%	46.8%	278.2	12.1
C	50	55.7%	-139.9%	315.3	7.4	12.6%	**81.3%**	445.9	8.1	32.9%	-50.2%	3.2	0.7	39.8%	23.9%	113.9	5.0
	75	54.8%	-146.4%	461.1	12.0	12.0%	**81.4%**	841.7	14.1	30.9%	-85.5%	5.6	1.1	35.8%	25.3%	227.1	10.0
	100	58.5%	-149.5%	348.3	11.5	11.7%	**81.1%**	341.8	7.2	28.3%	-8.2%	**3.6**	**0.6**	42.6%	11.4%	100.9	5.1

NSGA-II using EFT

P	n	best power solution				best temperature solution				best QoS solution				best trade-off solution			
		power	temp.	dv_T	dv_n	power	temp.	dv_T	dv_n	power	temp.	dv_T	dv_n	power	temp.	dv_T	dv_n
A	50	77.4%	-119.2%	120.0	8.0	25.7%	**84.1%**	200.8	10.9	48.5%	-9.7%	**0.0**	**0.0**	62.2%	24.7%	60.2	4.6
	75	75.8%	-105.4%	338.2	12.4	26.2%	**85.5%**	645.2	15.5	48.1%	20.1%	1.8	0.7	61.0%	34.2%	97.0	8.1
	100	74.9%	-169.3%	293.2	15.3	21.7%	**81.3%**	495.4	18.6	39.2%	13.8%	0.3	0.1	57.0%	15.7%	93.8	10.9
B	50	54.1%	1.8%	171.0	9.7	12.8%	75.9%	268.4	10.0	30.9%	26.9%	4.6	2.0	45.8%	39.4%	49.2	6.2
	75	51.4%	-26.1%	268.6	14.9	10.5%	74.7%	43.2	17.7	31.1%	31.6%	2.0	3.5	41.4%	38.1%	60.6	8.5
	100	56.7%	-9.3%	860.0	17.2	12.0%	76.4%	231.6	22.8	39.2%	22.4%	**4.2**	5.5	45.4%	38.0%	160.6	10.1
C	50	57.5%	-339.4%	105.2	8.7	9.1%	76.0%	147.2	11.8	24.6%	-43.6%	1.8	2.1	42.9%	-27.4%	59.4	8.0
	75	56.5%	-297.1%	253.2	16.9	11.8%	75.3%	212.6	19.7	37.1%	-54.6%	2.8	4.7	42.5%	-34.2%	108.2	14.6
	100	54.9%	-268.7%	214.6	28.5	3.7%	75.7%	199.6	25.5	26.4%	-46.3%	6.8	10.1	38.2%	-29.5%	77.4	19.3

analyze the best trade-off solutions defined as the nearest to the (normalized) ideal objective vector [5] for each problem instance, which corresponds to an ideal solution that equally weights power, temperature, and QoS.

The results in Table 2 demonstrate that NSGA-II+BFH computes the best power-aware solutions, up to **77.8%** better than the BAU strategy, and NSGA-II+BD obtains the best temperature results, up to **85.8%** over the BAU strategy. However, those solutions have a significant impact on the other objectives. Accurate QoS values are obtained using NSGA-II+BD when admitting reasonable temperature deviations, for both non-deferrable and deferrable workloads.

Regarding the best trade-off solutions, NSGA-II+EFT accounts for the lower impacts on QoS (in average, 8.4% for non-deferrable workloads, and 10.0% for deferrable workloads), while achieving important improvements on energy (between **38–62%**) and temperature (up to **49%**) when compared against the BAU strategy. NSGA-II+BD is an acceptable second option. The results also indicate that no significant differences on the objective function values are obtained when considering deferrable and non-deferrable tasks using the proposed schedulers.

The reported results indicate that NSGA-II+ETF is a promising technique for datacenter controlling, to decide the most appropriate trade-off between objectives (e.g., during short periods of very high electricity price, it might be useful to drop power demand at the expense of QoS and temperature).

Fig. 3 presents examples of Pareto fronts computed for two different (representative) problem instances. The figures show that a good coverage of trade-off solutions is obtained, correctly sampling the region of (equally-weighted) best compromise solutions for the problem. When comparing the three schedulers, we see that NSGA-II+EFT generally outperforms NSGA-II+BSD and NSGA-II+BFH in terms of QoS. For example, for power profile A, EFT (blue) delivers solutions with very low QoS impact all across the Pareto front, making the front almost a 2D curve of trade-off between temperature and power violations.

Solution analysis. Fig. 4 presents four illustrative solutions from the Pareto front obtained using NSGA-II+EFT for a problem instance with 75 tasks and power profile A. Figs. 4(a)-4(c) show the extremes of the Pareto front. Fig. 4(a)

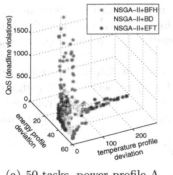
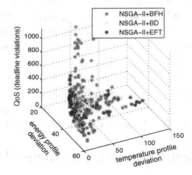

(a) 50 tasks, power profile A   (b) 50 tasks, power profile B

Fig. 3. Sample Pareto fronts computed by NSGA-II+EFT for representative instances

shows that the power closely follows the step-changing reference power, enabling the datacenter to reduce electricity costs, maximize renewable utilization, or participate in the electricity market. For example, if the electricity price was to change from 0.4 \$/kWh during peak time to 0.23 \$/kWh during off-peak time (the case for some electricity retailers in Australia) the solution in Fig. 4(a) would reduce the energy cost in the electricity bill of the datacenter by **16.5%**.

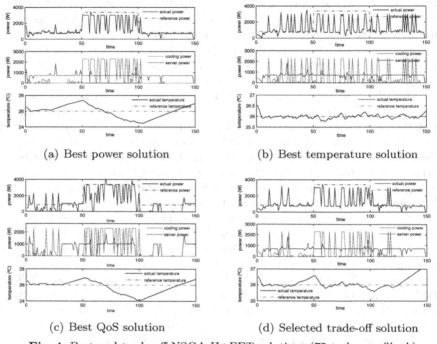

(a) Best power solution   (b) Best temperature solution

(c) Best QoS solution   (d) Selected trade-off solution

Fig. 4. Best and trade-off NSGA-II+EFT solutions (75 tasks, profile A)

Fig. 4(b), which gives maximum priority to temperature, shows a tight regulation within less than 0.5 C from the reference. It is 81% better than the BAU solution with respect to temperature. However, it being an extreme of the Pareto front, we observe poor power tracking for this solution. Fig. 4(c) shows the best solution in terms of QoS (zero violated deadlines). Finally, Fig. 4(b) presents the selected trade-off solution from the Pareto front which is closest to the ideal vector. While, as expected, this solution does not follow the reference power or temperature as closely as Fig.s 4(a) and 4(b) respectively, it roughly tracks power while maintaining the temperature deviation from the reference at less than 1 C at all times except for a 1.2 C excursion at the end of the simulation.

6   Conclusions and Future Work

This article presented a multiobjective optimization approach for operating a datacenter taking into account power profiles, temperature and QoS. The proposed method combines the NSGA-II evolutionary algorithm with ad-hoc QoS schedulers. The experimental analysis compared three variants of the proposed algorithm against a BAU planning strategy over realistic problem instances.

Accurate solutions were computed regarding the studied objectives (extremes of the Pareto front) as well as interesting trade-off solutions which are clearly superior than the BAU strategy. NSGA-II+ETF computed better results regarding both the multiobjective optimization metrics studied, and the best trade-off solutions. NSGA-II+BD was the second best planning strategy overall.

The main lines for future work are related to further improving the control approach, by including more decision variables in the evolutionary optimization, in order to extend the planning flexibility, among them dynamic voltage and frequency scaling, battery state of charge, and the scheduling itself. The model can be extended to support virtual machines and multi-core architectures, where there is not a one-to-one correspondence between tasks and servers.

The ultimate goal of our research is to design and implement a model predictive control to dynamically regulate the datacenter operation, allowing to update the state of the system and solving the optimization problem as more information arrives. High performance computing techniques should be applied in order to speed up the optimization process, allowing to take decisions on-the-fly and act/react when unpredictable events occur.

References

1. Ahmad, I., Ranka, S.: Handbook of Energy-Aware and Green Computing. Chapman & Hall/CRC (2012)
2. Aikema, D., Simmonds, R., Zareipour, H.: Datacenters in the ancillary services market. In: Int. Green Computing Conf., pp. 1–10 (2012)
3. Bäck, T., Fogel, D., Michalewicz, Z. (eds.): Handbook of evolutionary computation. Oxford University Press (1997)
4. Coello, C., Van Veldhuizen, D., Lamont, G.: Evolutionary algorithms for solving multi-objective problems. Kluwer, New York (2002)
5. Deb, K.: Multi-Objective Optimization using Evolutionary Algorithms. J. Wiley & Sons, Chichester (2001)
6. Dorronsoro, B., Nesmachnow, S., Taheri, J., Zomaya, A., Talbi, E.G., Bouvry, P.: A hierarchical approach for energy-efficient scheduling of large workloads in multicore distributed systems. Sust. Computing (2014)
7. Ghamkhari, M., Mohsenian-Rad, H.: Data centers to offer ancillary services. In: 3rd Int. Conf. on Smart Grid Communications, pp. 436–441 (2012)
8. Goiri, I., Katsak, W., Le, K., Nguyen, T., Bianchini, R.: Parasol and GreenSwitch: managing datacenters powered by renewable energy. In: 18th Int. Conf. on Architectural Support for Programming Languages and Operating Systems, pp. 51–64 (2013)
9. Goiri, I., Le, K., Haque, M., Beauchea, R., Nguyen, T., Guitart, J., Torres, J., Bianchini, R.: GreenSlot: Scheduling energy consumption in green datacenters. In: Int. Conf. for High Performance Computing, Networking, Storage and Analysis (2011)
10. Goiri, I., Le, K., Nguyen, T., Guitart, J., Torres, J., Bianchini, R.: GreenHadoop: Leveraging green energy in data-processing frameworks. In: 7th European Conf. on Computer Systems, pp. 57–70 (2012)

11. Iturriaga, S., Nesmachnow, S., Dorronsoro, B., Bouvry, P.: Energy efficient scheduling in heterogeneous systems with a parallel multiobjective local search. Computing and Informatics Journal 32(2), 273–294 (2013)
12. Khan, S., Ahmad, I.: A cooperative game theoretical technique for joint optimization of energy consumption and response time in computational grids. IEEE Trans. Parallel Distrib. Syst. 20, 346–360 (2009)
13. Kim, J.K., Siegel, H., Maciejewski, A., Eigenmann, R.: Dynamic resource management in energy constrained heterogeneous computing systems using voltage scaling. IEEE Trans. Parallel Distrib. Syst. 19, 1445–1457 (2008)
14. Koomey, J.: Growth in data center electricity use 2005–2010. Analytic Press (2011)
15. Krioukov, A., Alspaugh, S., Mohan, P., Dawson, S., Culler, D., Katz, R.: Design and evaluation of an energy agile computing cluster. Tech. Rep. UCB/EECS-2012-13, University of California, Berkeley (2012)
16. Le, K., Bianchini, R., Zhang, J., Jaluria, Y., Meng, J., Nguyen, T.: Reducing electricity cost through virtual machine placement in high performance computing clouds. In: Int. Conf. for High Performance Computing, Networking, Storage and Analysis (2011)
17. Lee, Y., Zomaya, A.: Energy conscious scheduling for distributed computing systems under different operating conditions. IEEE Trans. Parallel Distrib. Syst. 22, 1374–1381 (2011)
18. Lennart, L.: System identification: theory for the user (1999)
19. Li, Y., Liu, Y., Qian, D.: A heuristic energy-aware scheduling algorithm for heterogeneous clusters. In: 15th Int. Conf. on Parallel and Distributed Systems, pp. 407–413 (2009)
20. Lindberg, P., Leingang, J., Lysaker, D., Khan, S., Li, J.: Comparison and analysis of eight scheduling heuristics for the optimization of energy consumption and makespan in large-scale distributed systems. The Journal of Supercomputing 59(1), 323–360 (2012)
21. Liu, Z., Chen, Y., Bash, C., Wierman, A., Gmach, D., Wang, Z., Marwah, M., Hyser, C.: Renewable and cooling aware workload management for sustainable data centers. Performance Evaluation Review 40, 175–186 (2012)
22. Mezmaz, M., Melab, N., Kessaci, Y., Lee, Y., Talbi, E., Zomaya, A., Tuyttens, D.: A parallel bi-objective hybrid metaheuristic for energy-aware scheduling for cloud computing systems. Journal Parallel Distribed Computation 71, 1497–1508 (2011)
23. Nesmachnow, S.: Computación científica de alto desempeño en la Facultad de Ingeniería, Universidad de la República. Revista de la Asociación de Ingenieros del Uruguay 61, 12–15 (2010)
24. Nesmachnow, S., Dorronsoro, B., Pecero, J.E., Bouvry, P.: Energy-aware scheduling on multicore heterogeneous grid computing systems. Journal of Grid Computing 11(4), 653–680 (2013)
25. Nesmachnow, S., Perfumo, C., Goiri, I.: Controlling datacenter power consumption while maintaining temperature and QoS levels. In: 3rd IEEE Int. Conf. on Cloud Networking (2014)
26. Pinel, F., Dorronsoro, B., Pecero, J., Bouvry, P., Khan, S.: A two-phase heuristic for the energy-efficient scheduling of independent tasks on computational grids. Cluster Computing 16(3), 421–433 (2013)
27. Wang, R., Kandasamy, N., Nwankpa, C., Kaeli, D.R.: Datacenters as controllable load resources in the electricity market. In: IEEE 33rd Int. Conf. on Distributed Computing Systems, pp. 176–185 (2013)
28. Zomaya, A.Y., Lee, Y.C.: Energy Efficient Distributed Computing Systems. Wiley-IEEE Computer Society Press (2012)

An Empirical Study of the Robustness of Energy-Aware Schedulers for High Performance Computing Systems under Uncertainty

Santiago Iturriaga, Sebastián García, and Sergio Nesmachnow

Universidad de la República
Montevideo, Uruguay
{siturria,sgarcia,sergion}@fing.edu.uy

Abstract. This article presents an empirical evaluation of energy-aware schedulers under uncertainties in both the execution time of tasks and the energy consumption of the computing infrastructure. We address an important problem with direct application in current clusters and distributed computing systems, by analyzing how the list scheduling techniques proposed in a previous work behave when considering errors in the execution time estimation of tasks and realistic deviations in the power consumption. The experimental evaluation is performed over realistic workloads and scenarios, and validated by in-situ measurements using a power distribution unit. Results demonstrate that errors in real-world scenarios have a significant impact on the accuracy of the scheduling algorithms. Different online and offline scheduling approaches were evaluated, and online approach showed improvements of up to 32% in computing performance and up to 18% in energy consumption over the offline approach using the same scheduling algorithm.

Keywords: HPC, scheduling, energy-aware, uncertainty.

1 Introduction

Nowadays, energy efficiency is a major concern when operating clusters, datacenters, and grid/cloud computing infrastructures. From a global perspective, all issues related to energy consumption raise several concerns for the scientific community, including economic, environmental, and system performance [11].

Energy consumption on computing systems does not only depend on the energy efficiency and features of the hardware, but also on the software used for task planning [1]. Among many different strategies for reducing the energy consumption,energy-aware scheduling techniques have emerged as useful alternatives for accurate planning and lowering the power required for operation [16]. Energy reduction techniques are usually based on limiting the computing power of the computing elements. They are in conflict with the system performance, so applying them has an impact on the Quality of Service (QoS) perceived by the user. Multi-objective formulations of the scheduling problem have been formulated to account for the specific features of the trade-off between energy utilization and performance [7].

G. Hernández et al. (Eds.): CARLA 2014, CCIS 485, pp. 143–157, 2014.
© Springer-Verlag Berlin Heidelberg 2014

The main trend on the scientific community in energy-aware scheduling is based on optimizing the energy consumption of the computing elements since the processor is the main energy consuming element among the hardware components. The processor also offers the most flexible options for energy management, such as dynamic voltage and frequency scaling (DVFS), dynamic power management, slack sharing and reclamation, and other techniques [20].

Many scheduling algorithms are based on assuming that the time required to perform every task is known in advance, and the planning is performed according to that input information. However, that assumption does not hold true in the case of computational infrastructures, where users submit their jobs to be executed on heterogeneous computing elements. Accurately predicting the execution time for individual tasks is a very hard problem, mainly because the actual execution time depends on many factors including the hardware features, communications and delays due to infrastructure and parallel execution, resource availability, among others. Estimation models using task profiling and benchmarking have been proposed since the early 1990's [9,10], but they rely on specific hardware features and computing models that are not fully reasonable for nowadays clusters and distributed computing infrastructures. Furthermore, current models for predicting the energy consumption do include some unrealistic approximations about the power utilization, especially in the case of complex multicore servers [16].

This article presents an empirical evaluation of energy-aware schedulers in heterogeneous computing (HC) scenarios that consider uncertainties in both the execution time of tasks and the energy consumption for a given computing infrastructure. We propose three variants of each of the best energy-aware list scheduling techniques proposed in our previous work [16]. Then, we analyze their behavior when addressing specific instances of the energy-aware scheduling problem in multicore HC systems, accounting for realistic errors in the estimation of the execution time of tasks, and specific deviations in the power consumption calculation when using a standard energy model for computing systems.

The main contribution of this article consists in proposing novel scheduling algorithms and reporting their experimental evaluation performed over realistic workloads and scenarios, validated by in-situ measurements using a power distribution unit. The empirical results demonstrate that error in real-world scenarios have a significant impact on the accuracy of the scheduling algorithms. Different scheduling approaches were evaluated, and the online approach showed improvements of up to 32% in computing performance and up to 18% in energy consumption over the offline approach using the same scheduling algorithm.

The paper is organized as follows. Section 2 describes the energy-aware scheduling problem under uncertainty. A review of related work is presented in Section 3. The heuristics for energy-aware scheduling in high performance computing systems are introduced in Section 4, just before the description of our model for uncertainty in Section 5. The experimental analysis of the proposed heuristics is reported in Section 6, Finally, Section 7 presents the conclusions and formulates the main lines for future work.

2   Robust Energy-Aware Scheduling under Uncertainty

This section describes the robust energy-aware scheduling problem in HC systems under conditions of uncertainty.

2.1   The Energy-Aware Scheduling Problem

In this article, we consider a multi-objective version of the scheduling problem in multicore HC systems, taking into account the minimization of the makespan and energy consumption. We call this problem the Makespan-Energy Heterogeneous Computing Scheduling Problem (ME-HCSP). The mathematical formulation for the problem considers the following elements:

- A HC system composed of a set of multicore machines $P = \{m_1, \ldots, m_M\}$; each machine having $NC(m_i)$ processing cores and processing speed $S(m_i)$.
- A collection of tasks $T = \{t_1, \ldots, t_N\}$ to be executed on the system, each task arrives in time $ARR(t_i)$.
- An *execution time function* $ET : T \times P \to \mathbf{R}^+$, where $ET(t_i, m_j)$ is the time required to execute task t_i on machine m_j.
- An *execution time error function* $\Delta_{ET} : T \times P \to \mathbf{R}^+$, where $\Delta_{ET}(t_i, m_j)$ is the error introduced when estimating $ET(t_i, m_j)$.
- An *energy consumption function* $EC : T \times P \to \mathbf{R}^+$, where $EC(t_i, m_j)$ is the energy required to execute task t_i on machine m_j, and $EC_{IDLE}(m_j)$ is the energy that machine m_j consumes in idle state.
- An *energy consumption error function* $\Delta_{EC} : T \times P \to \mathbf{R}$, where $\Delta_{EC}(t_i, m_j)$ is the error introduced when estimating $EC(t_i, m_j)$.

The goal of the ME-HCSP is to find an assignment function $f : T^N \to P^M$ which simultaneously minimizes the *makespan* and the *total energy consumption* metrics. The assignment function f should schedule each task t_i to be executed without preemption on some machine m_j at some time $ST(t_i)$, with $ST(t_i) \geq ARR(t_i)$. The makespan metric is defined as the maximum completion time $C_{max} = \max_{t_i \in T} C(t_i)$, where the completion time of task t_i is $C(t_i) = ST(t_i) + ET(t_i, m_j)$. The energy required to execute the task t_i in the machine m_j, given by $EC(t_i, m_j)$, depends on the execution time of the task t_i in machine m_j, $ET(t_i, m_j)$, and the energy consumption of the machine m_j. The *total energy consumption* is defined as shown in Equation 1.

$$\sum_{\substack{t_i \in T: \\ f(t_i) = m_j}} EC(t_i, m_j) + \Delta_{EC}(t_i, m_j) + \sum_{m_j \in P} EC_{IDLE}(m_j) \qquad (1)$$

Regarding the energy consumption, in this work we apply the model for multicore computing systems introduced in our previous work [16]. In this model, the energy consumption of a task is estimated by assuming the task is CPU-bound and approximating its energy consumption by the energy consumption of the CPU when executing that task. This was found to be an accurate approximation in an HPC systems where most tasks are CPU intensive and where the

CPU is the most energy consuming device. This model states that the total energy consumption accounts for both the energy required to execute the assigned tasks, and the energy that each machine consumes in idle state. Therefore, we do estimations for the worst case scenarios because in real systems idle machines can be changed to an energy saving mode (or switched off).

In the previous formulation all tasks can be independently executed, disregarding the execution order. The independent task model is common in grid and volunteer-based computing infrastructures, as well as in BoT applications.

2.2   Robust Scheduling

Most modern High Performance Computing (HPC) systems are comprised of a large number of distributed and heterogeneous computing elements. The execution times of tasks in these HPC systems is inherently unpredictable [5,15]; computing element heterogeneity and network communication delays contribute a great deal to task execution time uncertainty. But arguably the major factor of uncertainty when scheduling tasks in HPC systems is introduced by the users of the system when specifying the *Estimated Execution Time* (EET), defined as $EET = ET + \Delta_{ET}$. The ET of all tasks is a very important component in order to compute an accurate task schedule, but because it is unknown for the scheduling algorithm, nowadays HPC systems relay on user estimates of tasks execution times, the EET. This is true for most of the modern scheduling products such as Load Leveler, Maui, Open Grid Scheduler, etc. [19].

Studies show the EET estimates are highly inaccurate, in some cases the ET of a significant number of jobs account for 10% or less of their EET [3]. There are a number of reasons for the high inaccuracy of the EET estimates. The first being that a significant number of tasks fail to execute because of task initialization errors. Though this is more related to configuring errors than to inaccurate EET, it still needs be considered by the scheduling algorithm. Another reason is that tasks that do execute correctly are largely overestimated. This is because many systems kill an executing task after its EET has been consumed, hence the EET estimate is not the true user estimate, but rather the maximum amount of time the user is willing to wait for the task execution output before it is acceptable for the task to be killed by the system [15]. Real-world execution traces show this is true even for tasks following the independent task model [19].

Energy consumption estimation is greatly affected by execution time estimation errors since energy consumption directly depends on the execution time of the scheduled tasks. But this is not the only uncertainty source; although the CPU is the most energy consuming device in HPC systems, certainly it is not the only one. Energy consumption is also affected by the use of peripheral devices (such as hard drives, network adapters, etc.) and by the use of cooling devices (such as cooling fans, air conditioning, etc.).

Uncertainty in the energy consumption and the execution time of tasks in HPC systems can lead to a considerable performance loss in task execution [19]. Hence, looking for scheduling solutions that are robust against such inaccuracies may help alleviate, or even neglect, the performance decrease they produce.

3   Related Work

Several works in the related literature have studied algorithms to find *flexible* solutions to the scheduling problem, i.e. they are able to handle some kind of uncertainties related to faults in the system, or they are expected to be less affected by these uncertainties than a regular scheduler.

Ali et al. [2] proposed a mathematical formulation of a metric for the robustness which can be applied to various parallel and distributed systems. The authors apply this metric to two example systems, one of them being the independent application allocation system that we are considering in this paper. When adopting this robustness metric, it is guaranteed that if the collective difference of the actual task execution times versus the estimated times is within a certain calculated range, then the given makespan requirement will be met. This metric has been used in a number of related works [7,13].

Several works aim at predicting an uncertainty value in order to include this prediction into the scheduling knowledge. All these works focus on predicting execution time uncertainty while considering a simple FCFS scheduling approach; they do not consider the energy consumption of the system. Tsafrir et al. [19] proposed a system-generated prediction system based on users' history and applied it to the EASY [8] algorithm. Using this approach they achieved a 25% average reduction in wait time and slowdown. Tran et al. [14] presented a method for predicting task execution time based on historical data. Using this predictor they were able to improve accuracy by up to 32%. The CREASY scheduler by Shmueli et al. [17] exploits knowledge on user behavior to improve QoS of the system. Using an alternative simulation methodology called site-level simulation they were able to improve user productivity by up to 50%. Tang et al. [18] analyzed the impact of execution time estimates in scheduling algorithms on the Blue Gene/P, designing and implementing a number of schemes for adjusting estimates. These schemes make use of historical workload data in order to predict the accuracy of a task estimation considering user and project information. The analysis showed the user estimates are highly inaccurate with only 31–33% of all the considered tasks having an estimation accuracy of 80% or more, and up to 21–28% having an accuracy of 20% or less. The experiments showed the adjusting schemes were able to improve up to 20% the performance of the system.

In our previous work [16], the model for multi-core computing systems that we apply in this article was introduced. Our approach did not apply DVFS nor other specific techniques for power/energy management. Instead, we proposed an energy consumption model (MIN/MAX model) based on the energy required to execute tasks at full capacity (E_{MAX}), the energy when not all the available cores of the machine are used, and the energy that each machine on the system consumes in idle state (E_{IDLE}). In our previous work, we proposed twenty fast list scheduling methods adapted to solve the bi-objective problem we also consider here, by simultaneously optimizing both makespan and energy consumption when executing independent BoT applications on a computing system composed of multi-core computers.

In this work we propose to study the impact on real-world scenarios of both execution time and energy consumption uncertainties when considering system performance and energy efficiency objectives. We evaluate a set of online and offline variants of scheduling algorithms proposed in [16] which simultaneously consider both objectives. To the best of our knowledge, this is the first work to evaluate energy consumption uncertainty in a computing scheduling problem.

4   Robustness of Energy Aware Scheduling Heuristics

In this work we consider three well-known scheduling approaches which can be classified as *offline*, *online greedy*, and *online batch* [12]. The offline approach assumes all tasks are known beforehand, hence the scheduling algorithm needs only to be executed once and is able to consider all the tasks simultaneously for the scheduling decisions. This approach is definitely the best in an uncertainty free problem, since the scheduling algorithm is provided with absolutely all the available information for making scheduling decision. Unfortunately, because the scheduling algorithm is executed only once, it is unable to dynamically adjust the scheduling to cope with uncertainty values.

On the other hand, in the online approach tasks are not known by the scheduling algorithm until they arrive. This requires the scheduling algorithm to be executed multiple times for completely scheduling a task workload. We tackle the online scheduling problems using two different techniques, one is a greedy technique and the other is a batch oriented technique. In the online greedy approach, tasks are scheduled one at a time as soon as they arrive and are never rescheduled. This approach is very simple and straightforward, and is able to react to some degree to uncertainty in the data. On the downside, the information available to the scheduler for making the scheduling decisions is minimal.

The online batch approach tackles some of the previously presented problems. In this approach the scheduling algorithm is re-executed after a predefined time step, all the tasks that arrive in a given time-step are delayed, are grouped as a batch, and are scheduled together by the scheduling algorithm. This way the online problem is treated as a succession of smaller offline problems. We consider two further improvements to this approach. The first being that in every scheduling batch not only the tasks that arrive in that time step are considered by the scheduler, but also all the tasks from previous batches already scheduled but which have not started their execution (i.e. are still queued). The second improvement is that the scheduling algorithm is not executed in every time step, it is executed only if in the current time step some meaningful event has occurred (i.e. at least one task has finished or at least a new task has arrived).

In this work we evaluate five different scheduling algorithms following the previous approaches. For the offline and online batch approaches we considered three multiobjective two-phase list-scheduling algorithms proposed in [16]: MaxMin, MaxMIN, and SuffMIN. Because a two-phase approach is not applicable to the online greedy approach, two simple single-objective algorithms were proposed: Min and MIN. The algorithms work as follows:

- *MaxMin* is a traditional two-phase heuristic which considers the makespan objective in both phases. In the first phase the task t with the largest compute time is selected. In the second phase task t is assigned to the machine which minimizes the makespan.
- *MaxMIN* is a two-phase heuristic which considers the makespan objective in the first phase and the energy consumption in the second. In the first phase the task t with the largest compute time is selected. In the second phase task t is assigned to the machine which minimizes the energy consumption.
- *SuffMIN* again considers the makespan objective in the first phase and the energy consumption in the second. In the first phase the task t which suffers the most if not assigned right away is selected. In the second phase task t is assigned to the machine which minimizes the energy consumption.
- *Min* and *MIN* are one-phase greedy heuristics that assign tasks as they arrive, considering the makespan (*Min*) and the energy consumption (*MIN*).

5   Modeling Uncertainty

In this work we consider two sources of uncertainty, the task execution time (ET) and the machine energy consumption (EC). We present here the task execution time model and the energy consumption model proposed in this work.

5.1   The Task Execution Time Uncertainty Model

One of the most popular models for modelling execution time uncertainty is the f-model [15]. This model assumes the task's EET is uniformly distributed within $[ET, (f+1)ET]$, where f is some positive factor. When $f = 0$ then $\Delta_{ET} = 0$ hence estimates are identical to execution times, and the larger the f-value the greater the user inaccuracy in the system. In this work we perform some empirical analysis and show the f-model does not fit the empirical data considered in the analysis, hence we deduce some simple model from the data in order to model task execution time uncertainty in this work.

In order to construct a model for uncertainty in the tasks execution time we performed an empirical study using workloads from three real-world HPC infrastructures. The analysis is two-fold, first we studied the EET of the tasks to characterize the user behavior when requesting execution time for their tasks, and second we studied the Δ_{ET} of the tasks considering their requested EET.

The first analyzed infrastructure is the CEA Curie system, a large HPC infrastructure with 93312 cores during the considered time span. A workload with 773138 tasks, which spans for 20 months (Feb. 2011–Oct. 2012), was used. We also studied the RICC infrastructure, a medium sized system with 9216 cores. A workload with 447794 tasks, which spans for 5 months (May 2010 to Sept. 2010) was used. Finally, we studied the Cluster FING system, a small sized system which was comprised of 408 cores during the considered time span. For the Cluster FING system a 31 months period was analyzed, in this period dated between November 2011 and June 2014, a total of 500000 tasks were executed.

The CEA Curie and RICC task workloads are available at the Parallel Workloads Archive http://www.cs.huji.ac.il/labs/parallel/workload while the Cluster FING workload is available at www.fing.edu.uy/cluster.

When analyzing the EET of the tasks in the studied real-world workloads, we found that most EETs are within either less than 20% or more than 80% of the maximum execution time allowed in the system. Hence, we propose grouping tasks in the workloads in 5 different groups: in the first group tasks which have EET between 0% and 20% of the maximum execution time, in the second groups tasks with EET between 20% and 40%, then between 40% and 60%, then between 60% and 80%, and finally between 80% and 100% (see Fig. 1).

When averaging the results for the three real-world workloads, we see that in average 50% of the tasks request less than 20% of the maximum allowed execution time, 45% of the tasks request more than 80% of the maximum execution time, and the remaining 5% is somewhat uniformly distributed.

Regarding Δ_{ET}, the workload analysis showed that the estimation errors are rather large and, again, not uniformly distributed. Further analysis showed that a significantly large number of tasks present either a quite accurate estimation or a very inaccurate estimation. This is shown in Fig. 1. This empirical findings are similar to the ones presented by Tsafrir [19]. Based on this data we propose three different error scenarios for our model: Δ_{ET}^{low} with an average error of 48%, Δ_{ET}^{med} with an average error of 56%, and Δ_{ET}^{high} with an average error of 67%.

relative EET	percentage of tasks
[0, 20%)	50%
[20%, 40%)	2%
[40%, 60%)	2%
[60%, 80%)	1%
[80%, 100%]	45%

relative EET error	percentage of tasks		
	Δ_{ET}^{low}	Δ_{ET}^{med}	Δ_{ET}^{high}
[0, 40%)	45%	35%	25%
[40%, 75%)	30%	25%	15%
[75%, 95%)	5%	10%	20%
[95%, 100%]	20%	30%	40%

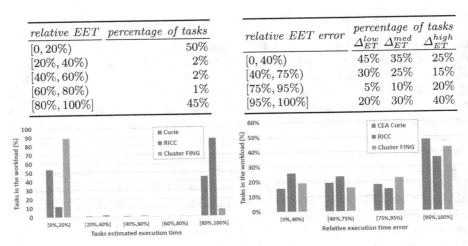

Fig. 1. Analysis of the proposed workloads

5.2 The Energy Consumption Uncertainty Model

We conducted a set of empirical evaluations in order to determine the uncertainty model for the energy consumption.

Our starting point was the high-level theoretical linear increasing model that we originally introduced in our previous work [16]. This model proposes a linear increase in the energy consumption (from E_{IDLE} to E_{MAX}) when using an increasing number of CPU cores. However, the model is only focused on the energy consumption of the processor; it does not take into account the energy consumption due to memory utilization and I/O devices. Thus, in this work we aim at validating the energy consumption model and estimate deviations from the previous model due to other energy consuming components.

In order to evaluate the model, three basic tests were executed using a server from our HPC infrastructure at Universidad de la República. The server is an HP Proliant DL385 G7 server with two AMD Opteron 6172 processors with 12 cores running at 2.1 GH, and 24 GB of RAM memory.

For the energy evaluation, a specialized Power Distribution Unit (PDU) was used: CyberPower PDU20SWHVIEC8FNET. We connected only the server running the tests to the PDU, as it lacks the capability of per outlet measurement. A specific application was developed to poll and log the energy consumption data, due to a limitation on the granularity of the logging capabilities of the PDU, which is only able to save log data at a rate of one measurement per minute. The logging application was executed in a separated computer also connected to the PDU, in order to avoid adding its own energy consumption to the measurements. Using the logging application, we were able to log a minimum of four and a mean of six instant energy measurements per second during each test.

The tests consist in executing an increasing number of applications in order to use different number of cores, from a single core up to twenty four cores. The applications used in the tests range from a simple mathematical operation to a complex transformation, in order to evaluate different scenarios:

1. *Single loop.* The first test consists on running a simple C++ loop performing a multiplication a huge number of times, this way ensuring a fully CPU-bound test using only one CPU.

2. *LINPACK.* The second test is based on an open source sequential implementation of the LINPACK benchmark [6]. We adjusted the LINPACK parameters to have an acceptable execution time while not using too much memory, to reduce the race for cache and RAM memories when running 24 instances.

3. *Fast Fourier Transform.* This test is similar to the previous one, but based on an open source implementation of the Fast Fourier Transform [4]. In this case, the evaluation was made using only up to 23 instances of the test, because the parameter setting resulted in an execution time for twenty-four instances that doubled the twenty-three one, due to race for RAM memory.

In the tests, the energy consumption was estimated from the logs obtained using the PDU by applying an interpolation of the instant power measurements. The graphics in Figure 2 shows the energy consumption when using an increasing number of cores for the three applications in the test (loop, LINPACK, and FFT, respectively). The fourth graphic in Figure 2 is an example of the instant power usage as function of time for the loop test case, where the execution of the tests using an increasing number of cores were performed one after the other.

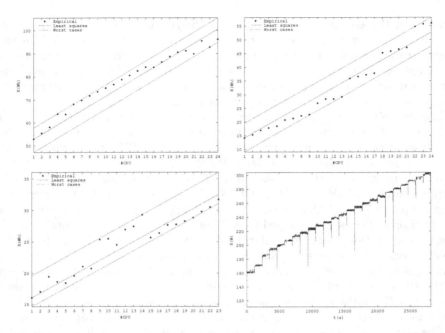

Fig. 2. Energy consumption for the three applications in the test (loop, LINPACK, and FFT, respectively), and instant power usage sample (loop test case)

Table 1 reports the maximum (worst case) and mean values for the error and the deviation from linearity in the energy consumption, along with the relative error values for each application in the test suite.

Table 1. Error results and deviation from linearity for the three tests performed

test	error		deviation from linearity		relative error	
	maximum	*mean*	*maximum*	*mean*	*maximum (%)*	*mean (%)*
simple loop	5.71	2.56	2.48	1.11	7.36	**3.34**
LINPACK	5.36	2.39	2.74	1.23	21.58	**7.98**
FFT	3.52	1.26	2.82	1.01	13.11	**4.88**

The numerical results validates the linear increasing energy consumption model, as we verify that the deviation from linearity when using real applications is below 3%; and the relative error on the energy consumption is below 8%, and about 5% in average. These results demonstrate that no significant impact is observed when executing CPU-oriented applications, such as the ones commonly executed in HPC facilities. Taking into account the results of the empirical analysis, we assume that the energy consumption error for multicore computers is in the range [-5%,5%].

6   Experimental Analysis

This section reports the experimental analysis of the proposed heuristics for robust energy-aware scheduling under uncertainty.

6.1   Problem Instances

We created a number of problem instances to evaluate the scheduling algorithm using the proposed uncertainty model. Each problem instance is defined by the task *workload*, describing the tasks to be executed in the system, and the machine *scenario*, describing the hardware infrastructure to execute the tasks.

The machine scenarios were created using the model for energy consumption in multicore computers [16] which makes use of a list of CPU and generates each scenario selecting machines using a uniform probability distribution. However, in this work we propose an alternative machine selection method for constructing each scenario: the CPUs are sorted according to their generation, the mean of the Gaussian probability distribution is uniformly selected, and two different standard deviation values are used, σ_{high} and σ_{low}. These σ values represent the machine heterogeneity in the generated scenario and they are defined as $\sigma_{high}=0.25 \times M$ and $\sigma_{low}=0.025 \times M$, where M is the number of machines in the scenario. This new machine selection method models a more realistic computing infrastructure comprised of sets of machines with similar computing power.

Scenarios of three different sizes were generated for this work following this new approach, $M \in \{8, 12, 16\}$. A total of **800** scenarios were generated for each of the considered number of machines, with the smallest 8-machine scenarios comprising an average of 131 cores per scenario, and the largest 16-machine scenarios comprising an average of 262 cores per scenario.

Regarding the task workload generation, 1024 tasks were generated for each workload using a Poisson probability distribution to model their arrival time. The experiments were performed using the lowest and highest average arrival rates of the three real-world workloads analyzed, $\lambda_{low} = 0.317$ and $\lambda_{high} = 0.634$. With this settings, the average simulation time of each 1024-tasks workload is around 53 minutes when using λ_{low} and around 26 minutes when using λ_{high}.

We fixed the maximum allowed time for each task execution to be 28 hours, which considering the proposed uncertainty model results in an average task EET of 13.7 hours and an average task ET of 7.8 hours.

A total of **400** task workloads were generated, 50 workloads for each combination of execution time error rate (Δ_{ET}) and arrival rate (λ). Each workload is evaluated with two machine scenarios, with high and low heterogeneity. Hence, a total of 800 experiments were conducted with different problem instances.

6.2   Results and Discussion

In this section we present and discuss the experimental analysis results for all the performed experiments.

Table 2. Average makespan and energy deviation for the offline algorithms

	num. machines	Δ_{ET}	offline heuristic		
			MaxMin	MaxMIN	SuffMIN
makespan	8	low	24.2%	**16.8%**	29.9%
		med.	31.4%	**22.2%**	37.9%
		high	38.4%	**28.0%**	46.6%
	12	low	22.1%	**13.1%**	28.9%
		med.	27.7%	**16.7%**	36.0%
		high	34.0%	**21.7%**	45.0%
	16	low	20.7%	**11.7%**	27.8%
		med.	23.6%	**13.1%**	33.3%
		high	29.2%	**18.1%**	42.0%
energy	8	low	33.7%	37.6%	**26.8%**
		med.	42.0%	45.5%	**35.9%**
		high	53.1%	54.8%	**48.5%**
	12	low	30.6%	35.7%	**15.5%**
		med.	38.1%	42.9%	**26.5%**
		high	50.1%	52.5%	**41.9%**
	16	low	28.5%	34.8%	**11.3%**
		med.	37.0%	41.5%	**20.0%**
		high	46.5%	50.5%	**32.3%**

First we explore the deviation from the expected schedule when using the offline scheduling algorithms. Table 2 presents the relative deviation between the expected and the actual makespan and energy consumption for each algorithm. Because of the nature of the problem the expected makespan and energy consumption is an upper bound of the actual values of the schedule, hence all deviation is an improvement form the expected schedule.

We can see the schedule deviation in both objectives increases as the error rate increases, and decreases as the problem dimension increases. When comparing the scheduling algorithms, results show the MaxMIN algorithm is the most robust for the makespan objective, while SuffMIN is the most robust for the energy consumption objective. However, the gap between the expected and the actual metrics of the schedules is significant for all the scenarios and all the scheduling algorithms. The best results are marked in **bold**.

Table 3 compares the considered algorithms showing their average relative improvement with respect to the worse performing algorithm for each scenario and objective. Results show the offline MaxMin computes the most accurate schedules for both objectives in every scenario when the error rate (Δ_{ET}) is none, increasing its accuracy as the problem dimension increases. This was expected as the offline algorithm is the one considering the greater amount of scheduling information. When considering problem scenarios with higher error rates, it can be seen that the online batch algorithms outperform the offline algorithms. The scheduling algorithms using the online approach are able to react to uncertainty and improve the accuracy of the schedule. The online batch MaxMin computes the most accurate schedules for the makespan objective, and the online batch MaxMIN computes the most accurate schedules for the energy consumption objective. It can be seen that the accuracy of the online batch algorithms increases with the problem dimension and the error rate, achieving an improvement of up

Table 3. Average makespan and energy consumption improvement

			heuristic							
			offline			online				
						batch			greedy	
		Δ_{ET}	MaxMin	MaxMIN	SuffMIN	MaxMin	MaxMIN	SuffMIN	Min	MIN
makespan	8 mach.	none	**34.7%**	22.0%	0.7%	34.4%	34.0%	29.8%	27.4%	28.0%
		low	23.1%	15.8%	2.4%	**44.4%**	44.2%	38.1%	22.7%	21.8%
		med.	22.0%	16.2%	3.4%	**47.2%**	46.3%	40.6%	22.2%	19.9%
		high	16.8%	15.0%	5.4%	**49.1%**	48.4%	43.2%	20.0%	19.3%
	12 mach.	none	**43.6%**	29.1%	1.3%	42.7%	40.9%	36.3%	35.1%	35.4%
		low	31.0%	23.3%	1.5%	**48.3%**	47.5%	42.1%	28.7%	28.0%
		med.	26.8%	19.9%	2.1%	**49.5%**	47.8%	43.2%	26.4%	25.3%
		high	21.7%	18.6%	3.5%	**48.6%**	47.9%	43.0%	24.1%	22.2%
	16 mach.	none	**48.4%**	32.9%	1.7%	47.0%	43.3%	39.3%	39.1%	38.9%
		low	33.2%	24.5%	1.2%	**47.9%**	46.0%	40.7%	28.9%	28.1%
		med.	32.0%	25.5%	1.2%	**50.2%**	48.5%	43.4%	29.6%	29.1%
		high	28.4%	22.7%	2.4%	**49.6%**	48.4%	44.5%	28.1%	27.0%
energy	8 mach.	none	**13.4%**	8.9%	0.6%	13.2%	13.1%	11.6%	10.8%	11.0%
		low	10.7%	8.0%	1.9%	21.7%	**22.1%**	19.1%	10.8%	10.2%
		med.	10.6%	8.8%	2.7%	24.4%	**24.5%**	21.4%	11.1%	9.7%
		high	9.0%	9.2%	4.2%	27.5%	**27.8%**	24.9%	11.2%	10.6%
	12 mach.	none	**19.4%**	13.9%	0.8%	19.0%	18.4%	16.5%	15.7%	15.9%
		low	15.8%	13.1%	1.2%	25.8%	**26.3%**	23.3%	15.1%	14.6%
		med.	14.4%	11.9%	1.9%	**27.9%**	27.8%	25.0%	14.5%	13.8%
		high	12.2%	11.6%	2.8%	28.7%	**29.2%**	26.2%	14.5%	13.2%
	16 mach.	none	**23.6%**	17.5%	1.1%	22.9%	21.6%	19.5%	19.5%	19.4%
		low	17.4%	14.2%	1.0%	**26.2%**	26.1%	23.0%	15.5%	14.9%
		med.	17.9%	15.7%	1.0%	**29.4%**	29.4%	26.1%	17.1%	16.8%
		high	17.6%	15.3%	2.1%	31.6%	**32.0%**	29.0%	18.1%	17.3%

Table 4. Number of problem instances in which each of the proposed heuristic compute the best makespan and energy consumption value

			heuristic							
			offline			online				
						batch			greedy	
		Δ_{ET}	MaxMin	MaxMIN	SuffMIN	MaxMin	MaxMIN	SuffMIN	Min	MIN
makespan	8 mach.	none	**153**	2	0	32	13	0	0	0
		low	1	0	0	**108**	89	4	0	0
		med.	2	0	0	**125**	70	5	0	0
		high	1	0	0	**102**	82	16	0	0
	12 mach.	none	**151**	1	0	24	23	1	0	0
		low	7	0	0	**115**	74	4	0	0
		med.	7	2	0	**122**	61	12	0	0
		high	4	0	0	91	89	16	0	1
	16 mach.	none	**170**	1	0	20	9	0	0	0
		low	18	0	0	**111**	69	2	0	0
		med.	11	0	0	**101**	85	7	0	0
		high	14	1	0	**96**	78	13	0	0
energy	8 mach.	none	47	13	2	**69**	58	11	0	0
		low	0	0	0	73	**117**	10	0	0
		med.	0	2	1	91	**100**	6	0	0
		high	0	0	0	77	**103**	20	0	0
	12 mach.	none	**80**	10	0	53	53	4	0	0
		low	5	0	0	66	**119**	10	0	0
		med.	2	2	0	85	**94**	16	0	1
		high	1	0	0	63	**108**	26	1	1
	16 mach.	none	**93**	22	3	33	46	3	0	0
		low	10	3	0	76	**101**	10	0	0
		med.	4	0	0	70	**114**	11	1	0
		high	7	4	0	62	**107**	19	0	1

to 50.2% for the makespan and up to 32.0% for the energy consumption. When comparing the online batch and offline approaches of the best algorithms, results show the online batch MaxMin is up to 32.3% more accurate than the offline MaxMin for the makespan, and the online batch MaxMIN is up to 18% more accurate than the offline MaxMIN for the energy consumption.

Table 4 shows the number of problem instances in which each algorithm is able to compute the most accurate schedule for each objective. It can be seen that the previous results hold. The most accurate heuristic is the offline MaxMin when no error level is considered. The online batch MaxMin is the most accurate for the makespan objective when higher error rates are considered, and the online batch MaxMIN is the most accurate for the energy consumption objective also when higher error rates are considered. Although the online greedy algorithms are able to compute competitive schedules in average, they are not able to compute the most accurate result for any problem instance.

7   Conclusions and Future Work

This work presented a formulation for the energy-aware scheduling problem considering uncertainties in the execution time of the tasks and in the energy consumption of the computing infrastructure. We analysed three real-world task workloads and proposed a workload generation model considering uncertainties. We also conducted empirical evaluations to validate and extend our previously proposed energy consumption model to consider uncertainty values.

In order to analyse the impact of these uncertainty values we evaluated a set of scheduling algorithms considering different scheduling approaches. Some of these scheduling approaches being better fitted to cope with uncertainties than others. Results show the uncertainty values in real-world scenarios significantly affects the accuracy of the scheduling algorithm, hence considering these uncertainty values may improve the accuracy of a scheduling algorithm.

In future work, we propose to extend our mathematical model to consider parallel non-independent tasks and to characterize the energy consumption of tasks which are not entirely CPU-bound, allowing us to model even more realistic problem instances and to take advantage of technologies such as DVFS. We will work on improving the accuracy of our proposed scheduling algorithms and compare them with some well-known commercial batch scheduler, e.g. Maui.

Acknowledgment. The work of S. Iturriaga, S. García and S. Nesmachnow is partly supported by ANII (project FSE_2013_1_10974) and PEDECIBA, Uruguay.

References

1. Ahmad, I., Ranka, S.: Handbook of Energy-Aware and Green Computing. Chapman & Hall/CRC (2012)
2. Ali, S., Maciejewski, A., Siegel, H., Kim, J.: Measuring the robustness of a resource allocation. IEEE Trans. Parallel Distrib. Syst. 51(7), 630–641 (2004)

3. Bailey Lee, C., Schwartzman, Y., Hardy, J., Snavely, A.: Are user runtime estimates inherently inaccurate? In: Feitelson, D.G., Rudolph, L., Schwiegelshohn, U. (eds.) JSSPP 2004. LNCS, vol. 3277, pp. 253–263. Springer, Heidelberg (2005)
4. Brigham, O.: The Fast Fourier Transform. Prentice-Hall, New Jersey (1974)
5. Cirne, W., Berman, F.: A comprehensive model of the supercomputer workload. In: International Workshop on Workload Characterization, pp. 140–148 (2001)
6. Dongarra, J.: The LINPACK benchmark: An explanation. In: Proceedings of the 1st International Conference on Supercomputing, pp. 456–474 (1988)
7. Dorronsoro, B., Bouvry, P., Cañero, J., Maciejewski, A., Siegel, H.: Multi-objective robust static mapping of independent tasks on grids. In: IEEE Congress on Evolutionary Computation, pp. 3389–3396 (2010)
8. Feitelson, D.G., Rudolph, L., Schwiegelshohn, U.: Parallel job scheduling a status report. In: Feitelson, D.G., Rudolph, L., Schwiegelshohn, U. (eds.) JSSPP 2004. LNCS, vol. 3277, pp. 1–16. Springer, Heidelberg (2005)
9. Ghafoor, A., Yang, J.: Distributed heterogeneous supercomputing management system. IEEE Comput. 26(6), 78–86 (1993)
10. Kafil, M., Ahmad, I.: Optimal task assignment in heterogeneous distributed computing systems. IEEE Concurrency 6(3), 42–51 (1998)
11. Lee, Y., Zomaya, A.: Minimizing energy consumption for precedence-constrained applications using dynamic voltage scaling. In: Proc. of the 9th International Symposium on Cluster Computing and the Grid, Shanghai, China, pp. 92–99 (2009)
12. Leung, J., Kelly, L., Anderson, J.H.: Handbook of Scheduling: Algorithms, Models, and Performance Analysis. CRC Press, Inc., Boca Raton (2004)
13. Mehta, A., Smith, J., Siegel, H., Maciejewski, A., Jayaseelan, A., Ye, B.: Dynamic resource allocation heuristics that manage tradeoff between makespan and robustness. Journal of Supercomputing, Special Issue on Grid Technology 42(1), 33–58 (2007)
14. Minh, T.N., Wolters, L.: Using historical data to predict application runtimes on backfilling parallel systems. In: 18th Euromicro International Conference on Parallel, Distributed and Network-Based Processing, pp. 246–252 (February 2010)
15. Mu'alem, A., Feitelson, D.: Utilization, predictability, workloads, and user runtime estimates in scheduling the ibm sp2 with backfilling. IEEE Trans. Parallel Distrib. Syst. 12(6), 529–543 (2001)
16. Nesmachnow, S., Dorronsoro, B., Pecero, J.E., Bouvry, P.: Energy-aware scheduling on multicore heterogeneous grid computing systems. Journal of Grid Computing 11(4), 653–680 (2013)
17. Shmueli, E., Feitelson, D.: On simulation and design of parallel-systems schedulers: Are we doing the right thing? IEEE Trans. Parallel Distrib. Syst. 20(7), 983–996 (2009)
18. Tang, W., Desai, N., Buettner, D., Lan, Z.: Job scheduling with adjusted runtime estimates on production supercomputers. Journal of Parallel and Distributed Computing 73(7), 926–938 (2013)
19. Tsafrir, D.: Using inaccurate estimates accurately. In: Frachtenberg, E., Schwiegelshohn, U. (eds.) JSSPP 2010. LNCS, vol. 6253, pp. 208–221. Springer, Heidelberg (2010)
20. Zhu, D., Melhem, R., Childers, B.: Scheduling with dynamic voltage/speed adjustment using slack reclamation in multiprocessor real-time systems. IEEE Trans. Parallel Distrib. Syst. 14, 686–700 (2003)

MBSPDiscover: An Automatic Benchmark for MultiBSP Performance Analysis

Marcelo Alaniz[1], Sergio Nesmachnow[2], Brice Goglin[3], Santiago Iturriaga[2], Verónica Gil Gosta[1], and Marcela Printista[1]

[1] Universidad Nacional de San Luis, Argentina
[2] Universidad de la República, Uruguay
[3] Inria Bordeaux–Sud-Ouest, University of Bordeaux, France

Abstract. Multi-Bulk Synchronous Parallel (MultiBSP) is a recently proposed parallel programming model for multicore machines that extends the classic BSP model. MultiBSP is very useful to design algorithms and estimate their running time, which are hard to do in High Performance Computing applications. For a correct estimation of the running time, the main parameters of the MultiBSP model for different multicore architectures need to be determined. This article presents a benchmark proposal for measuring the parameters that characterize the communication and synchronization cost for the model. Our approach discovers automatically the hierarchical structure of the multicore architecture by using a specific tool (hwloc) that allows obtaining runtime information about the machine. We describe the design, implementation and the results of benchmarking two multicore machines. Furthermore, we report the validation of the proposed method by using a real MultiBSP implementation of the vector inner product algorithm and comparing the predicted execution time against the real execution time.

1 Introduction

Performance prediction is an important tool for performance analysis of parallel applications [5]. This technique involves modeling program performance as a function of the hardware and software characteristics of a system. By changing these characteristics in the model, the execution time of standard programs can be accurately predicted for a variety of platforms and configurations.

The Bulk Synchronous Parallel (BSP) model [7], is one of the most popular among several analytical models proposed. The model assumes a BSP abstract machine with identical processors. Each processor has access to its own local memory and they communicate with each other through a all-to-all network, providing uniform point-to-point access time and bandwidth capacity.

The BSP model was introduced for distributed computers, but assuming only one core per computing node. Although the model was very successfully used in the 1990s, it gradually became less used with the emergence of new multicore architectures in the last decade. As the evaluation of computers gained renewed importance, the BSP model was extended to MultiBSP by Valiant [8]. MultiBSP

G. Hernández et al. (Eds.): CARLA 2014, CCIS 485, pp. 158–172, 2014.

extends BSP in two ways: i) it is a hierarchical model, with an arbitrary number of components, taking into account the physical structure of multiple memory and cache levels within single chips as well as in multi-chip architectures; and ii) at each level, MultiBSP incorporates memory size as an additional parameter in the model, which was not included in the original BSP.

In this line of work, the research reported in this paper is focused on solving the problem of characterizing multicore computing architectures, which are described by a series of parameters such as size, latency, and memory levels. When a parallel algorithm based on the MultiBSP computational model is designed, the programmer needs to know the value of the parameters that describe the architecture, since the performance of the resulting algorithm depends on these parameters. Moreover, the MultiBSP programmer needs to conceive his application with multiple levels of abstraction that require the appropriate use of threads, cache memories and the cores that share these caches.

The proposed benchmark has the following features: a) it computes the Multi-BSP parameters using a bottom-up technique for discovering the architecture and building the hierarchy levels using the MultiBSP approach and b) it is implemented using the same library that implements the abstraction levels of the application, so it measures the critical operations taking into account not only the theoretical aspects, but also the specific implementation.

In order to develop the proposed benchmark, we address the following topics: i) based on the detection of the hierarchy of levels in a multicore machine, we show how to translate the hierarchy into the components of an abstract MultiBSP machine. ii) we explain formally all parameters, specially focusing on communication and synchronization costs. iii) we introduce the concept of h-communication, which is an adaptation of the h-relation of BSP for the specific case of shared-memory relations within a single node.

Our benchmark is applied to characterize two High Performance Computing (HPC) multicore machines. We also report the validation of the proposed method by using a real MultiBSP implementation of the vector inner product algorithm and comparing the predicted execution time against the real execution time.

The research reported in this article is developed within the project "Scheduling evaluation in heterogeneous computing systems with hwloc" (SEHLOC[1]). The main goal consists in the development of runtime systems that allow combining characteristics of the software applications and topological information of the computational platforms, in order to get scheduling suggestions to profit from software and hardware affinities and provide a way for efficiently executing realistic applications.

The paper is organized as follows. Section 2 introduces the BSP and Multi-BSP models, and relevant related work about BSP benchmarking. Section 3 describes the design and implementation of the MBSPDiscover benchmark. Section 4 reports the application of the proposed benchmark for two case studies and the validation using a real MultiBSP application. Finally, Section 5 presents the conclusions and formulates the main lines for future work.

---

[1] http://runtime.bordeaux.inria.fr/sehloc/

2   BSP and MultiBSP Models

To set the scope of this paper, this section describes the BSP and MultiBSP models. We start with a brief description of the flat BSP model and how it evolved into the concept of multicore, which emphasizes hierarchies of components.

2.1   The Original BSP Model

The BSP model considers an abstract parallel computer, which is fully modeled by a set of parameters: p—number of processors, s—processor speed, g—communication cost, and l—synchronization cost. Using these parameters, the execution time of any BSP algorithm can be calculated.

In the BSP model, the computations are organized in a sequence of global *supersteps*, which consist of three phases: *i*) every participating processor performs local computations, i.e., each process can only make use of values stored in the local memory of the processor; *ii*) the processes exchange data between themselves to facilitate remote data storage capabilities and *iii*) every participating process must reach the next synchronization barrier, i.e., each process waits until all other processes have reached the same barrier. Then, the next superstep can begin.

The practical model of programming is Single Program Multiple Data (SPMD), implemented as C/C++ program copies running on p processors, wherein communication and synchronization among copies are performed using specific libraries such as BSPlib [4] or PUB [2]. In addition to defining an abstract machine and imposing a structure on parallel programs, the BSP model provides a cost function modeled by the architecture parameters.

The total running time of a BSP program can be calculated as the accumulative sum of the cost of its supersteps, where the cost of each superstep is the sum of three quantities: *i*) w, the maximum number of calculations performed by each processor; *ii*) $h \times g$, where h is the maximum of the messages sent/received by each processor, with each word costing g units of time; and *iii*) l, the time cost of the barrier synchronizing the processors. The effect of the computer architecture is included by the parameters g and l. These values, along with the processor speed s, can be empirically determined for each parallel computer by executing benchmark programs at installation time.

2.2   The New MultiBSP Model

Modern supercomputers are made of highly parallel nodes with tens of cores. The efficiency of these nodes required improvements of the memory subsystem by adding multiple hierarchical levels of caches as well as a distributed memory interconnect causing Non-Uniform Memory Access (NUMA). In 2010, Valiant updated the BSP model to account for this situation, resulting in the MultiBSP model. It was defined with the same abstractions and bridge architecture as the original BSP, but adapted to multicore machines.

The MultiBSP Model describes a model instance as a tree structure of nested components, where the leaves are processors and each internal node is a BSP computer with local memory or some storage capacity.

Formally, a MultiBSP machine is specified by a list of tuples (levels) where each tuple has four parameters (m_i, p_i, g_i, L_i) where:

- p_i is the number of i-1th level components inside an ith component. For $i = 1$, these 1st level components consist of p_1 raw processors, which can be regarded as 0th level components. One computation step of such a processor on a word in level 1 memory is taken as one basic unit of time.
- g_i is the communication cost parameter, it is defined as the ratio of the number of operations that a processor can perform in a second and the number of words that can be transmitted in a second between the memories of a component at level i and its parent component at level $i + 1$. A *word* here is the amount of data on which a processor operation is performed. We assume that the level$_1$ memories can keep up with the processors, and hence that the data rate (corresponding to the notation g_0) has the value one.
- L_i is the cost for the barrier synchronization for a level i superstep. The definition requires barrier synchronization of the subcomponents of a component, but no synchronization across above branches in the component hierarchy.
- m_i is the number of words of memory inside an ith level component that is not inside any $i - 1^{th}$ level component.

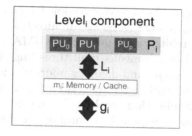

Fig. 1. Schematic view of the ith component level of MultiBSP model

Fig. 1 shows a component of level i. A level i superstep is a construct running at a level i component that allows each of its p_i level $i - 1$ components to execute independently (including supersteps of level $i - 1$). Once all p_i finish their computation, they can all exchange information with the m_i memory of the level i component with a communication cost determined by g_{i-1}. The cost charged will be mg_{i-1}, where m is the maximum number of words communicated between the memory of the ith level component and any one of its level $i - 1$ subcomponents. After a barrier between the p_i components, the next superstep may begin.

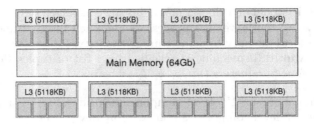

Fig. 2. MultiBSP model: $(5118\text{KB}, 4, g_1, L_1),(64\,\text{GB}, 8, g_2, L_2)$

For instance, Fig. 2 shows a machine, whose architecture can be specified by three MultiBSP components (level_0, level_1 and level_2): $(0, 1, 0, 0)$, $(5118\text{KB}, 4, g_1, L_1)$ and $(64\,\text{GB}, 8, g_2, L_2)$. We can ignore the level_0 because it represents only one processing unit and thus does not involve internal synchronization or communication. Therefore we only have two components, which corresponds to the two level of hierarchy in the architecture.

A benchmarking algorithm for the MultiBSP model will need an automatic process for discovering the specific hardware architectures. Accordingly, in our work we use the *portable HardWare LOCality* (`hwloc`) tool [3][2] that allows obtaining runtime information about the architecture of the machine, such as processors, caches, memory nodes, etc. in an abstract way.

The use of the hwloc software package has been proposed in the SEHLOC project in order to have a tool for automatically detecting the architecture features of multicore systems, defining the interconnection topologies and the hierarchies for neighboring cores. We use the version 1.7.2 of hwloc, which provides a portable abstraction (across OS, versions, architectures, etc.) of the hierarchical topology of modern architectures, including NUMA memory nodes, sockets, shared caches, cores and simultaneous multithreading. It also gathers various system attributes such as cache and memory information as well as the locality of I/O devices such as network interfaces, InfiniBand HCAs or GPUs. It primarily aims at helping applications with gathering information about modern computing hardware so as to exploit it accordingly and efficiently.

2.3 Related Work

The program `bspbench` from BSPEdupack[4] has been the main benchmarking program on BSP model. The proposed benchmark measures a full h-relation, where every processor sends and receives exactly h data words. The methodology tries to measure the slowest possible communication, putting single data words into other processors in a cyclic fashion. This reveals whether the system software indeed combines data for the same destination and whether it can handle all-to-all communication efficiently. In this cases the resulting g obtained by benchmarking program `bspbench` is called pessimistic. The Oxford BSP toolset

---

[2]   Available under the BSD license at http://www.open-mpi.org/projects/hwloc

[4] has another benchmarking program, bspprobe, which measures optimistic g values using larger packets insted of single words. BSP benchmarking also can be done by using mpibench from MPIedupack[4].

The benchmarking of the MultiBSP computational model has been recently addressed in the article by Savadi and Hossein [6], using a similar approach as the one we apply here. The classic BSP benchmarking is used as a baseline, but the specification of a model instance is different. Unlike the benchmarking methodology followed in our work, the authors consider deep architecture details such as cache coherency, for instance for propagation of values in the memory hierarchy. In their approach, the analysis of results is made by comparing the real values obtained by the process of benchmarking against theoretical values of the g and L parameters, which are computed as optimistic lower bounds (i.e. the authors suppose that the memory utilization is always lower than the cache size, and that all cores work at maximum speed). Our approach differs since we do not make any assumption about the underlying hardware platform but rather hide its characterics inside the output of will chosen benchmarks. We believe this strategy is well suited to modern architectures that are too complex for precise models depending on their advanced, hidden and/or rarely well documented features.

From a practical point of view, the main advantage of our proposal is to evaluate real MultiBSP operations implemented for the library MulticoreBSP for C [9]. In addition, our results are validated using a real MultiBSP program, comparing the real execution time of the inner product algorithm against the predicted running time using the theoretical MultiBSP cost function.

3   The MBSPDiscover Benchmark for MultiBSP

This section presents the design and implementation of the MBSPDiscover benchmark to estimate the g and L parameters that characterize a MultiBSP machine.

3.1   Motivation

Multicore architectures are widely used for HPC applications, and both the number of cores and the cache levels have been steadily increasing in the last years. Therefore, there is a real need to identify and evaluate the different parameters that characterize the structure of cores and memories, not only to understand and compare different architectures, but also for using them wisely for a better design of HPC applications. This characterization is motivated by the fact that the performance improvements when using a multi-core processor strongly depend on software algorithms, their implementation, and the utilization of the hardware capabilities.

As mentioned previously, this work follows the MultiBSP model which specifies the parameters needed to characterize a multicore machine. In this model, the performance of a parallel algorithm depends on parameters such as communication and synchronization costs, number of cores, and the size of caches.

Because it is hard to build analytical equations involving those variables, performing computer benchmarking via a computational model is therefore a reasonable method to evaluate performance and characterize the architecture.

It is important to emphasize that the quality of a benchmarking tool should not depend on particular architecture. This extra requirement is solved by discovering the relations of the different cores within each level of cache.

3.2   MBSPDiscover Design

The existing benchmark BSPbench for the standard BSP model [1] was used as a reference baseline to design the MBSPDiscover tool. The obvious difference between the existing benchmark and the new one is the need of obtaining pairs of values for the g and L parameters for each level of components in the Multi-BSP model. In addition, in the MultiBSP case, the processing is made inside of multicore nodes instead of outside nodes through the network.

Software Architecture and Modules. Fig. 3 shows the software architecture for the kernel of the MBSPDiscover proposal. The functionality for each of the processes displayed in the figure is explained below:

- *Discovering module*: the hardware architecture is collected by using hwloc and it is loaded in a tree of resources. This structure is inside the hwloc API box.
- *Interface*: Once the tree structure is generated, a set of functions walk across the tree using a bottom-up process for building a new tree named MBSPTree that contains all the information needed to support the MultiBSP model.
- *Benchmarking module*: It retrieves core indexes and memory size from the MBSPTree for each level. Then it measures communication and synchronization cost through a MultiBSP submodule, as well as an affinity submodule for pinning levels on the right cores. Finally it computes the resulting g and L parameters.

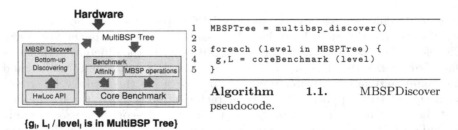

Fig. 3. Schematic view (left) and pseudocode (right) of the MBSPDiscover process

MBSPTree acts as the interface between both modules. Fig. 4 shows the structure corresponding to the hardware architecture presented in Fig. 5.

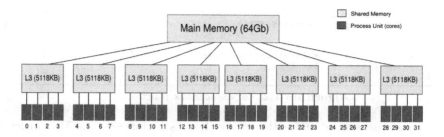

Fig. 4. MBSPTree structure generated by MBSPDiscover

The Corebenchmark Module. We explain in detail the implementation of the `coreBenchmark` module for computing the parameters g_i and L_i.

The `coreBenchmark` function is shown in Algorithm 1.2. It receives as parameters the information of the corresponding level based in the MultiBSP Model, and data for affinity like the core indexes and the size of cache memory, which are stored in the `MBSPTree` structure. At the beginning (line 2), `coreBenchmark` uses the `setPinning` function from the `affinity` module. `setPinning` binds the threads spawned by the `begin` function (line 3) to the cores corresponding to the current level. The function spawns one thread per core in that level and calculates the computing rate of the MultiBSP component using `computingRate` function (line 4). Each level has a set of cores sharing one memory, then for benchmarking a level, only those cores are considered.

The `computingRate` function measures the time required to perform $2 \times n \times$`DAXPY` operations. The `DAXPY` routine performs the vector operation $y = \alpha * x + y$, adding a multiple of a double precision vector to another double precision vector. `DAXPY` is a standard BLAS1 operation [3] for estimating the platform efficiency when performing memory-intensive floating point operations.

```
1   function coreBenchmark(level) {
2     setPinning(level.cores_indexes)
3
4     begin(level.cores)
5     rate = computingRate(level)
6     sync()
7
8     for (h=0; h<HMAX; h++) {
9
10      initCommunicationPattern(h)
11      sync()
12
13      t0 = time()
14
15      for (i=0; i<NITERS; i++) {
16        communication()
17        sync()
18      }
19
20      t = time() - t0
21
```

---

[3] BLAS operations are described at http://www.netlib.org/blas/

```
22      if (master) {
23          times.append(t*rate/NITERS);
24      }
25    }
26    level.g, level.L = leastSquares(times)
27    return (level.g, level.L)
28  }
```

Algorithm 1.2. coreBenchmark function.

Then a synchronization for the current level is performed (line 5) in order to assure that all threads have the computing rate value.

The coreBenchmark function measures a full h-communication, which we define as the extension of a h-relation for the shared-memory case within a single node. It is implemented as a communication where every core writes/reads exactly h data words. We consider the worst case, measuring the slowest communication possible by cyclically reading single data words into other processors. In that way, the values of g_i and L_i computed using the benchmark are pessimistic values, and the real values will be always better. The variable h represents the largest number of words read or written in the shared memory of the level. HMAX is the maximum value for all h parameters used in the communications patterns for each level. It may need to be different for different levels of the hierarchy, we plan to find suitable values by trial and error.

The communication times using the h-communication pattern are initialized by the initCommunicationPattern routine (line 7). This process is repeated NITERS times (lines 10–13), because each operation is too fast to be measured with proper precision. After that, the master thread in each level saves the flops used for each h-communication (line 16).

Finally, the parameters g and L are computed using a traditional least squares approximation method (line 19), to fit the data to a linear model, according to the related works [1,6], providing an accurate approximation for g_i and L_i.

3.3   Methodology for the Empirical Evaluation of h-Communications

The methodology applied to measure the h-communications and then estimate the parameters g and L is based on measuring the implementation of *MultiBSP operations*. We refer to MultiBSP operations as the functions/procedures need to implement an algorithm designed with the MultiBSP computational model. In our software design, the MBSP operations module contains the implementation of these functions, including operations provided by the MulticoreBSP for C library [9]. This library establishes a methodology for programming according to the MultiBSP computational model.

The software design shown in Fig. 3 is important here because when MultiBSP algorithms are programmed using other libraries, it is possible to reconfigure the tool, changing the MBSP operation module and re-characterizing the architecture by running the benchmark with this new configuration.

4 Experimental Analysis

This section reports the experimental analysis of the proposed MultiBSP benchmark. First, we introduce the problem instances by describing the main features of the architectures used to test the benchmark. After that, the numerical results and the values for the g and L parameters are reported. Finally, the validation of our results using a real MultiBSP program is presented.

4.1 MultiBSP Architectures Used in the Experimental Analysis

For our experiments, the hierarchical levels of the considered architectures are specially relevant. The main goals of the experimental analysis are to verify the proper functionality of the proposed benchmark and also to compute the corresponding values for the parameters of the MultiBSP model.

We selected two real infrastructures for the experimental analysis, which feature a reasonably large number of cores and interesting cache levels:

- Instance #1 is *dell32*, whose architecture is shown in Fig. 5. *dell32* has four AMD Opteron 6128 *Magny-Cours* processors with a total of 32 cores, 64 GB RAM, and two hierarchy levels.
- Instance #2 is *jolly*, whose architecture is shown in Fig. 6. *jolly* has four AMD Opteron 6272 *Interlagos* processors with a total of 64 cores, 128 GB RAM, and three hierarchy levels.

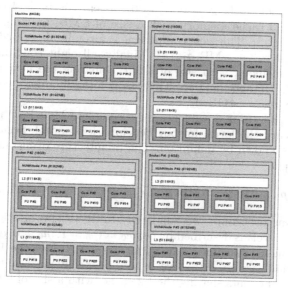

Fig. 5. `hwloc` output describing the topology of the *dell32* multicore machine

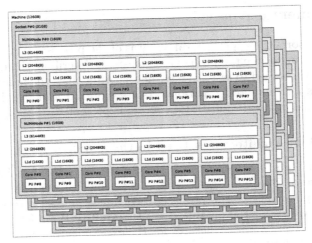

Fig. 6. `hwloc` output describing the topology of the *jolly* multicore machine

For each of those architectures, we need to specify the instances in MultiBSP. We proceed step by step for a better understanding of the MultiBSP formulation.

For *dell32* we start from bottom (cores) to upper levels and build the components in tuples that share a memory space. The first tuple is made of a single core at $level_0$. It does not shared any memory with any other component, so its shared memory is 0 and both parameters g and L are zero by definition: $tuple_0 = \langle p_0 = 1, m_0 = 0, g_0 = 0, L_0 = 0 \rangle$. Then, the basic 4 components in $level_0$ share the L3 cache memory with a size of 5 MB, building a new Multi-BSP component $level_1$. This new component is formally described by the tuple: $tuple_1 = \langle p_1 = 4, m_1 = 5 \text{ MB}, g_1, L_1 \rangle$. Finally, all eight components in $level_1$ share the RAM memory, with size of 64 GB, building the next and last level, $level_2$, in a MultiBSP specification. This one is formally described by the tuple: $tuple_2 = \langle p_2 = 8, m_2 = 64 \text{ GB}, g_2, L_2 \rangle$.

We join all tuples using a sequence for a complete MultiBSP machine specification and discard the $level_0$ for our benchmark proposal, because the values of g_0 and L_0 are known by definition. The architecture of instance #1 is then described by Eq. 1.

$$M_1 = [\langle p_1 = 4, m_1 = 5 \text{ MB}, g_1, L_1 \rangle, \langle p_2 = 8, m_2 = 64 \text{ GB}, g_2, L_2 \rangle] \qquad (1)$$

Using the same procedure, we build the MultiBSP specification for instance #2, *jolly*. Again, $level_0$ is described by $tuple_0 = \langle p_0 = 1, m_0 = 0, g_0 = 0, L_0 = 0 \rangle$. It is the same in all machines, except for cores that use the hyperthreading technology (in that case, an extra level is need to specify physical threads). Then, there are two components sharing the L2 cache, with a size of 2 MB. The $level_1$ is described by $tuple_1 = \langle p_1 = 2, m_1 = 2 \text{ MB}, g_1, L_1 \rangle$ The components at $level_1$ are grouped by sharing four L3 cache memories, with a size of 6 MB, building the $level_2$, as defined by $tuple_2 = \langle p_2 = 4, m_2 = 6 \text{ MB}, g_2, L_2 \rangle$. In the last level

(#3), eight components from $level_2$ are grouped. They share the RAM memory, with a size of 128 GB, as specified by $tuple_3 = \langle p_3 = 8, m_3 = 128\,\text{GB}, g_3, L_3 \rangle$.

Finally, using the same procedure we previously applied to the dell32 architecture (i.e. joining all tuples and discarding $level_0$), we get the MultiBSP specification in Eq. 2.

$$M_2 = [\langle p_1 = 2, m_1 = 2\,\text{MB}, g_1, L_1 \rangle, \langle p_2 = 4, m_2 = 6\,\text{MB}, g_2, L_2 \rangle,$$
$$\langle p_3 = 8, m_3 = 128\,\text{GB}, g_3, L_3 \rangle] \quad (2)$$

Using these instances of the MultiBSP model, we can predict the running time of a MultiBSP algorithm executed in each machine. The g_i and L_i parameters in each tuple must be previously calculated using the benchmarking procedure explained in the previous section. Next section reports the values of g and L obtained for both architectures at each level.

4.2   Results

We report the time to perform h-communications in each level, increasing the number h as in the `coreBenchmark` function. Reporting the flops for each h-communications is important because we compute the g_i and L_i using least squares to estimate the parameters at each level.

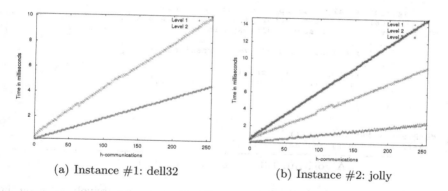

(a) Instance #1: dell32   (b) Instance #2: jolly

Fig. 7. Time to perform from h-communications per level in a MultiBSP tree, with h between 0 and 256

Figure 7 show the h_i communications in each level for *dell32* ($level_1$ and $level_2$) and *jolly* (levels 1, 2, and 3). In $level_1$ of *dell32*, the communications are within the shared memory (L3 cache), so they are twice faster than in $level_2$, which use the RAM memory. For *jolly*, the communications in $level_1$ are within the L2 cache, thus they are three times faster than in $level_2$, where communications are performed through the L3 cache. In turn, they are 1.5× faster than those in $level_3$ of the hierarchy, which are performed by accessing the RAM memory.

Table 1. Computed values for g and L parameters for the studied architectures

dell 32			jolly		
level	g (flops/word)	L (flops)	level	g (flops/word)	L (flops)
2	977.5	15550.2	3	1315.9	16184.4
1	334.9	7792.9	2	549.9	7157.9
			1	105.3	498.2

Finally, using the least squares method we estimate the values of g_i and L_i over the h-communications for each level. The final values for *dell32* and *jolly* are reported in Table 1.

4.3 Validation of Results

For validating the results computed in the previous subsection, we conducted an experiment using a real application, the *vector inner product* from BSPedupack (actually the computation of the norm of a vector), described in Algorithm 1.3 in the MultiBSP programming model. We plan to extend the validation by considering a set of benchmark applications as future work.

```
1   innerProduct(level, vector) {
2     if (level.next == NULL ) {
3       return sequentialInnerProduct(vector);
4     } else {
5       begin_parallel_multibsp ( level.sons.length )
6         ownslice = split_vector(vector, multibsp_pid );
7         level = level.sons[ multibsp_pid ];
8         sync()
9         results = innerProduct(level, ownslice)
10        sync()
11        if (multbsp_id == master) {
12          return sequentialInnerProduct(results);
13        }
14      end_parallel_multibsp
15    }
16  }
17  MBSPTree = MBSPDiscover()
18  innerProduct(MBSPTree, data_vector)
```

Algorithm 1.3. Vector Inner Product.

Algorithm 1.3 applies the MultiBSP programming model recursively, crossing the MCBSPTree obtained with MBSPDiscover in the proposed benchmark. Using the tree structure, the data vector is split in slices for each thread at level i. For $i > 0$, the data splitting is applied recursively. In level 0, a sequential inner product algorithm is used to compute a partial result. Then, after synchronizing all threads in each level, the result is the inner product for the whole data vector. The master thread applies a reduction phase, combining all results using the sequential inner product and then returns the result to the upper level.

The validation involves the following steps (applied for different vector sizes):

1. Estimate the amount of communications and synchronizations at each level, by using hardware counters.

2. Compute the values of g_i and L_i parameters using the proposed benchmark.
3. Compute the runtime of the algorithm using the theoretical cost model of tje MultiBSP [8].
4. Run the vector inner product algorithm.
5. Compare the results with the theoretical prediction.

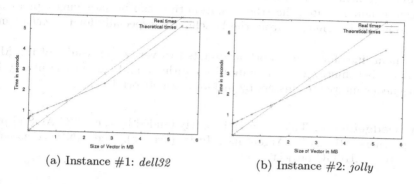

(a) Instance #1: *dell32*   (b) Instance #2: *jolly*

Fig. 8. Comparison between the real execution time against the theoretical execution time

Fig. 8 graphically presents the comparison between the real execution time against the theoretical execution time for both studied architectures.

The results show that when using a vector with less than 2^8 elements, the real execution time is larger than the theoretical time. This happens mainly because with few data, the time for spawning threads adds a significant overhead compared with the time to calculate a vector slice at $level_i$. For *dell32*, when computing vectors with more than 2^8 elements, both curves have the same slope, then we can say that both times are relative and the measure is stabilized. For *jolly*, the predicted and execution times have a different behavior. There is an ideal point where both measures are the same, but when the vector is larger than 2^8 elements, the execution time increases slower than the predicted time. The good results in Fig. 8(a) validates the proposed approach, as the values g_i and L_i used in the predicted time are very close to the real time. On other hand, in Fig. 8(b) the predicted time is not as close to the real time as we expect. However, the theoretical time is always greater than the real time, so it is useful as an accurate lower bound for predictions.

5   Conclusions and Future Work

This work presented MBSPDiscover[4], an automatic tool for characterizing multicore architectures based in the MultiBSP computational model. The proposed

---

[4] Available from http://runtime.bordeaux.inria.fr/sehloc/

benchmark computes the parameters g and L (communication and synchronization cost) for the MultiBSP model. It is adaptable to any hierarchical architecture and its output is a structure with the information of each level, useful for programming applications following the MultiBSP model.

We applied the benchmark to characterize and evaluate two actual HPC multicore systems. In order to validate the results, we designed and implemented a particular problem in the MultiBSP model, and predicted its execution costs. The results demonstrated that the execution time can be satisfyingly predicted when using the information from the benchmark, especially for the *dell32* machine.

The main lines for future work are related to verify the results of the MBSPDiscover benchmark using a suite of algorithms, and extend the library for heterogeneous multicore clusters by including a network level.

Acknowledgements. This research is partly funded by the STIC-AmSud program partners MINCyT (Argentina), Inria (France), and ANII (Uruguay), through the SEHLOC project.

References

1. Bisseling, R.: Parallel scientific computation: a structured approach using BSP and MPI. Oxford University Press, Oxford (2004)
2. Bonorden, O., Juurlink, B., von Otte, I., Rieping, I.: The Paderborn University BSP (PUB) Library. Parallel Comput. 29(2), 187–207 (2003)
3. Broquedis, F., Clet-Ortega, J., Moreaud, S., Furmento, N., Goglin, B., Mercier, G., Thibault, S., Namyst, R.: Hwloc: A generic framework for managing hardware affinities in HPC applications. In: 18th Euromicro Conference on Parallel, Distributed and Network-based Processing, pp. 180–186 (2010)
4. Hill, J., McColl, B., Stefanescu, D., Goudreau, M., Lang, K., Rao, S., Suel, T., Tsantilas, T., Bisseling, R.: BSPlib: The BSP programming library. Parallel Computing 24(14), 1947–1980 (1998)
5. Lobachev, O., Guthe, M., Loogen, R.: Estimating parallel performance. J. Parallel Distrib. Comput. 73(6), 876–887 (2013)
6. Savadi, A., Deldari, H.: Measurement latency parameters of the MultiBSP model: A multicore benchmarking approach. J. Supercomput. 67(2), 565–584 (2014)
7. Valiant, L.: A bridging model for parallel computation. Commun. ACM 33(8), 103–111 (1990)
8. Valiant, L.: A bridging model for multi-core computing. J. Comput. Syst. Sci. 77(1), 154–166 (2011)
9. Yzelman, A.N.: Fast sparse matrix-vector multiplication by partitioning and reordering. Ph.D. thesis, Utrecht University, Utrecht, the Netherlands (October 2011)

Flexicache: Highly Reliable and Low Power Cache under Supply Voltage Scaling

Gulay Yalcin[1,2], Azam Seyedi[1,2], Osman S. Unsal[1], and Adrian Cristal[1,3]

[1] Barcelona Supercomputing Center
[2] Universitat Politecnica de Catalunya
[3] IIIA - Artificial Intelligence Research Institute - Spanish National Research Council
{gyalcin,aseyedi,ounsal,acristal}@bsc.es

Abstract. Processors supporting a wide range of supply voltages are necessary to achieve high performance in nominal supply voltage and to reduce the power consumption in low supply voltage. However, when the supply voltage is lowered below the safe margin (especially close to the threshold voltage level), the memory cell failure rate increases drastically. Thus, it is essential to provide reliability solutions for memory structures. This paper proposes a novel, reliable L1 cache design, Flexicache, which automatically configures itself for different supply voltages in order to tolerate different fault rates. Flexicache is a circuit-driven solution achieving in-cache replication with no increase in the access latency and with a minimum increase in the energy consumption. It defines three operating modes: Single Version Mode, Double Version Mode and Triple Version Mode. Compared to the best previous proposal, Flexicache can provide 34% higher energy reduction for L1 caches with 2× higher error correction capability in the low-voltage mode.

1 Introduction

As energy is a key design concern for computer systems, microprocessors started to provide 1) high-performance and 2) low-power operating modes [20]. Processors run at a high frequency by using the nominal supply voltage (V_{dd}) in the high-performance mode, and they reduce V_{dd} in the low-power mode to reduce the energy consumption by trading-off performance. However, this energy reduction comes with a drastic increase in the number of failures especially in memory structures (i.e on-chip SRAM memories such as L1 and L2 caches) [11,15]. These memory failures can be persistent (i.e. yield loss or hard errors) or non-persistent (i.e. soft errors or erratic bits) while rates of both failures increase as the V_{dd} is decreased. Moreover transistor scaling increases the vulnerability of transistors to radiation events since it increases the likelihood of having multibit soft errors on adjacent bits [7]. Thus, it is essential to implement reliability solutions addressing both persistent and non-persistent failures in caches in order to reduce the V_{dd} and provide reliable cache operation for future technology nodes. There are two main techniques to deal with high fault rates stemming from the above issues: 1) Coding techniques such as parity or ECC, 2) In-cache replication. While they are effective, both mechanisms have issues.

G. Hernández et al. (Eds.): CARLA 2014, CCIS 485, pp. 173–190, 2014.
© Springer-Verlag Berlin Heidelberg 2014

Error Correction Codes (ECCs) are the most widely used techniques for detecting and correcting both persistent and non-persistent failures with additional area, power and encoding/decoding time overhead [12,18,23]. However, the increase in the error correction capability of ECC is much lower than the increase in power and area consumption. For example, in 8-byte data, correcting a double-bit error costs 19% area overhead while three-bit error correction requires a stronger and a more complex ECC with 100% area overhead [7]. Intel's latest 22nm 15-core Xeon processor uses Double Error Correction, Triple Error Detection (DECTED), a very strong ECC, for its L3 cache data tag array; however, the computational cost of DECTED ECC impacts the L3 data accesses, whose latency is variable, thus significantly complicating the micro-architecture [25]. Due to the diminishing benefits of stronger ECCs, providing reliability in an environment with a very high fault rate (i.e. more than 10^{-3} failure probability for each bit) such as when the processor is operating in a very low power mode, is not trivial. Thus, only a few ECC solutions address large-scale multibit errors in a line [12,23]. However, they require a complex encoder/decoder with a high energy consumption which diminish the energy saving potential of the low-power mode execution. The second mechanism, in-cache replication such as triplication, is a conventional way of providing high reliability with a minimum fault recovery latency in which replicated cache lines are corrected via bitwise majority voter [9,31]. However, replication schemes have two main problems: (1) Writing/reading more than one cache line increases access latency and energy consumption. (2) When processors operate with a very low V_{dd}, the number of uncorrectable lines increases due to the multiple failures in the same bit-position.

In this study, our goal is designing on-chip SRAM memories which can tolerate very high bit failure rates of ultra-low voltage execution with minimum overhead, and without harming the cache capacity in the nominal mode. To this end, we present Flexicache, a new cache design which avoids the problematic aspects of coding and in-cache replication through a two-tiered approach. First, Flexicache proposes a circuit-driven solution that duplicates/triplicates all the available cache lines and achieves read/write accesses to multiple lines without increasing access latency and with a minimum increase in the access energy. Flexicache automatically configures itself for different supply voltages in order to tolerate different fault rates. It works in one of the three modes:(1) Single Version Mode (SVM), (2) Double Version Mode (DVM) or (3) Triple Version Mode (TVM). Second, Flexicache divides each cache line into single-parity-protected partitions to increase the error correction capability of replication schemes.

The main contributions of this study are the following:

- We present a novel, reliable cache design, Flexicache, which configures itself for different supply voltages from the nominal to the near threshold voltage levels in order to duplicate or triplicate each data line when higher reliability is required.
- Flexicache provides significantly higher cache capacity with less error correction energy compared to OLSC [12] and conventional triplication.

- Flexicache allows cache operating down to 320 mV (10% failure rate) by presenting, on average, 63% energy reduction in cache operations. The area overhead of Flexicache is only 12% compared to a typical L1 cache.

2 Background and Related Work

In this section, we first explain the nomenclatures of failures in memory structures. Then we present the previous schemes used for scaling V_{dd}.

Memory Failures: Bit failures are classified into two broad categories [12]:

Persistent Failures: The random variation in the number and location of dopant atoms in the channel region of the device leads to the random variations in transistor threshold voltage. It causes threshold voltage mismatch between the transistors close to each other. In a SRAM cell, a mismatch in the strength between the neighbouring transistors caused by intra-die variations can result in the failure of the cell [4]. A cell failure can occur due to: (1) An increase in the cell access time, (2) unstable read operation, (3) unstable write operation, (4) failure in the data holding capability of the cell. Further details can be found in [30]. On the other side, open or short circuits cause irreversible physical changes in the semiconductor devices. These permanent failures tend to occur early in the processor lifetime due to manufacturing faults (called the infant mortality), or late in the lifetime due to thermal and process related stress. The location of a persistent failure is random and independent of whether the neighbouring bit is faulty or not [20]. The locations of persistently defective bits can be detected by performing built-in self test (BIST) [17].

Non-Persistent Failures: Radiation events or power supply noise can cause a bit flip and corrupt a data stored in a device until a new data is written [8]. As transistor dimensions and operating voltages shrink, sensitivity to radiation events increases drastically. On the other side, process variation or in-progress wear-out, combined with voltage and temperature fluctuations might cause correlated faults of short duration. They are termed intermittent faults (or erratic failures), that last from several cycles to several seconds [13]. Diagnosing an intermittent fault by BIST is hard since it does not persist and conditions that cause the fault are hard to regenerate. As V_{dd} decreases, the bit failure rate increases rapidly for both intermittent faults and persistent failures [23,12].

Related Work: In this section, we discuss architecture-based schemes utilized under scaling voltage and compare their main characteristics with Flexicache in Table 1. Orthogonal Latin Square Code (OLSC) [18] is a state of the art ECC scheme used for level-1 caches when the supply voltage is lower than the safe margin. Multi-Bit Segmented ECC (MS-ECC) [12] utilizes OLSC at a finer granularity in order to increase the error correction capability of OLSC to be used for ultra-low voltage level. Thus MS-ECC can reduce the supply voltage until 350 mV in 35nm technology by providing 6.5% useful cache capacity (We define useful cache capacity as the portion of the cache which is not disabled) [23]. Kim, et al. [19], propose two-dimensional (2D) ECC to correct multi-bit errors with a minimum area overhead in check bits. However, the correction capability

Table 1. Comparison of Flexicache with Architecture Based Error Correction Schemes for Scaling Vcc (Bold is better)

	Segmented ECC	2D ECC	Disabling/ Bit-Fix	Flexicache
Persistent Failures	**yes**	yes	yes	**yes**
Non-Persistent Failures	**yes**	yes	no	**yes**
Minimum V_{dd}	375 mV	–	400 mV	**320 mV** (see Section 5)
Latency in the Low-Power Mode	1 cycle	1 cycle	**0 cycle**	1 cycle
Other Latency	**no**	read-modify-write	**no**	**no**

of this scheme is strongly dependent upon the location of defective bits. So that, it is not convenient to use in low-power mode when failures are random. Also, it requires a read-modify-write operation for all Stores and for every cache miss which increases the delay and power consumed by all write operations. Miller et al. [23] proposed Parichute which utilizes Turbocodes for reducing V_{dd} of the second and higher level caches. Although this scheme provides a very high error correction rate supporting a voltage reduction significantly, its error correction latency can be couple of cycles (i.e. more than 5 cycles [23]) in the near-threshold voltage level. Thus, Parichute is not convenient to be used in time-critical L1 caches. Several disabling schemes have been proposed for tolerating only persistent failures [30,3,5]. Wilkerson et al. [30] disables the faulty words in order to combine two consecutive cache lines to form a single cache line where only non-failing words are used. Although the area overhead of word-disable in high-power mode is only 8%, in the low power mode the available cache size shrinks to the half when the error rate is lower than 0.01%. Abella, et al. [3] disables sub-blocks instead of words in order to utilize more capacity in the low-power mode. Both disabling schemes need to access a fault map in parallel. ZerehCache [5] employs fine granularity re-mapping of faulty bits and relies on solving a graph coloring problem to find the best re-mapping of defects to spare lines. Bit-fix [30] stores the location of defective bits and their correct values to the quarter of cache ways. Circuit-based hardening approaches have also been proposed such as using 8T SRAM cells [24] which are more stable against parameter variations than 6T cells. 8T cells are useful for noisy places and specially designed for low V_{dd} modes while it presents high area overhead in the nominal voltage.

In this study, we propose Flexicache, a circuit-driven solution that duplicates or triplicates all the available lines in the cache with no increase in the access latency. We presented the preliminary sketch of the idea for the circuit design in a previous event without precluding further submissions [26]. In this study, besides elaborating the circuit design, we present the details of the address decoder and the architectural extensions of Flexicache.

3   Architecture of Flexicache

Flexicache allows three modes of error protection according to the resilience level of the applied V_{dd}: Single Version Mode (SVM), Double Version Mode (DVM)

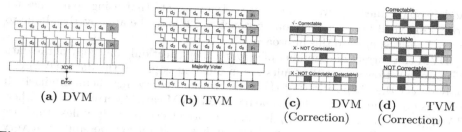

Fig. 1. The figure presents the basics Flexicache for DVM (Figure.1a) and TVM (Figure.1b) for 8-bit partitions. Also, it presents examples for correctable and non-correctable faults.

and Triple Version Mode (TVM). Flexicache divides each cache line into parity-protected-partitions akin to many commercial L1 caches protected by single-bit parity in block, word or byte granularity [21]. Figure 1 presents the design of DVM and TVM for a hypothetical 8-bit partition. SVM, which is not presented in the figure, provides reliability solely based on single bit interleaved parity. In this study, Flexicache runs in SVM in the nominal voltage when the failure rate is minimum in order to provide full cache capacity for the applications. Note that instead of parity, a stronger code can also be utilized to provide a higher reliability for mission critical applications.

Flexicache runs in DVM when the V_{dd} is medium-low and writes data to two cache lines. Note that the circuit design allows writing/reading multiple lines simultaneously (i.e. without increasing the access time) as we explain in the following section. In a read, DVM compares two duplicated, parity-protected partitions through the XORs to check if there is any fault. In case of the complete match, Flexicache dispatches one of the partitions to the output buffer. Otherwise, Flexicache calculates the parity of each partition and sends out the partition which has the correct parity. DVM provides a backup copy for each partition. For instance, when a particle strike effects several adjacent bits in a line, the correct value is read from its replica without requiring any decode-and-correct time. In order to avoid the possibility of a strike affecting both coupled lines, Flexicache couples the lines with spatially distant locations. (e.g 0th and 63th lines.)

When the V_{dd} is near threshold, in order to tolerate the drastically increased error rate, Flexicache runs in TVM by writing the data to three cache lines simultaneously. On a read, Flexicache uses bitwise majority voting to obtain the correct data and calculates the parity of the data. Unless parity confirms that the result is correct, Flexicache calculates the parities of three partitions and sends out the correct partition. In TVM, the whole cache should be divided into three which is not trivial for a cache having 2^n lines. One solution can be manually connecting lines by taking into account that the lines in the same group should be in distinct positions (e.g. 0th, 42th and 84th lines for a 128-line cache). However, this considerably increases the complexity of the address decoder. Instead, we add spare lines to make the cache dividable into three. For instance, for a 128-line cache, we add 16 spare lines and we connect every 48 lines.Note that using spare lines for tolerating yield loss is a common approach [5,22] and, the area overhead due to extra lines is similar to this approach.

DVM can correct odd number of errors if they effect only one copy of the data (Figure 1c). However, if the faults are in different copies of the data, DVM can only detect the bit-positions of the faults without correcting them. Similarly, if there is even number of faults in one partition DVM cannot correct them, either. TVM (Figure 1d), on the other hand, can correct errors easily unless they are affecting the bits in the same position (it has a significant possibility in very high bit failure rate). Otherwise, after calculating the parity, TVM detects that the result of majority voter is not correct, and it can correct errors if one of the three copies is error-free. If all three copies are erroneous, and some errors are in the same bit position, TVM can not correct the partition.

When there is an uncorrectable partition in a line, we utilize a partition-fix mechanism in DVM and TVM to avoid wasting the correct partitions. Partition-fix is similar to the bit-fix proposed by Wilkerson et al [30]. It uses a quarter of the cache ways to store locations and the correct values of defective partitions. This reduces both the cache size and associativity in the low-power mode. Thus, we utilize partition-fix mechanism only for the lines which have uncorrectable partitions. Note that, our partition-fix mechanism is different from the bit-fix for a non-persistent bit failure correction. In bit-fix, the cache lines are not protected by any other means, they only rely on memory tests and fixing the detected failures. In Flexicache, the fixed partitions are also protected by DVM or TVM which can still correct non-persistent failures. Previous triplication schemes [9,31] write data to three cache lines and read the correct value from the majority voter. In Flexicache, partitioning and parity protection of each partition present higher error correction capability.

Persistent-fault tolerating proposals perform BIST [17] either postmanufacturing or at boot time to determine the uncorrectable cache lines at each voltage level [3,30,23]. These lines are stored in on-chip ROM or main memory and loaded before the processor transitions into near-threshold. For non-persistent failures, if the system can not correct a fault in L1 cache, either the correct value is re-fetched from L2 cache if the write-through cache is utilized or the system issues a machine check exception unless other means are utilized. Flexicache performs BIST test as in previous proposals to determine faulty partitions in order to fix them or disable the cache ways/lines including them. In runtime, Flexicache can detect and correct non-persistent failures, as well. For uncorrected non-persistent failures, Flexicache can utilize lightweight, global checkpointing such as SafetyNet [28].

4   Circuit Design

Conventional triplication schemes either write three lines sequentially [31] (harms application performance) or increases the number of read/write ports [9] (increases energy consumption). Previously, we designed dvSRAM which includes

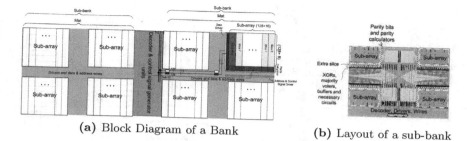

(a) Block Diagram of a Bank   (b) Layout of a sub-bank

Fig. 2. The figure shows the block diagram of a bank in a 64KB, 4-way Flexicache and the layout of a sub-bank and address decoder of Flexicache

two values in each cell, primary value and secondary value [27]. These two values can be accessed, modified, moved back and forth between the main and secondary cells within the access time of the cache. Ergin et al. [16] also proposed similar work using a shadow cell SRAM design for checkpointed register files. Similarly, Flexicache needs to access replicated data within the cache access time with minimum energy. Armejach et al [6] present how a reconfigurable cache using dvSRAM circuits can be designed so that it can dynamically switch its configuration between a 64KB general purpose data cache and a 32KB special purpose, dual version using data cache. Flexicache also requires a reconfigurable cache design so that it can provide three different execution modes (i.e. SVM, DVM, TVM) not to sacrifice the cache capacity in the high-performance execution mode.

In this section, we elaborate how we can design the circuit of Flexicache for L1 data cache so that it can replicate cache lines without increasing access latency and with minimal energy overhead. Note that it is straightforward to extend the design for the instruction cache and the L2 cache. Felxicache can also be designed orthogonally to dvSRAM so that it can support both optimistic concurrency and near-threshold voltage execution that we leave it out of the scope of this study.

In this section we present the design of Flexicache for 4-way, 64-KB data cache with 64-byte cache lines, and two clock cycle access time. Figure 2a presents the block diagram of one of 4 ways. We use Cacti [29] to determine the optimal number and size of Flexicache components (e.g. number of sub-banks) and the cache architecture with optimal access time and power consumption. For a one-bank array, Cacti suggests 2 identical sub-banks, 1 mat for each sub-bank and 4 sub-arrays in each mat (Figure 2a). We utilize these high-level CACTI results as inputs to subsequent cache circuit design steps: we construct for one way Hspice transistor level netlist using 45-nm Predictive Technology Model [2]. During an access, only one of the two sub-banks (i.e. left sub-bank and right sub-bank) and four identical sub-arrays of the mat (i.e. each sub-array holds a part of the cache line) are activated. The address decoder and control signal generator units are placed in the middle part of the array. Necessary data and address wires and drivers are placed in the middle part of each sub-bank. Flexicache divides each

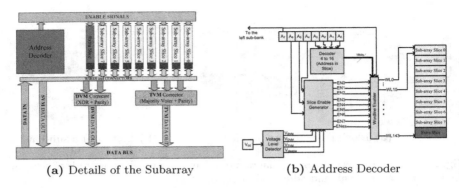

(a) Details of the Subarray   (b) Address Decoder

Fig. 3. The figure presents the basic components of Flexicache such as buses, decoder and Address Decoder

sub-array to eight equal slices (i.e sub-array slice) each containing 16 lines with the individual precharged circuit, the write circuit, the sense amplifier circuit and input and output buffers. Also, it extends each sub-array with an extra slice (i.e. to make it divisible by 3). In Figure 2b, we show the layouts of one sub-bank [1] for Flexicache; the second symmetric sub-bank is omitted.

Figure 3a presents the abstract view of the block diagram of one sub-array in Flexicache (For the details of the required buffers and the interfaces please see Appendix 6). According to the decoded addresses and the V_{dd} level, one, two or three slice(s) are activated and the data coming from the bus is written to the enabled slice(s). Cosemans et al. [14] evaluated the energy consumption of the cache elements during read or write operations in a design based on 90nm technology. For instance, during the read operation, timing components (including delay elements and control wires) is the most energy consuming element (i.e. 30%). Similarly, address decoder consumes around 25% of the read/write energy. Since Flexicache still uses the most of the energy-hungry components (e.g. buses, data drivers and the address decoder) only once in DVM and TVM, it slightly increases the energy consumption of timing elements and the address decoder. On the other side, Flexicache only duplicates (triplicates) the energy consumption of cells and sense amplifiers which consumes less than 15% of the read/write energy. Thus, Flexicache presents modest additional energy consumption in DVM and TVM.

Figure 3b presents an abstract view of the address decoder (The detailed view of the decoder can be seen in Appendix 6). In the figure, A_0 to A_7 represents the addresses bits. The decoder uses the 4 least significant bits (i.e A_0 to A_3) in order to address the line number within a slice. Also, it uses A_7 to activate either the left sub-bank or the right sub-bank. *Voltage Level Detector* activates either SVM, DVM or TVM. These three signals together with A_4 to A_6 generates enable signals (EN0 to ENex) which activate slice(s). At each time, depending on the mode, one, two or three Enable Signals are high and data is written to (and read from) one two or three cache lines simultaneously.

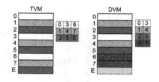

Fig. 4. Slices activated at a time in DVM and TVM

4.1 Switching Between Modes

The V_{dd} can be increased or decreased in the runtime, thus, Flexicache needs to switch between modes. In a naïve approach, before mode switching, the whole cache is flushed which presents a cache warm-up performance overhead immediately after switch. In this section, we present a more efficient approach. We organized the activated slices in each mode in order to ease the switching. In Figure 4, we present the activated slices at a time during the read/write operation of DVM and TVM.

In order to switch TVM→DVM→SVM, it is adequate to flush the slices in the last column of the old mode in the tables shown in Figure 4. In another word, when Flexicache switches from DVM to SVM, slices 3, 4, 5 and 7 are flushed from the cache. Similarly, when Flexicache switches from TVM to DVM, slices 6, 7 and Extra slice are flushed. Also, if Flexicache switches from TVM to SVM (although many systems do not allow this fast voltage increase), combination of both columns (i.e. slices 3, 4, 5, 6, 7, Ex) are flushed. Obviously, before this flushing operation, the slices which are not flushed (i.e staying slices) should be corrected with the old mode. One option can be stopping the execution of the application right after the voltage increase, using the to-be-flushed lines for correcting the staying lines by utilizing the old mode and continuing the application execution after all staying lines are corrected. In the second option, in order to avoid this stopping overhead, all staying lines are traced after changing the mode. When a line is read for the first time after the mode change (or a dirty line is evicted from the cache), this line is corrected by using the old mode. The second or the third replica of the line can be flushed after this correction. If a line is written without reading after changing the mode, the flushing can be done without requiring any correction.

However switching SVM→DVM→TVM is not that trivial since the correct data should be updated in the second or third replica before reducing the supply voltage. Thus, for instance, when Flexicache switches from DVM to TVM, before reducing the supply voltage, lines in the slices 6, 7 and Ex are first evicted from the cache. Then, these lines are updated as the third copy. As an example, lines in slice 6 should be updated by reading the lines in slices 0 and 3 and obtaining the correct data via DVM circuit. It is only safe to reduce the supply voltage after that. Although switching SVM→DVM→TVM present the performance overhead of a runtime barrier for updating the second or third copies, it is not a show-stopper since this switch operation is required when going towards low-power mode from the high-performance mode meaning that the application can trade off the performance for power.

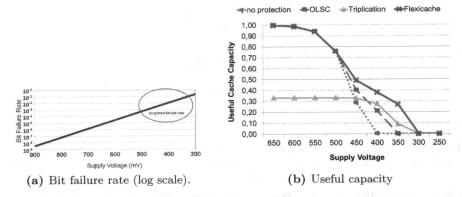

(a) Bit failure rate (log scale).   (b) Useful capacity

Fig. 5. Bit Failure Rate due to scaling voltage and he Useful cache capacity provided by Flexicache after disabling uncorrectable lines under this bit failure rate

5   Evaluation

In this section, we compare Flexicache against a conventional triplication scheme (TMR) and MS-ECC [12]. We use 4-way set associative, 64KB L1 cache with 2-cycle access time, 64B line size. We divide each line into 32 partitions for both OLSC and Flexicache with the partition size of 16 bits.

Miller et al [23] examined the persistent bit failure rate in the given V_{dd} for 32nm technology (Figure 5a). As V_{dd} is lowered, the bit failure rate increases exponentially. Flexicache targets to tolerate ultra high bit failure rates occurring in the near-threshold voltage level without harming the performance of the cache in the low error rate. For the calculation of the V_{dd} that Flexicache operate reliably, we reference these previous results. We inject persistent faults into random locations according to bit failure rate (i.e. probability that a single bit fails) given in [23]. We calculate the useful cache capacity as the portion of the cache which is not disabled. For non-persistent failure such as soft errors, we inject multi-bit failures varying between 1 to 10 bits. We present the experimental results for the aspects of 1) useful cache capacity, 2) error correction latency, 3) energy reduction of cache operations, and 4) reliability against non-persistent faults (mean time to failure) and 5) uniform view of the cache. 6) area overhead,

Useful Cache Capacity: Figure 5b compares the cache capacities. We extend Flexicache with extra slices in order to make it divisible to three, and we normalized the useful cache capacity to the non-extended capacity for fair comparison. First, when the V_{dd} is high, Flexicache do not sacrifice the useful cache capacity due to its flexible circuit design which dynamically switch its configuration to 64KB general purpose data cache (i.e. SVM). Second, due to the partitioning and partition-fix mechanism of Flexicache, it provides higher cache capacity than the conventional triplication schemes even in the low-power mode. Third, Flexicache can operate until the persistent bit failure rate is 12% while TMR can operate until 6% bit failure rate and MS-ECC can operate

Table 2. The figure analysis the area overhead and latency

	Flexicache		MS-ECC	
	Encoder	Decoder	Encoder	Decoder
Number of Gates in the Critical Path	4 XORs	7 XORs + 2 ANDs + 2 ORs	2 XORS	2 XORs + 2 ANDs + 4 ORs
Total Number of Gates	480 XORs	3K XORs + 1,5K ORs + 3,5K ANDs	1,5K XORs	6K XORs + 4,5K ORs + 10K ANDs
Latency	1 cycle	1 cycle	1 cycle	1 cycle
Energy Overhead (In the nominal voltage)	2,5%	20%	5,5%	50%
Area Overhead (Encoder+Decoder)	0.06%		0.12%	

until 2% bit failure rate (Bit failure rates are not shown in the graph). Therefore, TMR and MS-ECC can provide more more than 20% of the cache capacity when the supply voltage is as low as 400mV while Flexicache can provide the similar amount of useful cache capacity when the supply voltage is 320 mV.

Error Correction Latency: In Table 2, we compare the area overhead and the latency presented by encoders and decoders in Flexicache and OLSC. We first present the number of gates in the critical paths. Although, in Flexicache, the number of gates in the critical path are higher than the one in MS-ECC, both encoding and decoding in each scheme can be accomplished in 1 cycle. Note that the decoding latency can be tolerated since decoding is done simultaneously with writing. On the other hand, total number of gates in the encoder and decoder of MS-ECC is much higher than the one in Flexicache which presents higher overhead in both read/write energies (4th line in the table) and area (5th line in the table). Both Flexicache and MS-ECC require changes in the address decoder of the cache to be able to write more than one line simultaneously. The overhead of these address decoders are similar in both schemes.

Energy Reduction: Figure 6 presents the energy consumption of cache operations (i.e. read/write energy and static energy). For read and write energies, TMR allocates three cache ways in a non-modified cache which triplicates the energy consumption. Similarly MS-ECC allocates two cache ways (1 data and the other for parity bits) when the supply voltage is lower than 700 mV, thus at this point MS-ECC also roughly duplicates reading and writing energies. This is mainly because the size of the in/out data is duplicated (or triplicated). Also, the energy consumption of the OLSC decoder is very high (i.e. 50%). Thus, which diminish the energy saving of scaling voltage for read energy as it can be seen at 600mV when OLSC is activated in MS-ECC (Figure. 6a and Figure. 6b). On the other hand, Flexicache accomplishes replication and fault recovery within a way without increasing the size of the data in/out bus coming to the way. Thus,

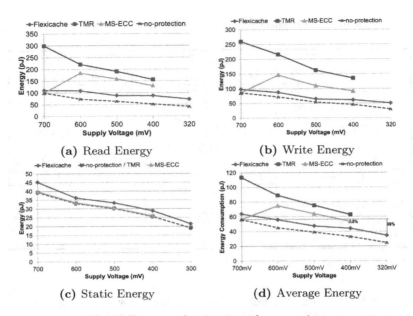

Fig. 6. Energy reduction in cache operations

reading and writing energies of Flexicache is much lower than MS-ECC and trip-lication. For the static energies (i.e. energy spent in one cycle when the cache is idle), Flexicache presents slightly higher energy consumption than an unmodi-fied cache mainly due to the additional extra slices (Figure. 6c). Note that these additional slices also increase the cache capacity that we excluded this increased capacity in our previous results. The static energy consumption of MS-ECC is negligibly higher than a non-modified cache due to OLSC encoder/decoder. It has been showed that dynamic energies are only the 30% of cache energy con-sumptions and among them they are mostly (two out of three) read operations. By considering that, in Figure 6d, we present the average energy consumption of a cache at a time. The figure shows that only Flexicache can operate when V_{dd} is 320 mV by presenting 39% reduction in the energy consumption of the cache compared to non-modified cache when it executes in the high-performance mode with the minimum safe V_{dd} (i.e. 700 mV). MS-ECC can reduce the energy consumption by only 5% compared to the same minimum safe voltage level.

Reliability against Particle Strike: In Figure 7, we inject non-persistent, multi-bit faults (i.e. size of the faults are between n=1-10 bits which means n adjacent bit become faulty due to a particle strike) to the non-disabled cache portion and, we present the fault coverage (i.e. the percentage of the injected faults) for error detection (Figure 7a) and error correction (Figure 7b). In the high-performance mode, MS-ECC can not detect or correct non-persistent faults since it does not extend the cache lines with ECC codes. On the other hand, each cache line is extended with ECC protection in the low-power mode when

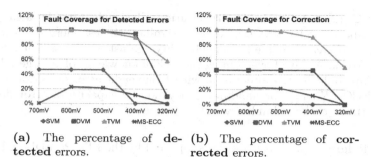

(a) The percentage of **de-tected** errors.

(b) The percentage of **cor-rected** errors.

Fig. 7. Non-persistent fault injection

the persistent fault rate is very high. At this point, additional multi-bit non-persistent faults leads the total number of faults in the cache line higher than OLSC can correct. Thus, non-persistent fault correction capability of MS-ECC is around 20% or less. Note that error detection capability and error correction capability of MS-ECC are identical since OLSC intends to produce the correct data without trying to detect if there was a fault or not. In SVM, Flexicache can not correct faults, but it can detect half of the injected faults (i.e. when the size of the fault is odd). In DVM, it can correct half of the injected faults since it uses parity for the error correction while it can detect more than 90% of the injected faults. TVM can provide more than 90% error correction capability until V_{dd} is 400mV. When V_{dd} is 320mV, only TVM can provide useful cache capacity. At this point, it can detect 58% of the injected non-persistent faults and can correct half of the injected faults. In this study, we switch from SVM to DVM when the V_{dd} is 600mV. One can decide to utilize DVM for higher V_{dd}s for reliability critical applications or systems in faulty environments in order to provide higher reliability with the cost of useful cache capacity.

Area Overhead: After adding parity bits, parity calculators, extra slices, XORs, majority voters, buffers and peripheral circuits, Flexicache presents 12% area overhead compared to the typical cache without any protection. The biggest portion of this overhead belongs to the extra slices which we add to make the cache dividable by three, therefore, actually increasing the size of the cache. This layout allows Flexicache dynamically switch between SVM, DVM and TVM which provides maximum 100%, 50% and 33% useful cache capacity as we presented in Figure 5b.

6   Conclusion

In this study, we present Flexicache, a novel, reliable cache design which configures itself for different supply voltages from the nominal to the near threshold voltage levels in order to duplicate or triplicate each data line if higher reliability is required. Flexicache can continue to operate reliably up to 10% bit failure rate. Therefore, it alters the possibility to operate in 320 mV. Compared to MS-ECC [12] and conventional triplication, Flexicache provides a cache with a higher capacity in low-power mode with significantly less energy consumption. Also, Flexicache can provide higher reliability against non-persistent faults.

Future Work: A way of overcoming the lack of knowledge of voltage-reliability relationship could be the integration with lightweight error detection schemes, such as ECC. When error handling is beyond the capacity of error detection schemes, the in-cache redundancy can be increased.

Acknowledgments. This work was supported by the FP7 ParaDIME Project, grant agreement no. 318693 and by the Ministry of Science and Technology of Spain and the European Union (FEDER funds) under contracts TIN2008-02055-E and TIN2012-34557.

References

1. The Electric VLSI Design System (2014), http://www.staticfreesoft.com
2. Predictive technology model (2014), http://ptm.asu.edu/
3. Abella, J., et al.: Low Vccmin Fault-Tolerant Cache with Highly Predictable Performance. In: MICRO, pp. 111–121 (2009)
4. Agarwal, A., et al.: Process Variation in Embedded Memories: Failure Analysis and Variation Aware Architecture. IEEE Journal of Solid-State Circuits 40(9), 1804–1814 (2005)
5. Ansari, A., et al.: ZerehCache: Armoring Cache Architectures in High Defect Density Technologies. In: MICRO, pp. 100–110 (2009)
6. Armejach, A., et al.: Using a Reconfigurable L1 Data Cache for Efficient Version Management in Hardware Transactional Memory. In: PaCT (2011)
7. Bajura, M.A., et al.: Models and Algorithmic Limits for an ECC-Based Approach to Hardening Sub-100-nm SRAMs. IEEE Trans. Nuclear Science 54(4), 935–945 (2007)
8. Baumann, R.: Soft Errors in Advanced Computer Systems. IEEE Design and Test 22, 258–266 (2005)
9. Chakraborty, A., et al.: E < mc2: Less energy through multi-copy cache. In: CASES, pp. 237–246 (2010)
10. Chen, C.L., Hsiao, M.Y.: Error-Correcting Codes for Semiconductor Memory Applications: A State-Of-The-Art Review. IBM Journal of Research and Development 28(2), 124–134 (1984)
11. Chen, G.K., et al.: Yield-Driven Near-Threshold SRAM Design. In: ICCAD 2007, pp. 660–666 (2007)
12. Chishti, Z., et al.: Improving Cache Lifetime Reliability at Ultra-Low Voltages. In: MICRO, pp. 89–99 (2009)
13. Constantinescu, C.: Trends and challenges in vlsi circuit reliability. IEEE Micro 23, 14–19 (2003)
14. Cosemans, S., Dehaene, W., Catthoor, F.: A 3.6 pJ/Access 480 MHz, 128 kb On-Chip SRAM with 850 MHz Boost Mode in 90 nm CMOS with Tunable Sense Amplifiers. IEEE Journal of Solid-State Circuits 44, 2065–2077 (2009)
15. Dreslinski, R.G., et al.: Near-Threshold Computing: Reclaiming Moore's Law Through Energy Efficient Integrated Circuits. Proceedings of the IEEE 98(2), 253–266 (2010)

16. Ergin, O., Balkan, D., Ponomarev, D., Ghose, K.: Early Register Deallocation Mechanisms Using Checkpointed Register Files. IEEE Transactions on Computers 55(9), 1153–1166 (2006)
17. Franklin, M., et al.: Built-in Self-Testing of Random-Access Memories. IEEE Computer 23(10) (1990)
18. Hsiao, M., et al.: Orthogonal Latin Square Codes. IBM Journal of Research and Development 14(4), 390–394 (1970)
19. Kim, J., et al.: Multi-bit Error Tolerant Caches Using Two-Dimensional Error Coding. In: MICRO (2007)
20. Kulkarni, J.P., et al.: A 160 mV Robust Schmitt Trigger Based Sub-threshold SRAM. IEEE Journal of Solid-State Circuits 42(10), 2303–2313 (2007)
21. McNairy, C., Soltis, D.: Itanium 2 Processor Microarchitecture. IEEE Micro 23, 44–45 (2003)
22. Mcnairy, C., Bhatia, R.: Montecito: A Dual-Core, Dual-Thread Itanium Processor. In: IEEE Micro (2005)
23. Miller, T., et al.: Parichute: Generalized Turbocode-Based Error Correction for Near-Threshold Caches. In: MICRO, pp. 351–362 (2010)
24. Morita, Y., Fujiwara, H., Noguchi, H., Iguchi, Y.: An Area-Conscious Low-Voltage-Oriented 8T-SRAM Design under DVS Environment. In: IEEE Symposium on VLSI Circuits, pp. 256–257 (June 2007)
25. Rusu, S., Muljono, H., Ayers, D., Tam, S., Chen, W., Martin, A., Li, S., Vora, S., Varada, R., Wang, E.: 5.4 Ivytown: A 22nm 15-core enterprise Xeon® processor family. In: IEEE International Solid-State Circuits Conference Digest of Technical Papers (ISSCC), pp. 102–103 (2014)
26. Seyedi, A., Yalcin, G., Unsal, O.S., Cristal, A.: Circuit Design of a Novel Adaptable and Reliable L1 Data Cache. In: Proceedings of the 23rd ACM International Conference on Great Lakes Symposium on VLSI, pp. 333–334 (2013)
27. Seyedi, A., et al.: Circuit Design of a Dual-Versioning L1 Data Cache for Optimistic Concurrency. In: GLSVLSI, pp. 325–330 (2011)
28. Sorin, D.J., et al.: SafetyNet: Improving the Availability of Shared Memory Multiprocessors with Global Checkpoint/Recovery. In: Proceedings of the 29th ISCA, pp. 123–134 (2002)
29. Thoziyoor, S., Muralimanohar, N., Ahn, J.H., Jouppi, N.P.: CACTI 5.1. Technical report, HP Laboratories (2008)
30. Wilkerson, C., et al.: Trading off Cache Capacity for Reliability to Enable Low Voltage Operation. In: ISCA, pp. 203–214 (2008)
31. Zhang, W.: Replication Cache: A Small Fully Associative Cache to Improve Data Cache Reliability. IEEE Transactions on Computers 54, 1547–1555 (2005)

A Appendix

In this section we explain the circuit details of Flexicache for a sub-array and for the address decoder that we used in the evaluation of energy and area overhead. In the main text, we present abstract views of these structures for simplicity.

A.1 Details of Sub-array

Figure 8 shows the block diagram of each sub-array structure. The figure presents the necessary buffers, comparators, parity calculators and control and data lines in detail.

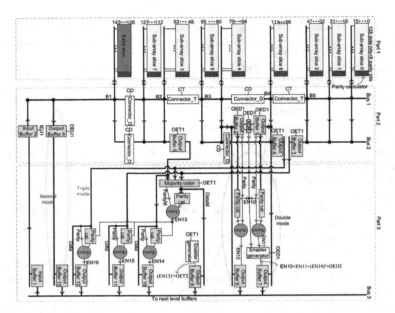

Fig. 8. Address Decoder and Sub-Array in Flexicache

For writing the selected cache line in SVM, signal IEU1 is high and activates input buffers IB1 and IB2 and data can transfer to the selected cache-line via Bus4 and Bus1; and similarly for reading the selected line, signal OEU1 is high and output buffers OB6 and OB13 are active and data is transferred from Bus1 to Bus3. Bus3 (Bus4) is connected to output data drivers (input data drivers) which are located close to each sub-array. At each access time, the enabler signals (CDE and CTE) are high and activate connector buffers, CD1, CD2, CD3, CD4, CT1 and CT2 and connect nodes B1, B2, B3, B4 and B5 to each other (Each connector buffer contains two series inverters with enablers). Similar to many typical L1 caches error protection is based on bit-parity calculation in order to achieve high performance. We divide each cache-line into 8 partitions each contains 16 bits where each interleaved parity protects one partition. At each reading time parity bit calculated and compared with the original parity bit.

For writing in DVM, signal IEU1 is high and data is transferred from Bus4 to Bus1 via IB1 and IB2 and is written to two selected lines at the same time. Parity calculator circuits generate parity bits and write them in parity bit cells as well. For reading the two selected lines, signals CTE is high and CDE is low, connector buffers, CD1, CD2, CD3 and CD4 disconnect B1 with B2 and also B3 with B4 while connector buffers, CT1 and CT2 connect B2 with B3 and also B4 with B5. With this method, Bus1 is divided into two parts; sub-array slices 0,1,2,6 are connected to the first part and sub-array slices 3, 4, 5, 7 are connected to the second part. Signal OED1 is high; output buffers OB1 and OB2 transfer two selected data to the XOR circuit to check the cell contents are identical. Signal EN10 activates two parity calculator circuits to calculate parity bits of selected lines. Then the result of these parity calculator circuits are compared with the original parity bits of each selected-lines. These two comparators generate two enable signals EN11 and EN12. Whenever one of comparator shows equality (when EN11 or EN12 is high), the related output buffer transfers its data to Bus3. If two compared data are equal, signal EN10 is low and output buffer OB7 transfers data to BUS3.

In TVM, for writing the selected cache-lines signal IEU1 is high and data is transferred from Bus4 to Bus1 via IB1 and IB2 and written in three selected lines simultaneously. Similar to SVM and DVM, signals CDE and CTE are high to connect separated Bus1 nodes with each other. At the reading time, CTE is low and CDE is high so Bus1 is divided into three parts; sub-array slices 0, 1, 2 are connected to the first part and sub-array slices 6, 4, 5 are connected to the second part and sub-array slices 3, 7 and extra slice are connected to the third part. CT1 and CT2 circuits disconnect B2 with B3 and B4 with B5. For reading the three selected lines, each from separate sub-array slice group, signal OET1 is high, OB3, OB4 and OB5 are active and data including parities are transferred to a majority voter (the correct value is decided by bit-wise majority voter). The majority voter output for cache-lines is DataM and for their parity-bits is ParityM. Then, the parity calculator circuit calculates the parity bits of DataM. Later one comparator circuit compares these results (the parity bits of DataM) with ParityM. If there are any differences, signal En13 will be high and the parity bits of selected lines are calculated and compared with their original parity bits. Whenever one of parity comparators shows equality, En14, En15 or En16 is high, the related output buffer (OB10, OB11 or OB12) is active and transfers data to Bus3. If signal En13 is low, DataM is transferred to Bus3 via OB9.

A.2   Detail of Address Decoder

The details of address decoder are present in Figure 9. Voltage level detector circuit generates four output signals V1, V2, V3 and V4 according to the supply voltage, V_{dd}; if V1 is high, the cache is in SVM and only one word-line address is activated at each access time; if V2 is high, the cache will be in DVM and two word-line addresses will be activated at each access time; if V3 is high, the cache will be in TVM and three word-line addresses will be activated at each access time; if V4 is high, the supply voltage level is lower than two threshold voltages and the memory cells operate in sub-threshold mode which is beyond our work in this paper and we leave it for future; so the cache-lines will be deactivated in this state. Pre-decoder 2, control signal generator unit 2 and control signal generator unit 3 and control signal generator unit 4 generate enabler signals, En1, En2 . . . and En9 to activate 144 word-line addresses. There are two groups of buffers located in the right and left side of the pre-decoder 1. Each buffers group contains 9 sub-groups, and each sub-group has 16 buffers. The outputs of pre-decoder 1 are connected to the buffers of each sub-group and generated 144 word-line addresses. All buffers of each sub-group are activated with one enabler signal. For example all buffers of sub-group 1 are enabled by signal En1. When partial address 0 and En1 are high, WL0 will be generated. In this way, all word-line addresses from 0 to 143 are generated. If A7 is high, the left part of each cache way is activated; similarly, If A7 is low, the right part of each cache way is activated. At each access time, depending on the mode, one, two or three Enable signals are high and data is written to (read from) one, two or three cache-lines simultaneously. For example in DVM, WL0 and WL48 are activated simultaneously; whenever one of the addresses 0 or 48 are activated, X1 or X4 are high and Vn1 is high so En1 and En4 are high. En1 and En4 are enablers for buffers and let partial address 0 pass and generates WL0 and WL48.

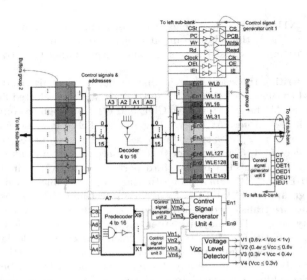

Fig. 9. Necessary decoders and control signal generators

A Parallel Discrete Firefly Algorithm on GPU for Permutation Combinatorial Optimization Problems

Pablo Vidal* and Ana Carolina Olivera

Universidad Nacional de la Patagonia Austral
Ruta N° 3 Acceso Norte, Caleta Olivia (9011), Santa Cruz, Argentina
{pjvidal,aolivera}@uaco.unpa.edu.ar
http://www.unpa.edu.ar

Abstract. The parallelism provided by low cost environments as multi-core and GPU processors has encouraged the design of algorithms that can utilize it. In the last time, the GPU approach constitutes an environment of proven successful progress in the implementation of different bio-inspired algorithms without major additional costs of performance. Among these techniques, the Firefly Algorithm (FA) is a recent method based on the flashing light of fireflies. As a population-based algorithm with operations without a high level of divergence, it is well suited as a highly parallelizable model on GPU. In this work we describe the design of a Discrete Firefly Algorithm (GPU-DFA) to solve permutation combinatorial problems. Two well-known permutation optimization problems (Travelling Salesman Problem and DNA Fragment Assembling Problem) were employed in order to test GPU-DFA. We have evaluated numerical efficacy and performance with respect to a CPU-DFA version. Results demonstrate that our algorithm is a fast robust procedure for the treatment of heterogeneous permutation combinatorial problems.

Keywords: Graphic Processing Units, Optimization, Permutations, DNA Fragment Assembly, Travelling Salesman Problem.

1 Introduction

In the last decades, metaheuristics have proved to be useful to solve combinatorial optimization problems [20,21,29,38]. In particular, nature-inspired algorithms have become very popular to solve this kind of problems [17,42]. These techniques usually need a high amount of computational resources and time in contrast with the need for answers in a "reasonable time" [39]. In this way, parallelization emerges as an attractive alternative in order to decrease the execution time and, in some cases it improves the accurate results of sequential algorithms. In this sense, interest has been growing in the development of parallel evolutionary algorithms by using Graphics Processing Units (GPUs) [39].

---

* Corresponding author: Pablo Vidal, pjvidal@uaco.unpa.edu.ar

G. Hernández et al. (Eds.): CARLA 2014, CCIS 485, pp. 191–205, 2014.

The GPUs represent a low cost environment for massively parallel computations with APIs and development kits for parallel applications. NVIDIA has created a parallel computing platform and programming model called CUDA (Compute Unified Device Architecture) [30] that allows the development of GPU routines called kernels. Each kernel defines instructions that are executed on the GPU device by many threads at the same time following the Simple Instruction Multiple Data (SIMD) model. NVIDIA has advertised its potential for bringing facilities for the programming in these devices and invested great efforts to create a programmable and transparent GPU architecture for programmers [30].

Several studies have presented ideas on how to port existing algorithms running on CPUs to the new GPU architecture: genetic algorithms [16], cellular genetic algorithms [40], particle swarm optimization [12] and some others [4,6,22,41]. In particular, there are contemporary contributions about GPUs that deal with permutation combinatorial problems [23,24,27,39].

The Firefly-Inspired Algorithms (FA), which were developed by Yang [42,43], are recent bio-inspired algorithms that have achieved outstanding results in various domains [8,11,25,45]. FAs have become an increasingly important tool of Swarm Intelligence that has been applied in almost all areas of optimization, as well as in engineering practice [44]. FA is a population-based Swarm Intelligence approach based on the flashing patterns and behaviour of fireflies [43]. FAs have some significant advantages over other metaheuristics, such as genetic algorithms and Particle Swarm Optimizers [9]. A couple of its distinctive advantages are: the automatic subgrouping and its ability to deal with multimodal problems [43]. Fireflies can randomly subdivide into sub-groups and each group can potentially swarm around a local optimum. All optima (obviously including the global optimum) can be obtained simultaneously if the number of fireflies is much higher than the number of subgroups [42,43]. Its characteristics become an attractive alternative to parallelize. In a few years, a lot of research around FA has been done with excellent results [2,10] in many different fields like Power Energy Systems [5,8], mobile networks [3] and permutations combinatorial problems [25,36,44]. However, parallel FA for general purposes and, in particular, for permutation combinatorial problems constitutes a new developing research area and there are relatively fewer papers published on this topic [13,32].

In this work, we present a Discrete Firefly Algorithm on GPUs (GPU-DFA) for permutation combinatorial problems. Therefore, here we show a parallel DFA running entirely on GPU, and demonstrate that the proposed optimization technique is quite amenable for massive parallelism to obtain larger performances and substantial improvements in gain times. We have also studied the behaviour of GPU-DFA over a set of combinatorial problems not only to establish the time reductions, but also the numerical advantages of this swarm intelligence algorithm. In particular, permutation combinatorial optimization problems are presented in the world in many ways, appearing as an excellent way to evaluate the performance of our GPU version with problems of interest related to current society [18]. In our case, the following well-known problems are analysed: Travelling Salesman Problem (TSP) and DNA Fragment Assembly Problem

(DNA-FAP) are employed to test the GPU-DFA. For TSP and DNA-FAP, instances of different sizes are used in order to test the behaviour and scalability of GPU-DFA in contrast with the CPU version. To the best of our knowledge, this is the first time that a GPU Firefly Algorithm is designed and developed especially for permutation combinatorial problems entirely over a GPU platform [13,32].

The remainder of this paper is organized as follows. Section 2 introduces the canonical DFA proposed by Yang [42]. Section 3 presents the general formulation of the GPU-Discrete Firefly Algorithm. In Section 4 we describe the experimental settings, including a brief explanation about TSP and DNA-FAP instances. The main details of the analysis and the results of the computational study are discussed in Section 5. Finally, Section 6 provides the conclusions and also highlights future research directions.

2   The Firefly Algorithm and Related Works

The Firefly Algorithm (FA) is a bio-inspired metaheuristic developed by Yang [42]. It was inspired by mimicking the flashing and attraction behaviour of fireflies. In the scheme of Yang [42,43,44] the fireflies have the following characteristics [9]:

1. All fireflies are unisex, so that one firefly is attracted to other fireflies regardless of their sex.
2. Attractiveness is proportional to their brightness. Hence, for any two flashing fireflies, the less bright one will move towards the brighter one (see Fig. 1(a)). The attractiveness is proportional to the brightness and they both decrease as their distance increases. If no one is brighter than a particular firefly, it moves randomly as shown in Fig. 1(b).
3. The brightness or light intensity of a firefly is affected or determined by the landscape of the objective function to be optimized.

(a)   (b)

Fig. 1. Firefly movement considering their attractiveness: (a) j moves to i, the most bright firefly close to it; (b) j has more brightness that the most attractive firefly i, so j moves randomly

A canonical FA works with two basic concepts: the variation of light intensity I, and the firefly attractiveness β between two fireflies i and j [42]. This attractiveness varies according to a distance r under a fixed light of absorption coefficient γ, that can be defined as follows:

$$I_j(r_{ij}) = I_0 e^{-\gamma r_{ij}^2} \quad (1) \qquad\qquad \beta_j(r_{ij}) = \beta_0 e^{-\gamma r_{ij}^2} \quad (2)$$

where I_0 is the light intensity and β_0 the original brightness of firefly (i.e., fitness) at $r = 0$, respectively. With respect to the light absorption coefficient γ, if $\gamma \to 0$ the attractiveness of a firefly i matches with its brightness (fitness), i.e., the brightness of a firefly will not decrease when viewed by another one. In the case of $\gamma \to \infty$, this means that the attractiveness value of a firefly is close to zero when viewed by another firefly in the sense that fireflies fly randomly in a very foggy region. In this case, the fireflies cannot see each other and fly in a random way. So, γ determines the speed of convergence and how the FA behaves. However, the distance between two fireflies i and j which are located in two different locations, can be expressed as an Euclidean distance. Taking into account the parameters like r, β and I. FA can define what kind of movement a firefly i can make with respect to a firefly j.

In a few years FAs have proven to be useful for continuous optimization [10,19,42]. For the case of FAs on GPU, only a few approaches have been performed on a GPU platform [13,32]. These models were tested over a continuous domain and good gain times were obtained.

Algorithm 1. CPU Firefly Algorithm

---

1. Initialize a population P of p fireflies
2. Define light absorption coefficient γ
3. **while** non stop condition **do**
4.   **for** $j = 1 : p$ **do**
5.   temp=$\emptyset$
6. $i =$ find the most attractive firefly near to j
7.   **if** $i \neq null$ **then**
8.   **for** $l = 1 : m$ **do**
9. $A = computedistance(j, i)$
10.   temp.add($movement_{Operator}(j, A)$)
11.   **end for**
12.   **else**
13.   **for** $l = 1 : m$ **do**
14.   temp.add($movement_{Random}(j)$)
15.   **end for**
16.   **end if**
17.   **end for**
18.   sort($temp$)
19.   select p fireflies from $temp$ and replace on P
20. **end while**
21. **return** The best of P

Discrete Firefly Algorithm. Discrete FA is a variation of canonical FA that may be used for combinatorial problems with success for diverse problems [8,14,36]. It is the base model used in this work for the implementation over GPU.

A pseudocode explanation of CPU-DFA can be seen in Algorithm 1. First, the p fireflies are initialized in population P (line 1). Next, the γ parameter is defined (line 2). Then, while the stop condition is not reached (line 3), the set *temp* is initialized to $\emptyset$ (line 5). For each firefly j, FA tries to find the brightest firefly i near j (line 6). FA calculates the attractiveness ($\beta_j(r_{ji})$) of firefly j with respect to i by using Equation 2. If $\beta_i(r_{ij}) > \beta_j(r_{ji})$ then firefly j will move toward firefly i (line 7); otherwise firefly j will move randomly ($i = null$, line 12). If j moves to i, m new fireflies are created by applying a specific operator considering the distance between j and i (lines 9 and 10). In the case when firefly j moves randomly, m new random fireflies are created (line 13 and 14) taking j as the base. After p fireflies have moved, there are $p \times m$ fireflies in *temp*. Then, the best p fireflies will be chosen based on their fitness (lines 18 and 19). When the evolutionary process ends, FA returns the best one of those p fireflies (line 21). In this context, DFA was shown to be efficient when solving various combinatorial problems [8,14,15,36].

3 GPU-Firefly Algorithm

The goal of this section is to present our algorithmic proposal, which has been called GPU-DFA. In short, our primary concern when designing DFA accelerated by GPU is to create an efficient model that runs the main processes of DFA entirely on GPU. The CUDA software model is employed so as to exploit maximum parallel execution and high arithmetic intensity of GPUs. One of the objectives is to minimize data transfers between the CPU and the GPU, thus avoiding communication bottlenecks.

We follow a coarse-grained parallelization scheme (one thread by firefly or pair of fireflies, respectively). The flowchart of the GPU-DFA model is presented in Fig. 2. The beginning of the proposed algorithm is the initialization of the FA and GPU parameters, respectively on the CPU side. Then, all parameters are transferred to the GPU main memory. Next, we use a group of CUDA *kernels* with the next tasks: At first, GPU-DFA creates and evaluates each solution in P per GPU thread. Afterwards, until the stop condition has been reached, GPU-DFA executes a series of kernels to evolve the current population. The division in multiple kernels is due to the heterogeneity of the tasks and the complexity thereof. In the evolution step, first GPU-DFA calculates parameters r, β and I between each pair of fireflies in parallel. When evaluating each pair of solutions in parallel, it is necessary to apply a method of parallel reduction in GPU so as to assess whether each solution of P found some brighter firefly it could get closer to or move randomly. Once each firefly j has a defined movement, we create and evaluate $p \times m$ new solutions (by disturbing each one with a specific operator or randomly) in a separate kernel and save them in *temp* population. Finally, *temp* is sorted according to its fitness by using parallel Bitonic Sort [33] and replaced over P with the p best fireflies from *temp*.

CUDA code's performance depends largely on the deployment of the threads in GPU, the number of kernels, the memory access schemes and the specific function optimized for GPU (as reduction, sorts or random generators). All methods presented here aim at exploiting fast-access local and global memory

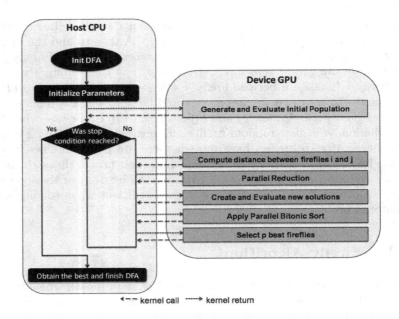

Fig. 2. GPU Discrete Firefly Algorithm Model

to the greatest possible extent. The local populations P and *temp* are stored in global memory. Due to the size of solutions that manage the use of shared memory, it becomes less feasible in our model, since the storage is limited when compared with solution size. However, this approach can be studied in the future with other kind of combinatorial problems or as an improvement in the model. In this work, we have considered the number of kernels as the main criterion to assess how well an algorithm can be parallelized. Due to the complexity of some operations that are completely different from each other, we have tried to write simple and small kernels since the kernel launch cost is negligible with the operations to perform and less registers are used.

On the other hand, the performance of a nature-inspired algorithm largely depends on the quality of its random number generations. For this work, we have utilized a Mersenne Twister random generator approach [35]. We have employed a global seed pass at the beginning of the GPU-DFA execution; then, each thread is initialized with different seed values (by modifying the initial global seed) in the device. Finally, they are invoked sequentially by each thread for subsequent random number generations.

4   Experimental Settings

In this section, two well-known permutation combinatorial problems are introduced in order to test the GPU-DFA.

4.1   Problems

We have selected two permutation problems that have been widely discussed in the literature, exhibiting multiple applications in both academic and industrial fields [7,37].

First, the TSP can be considered one of the most popular permutation combinatorial problems in the literature [15]. TSP is defined as a permutation problem with the objective of finding, given a list of cities and the distances between each pair of cities, the path of the shortest length (or the minimum cost) that a salesman has to take by visiting all the cities exactly once and returning to the starting point. The fitness of a TSP solution is calculated as usual (i.e., as the sum of edges' weights in the solution tour).

In another sense, DNA-FAP is one of the fundamental problems in computational molecular biology. This problem involves the combination of the partial information from known fragments to find a consistent total DNA chain. Hence, large DNA strands need to be broken into small fragments for sequencing in a process called shotgun sequencing [34]. But this process does not keep either the ordering of the fragments or the portion a particular fragment came from. This leads to the DNA fragment assembly problem [17] where these short sequences have to be then reassembled in order, by using the overlapping portions as landmarks. Most fragment assembly algorithms consist of the following steps:

- **Overlap**: Finding potentially overlapping reads
- **Layout**: Finding the order of reads along DNA
- **Consensus**: Deriving the DNA sequence from the layout

The overlap problem consists in finding the best match between the suffix of one read and the prefix of another one. The common practice is to filter out pairs of fragments that do not share a significantly long common substring.

Constructing the layout is the hardest step in fragment assembly [28]. The difficulty is encountered when deciding whether two fragments really overlap (i.e., their differences are caused by sequencing errors) or they actually come from two different copies of a repeat. Repeats represent a major challenge for whole genome shotgun sequencing and make the layout problem very difficult.

The final consensus step of fragment assembly amounts to correcting errors in sequence reads. To measure the quality of a consensus, we can look at the coverage distribution. Coverage at a base position is defined as the number of fragments at that position. It is a measure of the redundancy of the fragment data, and it denotes the number of fragments, on average, where a given nucleotide in the target DNA is expected to appear. It is computed as the number of bases read from fragments over the target DNA's length [17]. For a firefly $i = [0, ..., a, a+1, ..., n]$ the Equation 3 shows the fitness (to maximize) of the sequence i for DNA-FAP.

$$Fitness(i) = \sum_{a=0}^{n-1} w_{a,a+1} \tag{3}$$

where $w_{a,a+1}$ is the pairwise overlap strength of fragments a and $a+1$ [31].

For the purpose of GPU-FA analysis, we have carried out several experiments with different instances of TSP extracted from TSPLib[1][1] and DNA-FAP benchmark data sets, which were described by Mallén-Fullerton et. al [26]. Table 1 summarizes the information of instances (number of cities, optimal) employed to evaluate the GPU-FA in contrast with the CPU-FA version.

Table 1. TSP and DNA-FAP instances

TSP				DNA-SA		
Instance	# of cities	Optimal		Instance	# of Fragments	Optimal
kroA100	100	21282		x60189_4	39	11478
d657	657	48912		m154216_6	173	48052
pr1002	1002	259045		bx842596_4	442	227920

4.2 Experimentation

In order to analyse both the behaviour and performance of the algorithms, we need to clarify some parameter definitions and mechanisms.

In both permutation problems, the distance between two fireflies is defined by Equation 4, where A is the number of different edges between fireflies i and j following the order brought by the array index or likewise, the number of consecutive differences in the array positions. For TSP, we need to evaluate one edge more in A when the last index and the first one do not coincide for both fireflies. n is the size of problem. Equation 4 scales r in the interval $[0, 10]$ [14].

$$r_{ij} = \frac{A}{n} \times 10 \qquad (4)$$

For DFA, the movement of a firefly attracted by another one depends on A. In this work we have applied a 2-opt movement k times, where k is a number generated randomly between 2 and A. Otherwise, random movement is generated by applying a 2-opt operator without restrictions.

In order to make a meaningful comparison among both FA versions, we have employed a common parametrization. We have used a maximum number of evaluations as the stop condition for both algorithms (1000000). As the population and the new solutions may vary, it has different sizes to see if there exists different behaviours of the algorithms and compare that exist some advantage or not to use different population sizes for each problem. FA works with two populations P and $temp$ respectively. Each one can be modified according to the parameters p and m. Then, following the philosophy of FA, we decided to work combining these two parameters with the follow values: 16, 32 and 48, to evaluate the scalability of each parameter by modifying the other.

We perform 30 independent runs to test TSP and DNA-FAP instances. Additionally we apply statistical analysis is of course very important to sustain

---

[1] http://www.iwr.uni-heidelberg.de/groups/comopt/software/TSPLIB95/

final claims; first, we apply the Kolmogorov-Smirnov test on the data to check their normality; if they are normally distributed the ANOVA test is performed, otherwise we will apply a Kruskal-Wallis test. The confidence level used for our claims is 95%.

We always consider in this work a confidence level of 95% (i.e., significance level of 5% or p-value under 0.05) in the statistical tests, which means that the differences are unlikely to have occurred by chance with a probability of 95%. Successful tests are marked with $+$ symbol, $\bullet$ means that no statistical confidence was found (p-value < 0.05).

The experiments was performed using the host with a CPU Intel(R) i7 CPU 920, with a total physical memory of 8192 MB. The operating system is Ubuntu Precise 12.04. In the case of the GPU, we have an NVIDIA GeForce GTX 680 with 2048 MB of DRAM on device and we used CUDA version 6.0.

5   Analysis and Results

In this section, we show the experimental results obtained by testing our proposed method and the behaviour of GPU-FAP is discussed. First, we present a detailed analysis about numerical and time performance for both DNA-FAP and TSP instances. Finally, we study the scalability of our approach and compare the gain times with respect to CPU-DFA version.

DNA-FAP Results. Table 2 shows the results for all the DNA-FAP instances with the different configurations for p and m. In the first column, we inform the name chosen for the instance, columns two and three show the diverse values assumed by parameters p and m. For CPU-DFA, columns four, five and six indicate in 30 independent runs the best fitness (Best) found, the average fitness value with its standard deviation and average runtime, respectively. In the case of GPU-DFA, the same data are exposed in columns seven, eight and nine.

Among the results for both implementations, they generate fitness values that are closer to the overall one, while even in some instances, they reach it. Table 2 shows that the two versions found the optimal value at least once for instance $x60189_4$ in all the configurations. For the rest of instances, both versions (CPU and GPU) obtain values located really quite near to the optimal one. In particular for the second DNA-FAP instance ($m154216_6$), both versions found the best known optimal value with one configuration. For the instance $bx8425964_4$ the increase in parameters p and m does not mean an improvement in the quality of the results; moreover, their quality worsens.

Regarding the results related to parameter p, for instance $x60189_4$ shows that there are no differences; all variations reach the optimum value. For the other two instances, the fitness values obtained are very close to the best optimum one with $p = 32$ for $m154216_6$ and $p = 16$ for $bx8425964_4$. With respect to parameter m, the best configuration is obtained with $m = 32$, exhibiting the same behaviour in most of the instances that are very close to the optimal one. We can also note that for parameter $m = 48$ we obtained shorter times for all the instances.

Table 2. DNA instance results for CPU-DFA and GPU-DFA

Instances			CPU-DFA			GPU-DFA			ST
	p	m	Best	Avg.	Time (sec.)	Best	Avg.	Time (sec.)	
	16	16	11478.00	$11084.93_{\pm81.12}$	4.13	11478.00	$11420.23_{\pm45.77}$	2.38	•
		32	11478.00	$11390.93_{\pm41.48}$	2.33	11478.00	$11469.60_{\pm25.63}$	1.51	•
		48	11478.00	$11469.83_{\pm25.95}$	1.76	11478.00	$11473.73_{\pm11.29}$	1.72	•
$x60189_4$	32	16	11478.00	$11464.93_{\pm58.19}$	7.73	11478.00	$11462.00_{\pm35.16}$	2.72	•
		32	11478.00	$11574.73_{\pm31.43}$	4.06	11478.00	$11466.80_{\pm28.80}$	1.59	•
		48	11478.00	$11467.93_{\pm16.75}$	2.90	11478.00	$11475.20_{\pm15.21}$	1.19	•
	48	16	11478.00	$11608.03_{\pm47.49}$	11.26	11478.00	$11470.23_{\pm23.87}$	1.25	•
		32	11478.00	$11444.47_{\pm39.73}$	5.79	11478.00	$11462.40_{\pm31.36}$	0.86	•
		48	11478.00	$11466.00_{\pm23.06}$	4.06	11478.00	$11463.93_{\pm27.71}$	0.77	•
	16	16	47963.00	$45230.90_{\pm312.77}$	52.37	47803.00	$46219.96_{\pm184.61}$	5.37	•
		32	47550.00	$47357.63_{\pm180.33}$	27.21	48050.00	$47935.93_{\pm90.40}$	12.62	•
		48	47811.00	$47593.13_{\pm112.79}$	18.88	47919.00	$47696.47_{\pm136.71}$	3.32	•
$m154216_6$	32	16	47521.00	$46255.50_{\pm297.18}$	104.34	47750.00	$47511.07_{\pm154.07}$	16.64	•
		32	48052.00	$47416.60_{\pm130.49}$	53.41	48052.00	$47673.57_{\pm114.99}$	8.96	•
		48	47881.00	$47651.07_{\pm117.43}$	36.51	47917.00	$47724.60_{\pm132.16}$	6.49	•
	48	16	46931.00	$46348.87_{\pm277.81}$	157.36	46817.00	$46223.69_{\pm296.13}$	11.85	•
		32	47569.00	$47204.63_{\pm183.40}$	80.54	47612.00	$47174.77_{\pm201.70}$	7.82	•
		48	47918.00	$47429.10_{\pm206.12}$	54.76	47961.00	$47688.36_{\pm100.61}$	6.98	•
	16	16	212802.00	$211408.97_{\pm863.62}$	393.18	213512.00	$211709.77_{\pm977.70}$	139.73	•
		32	225918.00	$224496.94_{\pm916.74}$	199.19	226165.00	$225110.91_{\pm1017.12}$	101.67	•
		48	218523.00	$216496.00_{\pm1054.03}$	134.93	217649.00	$216800.73_{\pm1100.46}$	72.70	•
$bx842596_4$	32	16	211857.00	$210783.79_{\pm1163.03}$	787.43	212381.00	$210599.81_{\pm1711.13}$	128.78	•
		32	213821.00	$211529.03_{\pm1887.81}$	395.64	212479.00	$210181.33_{\pm1281.12}$	66.22	•
		48	212659.00	$211233.76_{\pm1291.36}$	266.27	212177.00	$211918.10_{\pm1151.91}$	45.03	•
	48	16	209954.00	$208333.23_{\pm990.41}$	1185.84	206025.00	$203691.00_{\pm1280.78}$	70.62	•
		32	207797.00	$204743.23_{\pm1293.12}$	596.09	207522.00	$206787.00_{\pm1484.26}$	46.31	•
		48	193276.00	$189610.83_{\pm1641.84}$	399.42	192587.00	$191152.00_{\pm1679.52}$	31.93	•

Table 2 indicates that the GPU-DFA algorithm obtains lower times in all the instances for all the configurations. These good times might be due to the FA operations that are translated into a parallel model that can maximize the efficiency of each thread and thus, the simplicity of each kernel is maintained. Concerning the amount of gain time obtained, we have computed this metric by dividing the time of the CPU-DFA with the GPU-DFA. The GPU-DFA gain time ranges from 1.02 to 16.79. In fact, the execution times in Table 2 confirm this fact, since the execution time when using GPU-DFA is much lower than the CPU's. The results clearly indicate that executing CPU-DFA is more expensive, when compared with the GPU version in all the DNA-FAP instances.

Additionally, in order to make a better comparison between both versions developed in this work, namely GPU-DFA and CPU-DFA, Fig. 3, Fig. 4 and Fig. 5 display the gain time factor obtained for each configuration among the three selected DNA-FAP instances, respectively. As an initial observation, we can say that the time gain values are above the value 1.00, which indicates that the CPU has always spent more execution time than GPU. In the same way, we see that the biggest gain factors of the time appeared in smaller parameter settings, especially those with $m = 16$. These figures clearly indicate that the GPU-DFA is the faster algorithm for all the instances. With respect to the time gain factor values, they range from 1.02 to 16.79.

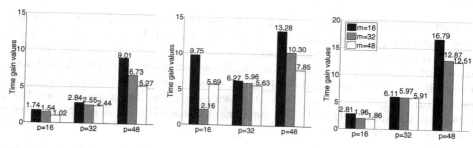

Fig. 3. Gain time results for $x60189_4$ **Fig. 4.** Gain time results for $m1542166_6$ **Fig. 5.** Gain time results for $bx8425964_4$

Table 3. TSP instance results for CPU-DFA and GPU-DFA

Instances	p	m	CPU-DFA			GPU-DFA			ST
			Best	Avg.	Time (sec.)	Best	Avg.	Time (sec.)	
	16	16	21858.00	22042.80±213.40	18.66	21778.00	21593.12±352.38	3.16	•
	16	32	21282.00	21639.60±381.12	9.93	21282.00	21497.69±429.79	2.89	•
		48	21336.00	21621.08±477.20	7.03	21402.00	21736.00±237.40	2.67	•
kroA100	32	16	21282.00	21582.33±360.48	36.88	21282.00	21401.40±228.60	3.85	•
	32	32	21282.00	21521.20±592.02	19.08	21282.00	22721.94±1281.12	3.78	•
		48	21395.00	21474.40±176.80	13.18	21631.00	22140.66±498.60	3.03	•
	48	16	21653.00	22114.20±567.60	54.85	21529.00	22071.39±562.48	2.98	•
	48	32	21477.00	22170.40±620.94	28.32	21438.00	22950.01±583.00	2.61	•
		48	21722.00	22290.80±477.38	19.47	21691.00	22266.20±502.80	2.20	•
	16	16	62346.00	63563.60±992.00	701.40	62198.00	63236.03±1113.40	129.09	•
	16	32	53019.00	55432.00±822.66	356.11	53919.00	54711.20±1964.40	82.11	•
		48	70824.00	73321.80±1958.05	240.50	69846.00	72198.20±1883.68	62.90	•
d657	32	16	59947.00	61889.60±2437,36	1415.81	59718.00	62617.21±2512.40	92.82	•
	32	32	50824.00	53321.80±1958.05	717.87	51282.00	54060.93±1926.02	59.21	•
		48	57406.00	59073.87±1032.66	482.90	61931.00	61420.94±1281.12	44.62	•
	48	16	66152.00	67607.00±1281.80	2134.44	66136.00	67204.20±1173.60	97.70	•
	48	32	55111.00	57073.59±2198.92	1087.16	55053.00	57771.03±2648.26	81.07	•
		48	73767.00	77686.00±3081.70	731.44	73896.00	77982.94±3443.19	65.71	•
	16	16	315113.00	327007.38±6680.03	1585.95	314822.00	323356.00±7320.00	292.66	•
	16	32	307182.00	314207.01±7279.82	801.31	309648.00	315094.19±8341.06	187.85	•
		48	333770.00	341904.93±6747.18	540.54	335412.00	343747.40±8580.93	147.91	•
pr1002	32	16	1451710.00	1481918.00±22179.53	3190.76	1478993.00	1528377.00±18649.91	138.18	•
	32	32	1063330.00	1117894.00±16308.92	1610.57	105938.00	1101450.38±15291.60	90.36	•
		48	1783723.00	1992019.00±16821.80	1083.88	1765683.00	1994320.94±19120.73	84.30	•
	48	16	991450.00	997701.38±6112.30	4835.04	995171.00	1118918.00±22179.53	237.49	•
	48	32	1563330.00	1576598.93±12728.05	2432.82	1589205.00	1601145.94±11273.20	138.32	•
		48	1961320.00	1995822.00±20345.82	1636.99	1968641.00	1996123.00±24837.80	112.79	•

TSP Results. Table 3 displays the results for all the TSP instances with different settings p and m. The first column shows the name chosen for the instance, columns two and three present the values taken for p and m. Columns four, five and six indicate the results for the best fitness (Best) found, the average fitness value with the standard deviation and the average runtime in 30 independent runs for the CPU-DFA approach. For GPU-DFA, the same kind of data is presented in columns seven, eight and nine.

Among the results of GPU-DFA implementation, we can clearly observe that this algorithm reaches an average fitness value that is really quite close to the best known optimal value in $kroA100$ and $d657$ instances. In particular, for configuration $p = 32$ and $m = \{16, 32\}$ the best fitness value has been achieved at least once in the executions. With respect to the largest TSP instance, we note that when the parameters take the values $p = 16$ and $M = \{16, 32, 48\}$ those are the settings that are more approximate to the optimal values. Probably, the reason why this happens is that these small configurations allow the algorithmic model iterate a greater number of times, thus generating subgroups that can perform further exploitation. Table 3 shows clearly the difference between the execution times of CPU and GPU implementations. GPU-DFA exhibits better times for all instances.

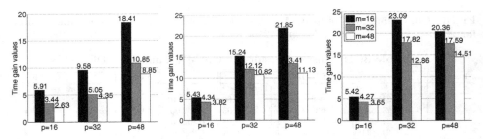

Fig. 6. Gain time results for $kroA100$

Fig. 7. Gain time results for $d657$

Fig. 8. Gain time results for $pr1002$

Regarding the gain of the times obtained in the TSP instances, Fig. 6, 7 and 8 show the respective values for each of those instances. We can observe the same behaviour as the one in the DNA instances. The gain factors range between 2 to 21 (GPU-DFA faster than CPU-DFA in all the instances).

The corresponding statistical tests included in the column ST in Tables 2 and 3 indicates that no statistical differences exists between them ($\bullet$ symbol). As espected, this confirms that they are the same numerical model.

As final remarks regarding our approach, these preliminary results demonstrate that GPU-DFA obtains best results in front of CPU-DFA. However, the numerical performance was not as good as expected, but we have confidence in the algorithmic performance since we have not yet introduced any specific function or operator related to any of the problems in particular. We have tested our approach with different problems and demonstrated that our approximation supports working with different instance sizes without a huge loss in time and solution quality by using smaller configuration parameters. The efficiency of the canonical DFA algorithm has shown that the model is perfectly suited to the GPU architecture.

6   Conclusions and Future Work

The work presented here is based on the Discrete Firefly Algorithm on GPU for Permutation Problems. We performed the tests over two well-known discrete problems: TSP and DNA-FAP. The algorithm was executed in a GPU platform designed for massive parallel arithmetic computing. The new algorithm is inspired by the successful experience gathered by the FA in different fields.

We compared our approach in accuracy and performance to the original single-threaded Discrete Firefly algorithm. Our comparative study between the CPU and GPU implementations shows that, in general terms, both yield numerical results closer to the overall and even in some instances reach it. The GPU-DFA obtains lower times than CPU implementation in the large instances. In this sense, our GPU implementation produced significantly better optimization results with significantly less time than CPU model, which in our experiments yielded a gain time between 1.02 and 21.85.

Besides, we have found that the GPU-DFA model provides a robust parallel model that would allows to solve instances of different sizes without a great degradation in the quality of the solutions.

In the future we will explore the expansion by hybridising this technique with others that can guide the search. Analysing the behaviour of several population sizes or the use of different natural inspired operators will also be part of future work. Besides, it would be interesting to evaluate the specific contribution over other kinds of problem domains or real scenarios to test the feasibility of using this type of technique.

Acknowledgments. Authors acknowledge funds from the ANPCyT for Grant PICT 2011-0639. Dra. Ana C. Olivera gratefully thanks CONICET (www.conicet.gov.ar). Pablo Vidal is thankful to Universidad Nacional de la Patagonia Austral (www.unpa.edu.ar).

References

1. Applegate, D., Bixby, B., Chvátal, V., Cook, B.: The Traveling Salesman Problem: A Computational Study. Princeton University Press (2007)
2. Baykasoglu, A., Ozsoydan, F.B.: An improved firefly algorithm for solving dynamic multidimensional knapsack problems. Expert Syst. Appl. 41(8), 3712–3725 (2014)
3. Bojic, I., Podobnik, V., Ljubi, I., Jezic, G., Kusek, M.: A self-optimizing mobile network: Auto-tuning the network with firefly-synchronized agents. Information Sciences 182(1), 77–92 (2012)
4. Cano, A., Olmo, J.L., Ventura, S.: Parallel multi-objective ant programming for classification using GPUs. J. Parallel Distr. Com. 73(6), 713–728 (2013)
5. Chandrasekaran, K., Simon, S.P.: Network and reliability constrained unit commitment problem using binary real coded firefly algorithm. International Journal of Electrical Power & Energy Systems 43(1), 921–932 (2012)
6. Delévacq, A., Delisle, P., Gravel, M., Krajecki, M.: Parallel Ant Colony Optimization on Graphics Processing Units. Journal of Parallel and Distributed Computing 73(1), 52–61 (2013), metaheuristics on GPUs
7. Donald, D. (ed.): Traveling Salesman Problem, Theory and Applications (2011)
8. Farhoodnea, M., Mohamed, A., Shareef, H., Zayandehroodi, H.: Optimum placement of active power conditioners by a dynamic discrete firefly algorithm to mitigate the negative power quality effects of renewable energy-based generators. International Journal of Electrical Power & Energy Systems 61, 305–317 (2014)
9. Fister, I.: Jr., I.F., Yang, X.S., Brest, J.: A comprehensive review of firefly algorithms. CoRR abs/1312.6609 (2013)

10. Gandomi, A., Yang, X.S., Talatahari, S., Alavi, A.: Firefly algorithm with chaos. Comm Nonlinear Sci Numer Simulat 18(1), 89–98 (2013)
11. García-Nieto, J.M., Olivera, A.C., Alba, E.: Optimal cycle program of traffic lights with particle swarm optimization. IEEE Transactions On Evolutionary Computation 17(6), 823–839 (2013)
12. Guerrero, G., Cecilia, J., Llanes, A., García, J., Amos, M., Ujaldón, M.: Comparative evaluation of platforms for parallel ant colony optimization. The Journal of Supercomputing, 1–12 (2014)
13. Husselmann, A., Hawick, K.: Parallel parametric optimisation with firefly algorithms on graphical processing units. In: Hamid (ed.) 2012 World Congress in Computer Science, Computer Engineering, and Applied Computing (2012)
14. Jati, G.K., Manurung, R.: Suyanto: Discrete firefly algorithm for traveling salesman problem: A new movement scheme. In: Yang, X.S., Cui, Z., Xiao, R., Gandomi, A.H., Karamanoglu, M. (eds.) Swarm Intelligence and Bio-Inspired Computation, pp. 295–312. Elsevier, Oxford (2013)
15. Jati, G.K., Suyanto: Evolutionary discrete firefly algorithm for travelling salesman problem. In: Bouchachia, A. (ed.) ICAIS 2011. LNCS, vol. 6943, pp. 393–403. Springer, Heidelberg (2011)
16. Johar, F., Azmin, F., Suaidi, M., Shibghatullah, A., Ahmad, B., Salleh, S., Aziz, M., Md Shukor, M.: A review of genetic algorithms and parallel genetic algorithms on Graphics Processing Unit (GPU). In: 2013 IEEE International Conference on Control System, Computing and Engineering (ICCSCE), pp. 264–269 (November 2013)
17. Jones, N.C., Preface, P.A.P.: An Introduction to Bioinformatics Algorithms. Massachusetts Institute of Technology (2004)
18. Kallrath, J., Schreieck, A.: Discrete optimisation and real-world problems. In: Hertzberger, B., Serazzi, G. (eds.) HPCN-Europe 1995. LNCS, vol. 919, pp. 351–359. Springer, Heidelberg (1995)
19. Kavousi-Fard, A., Samet, H., Marzbani, F.: A new hybrid modified firefly algorithm and support vector regression model for accurate short term load forecasting. Expert Systems with Applications 41(13), 6047–6056 (2014)
20. Kessaci, Y., Melab, N., Talbi, E.G.: A pareto-based metaheuristic for scheduling HPC applications on a geographically distributed cloud federation. Cluster Computing 16(3), 451–468 (2013)
21. Liao, T., Chang, P., Kuo, R., Liao, C.J.: A comparison of five hybrid metaheuristic algorithms for unrelated parallel-machine scheduling and inbound trucks sequencing in multi-door cross docking systems. Appl Soft Comput 21(0), 180–193 (2014)
22. Luo, G.H., Huang, S.K., Chang, Y.S., Yuan, S.M.: A parallel bees algorithm implementation on {GPU}. Journal of Systems Architecture 60(3), 271–279 (2014), real-Time Embedded Software for Multi-Core Platforms
23. Van Luong, T., Melab, N., Talbi, E.-G.: GPU-based approaches for multiobjective local search algorithms. A case study: The flowshop scheduling problem. In: Merz, P., Hao, J.-K. (eds.) EvoCOP 2011. LNCS, vol. 6622, pp. 155–166. Springer, Heidelberg (2011)
24. Ma, W., Krishnamoorthy, S., Villa, O., Kowalski, K., Agrawal, G.: Optimizing tensor contraction expressions for hybrid cpu-gpu execution. Cluster Computing 16(1), 131–155 (2013)
25. Maher, B., et al.: A firefly-inspired method for protein structure prediction in lattice models. Biomhc. 4(1), 56–75 (2014)
26. Mallén-Fullerton, G.M., Hughes, J.A., Houghten, S., Fernández-Anaya, G.: Benchmark datasets for the DNA fragment assembly problem. International Journal of Bio-Inspired Computation 5(6), 384–394 (2013)

27. Mezmaz, M., Mehdi, M., Bouvry, P., Melab, N., Talbi, E.G., Tuyttens, D.: Solving the three dimensional quadratic assignment problem on a computational grid. Cluster Computing 17(2), 205–217 (2014)
28. Minetti, G., Alba, E.: Metaheuristic assemblers of DNA strands: Noiseless and noisy cases. In: Proceedings of the IEEE Congress on Evolutionary Computation, CEC 2010, Barcelona, Spain, July 18-23, pp. 1–8 (2010)
29. Neumann, F., Witt, C., Neumann, F., Witt, C.: Combinatorial optimization and computational complexity. In: Bioinspired Computation in Combinatorial Optimization. Natural Computing Series, pp. 9–19. Springer, Heidelberg (2010)
30. NVIDIA Corporation: NVIDIA CUDA C Programming Guide (June 2011)
31. Parsons, R., Forrest, S., Burks, C.: Genetic algorithms, operators, and DNA fragment assembly. Machine Learning 21(1-2), 11–33 (1995)
32. de Paula, L., et al.: Parallelization of a modified firefly algorithm using GPU for variable selection in a multivariate calibration problem. International Journal of Natural Computing Research (IJNCR) 4(1), 31–42 (2014)
33. Peters, H., Schulz-Hildebrandt, O., Luttenberger, N.: Fast in-place sorting with CUDA based on bitonic sort. In: Wyrzykowski, R., Dongarra, J., Karczewski, K., Wasniewski, J. (eds.) PPAM 2009, Part I. LNCS, vol. 6067, pp. 403–410. Springer, Heidelberg (2010)
34. Pop, M.: Shotgun sequence assembly. Advances in Computers 60, 193–248 (2004)
35. Saito, M., Matsumoto, M.: Variants of mersenne twister suitable for graphic processors. ACM Trans. Math. Softw. 12, 1–12 (2013)
36. Sayadi, M.K., Hafezalkotob, A., Naini, S.G.J.: Firefly-inspired algorithm for discrete optimization problems: An application to manufacturing cell formation. Journal of Manufacturing Systems 32(1), 78–84 (2013)
37. Stojanovic, N.: The human genome project: software challenges and future directions. In: 2005 ACS / IEEE International Conference on Computer Systems and Applications (AICCSA 2005), Cairo, Egypt, January 3-6, p. 128. IEEE Computer Society (2005)
38. Talbi, E.G.: Metaheuristics: From Design to Implementation. Wiley (2009)
39. Talbi, E.G., Hasle, G.: Metaheuristics on GPUs. J. Parallel Distrib. Comput. 73(1), 1–3 (2013)
40. Vidal, P., Alba, E.: Cellular genetic algorithm on graphic processing units. In: González, J.R., Pelta, D.A., Cruz, C., Terrazas, G., Krasnogor, N. (eds.) NICSO 2010. SCI, vol. 284, pp. 223–232. Springer, Heidelberg (2010)
41. Vidal, P., Luna, F., Alba, E.: Systolic neighborhood search on graphics processing units. Soft Computing 18(1), 125–142 (2014)
42. Yang, X.S.: Nature-Inspired Metaheuristic Algorithms. Luniver Press (2008)
43. Yang, X.S.: Firefly algorithm, stochastic test functions and design optimisation. Int. J. Bio-Inspired Comput. 2(2), 78–84 (2010)
44. Yang, X.S., He, X.: Firefly algorithm: Recent advances and applications. Int. J. Swarm Intelligence 1, 36–50 (2013)
45. Yang, X.S., Hosseini, S.S.S., Gandomi, A.H.: Firefly algorithm for solving nonconvex economic dispatch problems with valve loading effect. Appl. Soft Comput. 12(3), 1180–1186 (2012)

A Parallel Multilevel Data Decomposition Algorithm for Orientation Estimation of Unmanned Aerial Vehicles

Claudio Paz[1], Sergio Nesmachnow[2], and Julio H. Toloza[1]

[1] Universidad Tecnológica Nacional, Facultad Regional Córdoba, Argentina
{cpaz,jtoloza}@scdt.frc.utn.edu.ar
[2] Universidad de la República, Uruguay
sergion@fing.edu.uy

Abstract. Fast orientation estimation of unmanned aerial vehicles is important for maintain stable flight as well as to perform more complex task like obstacle avoidance, search, mapping, etc. The orientation estimation can be performed by means of the fusion of different sensors like accelerometers, gyroscopes and magnetometers, however magnetometers suffer from high distortion in indoor flights, therefore information from cameras can be used as a replacement. This article presents a multilevel decomposition method to process images sent from an unmanned aerial vehicle to a ground station composed by an heterogeneous set of desktop computers. The multilevel decomposition is performed using an alternative hierarchy called Master/Taskmaster/Slaves in order to minimize the network latency. Results shows that using this hierarchy the speed of traditional Master/Slave can be doubled.

Keywords: orientation estimation, unmanned aerial vehicles, high performance computing.

1 Introduction

Nowadays, unmanned aerial vehicles (UAV) generate great interest because they can replace traditional vehicles which carry out dangerous task like early impact analysis after a disaster [1], [2], [3], high cost assessment task like atmospheric surveys [4] or simply for crops analysis [5].

Quadrotors are low cost aerial vehicles, easy to build and maintain because they consist of a cross shape chassis with four rotors in the corners as shown in Fig. 1. Due to this shape quadrotors are able to maintain a hovering flight and perform aggressive maneuvers. Quadrotors flight can be classified in hovering, navigation and vertical take-of and landing. Fast orientation estimation of a quadrotor is important for two reason, first, hovering flight demands high speed controlled thrust on each motor for balance it, and second, in many applications like autonomous navigation, search, mapping, etc. it is useful to known the full orientation of the vehicle.

G. Hernández et al. (Eds.): CARLA 2014, CCIS 485, pp. 206–220, 2014.
© Springer-Verlag Berlin Heidelberg 2014

Fig. 1. QA3 Mini, quadrotor under development at IT Research Center

There are different orientation representation methods including Euler axis, Euler angles, direct cosine matrix and quaternion [6]. Euler angles orientation representation exceeds other methods in clarity and with some constraints can be used for quadrotor flight control in hovering mode. Orientation of a rigid body referred to a global reference can be represented by Euler angles by a sequence of three elemental rotations (yaw, pitch and roll) about the axes of the coordinate system of the body (z, y and x, respectively). Usually, in the body reference system the x-axis points forward and y-axis points right and to complete the right-hand rule, z-axis points down.

The quadrotor can carry large number of sensors on board, accelerometers, gyroscopes and magnetometers among them. This sensors are generally mounted in an arrangement to measure vehicle attitude and motion. It is well known that MEMS (Micro Electro Mechanical Systems) gyroscopes are cheap and lightweight but have large bias due to its operating principle. As a consequence of this bias, the estimation of attitude angles has an important drift and grows without limits. To eliminate this bias, accelerometers complement the gyroscopes to estimate roll and pitch, and magnetometers are used to correct yaw angle. Nevertheless, magnetometers suffer high distortion in indoor navigation due to power wires and electric and electronic devices [7]. Thus, in this cases, another sensor must be used to assist gyroscopes. Cameras are lightweight and cheap sensors which are able to provide big amount of information. There are numerous methods that can be used to recover camera rotations from two successive images like feature tracking and optical flow [8]. In hovering flight, given the slow variation of the yaw angle respect to the frame rate of the camera, it is possible estimate this angle using images taken by a downward looking camera attached to the quadrotor chassis. Gyroscopes can be aided with this information to obtain drift-free yaw angle estimation. For the case of low altitude indoor flight, it is hard to find features to track due to the regularity of ground (tiling or carpet). In this cases, frequency domain representation of the images can detect displacement of the camera using the Fourier Transform and the so called Cross Power Spectrum [9]. This method can be used on small portions of the images to obtain the displacement the so called spectral features to aid gyroscope readings [10]. However, this approach can be computationally expensive and may not run efficiently on a single computer.

Commodity cluster computing is a paradigm for parallel/distributed computing that proposes using a reasonable large number of available computing resources to perform parallel computation at low cost, since those resources are suppose to be already available for non-high performance computing tasks (i.e., office equipment, educational computers, personal notebooks) [11]. Commodity cluster infrastructures, usually built by integrating low-cost personal computers and other devices using a local-area network (LAN), have been used since the mid-1990s for solving a wide range of problems in different application domains, including the scientific and industrial ones [12]. They are characterized as *Beowulf clusters*, from the pioneering work by Sterling and Becker at NASA [13].

In this work a parallel implementation of yaw angle determination is presented. This system runs in a ground station which receive images from the camera mounted in the quadrotor, performs the yaw angle estimation and sends the result again to the quadrotor. The implemented parallel application was evaluated over a Beowulf cluster using two benchmark sets: the specific public data-set by Lee et al. [14] and a benchmark set built with own images. In order to mitigate the latency of the LAN a multilevel data decomposition is proposed using a pyramidal hierarchy called Master/Taskmaster/Slaves. The experimental evaluation indicates that significant reductions in the execution time are achieved when using this hierarchy instead of the classical Master/Slave. The speedup analysis demonstrates that using a multilevel data decomposition an improved of 2× can be achieved.

The paper is organized as follows. Section 2 presents the basis for camera orientation estimation and particularly for the case of yaw angle estimation, besides a brief explanation of the spectral features. Section 3 gives an overview of the proposed approach to implement a parallel orientation estimation algorithm. The experimental analysis of the proposed parallel algorithm is reported in Sect. 4 using a precise public data set of images and orientation, as well as using own images with an ad hoc orientation method for reference. Finally, Sect. 5 presents the conclusions and formulates the main lines for future work.

2 Homography Based Yaw Angle Determination

Given two images of the same plane taken with a camera from different points of view, each characteristic point m_a belonging to image i_a and their corresponding m_b belonging to image i_b are related by a plane induced homography H_{ba} [8] such that $m_a = H_{ba}m_b$.

The homography H_{ba} represents the spatial translation and the rotation between the different camera positions. Particularly, if camera movement is limited to a plane parallel to the plane containing the characteristics and the rotation is around a normal vector to this plane, the homography H_{ba} is defined by

$$H_{ba} = \begin{bmatrix} R_z & t \\ 0 & 1 \end{bmatrix} \tag{1}$$

where t is the vector representing the spatial translation and R_z is the rotation matrix of the camera around z-axis. Matrix R_z is defined by

$$R_z = \begin{bmatrix} \cos\psi & -\sin\psi \\ \sin\psi & \cos\psi \end{bmatrix} \tag{2}$$

where ψ is the rotation angle between images.

In the ground station, corresponding characteristics m_a and m_b must be found in order to determine the homography matrix H_{ba} from which rotation matrix R_z can be obtained. Finally, the yaw angle ψ can be isolated from any element of rotation matrix R_z

Characteristics, also named features, are key points based on intensity changes extracted from an image, easily recognizable in subsequent frames. Occasionally, in the case of downward looking camera attached to a quadrotor in low altitude hovering flight, features are hard to find because of that terrains like lawn in outdoor or carpets in indoor are too regular for feature tracking. To deal with this problem, the frequency domain representation, obtained by Fourier Transform and Fourier shift theorem can be used. Fourier shift theorem claims that given two identical images i_a and i_b displaced one of each other a distance (u, v)

$$i_a(x, y) = i_b(x + u, y + v) \tag{3}$$

and the Fourier Transform of both images are related by

$$I_a(\omega_x, \omega_y) = e^{j(u\omega_x + v\omega_y)} I_b(\omega_x, \omega_y) \tag{4}$$

where I_a and I_b are the Fourier transform of i_a and i_b, respectively. The displacement $\Delta d = (u, v)$ can be calculated first using the *Cross Power Spectrum* (CPS) as follows

$$C(I_a, I_b) = \frac{I_a(\omega_x, \omega_y) I_b^*(\omega_x, \omega_y)}{|I_a(\omega_x, \omega_y)||I_b^*(\omega_x, \omega_y)|} = e^{j(u\omega_x + v\omega_y)} \tag{5}$$

and finally using the inverse Fourier transform.

Given that, to recover the homography at least four point are required, images are divided into patches p_i and the Fourier transform is calculated on each one of them. Hence, a Δd_i displacement is found for each patch as is shown in Fig. 2. By adding this displacements to some point of the patches of the first image, correspondence characteristics set between images are found. Formally,

$$\{m_{a_i} \leftrightarrow m_{a_i} + \Delta d_i = m_{b_i}\} . \tag{6}$$

Finally, from the homography matrix, rotation matrix R_z is obtained and from (2) the ψ angle is isolated.

Algorithm 1 summarizes the described method using Algorithm 2 for displacement determination.

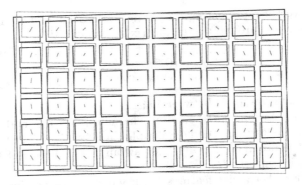

Fig. 2. Patches displacement between two images

Algorithm 1. Yaw angle estimation

---

function YAW_ESTIMATION(i_t, i_{t-1})
    Obtain patches $p_{i\,t}$ and $p_{i\,t-1}$ from i_t and i_{t-1}
    for all $\{p_{i\,t}, p_{i\,t-1}\}$ **do**
        $\Delta d_i \leftarrow$ FINDDISPLACEMENT($p_{i\,t}, p_{i\,t-1}$)
        $m_{i\,t} \leftarrow m_{i\,t-1} + \Delta d_i$
    end for
    $\psi \leftarrow R_z \leftarrow H \leftarrow$ FINDHOMOGRAPHY($m_{i\,t}, m_{i\,t-1}$)
    return ψ
end function

Algorithm 2. Displacement determination between patches

---

function FINDDISPLACEMENT($p_{i\,t}, p_{i\,t-1}$)
    $P_{i\,t} \leftarrow FFT(p_{i\,t})$
    $P_{i\,t-1} \leftarrow FFT(p_{i\,t-1})$
    $C \leftarrow CPS(P_{i\,t}, P_{i\,t-1})$
    $r \leftarrow IFFT(c)$
    $\Delta d_i \leftarrow$ MAX(r)
    return Δd_i
end function

---

3   A Multilevel Decomposition Algorithm

This work proposes a parallel algorithm to calculate the homography based yaw
angle determination equations described in the previous section, over a parallel
architecture. This algorithm take advantage of the natural division of the image
in patches using a domain decomposition method, following the data-parallel
approach. The parallel algorithm is implemented in a ground station which is
composed by office desktop computers connected with a pre-existing LAN to
form a distributed system. From now on, we refer to the computers as *nodes*
and each node has multiple processors running one thread each.

The successive images sent by the quadrotor are received by just one thread in the node containing the UHF receiver and the video digitalizer card. This requires designing the system with a master-slave hierarchy in which the master thread receives and divides the image, and then distributes the patches between threads. The main drawback of this hierarchical approach is that the latency of the network to send each individual patch can significantly increase the execution times.

In order to mitigate the latency problem of the legacy infrastructure, a multilevel domain decomposition approach is proposed. Furthermore, a pyramidal Master/Taskmaster/Slave hierarchy to distribute the patches are used. The proposed hierarchy uses one taskmaster per node, which is in charge of partitioning data for the slave threads executing on that node, as shown in Fig. 3.

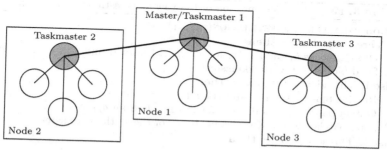

Fig. 3. Master/Taskmaster/Slave hierarchy example. Circles represent threads, gray ones are the taskmasters. Wide lines represent connections over Ethernet and the thin lines symbolize shared memory connections.

Thus, once the image is received, it is divided into blocks by the master thread and each block is sent to the corresponding taskmaster. This previous division of the image into blocks minimizes the number of messages sent by the master. In the Master/Taskmaster/Slave hierarchy example shown in Fig. 3 only two messages are sent over Ethernet against eight if the traditional Master/Slave were used. After this, each taskmaster divides the received block into patches and sends each patch to the slaves. The partitioning process is shown in Fig. 4.

Later, each slave performs the FFT, CPS and IFFT of the patch to find Δd_i and then each displacement is sent back to the taskmasters and finally to master. Once all the distances have been collected, the master thread calculates the homography and isolates the ψ angle.

Algorithm 3 summarizes the described method in Sect. 2 with the proposed multilevel decomposition approach. As in the sequential approach the displacements are calculated using the Algorithm 2.

4 Experimental Analysis

This section reports the experimental analysis of the proposed parallel algorithm for yaw angle estimation.

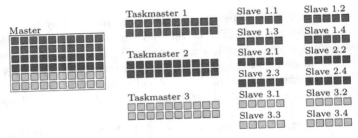

Fig. 4. Domain Multilevel Decomposition example. Image is partitioned into blocks before being sent to taskmasters. Each taskmaster divides the block into patches and sends them to slaves in order to hide network latency.

Algorithm 3. Parallel implementation of the yaw angle estimation algorithm

---

   function PARALLEL_YAW_ESTIMATION(i_t, i_{t-1})
      if Thread == Master **then**
         Obtain blocks $b_{j\,t}$ and $b_{j\,t-1}$ for $j = 1 \ldots J$ from I_t and I_{t-1}
         Send blocks to the J taskmasters
      else if Thread == Taskmaster **then**
         Receive block j from master thread
         Obtain patches $p_{i\,t}$ and $p_{i\,t-1}$ for $i = 1 \ldots K$ from $b_{j\,t}$ and $b_{j\,t-1}$
         Send patches to the K slaves in charge of the j−th taskmaster
      else if Thread == Slave **then**
         $\Delta d_i \leftarrow$ FINDDISPLACEMENT($p_{i\,t}, p_{i\,t-1}$)
      end if
      GATHER(Δd_i)
      if Thread == Master **then**
         $m_{i\,t} \leftarrow m_{i\,t-1} + \Delta d_i$
         $\psi \leftarrow R_z \leftarrow H \leftarrow$ FINDHOMOGRAPHY($m_{i\,t}, m_{i\,t-1}$)
         return ψ
      end if
   end function

4.1 Development and Execution Platform

The proposed algorithm was implemented in the C programming language, using the PHASECORRELATE() function from OpenCV library [15] for both the sequential and parallel version. In both Algorithm 1 and Algorithm 3, the FIND-HOMOGRAPHY() function was implemented with its homonym function from OpenCV library as well.

The parallel version was implemented using the MPICH version of the Message Passing Interface (MPI) library for parallel and distributed computing [16].

The experimental evaluation was performed on a commodity cluster made with desktop computers with 3rd generation Intel i5 processors and 8GB of RAM connected to a 100Mb/s Ethernet LAN. In order to increase the amount of nodes and threads, an old Dell Power Edge rack server with 2 AMD Opteron

6128 and 16GB of RAM was also connected. Given the heterogeneous platform, a simple load balance method based on the execution time was also implemented.

To denote the number of nodes and number of threads in the graphics, uppercase letter N and T were used, respectively (e.g. 1N4T for one node and four threads, 3N24T for three nodes and twenty four threads, etc.).

4.2   Problem Instances

The experimental analysis was performed using the *sFly* data sets by Lee et al. [14] (http://www.sfly.org/mav-datasets), which were taken by an UAV and consist of different images sequences from a front looking and downward looking cameras, together with measurements from an IMU as well as the ground truth information given by a precision external reference system called Vicon system.

The sequence of images used is named hoveringDown; it consists of 2041 image frames of 752 × 480 pixels of resolution taken at approximately 20fps by the downward looking camera. The IMU and Vicon system sample rate are 200Hz, resulting in a total of 21388 samples. They correspond to a flight period of approximately 106 seconds, where the UAV takes off, performs a hovering flight and ends landing near to the same place. The total amount of yaw angle change during the flight is approximately 1.4rad.

Furthermore, a data set with own images was also tested. The images were taken with a 640 × 480 downward looking camera attached to a quadrotor over a carpet at approximately 15fps. In Fig. 5 two consecutive images of the data set are shown where it is possible to see the total absence of intensity features. In this conditions traditional feature trackers are hard to use. The flight period of the data set is around 40 seconds resulting in a total of 600 images without features. The quadrotor is named QA3 and it is under development at IT Research Center (http://ciii.frc.utn.edu.ar).

(a)   (b)

Fig. 5. Consecutive images of the QA3 data set carpet, which are rotated 0.008rad between them. The lack of intensity features make very difficult the use of traditional feature trackers

Two mains goals were taken into account: maintain the accuracy of the sequential algorithm presented by Araguás et al. [10] and ensure a processing time of no more than 0.10 seconds which is enough time to close the yaw angle control loop on-board of the UAV.

4.3   Performance Metrics

In this work, we apply two standard metrics to evaluate the performance of the proposed multilevel data decomposition: *speedup* and *efficiency*. Both are common metrics used by the research community to evaluate the performance of parallel algorithms [17].

The speedup evaluates how much faster is a parallel algorithm than its sequential version. The *relative speedup* (SRS) is defined as the ratio of the execution times of the sequential algorithm (TS_1) and the parallel version executed on m computing elements (threads or processors) (TP_m) (7). We also evaluate the parallel capabilities/scalability of the proposed algorithm by comparing the execution times of the parallel algorithm executing on one (TP_1) and m computing resources (TP_m), which we call *Parallel Relative Speedup* (PRS) (8). When applied to non-deterministic algorithms (i.e., due to non-deterministic situations in the computing environment or non-deterministic bifurcations in the algorithm itself), the speedup should compare the *mean* values of the sequential and parallel execution times, obtained in a reasonable number of independent executions. The ideal case for a parallel algorithm is to achieve linear speedup $(SPS_m = m)$, but the common situation is to achieve sublinear speedup $(SPS_m < m)$, due to the times required to communicate and synchronize the parallel processes.

The efficiency (9) is the normalized value of the speedup, regarding the number of computing elements used for execution. This metric allows comparing algorithms executed in non-identical computing platforms. The linear speedup corresponds to $e_m = 1$, and in usual situations $e_m < 1$.

$$SPS_m = \frac{TS_1}{TP_m} \quad (7) \qquad PRS_m = \frac{TP_1}{TP_m} \quad (8) \qquad e_m = \frac{SPS_m}{m} \quad (9)$$

4.4   Results and Discussion

To validate the parallel implementation, previous to the performance analysis, the yaw angle estimation of the sequential application and various of the parallel configurations were compared using the sFly and QA3 data sets, and the results are reported in Fig 6 and Fig. 7, respectively.

Figure 6a shows that the different estimates are almost coincident and most of the time are overlapped. In Fig. 7a is also possible to see the overlapping of the parallel and sequential versions. Black lines show in both cases the actual orientation. These results validate the parallel implementations and they lead to use any parallel configuration as a reference baseline, provided that time is not being measured like in Fig. 6b and Fig. 7b where the absolute error is shown.

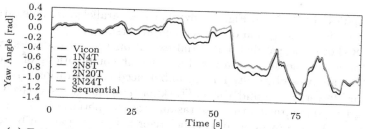

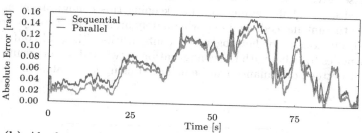

(a) Estimation performed by different configurations as well as the actual orientation given by the Vicon system

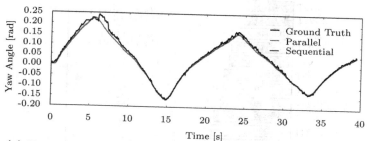

(b) Absolute error comparing the actual orientation against any parallel implementation along with against sequential

Fig. 6. Yaw angle estimation performed by different algorithms using sFly data set to validate parallel implementations

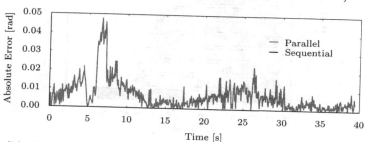

(a) Yaw angle estimation performed by parallel and sequential implementations as well as the actual orientation (*Ground Truth*)

(b) Absolute error comparing the actual and estimated orientation

Fig. 7. Yaw angle estimation performed by different algorithms using QA3 data set where the complete overlapping of the serial and parallel estimation can be seen

The graphics in Fig. 6 and Fig. 7 show that the parallel yaw angle estimation is an accurate implementation of the sequential version.

Figure 8 shows the parallel and serial execution times to process two consecutive frames of the sFly data set, for different combinations of nodes and threads. The analysis of results for the unbalanced configurations (i.e., orange and lilac for Master/Slaves and Master/Taskmasters/Slaves, respectively) allows concluding the configuration that use taskmasters outperform in 2× those that not use them. A good example of this behavior is the comparison between the different configurations of 2N8T and the different configurations of 3N24T. In the last case, given that it is an heterogeneous configuration, the best result is performed with a balance method, but keeping this configuration apart and taking only the unbalanced, again approximately an increase 2× of performance is achieved. Obviously, for heterogeneous configurations (i.e., all configurations with three nodes together with the configuration of two nodes and twenty threads (2N20T)) a better performance can be achieved using load balancing.

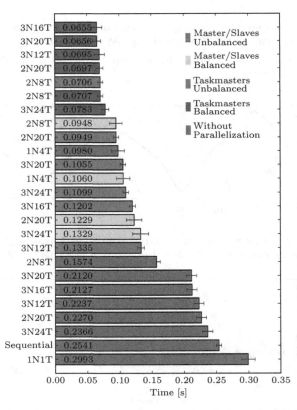

Fig. 8. Execution times to process two consecutive frames of each implemented configuration using the sFly data set

Table 1. Speedup and efficiency achieved with the different configurations

	SRS	PRS	efficiency
3N16T Taskmasters Balanced	3.88	4.57	0.2425
3N20T Taskmasters Balanced	3.88	4.56	0.1940
3N12T Taskmasters Balanced	3.66	4.31	0.3050
2N20T Taskmasters Balanced	3.65	4.29	0.1825
2N8T Taskmasters Unbalanced	3.60	4.24	0.4500
2N8T Taskmasters Balanced	3.59	4.23	0.4487
3N24T Taskmasters Balanced	3.24	3.82	0.1350
2N8T Balanced	2.68	3.16	0.3350
2N20T Taskmasters Unbalanced	2.68	3.15	0.1340
1N4T Unbalanced	2.59	3.05	0.6475
3N20T Taskmasters Unbalanced	2.41	2.84	0.1205
1N4T Balanced	2.40	2.82	0.6000
3N24T Taskmasters Unbalanced	2.31	2.72	0.0962
3N16T Taskmasters Unbalanced	2.11	2.49	0.1318
2N20T Balanced	2.07	2.43	0.1035
3N24 Balanced	1.91	2.25	0.0796
3N12T Taskmasters Unbalanced	1.90	2.24	0.1583
2N8T Unbalanced	1.61	1.90	0.2000
3N20T Unbalanced	1.20	1.41	0.0600
3N16T Unbalanced	1.19	1.41	0.0743
3N12T Unbalanced	1.14	1.34	0.0949
2N20T Unbalanced	1.12	1.32	0.0560
3N24T Unbalanced	1.07	1.26	0.0445

Table 1 reports the SRS, PRS and efficiency metrics of the different configurations based on Fig. 8.

The comparison between the sequential version of the yaw angle estimation algorithm against the best parallel implementation (i.e., 3N16T with Taskmasters and load balance) reported in Table 1 demonstrates that approximately 4× of speedup can be achieved. In terms of efficiency, it can be seen comparing all the unbalanced configurations with and without taskmasters, that using the lasts the performance was increased at least 2×. Obviously, the best efficiency (0.64) was achieved avoiding the use of the network (i.e., the configuration 1N4T which has only one node and no load balance). Nevertheless, this configuration is not able to ensure enough speed to process the images in less than 0.1s to close which is a constraint to use the yaw angle control loop. This speed could be accomplished only with the configurations that uses more than one node like 3N16T, 3N20T, 3N12T, 2N20T, 2N8T and 3N24T using Master/Taskmasters/Slaves hierarchy.

Similar results are obtained when processing the QA3 data set. They are presented in Fig. 9. Given that this data set has smaller images, the processing time is slightly lower.

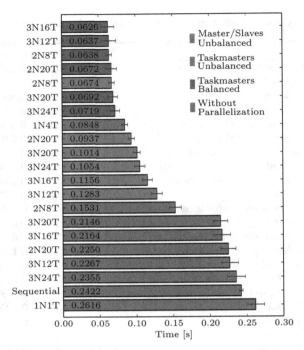

Fig. 9. Execution times to process two consecutive frames of each implemented configuration using the data set composed of own images

5   Conclusions and Future Work

In this work, a parallel implementation of an algorithm able to estimate the orientation of a unmanned aerial vehicle was presented. The estimation is performed by using a remote processing of images taken from an on-board camera. A multilevel decomposition method to process the images in an heterogeneous set of desktop computers was proposed. This method uses an alternative hierarchy called Master/Taskmaster/Slaves which has as main goal the reduction of the messages sent over Ethernet in order to minimize the latency of the network. To test the algorithm two data sets were used.

The results show that using the proposed hierarchy and the multilevel data decomposition method the speed of the process using the traditional hierarchy Master/Slaves can be doubled. This method can be used for any type of parallel implementation with large amounts of information passing from one node to another. Moreover, for the evaluated case of an UAV along with a ground station, given the processing speed achieved, a close loop for full control of the yaw angle of the UAV can be implemented.

Currently, as a direct application of the research reported in this work, a full orientation control loop for the QA3 quadrotor is under development.

Acknowledgments. The first author is supported by the National Technological University grants program. The work of S. Nesmachnow is partly funded by ANII and PEDECIBA, Uruguay. This work was partially funded by the Argentinean National Agency for the Advance in Science and Technology under project "Autonomous Vehicle Guidance Fusing Low-cost GPS and other Sensors", PICT-PRH-2009-0136), currently developed at the Center for IT Research (CIII), Córdoba, Argentina.

References

1. Bendea, H., Boccardo, P., Dequal, S., Tonolo, F., Marenchino, D., Piras, M.: Low cost UAV for post-disaster assessment. In: International Society for Photogrammetry and Remote Sensing Congress (2008)
2. Mase, K.: Wide-area disaster surveillance using electric vehicles and helicopters. In: 2013 IEEE 24th International Symposium on Personal Indoor and Mobile Radio Communications (PIMRC), pp. 3466–3471 (September 2013)
3. Neto, J., da Paixao, R., Rodrigues, L., Moreira, E., dos Santos, J., Rosa, P.: A surveillance task for a UAV in a natural disaster scenario. In: 2012 IEEE International Symposium on Industrial Electronics (ISIE), pp. 1516–1522 (May 2012)
4. Corrigan, C.E., Roberts, G.C., Ramana, M.V., Kim, D., Ramanathan, V.: Capturing vertical profiles of aerosols and black carbon over the indian ocean using autonomous unmanned aerial vehicles. Atmos. Chem. Phys. 8(3), 737–747 (2008)
5. George, E., Tiwari, G., Yadav, R., Peters, E., Sadana, S.: UAV systems for parameter identification in agriculture. In: 2013 IEEE Global Humanitarian Technology Conference: South Asia Satellite (GHTC-SAS), pp. 270–273 (August 2013)
6. Phillips, W.F., Hailey, C.E.: Review of attitude representations used for aircraft kinematics. Journal of Aircraft 38(4), 718–737 (2001)
7. Yamazaki, K., Kato, K., Ono, K., Saegusa, H., Tokunaga, K., Iida, Y., Yamamoto, S., Ashiho, K., Fujiwara, K., Takahashi, N.: Analysis of magnetic disturbance due to buildings. IEEE Transactions on Magnetics 39(5), 3226–3228 (2003)
8. Hartley, R., Zisserman, A.: Multiple View Geometry in Computer Vision. Cambridge University Press (2003)
9. Kuglin, C.D., Hines, D.C.: The phase correlation image alignment method. In: IEEE International Conference on Cybernetcis and Society, pp. 163–165 (1975)
10. Araguas, G., Paz, C., Gaydou, D., Paina, G.P.: Orientation estimation fusing a downward looking camera and inertial sensors for a hovering UAV. In: 2013 16th International Conference on Advanced Robotics (ICAR), pp. 1–6 (November 2013)
11. Gray, J.: Super servers: Commodity computer clusters pose a software challenge. In: BTW, pp. 30–47 (1995)
12. Plaza, A., Valencia, D., Plaza, J., Martinez, P.: Commodity cluster-based parallel processing of hyperspectral imagery. J. Parallel Distrib. Comput. 66(3), 345–358 (2006)
13. Sterling, T.L., Savarese, D., Becker, D.J., Dorband, J.E., Ranawake, U.A., Packer, C.V.: BEOWULF: A parallel workstation for scientific computation. In: Banerjee, P. (ed.) Proceedings of the 1995 International Conference on Parallel Processing, pp. 11–14 (1995)

14. Lee, G.H., Achtelik, M., Fraundorfer, F., Pollefeys, M., Siegwart, R.: A benchmarking tool for mav visual pose estimation. In: 2010 11th International Conference on Control Automation Robotics & Vision (ICARCV), pp. 1541–1546 (2010)
15. Bradski, G.: The OpenCV Library. Dr. Dobb's Journal of Software Tools (2000)
16. Gropp, W., Lusk, E., Skjellum, A.: Using MPI: Portable Parallel Programming with Message-Passing Interface. MIT Press (1999)
17. Foster, I.: Designing and Building Parallel Programs: Concepts and Tools for Parallel Software Engineering. Addison-Wesley Longman, Boston (1995)

A Numerical Solution for Wootters Correlation

Abdul Hissami, Alberto Pretel, and E. Tamura

Pontificia Universidad Javeriana – Cali
Calle 18 118-250, Santiago de Cali, Colombia
{abdulh,apretel,tek}@javerianacali.edu.co
http://www.javerianacali.edu.co

Abstract. This paper describes QDsim, a parallel application designed to compute the quantum concurrence by calculating the Wootters correlation of a quantum system. The system is based on a two-level two quantum dots inside a resonant cavity. A Beowulf-like cluster was used for running QDsim. The application was developed using open, portable and scalable software and can be controlled via a GUI client from a remote terminal over either the Internet or a local network. A serial version and three parallel models (shared memory, distributed memory and hybrid –distributed/shared memory) using two different partitioning schemes were implemented to assess their performance. Results showed that the hybrid model approach using domain decomposition achieves the highest performance ($12.2X$ speedup in front of the sequential version) followed by the distributed memory model ($6.6X$ speedup). In both cases, the numerical error is within 1×10^{-4}, which is accurate enough for estimating the correlation trend.

Keywords: Quantum Computing, Wootters Correlation, Density Matrix, Parallel Algorithms, Parallel Models, Cluster Computing.

1 Introduction

Quantum Computing is a revolutionary field of Physics whose goal is increase enormously the computing performance by using quantum mechanics laws to create very small-scale processing units (a few atoms in size) thus surpassing the limits of classic computing. This field studies different topics on the classic information theory and its processing, e.g., quantum algorithms, quantum teleportation, quantum codes and error detection, and realization of quantum computers. The latter topic investigates new forms of processing and information storage at the nano scale. A variety of future candidate technologies for implementation are currently being explored [1]; for example, superconductor quantum computer, trapped-ion quantum computer, solid state Nuclear Magnetic Resonance (NMR), Kane Quantum computers and Quantum Dot computers.

Nowadays, Quantum Dot computers are a promising technology for the realization of quantum computers. Unfortunately, a Quantum Dot (QD) is not able to retain its state for a long time. Consequently, the information is destroyed [1].

G. Hernández et al. (Eds.): CARLA 2014, CCIS 485, pp. 221–235, 2014.
© Springer-Verlag Berlin Heidelberg 2014

This effect is known as *Decoherence*. To provide an insight into this phenomenon, an application called QDsim was created.

QDsim is a numerical application designed to study the quantum dynamics of concurrence for a bipartite system composed of two quantum dots under external interactions. It is important to highlight that the concurrence is the best known indirect measurement of entanglement[1] of any bipartite system. By using the density operator Master Equation (ME), QDsim is able to compute the concurrence in the bipartite system using the analytical formula derived by Wootters[2].

Electromagnetic radiations from any source, can produce a series of resonant effects inside the quantum cavity (where the QDs are embedded) thus causing interactions. Furthermore, even the laser beam used to control the operation of the QD may cause such interactions. The aforementioned resonant effect is composed of infinite light modes (Fock states) or degrees of freedom that perturb the quantum state of the QDs. For this reason, solving this kind of system is a time-consuming task; from hours to even days.

This paper thus proposes an algorithm to solve Wootters Concurrence using parallel techniques that runs over a Beowulf-like cluster composed of shared memory processors in order to reduce the processing time. Section 2 gives a brief introduction of the quantum system, sections 3, 4 and 5 show how the computation was parallelized, and finally sections 6, 7 and 8 discuss the results and how performance was measured.

2   System Model

Using the analogy of the binary representation, where bits (represented by "0" logic and "1" logic) are the cornerstone of the information in classical computation, excitonic states are the foundation of the quantum information through quantum bits or Qbits. The model under study has two QDs embedded in a three dimensional semiconductor microcavity as shown schematically in Fig. 1. Qbits have two levels: the first, represented by $|0\rangle$, corresponds to the absence of excitons; on the other hand, the $|1\rangle$ state indicates the presence of excitons.

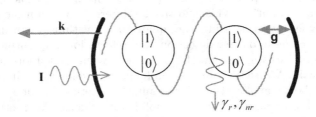

Fig. 1. Model of a QD into quantum cavity taken from [3]

---

[1] A phenomenon in which the quantum states of two or more QDs are correlated.

The dynamics of the quantum system depicted in Fig. 1 is described in more detail in [3] where it is analyzed with the coupling constant of the resonant cavity with the environment (denoted by **k**) and the external radiation field (denoted by **I**). Both QDs are coupled to the cavity and the coupling is represented by **g**. Since the cavity and external fields interact with the QDs, the excitonic states are affected by the radiative and non-radiative decays (γ_r and γ_{nr} respectively).

From this model, the Hamiltonian is given by: $H = H_0 + H_1 + H_2$, where H_0 represents the free energy of the QD, the cavity, the phonons and the electromagnetic bath; H_1 represents the internal QD-cavity and QD-QD interactions; and H_2 is the interaction between QD and cavity with the electromagnetic bath and phonons. The master equation for the evolution of the systems dynamics is given by:

$$\frac{d\rho}{dt} = \frac{-i}{\hbar}[H, \rho] + \frac{\gamma_r(t)}{2} \langle n_{phot,we} \rangle \sum_{p=1}^{2}[(\sigma_+^p \rho \sigma_-^p - \sigma_-^p \sigma_+^p \rho) + h.c]$$

$$+ \frac{\gamma_r(t)}{2}(\langle n_{phot,we} \rangle + 1) \sum_{p=1}^{2}[(\sigma_-^p \rho \sigma_+^p - \sigma_+^p \sigma_-^p \rho) + h.c]$$

$$+ \frac{k(t)}{2} \langle n_{phot,wc} \rangle (a^\dagger \rho a - a a^\dagger \rho + h.c) \tag{1}$$

$$+ \frac{k(t)}{2}(\langle n_{phot,wc} \rangle + 1)(a \rho a^\dagger - a^\dagger a \rho + h.c)$$

$$+ \frac{\gamma_{nr}(t)}{2}(2 \langle n_{phon,we} \rangle + 1) \sum_{p=1}^{2}[(\sigma_z^p \rho \sigma_z^p - \sigma_z^p \sigma_z^p \rho) + h.c] \ .$$

Where H is the Hamiltonian of the quantum system, γ_r and γ_{nr} are the radiative and non-radiative exciton decay rates, $\langle n_{phot}, \omega_e \rangle$ is the average number of photons with excitonic Bohr frequency, ω_e is the Bohr frequency related to the energy difference among "1" and "0" levels, a and $a^\dagger$ are the creation and annihilation operators, $k(t)$ is the cavity decay rate, ω_c is the cavity radiation frequency, $\langle n_{phot}, \omega_c \rangle$ is the average number of photons with cavity frequency and $\langle n_{phon}, \omega_e \rangle$ is the average number of phonons with excitonic Bohr frequency, σ_+ and σ_- are the excitation and de-excitation operators (excitonic operator) respectively. Finally, $h.c$ is the hermitian conjugate of the preceding term. Equation (1) is time dependent but it is normalized regarding the spontaneous emission rate for excitons in the empty electromagnetic field.

Projecting (1) on the Fock states, the density matrix is obtained. From it the dynamics of the base states of the QD can be extracted to compute the quantum dynamics of Wootters concurrence [4], which is defined by:

$$C(t) = max\left(0, \sqrt{\lambda_1(t)} - \sqrt{\lambda_2(t)} - \sqrt{\lambda_3(t)} - \sqrt{\lambda_4(t)}\right) \ . \tag{2}$$

Where λ_i are the eigenvalues of the matrix R defined by:

$$R = \hat{\rho} \cdot \sigma_y \cdot \hat{\rho}^* \cdot \sigma_y \ . \tag{3}$$

where σ_y is the Pauli spin matrix:

$$\sigma_y = \begin{pmatrix} 0 & 0 & 0 & -j \\ 0 & 0 & 1 & 0 \\ 0 & 1 & 0 & 0 \\ -j & 0 & 0 & 0 \end{pmatrix}. \qquad (4)$$

3   The Application

QDsim was designed to solve the density matrix and compute the quantum dynamics of concurrence as a function of time and a physical variable of the QD system that is chosen by the user. For example, Fig. 2 shows in the vertical axis, the concurrence, whose values oscillate between 0 and 1; the two horizontal axes represent time (given in picoseconds) and the physical variable VX (e.g., the degree of purity of the Extended Werner-like state, probability amplitude, the quotient between photon emission decay rate and radiative quantum dot decay rate, the quotient between phonon emission decay rate and non-radiative quantum dot decay rate, the quotient between dots coupling and dot-cavity coupling. For more details about these variables, see [9] and [3].)

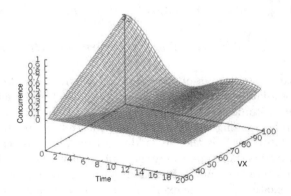

Fig. 2. Surface plot of quantum concurrence

The system allows setting up different simulation parameters. The physical variable to simulate (given by VX) is adjustable through a Graphical User Interface (GUI) with their respective limits called VLL (VX Lower Limit) and VUL (VX Upper Limit) and the step increment ($VINC$). In addition, other variables such as integration method, integration error, time intervals (TLL, TUL) and other simulation variables can also be defined using the GUI.

The basic flow diagram of the application is composed of five tasks (see Fig. 3):

1. An initialization process where a set of parameters regarding the simulation is defined (e.g., time intervals, VX intervals, integration method, definition of physical parameters, etc.)
2. Generate the system equations or ME
3. Solve the ME using Ordinary Differential Equation (ODE) solvers
4. Computation of the quantum concurrence where a set of system equations (master equation) to be solved using a specific integration method are generated and then the concurrence is computed using Wootters concurrence [4]. Results are temporarily stored in hard disk.
5. From the results stored in hard disk, generate the surface plot using GNU-plot[2].

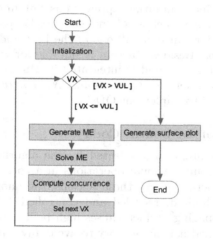

Fig. 3. Basic flow diagram of QDsim

4 Parallelization Features

The computational complexity of the algorithm depends on several variables (e.g the degree of freedom of the system, the number of interactions of the QD, the numerical error of the integrator). The problem is that the complexity is not easy to derive a priori: the number of equations to generate can be known in a static manner; on the other hand, the number of terms and factors is only known at runtime, and worst yet, some of the factors could be simulation-time dependent functions. Since using the estimated worst-case execution time can be overly optimistic, a proof-of-concept was implemented using Mathematica[3], to

---

[2] See http://www.gnuplot.info
[3] See: Wolfram Mathematica, http://www.wolfram.com/mathematica/

have an idea about the computational complexity. Its execution required hours and even days for processing.

Three key elements were used to improve the processing time of the application as follows:

- The programming language
- Optimization of the source code
- Use of parallel algorithms and architectures

4.1   The Programming Language

During the early stages of the project development, to overcome the higher execution times of using Mathematica, the algorithm was partially implemented in different languages such as R[4] and Python[5]. They are two widely used languages in many scientific computing applications but unfortunately, they are slower than other languages such as *C* and *Fortran*. Despite that *Fortran* is an older language, its performance is still one of the best and is currently used in many HPC applications. Besides, *Fortran* is suitable for working in distributed memory parallel architectures and is integrated into many Linux distributions using GNU Fortran compiler. For this reason, *GNU Fortran 4.1*, which is based on Fortran 95, was used to implement QDsim.

4.2   Optimization of the Source Code

The performance of a program is affected by the algorithm complexity (i.e., number of loops and computational operations in a code) and the location of data in the memory hierarchy. For these reasons, the number of variables and operations should be limited, recycled and controlled. This approach avoids, on one hand memory paging[6], which causes high penalties in execution performance; on the other hand it is mandatory to avoid any unnecessary operations. For example, (1) is composed of many factors, which depending upon system parameters, sometimes yield multiplied by zero at runtime. Unfortunately, neither the compiler (in spite of the optimization flags) nor the Control Unit[7] are aware of finding an efficient way of minimizing such operations. Being unaware of this, the program wastes valuable clock cycles in a fruitless manner. Thus, the proposed algorithm avoids those redundant operations to increase significantly its performance. From (1), the elements of the density matrix are obtained and represented (in a compact manner) as a set of i terms [3], where each term is composed of a set of a_j factors as shown in (5).

$$F(t, \rho_k) = \frac{d}{dt}\rho_k = \sum_i \left[\prod_j a_{j,i} \right] \cdot \rho_i \ . \tag{5}$$

---

[4] See: The R Project for Statistical Computing, http://www.r-project.org

[5] See: http://www.phyton.org

[6] Reading from the lower levels of the memory hierarchy instead of doing so from the higher ones.

[7] Internal circuitry that allows the operations inside the CPU and the data flow.

Since some a_j can be either functions (composed of hyperbolic and exponential operations) or constants, the approach is to compute first those a_j with lower CPI[8] and then, compute the functions with higher CPIs (for example, math operations such as "$\times$", "$+$", "$-$", "$\div$" have lower CPI than "$sinh(x)$" and "e^x".) When $a_j = 0$, the algorithm skips the product operator and computes the next i-th term as shown in Fig. 4.

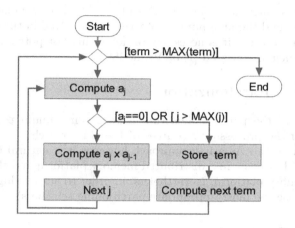

Fig. 4. Flow diagram of the optimization of the number of operations

This method reduces unnecessary operations when there is a multiplication by zero, thus decreasing the waste of valuable clock periods.

4.3   Use of Parallel Algorithms and Architectures

In order to reduce the processing time of complex computations, parallel techniques can be applied. For a computational problem, the parallelization can be achieved using compiler directives [6] or manually. The former approach is not recommended in this particular problem because it yields lower performance in complex problems like this since the parallelization process depends on many factors such as algorithm structure[9], the parallel computer architecture[10] and the parallel programming model. Since there is no general method for parallelization, there are a series of steps described in [5] that were used for the parallelization process.

Based on the flow diagram of Fig. 3, there are two types of partition schemes: Loop Partitioning (called LP) on VX loop and Task Partitioning (called TP) where the tasks (see Fig. 3) are parallelized. As mentioned previously, these

---

[8] Acronym of Clocks Per Instruction.

[9] Regarding the data and task dependencies in a code.

[10] Architectures based on distributed memory, shared memory, number of processing units and interconnection topology.

partitions depend of the algorithm structure and computer architecture. Fortunately, the loop only sets a given value in the physical variable VX of the ME and consequently, there are no loop dependencies in LP between one iteration and the subsequent ones. The LP scheme is easy to implement in a distributed memory scheme (MP); furthermore, since there are no loop dependencies, the communication cost is low. On the other hand, implementing LP in a shared memory platform (MC) is not straightforward due to resource constraints (e.g. resources such as cache size –level 1, 2 and 3–, bus access policies and data flow restrictions) and the high number of variables involved in the computation. Nevertheless, in any case, it is necessary to determine hotspots and bottlenecks using profilers such as Valgrind [7] or Vtune [8].

5   Algorithm Parallelization

The main idea of the parallel algorithm is to get maximum performance by exploiting all of the processing resources of the cluster architecture (computer nodes and their cores.) As a first approach however it is natural that the algorithm uses the LP scheme in a distributed memory platform and the TP scheme in a shared memory platform. Nevertheless, in order to achieve higher speedups it is critical to use the most appropriate partitioning scheme(s).

5.1   LP Partitioning Scheme

Figure 3 suggests that the majority of code is placed inside the loop. This is indeed the case, as Valgrind shows that, for the worst-case execution time scenario, 95.16%[11] of processing time occurs inside this loop. This fact is beneficial for parallelization purposes to achieve higher speedups.

The LP partitioning uses domain decomposition to split the range $[VLL, VULL]$ of the physical variable VX in several sub-domains and then assign them to every processing unit (computer nodes or cores) as shown in Fig. 5. The number of chunks per processing unit is determined by $VINC$ (step increment) and the number of computers, np. These chunks are uniformly distributed among the processing units to keep the processing load balanced.

5.2   TP Partitioning Scheme

The results of the measurement analysis by executing Valgrind showed that "Solve ME" is a hotspot (with the 91.3% of processing time). Inside of this function, the integration method consumes roughly 78% of the processing time, while the rest of code (13.3%) are strictly serial statements. Therefore, the optimization efforts need to be focused there. This task solves a large coupled ODE system of the ME[12] using an integration method. To solve the ME, QDsim implements different integration methods such as Adams-Bourdon for stiff systems, Backward Differentiation Formula and Euler.

---

[11] $95.16_{loop} = 0.02_{generateME} + 91.3_{solveME} + 3.84_{computeConcurrence}.$

[12] Generated by the task "Generate ME".

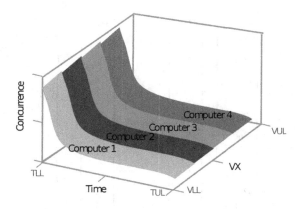

Fig. 5. Partitioning using domain decomposition. Every processing element computes a non-dependent chunk.

The latter method was chosen for all of the experiments due to its good numerical convergence in the analysis of quantum concurrence. Despite the Euler is strictly serial, the large number of equations allowed the parallelization using only a shared memory scheme. Besides, the TP partitioning leads to a cumbersome implementation in a distributed memory scheme since the high quantity of data dependencies will increase the execution time due to a higher latency in the interconnection network. For these reasons, a shared memory scheme is used for this partitioning.

Figure 6 shows the Euler method for a linear system where $\rho(i,j)$ is the dependent variable for the i-th equation in the j-th iteration, Δt is the time step, F is an ODE function that depends on the previous values of $\rho(i,j)$ and the current time t. The length of the vector ρ depends on the degree of freedom of the light modes (ideally, it is infinity) and is limited to n modes by statistical experiences. The number of equations increases proportionally to the number of modes and it is limited to n equations (in Fig. 6, $n = 40$.)

Since the number of equations is large, the domain of n is split into blocks. Each block has a number of pieces that is equal to the number of cores; a block is then assigned to each core. The problem arises during the evaluation of the function F where the system equations are produced. For example, the k-th derivate –see (5)– is compound of j factors, whose number varies significantly from 0 to many factors. Worst yet, a factor may be a function.

Since the complexity of evaluating each equation is not even from a computational viewpoint, the performance of the system is reduced significantly because of this imbalance. For this reason, to keep the load balancing, it is not enough to distribute an equal number of equations among the cores. Ideally, to get a perfect balance one should distribute a number of operations per core such that the computational cost in every core is the same. This of course, is unfeasible in this particular case. A pragmatic solution was to attempt to distribute an equal

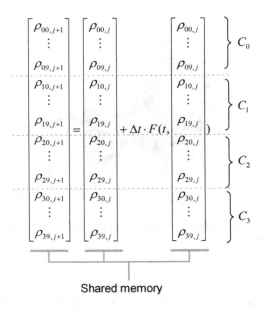

Fig. 6. Vectorial form of the ODE system in a shared memory

number of terms per core, which resulted in a fair balance. The allocation of terms uses a fine-grained round-robin scheduling.

Since the matrix ρ is a strongly coupled system, it should be stored in a shared memory to allow that every core can read the vector $\rho(i, j)$ simultaneously[13].

6   Experimental Setup

Three models of QDsim were implemented to analyze its performance under different environments and applying two partition schemes (LP and TP):

- A shared memory model using OpenMP [14]
- A distributed memory model using OpenMPI [15]
- A hybrid model (distributed/shared memory) using OpenMPI & OpenMP

Basically, these versions tried to answer the following questions:

1. Has a shared memory architecture the same performance as a distributed memory architecture?
2. Does hyper-threading technology contributes in the computing performance?

---

[13] The simultaneity depends on the size of the level 2 cache and the data size to be mapped into it.
[14] See: http://openmp.org
[15] See: http://www.open-mpi.org

3. How much performance can achieve a distributed memory/shared memory model?

These versions plus the serial version were executed in a cluster architecture that is composed of seven Symmetric Multi-Processing (SMP) heterogeneous nodes (three nodes with Intel Xeon SL8SV dual-core processors with Hyperthreading technology[16] and four nodes with two AMD Opteron250 single-core processors.) Every node has 64-bit Scientific Linux 5.6 executing runlevel 3 (text mode) to decrease the system workload caused by the GUI. Of these nodes, one node is used as Master and another is used as a Storage Node. The nodes are connected via a dedicated 8-port Gigabit switch. To measure the elapsed time, the time command on Linux is used. Unfortunately, no profilers were executed at runtime due to the high volume of operations. To reduce the time error measurement, the elapsed time was measured repeatedly (10 trials). Valgrind was used during the debugging phase only to compute the percentage of the serial and parallel sections. To minimize unexpected behaviors in performance, CPU throttling was disabled during the measurement process.

To validate the numerical results of the proposed algorithm, the data was compared with analytical results from [9]; it has a sound research in bipartite systems of quantum dots. From there, eight experiments were performed to validate QDsim using different configurations. Each simulation changes a specific parameter of the quantum system such as the Purity level, the QD decay rate, the amplitude of probability, the radiative decay rate and the quotient between photon emission decay rate and radiative quantum dot decay rate. The physical parameters to feed the model are based on a InAs/GaAs semiconductor.

7   Results

From a partitioning viewpoint there are four implementations:

- Loop Partitioning
  - on a shared memory model using OpenMP (LPMC)
  - on a distributed memory model using OpenMPI (LPMP)
  - on a hybrid (distributed/shared memory) version using OpenMPI & OpenMP (LPMP + LPMC)
- Loop/Task Partitioning
  - on a hybrid (distributed/shared memory) version using OpenMPI & OpenMP (LPMP + TPMC)

Performance is measured using speedup as a metric. The speedup S is the quotient between the time of the serial algorithm Ts and the time of the parallel version Tp ($S = Ts/Tp$). The time of the parallel version is a function of the number of computer nodes np and the number of cores nt used in the computation.

---

[16] Increases the performance of physical cores by using abstract cores called *Logical Cores*.

7.1   Loop Partitioning

Figure 7 shows the behavior of the three parallel models (LPMC, LPMP and LPMC+LPMP.) The x axis shows the variations of either np or nt; note that only the hybrid model shows the variation of np when $nt = 2$. The y axis shows the variation of speedup S as the number of Processing Units (np or nt) increases.

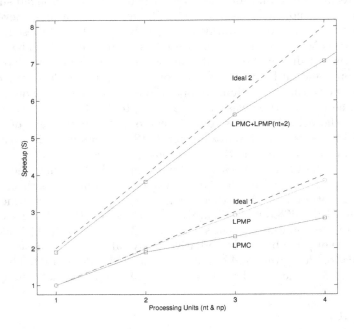

Fig. 7. Performance comparison among parallel models as $np(nt)$ increases

For this implementation, according to Amdahl's law, a linear behavior on speedup is expected in every model since the parallel section covers more of the 91.3% of the coding. For example, the LPMP model is closer to the ideal behavior when $1 \leq np < 4$. Nevertheless, there is an inflection point in the linearity for the LPMC model when $nt > 2$ (see Fig. 7). This indeed is caused by the performance of the logical cores[17] when the available physical cores are oversubscribed. Only when $nt = 2$, the speedup for the LPMC model gets closer to that for the LPMP model but with a downtick: the LPMP model got $S = 1.97X$ approximately whereas the LPMC model got $S = 1.90X$ (see Table 1) using either two computer nodes or two cores respectively. The relative error of the speedup between the Ideal and LPMC models increases as the number of cores increase and consequently the parallel efficiency decreases. The hybrid model (LPMP + LPMC) gets the highest performance since every core contributes to the total efficiency of the processing.

---

[17] Hyper-threading technology on Xeon processors.

Observe that for this simulation, Table 1 shows that logical cores only contribute $0.5X$ to speedup while physical cores contribute $1.0X$. Regarding the LPMP + LPMC scheme, its performance increases roughly proportional to $np \cdot nt$ (e.g., $S \approx 4$ when $np = 2$ and $nt = 2$) and the speedup increases faster than both LPMP and LPMC.

Table 1. Speedup values for Loop Partitioning

	nt=2	nt=3	nt=4	nt=5	nt=6	nt=7
S_{LPMC}	1.90X	2.31X	2.82X	-	-	-
$S_{theoretical}$	2.00X	3.00X	4.00X	-	-	-
$Error_{relative}$	5.00%	23.0%	29.5%	-	-	-
	np=2	np=3	np=4	np=5	np=6	np=7
S_{LPMP}	1.95X	2.85X	3.81X	4.71X	5.50X	6.61X
$S_{theoretical}$	2.00X	3.00X	4.00X	5.00X	6.00X	7.00X
$Error_{relative}$	2.13%	4.71%	4.62%	5.70	8.21	5.51
	np=2 nt=2	np=3 nt=2	np=4 nt=2	np=5 nt=2	np=6 nt=2	np=7 nt=2
$S_{LPMC+LPMP}$	3.74X	5.48X	7.09X	8.93X	9.82X	12.20X
$S_{theoretical}$	4.00X	6.00X	8.0X	10.0X	12.0X	14.0X

7.2   Loop/Task Partitioning

Since the parallelizable section (task "solve ME") is around 78%, the expected speedup behavior is asymptotic but it is mixed up with the effects of core over-subscription. When the percentage of the parallel section decreases, the speedup is reduced. For the Loop Partitioning, each core contributed with $1X$; now one can say that each core contributes with $0.8X$ approximately when $nt = 2$. This contribution of course decreases when the computations use the logical cores. Figure 8 shows the speedup when the number of threads increase from 0 to 4 and the number of computer nodes increases up to 7. The black squares represent the measured values while the dashed line only represents the tendency. The maximum speedup, $10.5X$ approximately, is reached when $np = 7$ and $nt = 2$.

8   Concluding Remarks

Regarding the three proposed questions, the numerical results show a small performance increment for the distributed memory model in front of the shared memory model for all of the trials. The reasons are the serialization effects on the code section. This serialization is mainly caused by constraints in the architecture, cache size, memory paging and hard disk access. Figure 9 shows the serialization effects when a processor tries to access the I/O interface. This snapshot from Vtune shows the states of the threads (in the upper part of the figure) as well as the thread concurrency[18] (in the bottom part of the figure.) Since the

---

[18] A measure of the level of parallelism between threads.

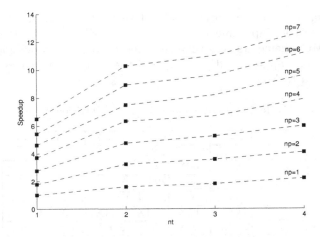

Fig. 8. Speedup for Loop/Task Partitioning

data bus can be accessed by one core only at any given moment, the other cores must wait for their turns (the sequential section S in the upper right half of the figure.) For this reason, thread concurrency decreases in this section. Nevertheless, the measurement error in the performance increases with the number of processing units. Logical cores always exhibited a lower performance than physical cores and can not be compared. Operating Systems always show these cores (logical and physical cores) as comparable and the general consumers usually get awry judgements about their real performance.

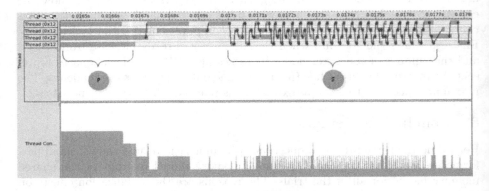

Fig. 9. Serialization effects

Regarding the parallelization of the density matrix, the use of hybrid models exhibited a good performance where the speedup increased until $10.5X$ (Task Partitioning) to $12.2X$ (Loop Partitioning) using the available cluster platform.

Selecting the appropriate partitioning scheme in accordance with the parallelization model is of utmost importance to yield good speedups.

Implementing the Loop Partitioning in a shared memory platform was a
painful task due to the number of variables and its declaration[19]. Furthermore,
the debugging process was also very difficult. For these reasons, the per core
allocated workload on a shared memory model should be a simple task. Despite
the Loop Partitioning got higher performance than Loop/Task Partitioning, the
latter has several advantages such as: it is controllable; easy to implement; lower
implementation time and an easier debugging process.

Further work may explore using Intel's Threading Building Blocks (TBB)[20]
to exploit dynamic load balancing among cores. On the other hand, to minimize
contentions regarding hard disk access, it can be worthwhile to use a dedicated
thread for that purpose.

References

1. Chen, G., Church, D., Englert, B., Henkel, C., Rohwedder, B., Scully, M., Zubairy,
   M.: Quantum Computing Devices: Principles, Designs, and Analysis. Chapman &
   Hall/CRC, New York (2006)
2. Hill, S., Wootters, W.K.: Entanglement of a Pair of Quantum Bits,
   http://arxiv.org/abs/quant-ph/9703041
3. Pretel, A., Reina, J.H., Aguirre-Contreras, W.: Excitonic dynamics of a quantum dot
   coupled to a laser-driven semiconductor microcavity. Microelectronics Journal 39,
   682–684 (2008)
4. Altintas, F., Eryigit, R.: Quantum Correlations in non-Markovian Environments.
   Physics Letters A 374, 4283–4296 (2010)
5. Intel Corp.: Optimizing Software for Multi-core Processors. White paper (2007)
6. Intel Corp.: Auto-parallelization overview. White paper (2007)
7. Valgrind Developers: Valgrind for dynamic analysis tools, http://valgrind.org/
8. Intel Corp.: Vtune performance profiler,
   https://software.intel.com/en-us/intel-vtune-amplifier-xe
9. Bellomo, B., Lo Franco, R., Compagno, G.: Entanglement dynamics of two independent qubits in environments with and without memory. Phys. Rev. A 77, 032342–
   032351 (2008)

---

[19] OpenMP requires the user to define which variables should be private to each core.
[20] See: https://software.intel.com/en-us/intel-tbb

Solving Nonlinear, High-Order Partial Differential Equations Using a High-Performanc Isogeometric Analysis Framework

Adriano M.A. Côrtes[1,2], Philippe Vignal[1,3], Adel Sarmiento[1,4],
Daniel García[1,5], Nathan Collier[1,6], Lisandro Dalcin[1,7], and Victor M. Calo[1,2]

[1] Center for Numerical Porous Media,
King Abdullah University of Science and Technology, Thuwal, Saudi Arabia
[2] Earth Sciences & Engineering,
King Abdullah University of Science and Technology, Thuwal, Saudi Arabia
[3] Material Science & Engineering,
King Abdullah University of Science and Technology, Thuwal, Saudi Arabia
[4] Applied Mathematics & Computational Science, Earth Science & Engineering,
King Abdullah University of Science and Technology, Thuwal, Saudi Arabia
[5] Mechanical Engineering,
King Abdullah University of Science and Technology, Thuwal, Saudi Arabia
[6] Oak Ridge National Laboratory, Oak Ridge, Tennessee, USA
[7] Consejo Nacional de Investigaciones Científicas y Técnicas and Universidad
Nacional del Litoral, Santa Fe, Argentina

Abstract. In this paper we present PetIGA, a high-performance implementation of Isogeometric Analysis built on top of PETSc. We show its use in solving nonlinear and time-dependent problems, such as phase-field models, by taking advantage of the high-continuity of the basis functions granted by the isogeometric framework. In this work, we focus on the Cahn-Hilliard equation and the phase-field crystal equation.

Keywords: Isogeometric analysis, high-performance computing, high-order partial differential equations, finite elements, phase-field modeling.

1   Introduction

The recent interest in Isogeometric Analysis (IGA) [1], a spline-based finite element method, motivated an efficient implementation of this numerical method PetIGA [2] pursues this goal. It is built on top of PETSc [3,4], an efficient an parallel library tailored for the solution of partial differential equations.

To highlight some of the features we have access to through the use of PetIGA we decided to focus on two phase-fields models of great interest in the materi science community, namely, the Cahn-Hilliard equation, and the phase-field cry tal equation. These are high-order and nonlinear partial differential equation Their discretization in space can be be simplified through the use of IGA whe compared to traditional finite elements, as the higher-continuous basis functio required can be trivially generated within this setting.

G. Hernández et al. (Eds.): CARLA 2014, CCIS 485, pp. 236–247, 2014.

In the second section we give a brief definition of what spline functions are, followed by a section that describes the main ideas behind the IGA framework. In the fourth section we describe some of the PetIGA data-structures and their parallelism. In the last section, we show how the framework can be applied to the phase-field models mentioned before.

2   Spline Spaces

To define a univariate B-spline basis one needs to specify the number n of basis functions wanted, the polynomial degree p of the basis and a knot vector

$$\Xi = \{\underbrace{\zeta_1, \ldots, \zeta_1}_{r_1 \text{ times}}, \underbrace{\zeta_2, \ldots, \zeta_2}_{r_2 \text{ times}}, \ldots, \underbrace{\zeta_m, \ldots, \zeta_m}_{r_m \text{ times}}\}, \tag{1}$$

with $\sum_{i=1}^{m} r_i = n + p + 1$ and $\zeta_i < \zeta_{i+1}$. The B-spline basis functions are piecewise polynomials of degree p on the subdivision $\boldsymbol{\zeta} = \{\zeta_1, \ldots, \zeta_m\}$.

A stable way of generating them involves using the Cox-de Boor recursion algorithm [5], which receives as inputs p and Ξ. Knot multiplicity is an essential ingredient in spline theory, since it allows to control the smoothness of the basis. Indeed, if a breakpoint ζ_j has multiplicity r_j, then the basis functions have at least $\alpha_j := p - r_j$ continuous derivatives at ζ_j. The vector $\boldsymbol{\alpha} := \{\alpha_1, \ldots, \alpha_m\}$ collects the basis regularities.

The space of spline functions is denoted by $\mathcal{S}_{\boldsymbol{\alpha}}^p := \text{span}\,\{B_i^p\}_{i=1}^n$. The multivariate cases are defined by tensor products of univariate spaces. As an example, the bivariate spline space is defined by $\mathcal{S}_{\boldsymbol{\alpha_1},\boldsymbol{\alpha_2}}^{p_1,p_2} = \mathcal{S}_{\boldsymbol{\alpha_1}}^{p_1} \otimes \mathcal{S}_{\boldsymbol{\alpha_2}}^{p_2}$.

3   Isogeometric Analysis Concept

Spline spaces are one of the main theories that the Computer Assisted Design (CAD) community uses to model geometries on a computer [5]. They are used as basis functions to parameterize euclidean subsets. The main concept behind Isogeometric analysis (IGA) is to use the same spline functions as basis functions for the Galerkin approximation of partial differential equations. As is done with isoparametric finite elements methods, the parameterization, hereafter denoted as $\mathbf{F} : [0,1]^d \to \mathbb{R}^n$, called **patch** by the CAD community and **geometric mapping** by the IGA community, can then be used to induce an approximation space on the domain of the equation, $\Omega = \mathbf{F}([0,1]^d)$.

It is important to note that the tensor product nature of a multivariate basis induces a structured grid on the parametric space. That is, we end up with a set of basis on a structured grid. An efficient implementation should take this into account.

Besides the possibility of h-refinement and p-refinement, spline functions also allow the possibility of a new type of refinement, called k-refinement in the IGA literature. Within k-refinement, the basis has a higher regularity than only continuous. This opened another pathway of application for the IGA framework, namely, the discretization of higher-order differential operators [8].

4   PetIGA

The Portable, Extensible Toolkit for Scientific Computation (PETSc) is a set of data structures and routines for the parallel solution of discrete problems, generally coming from some discretization of a partial differential equation. With respect to parallelism, PETSc is built on top of MPI, the standard message passing interface framework. Its main goal is to provide the user with a complete set of tools for the solution process, freeing the programmer from the burden of parallel implementation.

PETSc is object-oriented in nature, with the main classes being: *IS, Vec, Mat, DM, KSP, PC, SNES, TS*. For example, once a *Vec* object is created, its contiguous chunks are spread throughout as many processors as the user has requested. The same is true of a *Mat* object. To access those objects, PETSc provides the *Set* and *Get* pair, such that the programmer does not have to think about the inter-process communication. More information on these objects and the PETSc framework can be found in [4].

PetIGA is a scalable implementation of NURBS-based Galerkin and Collocation finite element methods, built on top of the PETSc library. Its main idea is to use the advantageous features one has access to through PETSc, while providing the user with a framework that only requires a variational formulation, specified through the coding of a residual and the Jacobian associated with the discrete problem.

4.1   PetIGA Data Structures

PetIGA also uses the object-oriented paradigm. The first main class, called *IGA*, is an abstraction of the notion of a **patch**. An *IGA* object contains all the information to build the basis functions in each direction (*IGABasis*), the control points to build the geometric mapping and the quadrature rule (*IGARule*) used, that is, the quadrature points and weights. Additionally, in terms of parallelization, we use a domain decomposition approach, splitting each direction in a way to guarantee a load balance between the processors.

Figure 1a shows an example using four processors, numbered from $P0$ to $P3$. In this simple case, each processor will have its own *IGA* object. To properly perform the parallel assembly of the global vectors and matrices, PetIGA makes extensive use of distributed structured grid data structures very similar to the built-in *DMDA* objects of PETSc (see [4], section 2.4), which manage all of the communication patterns on a structured grid between the processors. The crosshatched regions in figure 1a show the neighboring (*ghost*) elements of processor $P0$. To complete its description, the *IGA* object has an *iterator* through *IGAElement* objects. This relationship is shown on the diagram of figure 1b.

The *IGAElement* class abstracts an element in the patch. It contains all the information needed from the element point of view, with the most important piece being the local degrees of freedom (i.e. the basis functions), whose support intercept the element, as well as their derivatives, evaluated at the quadrature points. To achieve good memory performance, since a structured grid is being

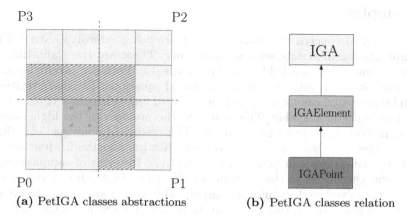

(a) PetIGA classes abstractions   **(b)** PetIGA classes relation

Fig. 1. Main concepts of PetIGA framework

considered, no connectivity array is stored, and everything is computed on the fly for each element. The *IGAElement* object has an *iterator* through the *IGAPoint* object, as expressed in figure 1b.

From the perspective of the user, the *IGAPoint* class is the most important one, and actually, the only one a PetIGA user must care about. An *IGAPoint* object gets all the information from the *IGAElement*, which refers to a specific quadrature (or collocation) point. Within that object, the *shape* field stores the shape functions and its nonzero derivatives on that quadrature point (see listing 1.1, lines 5,6). The rationale behind these abstractions stems from wanting the user to only have to focus on the variational formulation of the problem.

As an example, let us consider the C function *SystemGalerkin*, shown in listing 1.1, that a user has to write to compute a discrete scalar Laplacian. This is part of the Poisson demo tutorial included in the PetIGA repository [2,17].

```
1  PetscErrorCode SystemGalerkin(IGAPoint p,PetscScalar *K,PetscScalar *F,
       void *ctx)
   {
3    PetscInt nen = p->nen;
     PetscInt dim = p->dim;
5    const PetscReal *N0       = (typeof(N0)) p->shape[0];
     const PetscReal (*N1)[dim] = (typeof(N1)) p->shape[1];
7
     PetscInt a,b;
9    for (a=0; a<nen; a++) {
       for (b=0; b<nen; b++)
11        K[a*nen+b] = DOT(dim,N1[a],N1[b]);
       F[a] = N0[a] * 1.0;
13   }
     return 0;
15 }
```

Listing 1.1. Callback function to build the discrete Laplacian and an unit force vector. Part of PetIGA demo code Poisson.c

5   Examples

The cases studied concern two equations that are being extensively studied by
the computational materials science community. These are the Cahn-Hilliard
equation [6], and the phase-field crystal equation [13]. Both are two high-order,
time-dependent and nonlinear partial differential equations. The discretizations
that will be presented cannot be done in a standard finite element setting, where
only C^0-continuity is available. This is due to the presence of the higher-order
operators in both variational formulations. The system of nonlinear equations
that is obtained in both cases is solved using Newton's method. More details
on the implementations can be found in [8,9,10,11]. In terms of computational
cost, we refer the reader to the work in [15,16], where in-depth analysis of the
linear systems solved while using both direct and iterative solvers can be found.
The examples presented in this work use the options PETSc has set by default,
which are:

- nonlinear solver tolerance with a value of 10^{-8},
- GMRES as linear solver, with a restart parameter of 30 and a 10^{-5} tolerance,
- block-Jacobi ILU(0) preconditioner.

5.1   The Cahn-Hilliard Equation

The Cahn-Hilliard equation is a fourth-order, nonlinear and time-dependent,
partial differential equation. In this work, we consider the dimensionless version, adapted from [8]. The Cahn-Hilliard equation has successfully been used to
model spinodal decomposition [12], a physical mechanism in which an immiscible binary fluid phase-separates when a critical transition parameter, θ, reaches
a certain threshold. The phase-field parameter c in the Cahn-Hilliard equation
represents concentration of one of the components in the mixture, and is related
to the dimensionless free energy functional of the system, $\mathcal{F}_{CH}$ by

$$\mathcal{F}_{CH} = \int_{\Omega} \left(c \log c + (1 - c)\log(1 - c) + 2\theta c(1 - c) + \frac{1}{2\chi}|\nabla c|^2 \right) d\mathbf{V} \quad (2)$$

where θ is given a value of 3/2, and $\chi = \dfrac{L_0^2}{2\theta\epsilon^2} = 100$ where L_0 is a representative
length, and will in this work be equal to one. Note that in this formulation,
the critical transition value for θ, θ_c, is one, such that the value assigned being
greater than θ_c, induces phase-separation. Following the phase-field framework
for generating the partial differential equation that models the interfacial behavior of the system [7], we now take the variational derivative of this free energy
with respect to c, such that

$$\frac{\delta \mathcal{F}_{CH}}{\delta c} = \mu_c - \frac{1}{\chi}\Delta c, \quad (3)$$

where μ_c represents the chemical potential, given by

$$\mu_c = \log\frac{c}{1 - c} + 2\theta\left(1 - 2c\right),$$

such that the partial differential equation is then defined as

$$\frac{\partial c}{\partial t} = \nabla \cdot \left(M_c \nabla \left(\frac{\delta \mathcal{F}_{CH}}{\delta c} \right) \right)$$

$$= \nabla \cdot \left(M_c \nabla \left(\mu_c - \frac{1}{\chi} \Delta c \right) \right), \tag{4}$$

where $M_c = c(1 - c)$ represents a mobility. Finally, the strong form of this equation, given that concentration must be conserved [7], can be expressed as: over the spatial domain Ω and the time interval $]0, T[$, given $c_0 : \Omega \longmapsto \mathbb{R}$, find $c : \Omega \times [0, T] \longmapsto \mathbb{R}$

$$\begin{cases} \dfrac{\partial c}{\partial t} - \nabla \cdot \left(M_c \nabla \left(\mu_c - \dfrac{1}{\chi} \Delta c \right) \right) = 0 & \text{on } \Omega \times]0, T] \\ c = c_0 & \text{on } \Omega \times \{t = 0\} \end{cases} \tag{5}$$

where c_0 denotes the initial condition, the natural boundary conditions are taken to be equal to zero, and periodic boundary conditions are considered in all directions. To derive the weak form for this equation, we let $\mathcal{V}$ denote the trial and weighting function spaces, and multiply the strong form (5) by a test function $w \in \mathcal{V}$ and integrate by parts,. The problem using the Galerkin method is then stated as: find $c \in \mathcal{V}$ such that $\forall w \in \mathcal{V}$,

$$\left(w, \frac{\partial c}{\partial t} \right)_\Omega + \left(\nabla w, M_c \nabla \mu_c + \frac{1}{\chi} \nabla M_c \Delta c \right)_\Omega + \left(\Delta w, \frac{1}{\chi} M_c \Delta c \right)_\Omega = 0, \tag{6}$$

where $(., .)_\Omega$ represents the $\mathcal{L}^2$ inner product over the domain Ω and $\mathcal{V}$ needs to be $\mathcal{H}^2$-conforming, where $\mathcal{H}^2$ represents the Sobolev space of square integrable functions with square integrable first and second derivatives. We now discretize the infinite dimensional problem in space, and derive the semidiscrete formulation which can be stated as: find $c^h \in \mathcal{V}^h \subset \mathcal{V}$ such that $\forall w^h \in \mathcal{V}^h \subset \mathcal{V}$

$$\left(w^h, \dot{c}^h \right)_\Omega + \left(\nabla w^h, M_c^h \nabla \mu_c^h + \frac{1}{\chi} \nabla M_c^h \Delta c^h \right)_\Omega + \left(\Delta w^h, \frac{1}{\chi} M_c^h \Delta c^h \right)_\Omega = 0. \tag{7}$$

We suppose that the discrete space $\mathcal{V}^h$ is spanned by the linear combination of basis functions N_A, which are $\mathcal{C}^1$-continuous B-spline basis functions.

With regards to PetIGA, if one is able to get equation (7) and an initial condition, testing of the residual can already be done to check if the system converges to a solution, or compare the results to a benchmark problem. Being a nonlinear time-dependent problem, the Cahn-Hilliard model requires the use of a Jacobian if a Newton-type scheme [8] is used. Nonetheless, by being built on top of PETSc, the user can use available functions to approximate the Jacobian. This can save valuable time while prototyping and debugging code, as the residual can be tested without explicitly coding the Jacobian [4]. With regards to the time-discretization, we employ the adaptive scheme from [8], which uses the generalized-α method. By setting an initial condition c_0 such that

$$c(t = 0, \mathbf{x}) = 0.63 + \eta, \tag{8}$$

over a unit square, with η a uniform random variable in $[-0.05, 0.05]$, phase separation can be observed. In Figure 2, snapshots of the evolution of an initiall mixed and immiscible binary fluid are shown. Notice that at steady state th phases have separated, which is consistent with the thermodynamics of this pro cess. Given the adaptive time-stepping algorithm used, and the highly nonlinea nature due to the logarithmic chemical potential of the problem, the number of nonlinear iterations per (accepted) time step varies between 2 and 10 throughou the simulation. More details on this particular method can be found in [8].

We present preliminary strong scaling results for this problem and show then on table 5.1. The code was run on Shaheen, a BlueGene/P supercomputer a King Abdullah University of Science and Technology, and the results show how PetIGA is well suited for high-performance applications.

Table 1. Scaling results for the two-dimensional Cahn-Hilliard equation. The compu tational mesh used consisted of $8192^2 C^1$-quadratic B-splines. The computational tim reported refers to the time taken for 10 time steps.

Cores (N)	Time t (s)	Speedup	Efficiency
512	2296	1.00	100%
1024	1207	1.90	95%
2048	578	3.97	99%
8192	147	15.62	98%

5.2   The Phase-Field Crystal Equation

The phase-field crystal equation is a sixth-order, nonlinear time-dependent pa tial differential equation. Although initially developed to solve solidificatio problems with both spatial and temporal scales orders of magnitude larger tha the ones available through molecular dynamics [13], it has since then been use to tackle issues in crack propagation, dislocation dynamics, and formation foams among others [14]. In this equation, the order parameter ϕ represents a atomistic density field, which is periodic in the solid state and uniform in th liquid one. The free energy functional used in this model is given by

$$\mathcal{F}_{PFC} = \int_{\Omega} \left(\frac{\phi^4}{4} - \epsilon \frac{\phi^2}{2} + \frac{1}{2} \left(\phi^2 - 2|\nabla\phi|^2 + (\Delta\phi)^2 \right) \right) dV$$

The same procedure shown in section 5.1 to derive the partial differential equa tion is again applied, such that the evolution in time of the atomistic densi field is defined as

$$\frac{\partial \phi}{\partial t} = \Delta \left((1 + \Delta)^2 \phi + \phi^3 - \epsilon\phi \right).$$

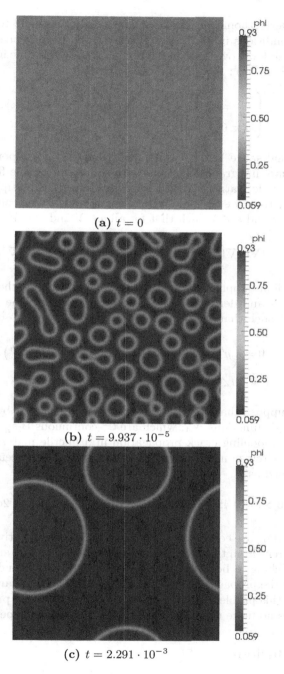

(a) $t = 0$

(b) $t = 9.937 \cdot 10^{-5}$

(c) $t = 2.291 \cdot 10^{-3}$

Fig. 2. Transient solution to the Cahn-Hilliard problem in two spatial dimensions, subject to a random initial condition and periodic boundary conditions. The weak form is discretized in space by a mesh of $128^2 C^1$-quadratic elements. The initially mixed fluid phase-separates.

By considering homogeneous boundary conditions equal to zero and periodic boundary conditions in all directions, the strong form of the problem can then be stated as follows: over the spatial domain Ω and the time interval $]0, T[$, given $\phi_0 : \Omega \longmapsto \mathbb{R}$, find $\phi : \Omega \times [0, T] \longmapsto \mathbb{R}$ such that

$$\begin{cases} \dfrac{\partial \phi}{\partial t} = \Delta \left[(1 + \Delta)^2 \phi - \epsilon \phi + \phi^3 \right] & \text{on } \Omega \times]0, T] \\ \phi(\mathbf{x}, 0) = \phi_0(\mathbf{x}) & \text{on } \bar{\Omega} \end{cases} \tag{11}$$

The functional space $V \in \mathcal{H}^3$ is defined, where $\mathcal{H}^3$ corresponds to the Sobolev space of square integrable functions with square integrable first, second derivatives and third derivatives. A weak form is obtained by multiplying equation (11) by a test functions $q \in \mathcal{H}^3$, and integrating by parts. One can state the problem as: find $\phi \in V$ and $\sigma \in V$ such that for all $q \in V$ and $w \in V$

$$\left(q, \frac{\partial \phi}{\partial t} \right)_\Omega + (\nabla q, \nabla((1 - \epsilon)\phi + \phi^3))_\Omega - 2(\Delta q, \Delta \phi)_\Omega + (\nabla^3 q, \nabla^3 \phi)_\Omega = 0 \tag{12}$$

To derive a finite approximation to the problem, we pick the finite dimensional space $V^h \subset V$ and derive a semi discrete formulation. The problem is then to find $\phi^h \in V^h$ such that for all $q^h \in V^h$

$$0 = \left(q^h, \frac{\partial \phi^h}{\partial t} \right)_\Omega + (\nabla q^h, \nabla((1 - \epsilon)\phi^h + (\phi^h)^3))_\Omega$$
$$- 2(\Delta q^h, \Delta \phi^h)_\Omega + (\nabla^3 q^h, \nabla^3 \phi^h)_\Omega = 0 \tag{13}$$

We again suppose that the discrete space V^h is spanned by the linear combination of basis functions N_A, which are C^2-continuous B-spline basis functions. An example modeling crack propagation in a ductile material [18] is shown in Figure 3. A circular notch of radius $20\pi/3$ is set at the center of a crystalline lattice, defined as

$$\phi(t = 0, \mathbf{x}) = 0.49 + \cos(q_x x)\cos\left(q_y y/\sqrt{3} \right) - 0.5\cos\left(2q_y y/\sqrt{3} \right). \tag{14}$$

where q_x and q_y are equal to $1.16/\sqrt{2}$ and $1.15/\sqrt{2}$, respectively. These assigned values, different from the equilibrium values that q_x and q_y are supposed to take, induce stretching in both the x and y directions of 16% and 15%, respectively, and explain the propagating crack in the domain. With regards to the numerical simulation, this problem is not as hard to solve as the one presented previously, and requires no more than 4 nonlinear Newton iterations per time step.

6   Conclusions

In this paper, a scalable implementation of isogeometric analysis is presented. The framework is built in such a way that so as to have the the user only worry about coding the discrete variational formulation of the problem. Besides

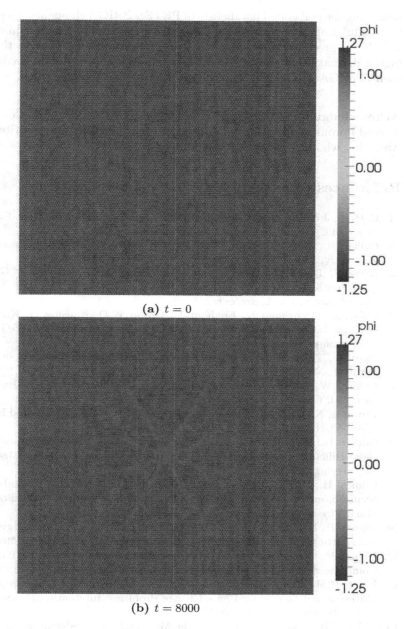

Fig. 3. Transient solution to the phase-field crystal equation in two spatial dimensions. A square domain $\Omega = [0, 1024\pi/3]^2$ is considered. The computational mesh is composed of $1024^2 \mathcal{C}^2$-cubic elements. The generalized-α method was used to handle the temporal integration, along with a time step size of $\Delta t = 5$. The initial crack propagates throughout the domain.

inheriting the embedded parallelism of PETSc, PetIGA choice also gives access to the modular options that PETSc has to solve partial differential equations, such as solvers, preconditioners and time-integration schemes. Due to the inherent high-order nature of phase-field models and the high-resolution needed to solve them, PetIGA is a sensible choice as a framework to handle them.

Acknowledgments. This work was supported by NumPor, the Center for Numerical Porous Media. We would also like to acknowledge the contribution of A. Ahmadia, who provided the strong scaling results.

References

1. Cottrell, J.A., Hughes, T.J.R., Bazilevs, Y.: Isogeometric Analysis: Toward Unification of CAD and FEA. John Wiley and Sons (2009)
2. Collier, N., Dalcin, L., Calo, V.M.: PetIGA: High-Performance Isogeometric Analysis. arxiv, 1305.4452 (2013)
3. Balay, S., Buschelman, K., Gropp, W.D., Kaushik, D., Knepley, M.G., McInnes, L.C., Smith, B.S., Zhang, H.: PETSc Web page (2014), http://www.mcs.anl.gov/petsc
4. Balay, S., Buschelman, K., Eijkhout, V., Gropp, W.D., Kaushik, D., Knepley, M.G., McInnes, L.C., Smith, B.S., Zhang, H.: PETSc Users Manual, ANL-95/11 - Revision 3.5, Argonne National Laboratory (2014)
5. Piegl, L., Tiller, W.: The NURBS Book. Monographs in Visual Communication. Springer, New York (1995)
6. Cahn, J.W., Hilliard, J.E.: Free energy of a nonuniform system. I. Interfacial free energy. J. Chem. Phys. 28, 258 (1958)
7. Provatas, N., Elder, K.: Phase-field Methods in Materials Science and Engineering. Wiley-VCH (2010)
8. Gómez, H., Calo, V.M., Bazilevs, Y., Hughes, T.J.R.: Isogeometric analysis of the Cahn-Hilliard phase-field model. Computer Methods in Applied Mechanics and Engineering 197(49-50), 4333–4352 (2008)
9. Gómez, H., Hughes, T.J.R.: Provably unconditionally stable, second-order time-accurate, mixed variational methods for phase-field models. Journal of Computational Physics 230(13), 5310–5327 (2011)
10. Vignal, P., Dalcin, L., Brown, D.L., Collier, N., Calo, V.M.: An energy-stable convex splitting for the phase-field crystal equation. arxiv, 1405.3488 (2014)
11. Vignal, P., Collier, N., Calo, V.M.: Phase Field Modeling Using PetIGA. Procedia Computer Science 18, 1614–1623 (2013)
12. Elliot, C.M.: The Cahn-Hilliard Model for the Kinetics of Pbase Separation. In: Mathematical Models for Phase Change Problems. International Series in Numerical Mathematics, vol. 88, pp. 35–73 (1989)
13. Elder, K.R., Katakowski, M., Haataja, M., Grant, M.: Modeling elasticity in crystal growth. Phys. Rev. Lett. 88 (2002)
14. Emmerich, H., Granasy, L., Lowen, H.: Selected issues of phase-field crystal simulations. The European Physical Journal Plus 126, 1–18 (2011)

15. Collier, N., Dalcin, L., Pardo, D., Calo, V.M.: The cost of continuity: performance of iterative solvers on isogeometric finite elements. SIAM Journal on Scientific Computing 35, 767–784 (2013)
16. Collier, N., Pardo, D., Dalcin, L., Paszynski, M., Calo, V.M.: The cost of continuity: A study of the performance of isogeometric finite elements using direct solvers. Computer Methods in Applied Mechanics and Engineering 213-216, 353–361 (2012)
17. PetIGA repository, https://bitbucket.org/dalcinl/petiga/
18. Gomez, H., Nogueira, X.: An unconditionally energy-stable method for the phase field crystal equation. Comput. Methods Appl. Mech. Eng., 249–252, 52–61 (2012)

Alya Multiphysics Simulations on Intel's Xeon Phi Accelerators

Mariano Vázquez[1,2], Guillaume Houzeaux[1],
Félix Rubio[1], and Christian Simarro[1]

[1] Barcelona Supercomputing Center, Spain
[2] IIIA-CSIC, Spain

Abstract. In this paper we describe the porting of Alya, our HPC-based multiphysics simulation code to Intel's Xeon Phi, assessing code performance. This is a continuation of a short white paper where the solid mechanics module was tested. Here, we add two tests more and asses the code on a much wider context. From the Physical point of view, we solve a complex multiphysics problem (combustion in a kiln furnace) and a single-physics problem with an explicit scheme (compressible flow around a wing). From the architecture point of view, we perform new tests using multiple accelerators on different hosts.

1 Introduction

Alya (see for instance [3,4,10,2,5,9]) is a multiphysics simulation code developed in Barcelona Supercomputing Center. Thanks to HPC-based programming techniques, it is able to simulate multi-physics problems with high parallel efficiency in supercomputers, being already tested up to one hundred thousand cores in Blue Waters supercomputer [10]. Alya simulates multiphysics problems such as fluid mechanics (compressible and incompressible), non linear solid mechanics, combustion and chemical reactions, electromagnetism, etc. Multiphysics coupling includes contact problem and deforming solids, fluid-structure interaction or fluid-solid thermal coupling. Its parallel architecture is based in an automatic mesh partition (using Metis [1]) and MPI tasks. Additionally it has an inner parallelization layer based on OpenMP threads, which combined with MPI tasks results in a hybrid parallelization scheme. In this paper we will focus in the pure MPI case.

Since years ago, heterogeneous systems with accelerators have been a very appealing alternative to more traditional homogeneous systems. Accelerators are hardware specifically designed to perform very efficiently a certain kind of operations, typical of number-crunching situations. In the last years, GPGPUs have emerged as the de-facto main alternative. NVIDIA, which is the largest manufacturer of GPGPUs, has been carrying out a huge effort to put all the computational power of its accelerators in the hands of scientists. They developed a powerful programming model, CUDA, to help programmers to adapt their codes to them. However, NVIDIA's GPGPUs' architecture is not well-suited for

G. Hernández et al. (Eds.): CARLA 2014, CCIS 485, pp. 248–254, 2014.

all the cases, being very efficient for a particular kind of algorithmics. The fact is that in GPGPUs regular data structures heavily condition parallel action on these structures. This fact penalizes a widespread use, although makes them the best option for such things such as simulation on cartesian meshes. As a supplementary drawback, in order to get the most of them, very heavy code re-engineering is required.

A second option that has appeared more recently is the INTEL Xeon Phi (IXP) accelerator, also known as MIC. Being based on the X-86 architecture, they do not require a special re-coding. IXP represents a very appealing architecture for codes such as Alya for several reasons. Firstly, Alya does not exploit mesh cartesian structure because it is specially designed for non-structured meshes, where connectivity bandwidth is not uniform and data access is more complex. Due to their flexibility, non-structured meshes are well suited for complex geometries. Secondly, due to the Physics that Alya solves, the numerical schemes cannot guarantee that all the threads will have the same amount of work. Finally, coupled multi-physics requires a lot of flexibility to program the different subproblems and, above all, the coupling schemes. It is worth to mention that Alya is around 500K lines, with more than 40 researchers working, experts in different disciplines. There is only one version of the code, which is standard enough to run in several platforms, and specifically designed to run in parallel and sequential in the same version. We made of portability, flexibility and code re-usage three of the main pillars of Alya. Therefore, we look for an accelerator where we can still keep the same flags up. This paper goes in this direction, exploring Intel Xeon Phi possibilities.

We attack the porting to Intel Xeon Phi in stages. In this paper and as a starting point, we focus in MPI parallelism. It is a relatively natural path, because Alya has already shown good scalability for cases where parallel work is distributed only through MPI tasks. Additionally, we observe that debugging a parallel application based on MPI tasks is easier than when based on OpenMP threads, so we can be sure where is the origin of differences in results, if any, and in performance. In a next paper we will address the hybrid case.

The tests have been carried out in native mode, where the code is compiled and run on the accelerator.

Briefly, we wanted to explore the following aspects:

- How much porting effort is required and how much of the code must be re-written and/or reengineered?
- As Alya is specially targetted to engineering simulations, would it be possible for a small company to upgrade a workstation just by buying a couple of IXP? Is it possible for them to run the same kind of problems with little effort but still scaling?
- Being under the same parallelization scheme, i.e. MPI-tasks, could IXP be considered as a "small cluster"?
- What is the behaviour of Alya when using accelerators hosted at different nodes?

2   Computational Aspects

2.1   Porting and Running on Intel Xeon Phi Coprocessor

Porting was not complex at all and no supplementary programming was required. At the moment of performing the tests, BSC's main supercomputer, Marenostrum, was being upgraded to include 84 Xeon Phi accelerators. For that reason, the main effort was indeed to provide feedback to the system administrators in order to do a clean set-up of the IXP. Alya is all written in Fortran 2003, strictly following the standard. Except for Metis [1] no third-party library is used. Alya has been compiled and tested in several supercomputer architectures using different compilers, including Intel products. Therefore, no special effort was required, except for adding the compiling option -mmic.

All cases were tested on Marenostrum III (MNIII), whose computing nodes are 2x Sandy Bridge-EP E5-2670, 2.6GHz/1600 20M 8-core, with 32 Gb. Each node has 2 PCIe x24, each one connected to a Xeon Phi 5110P with 8Gb memory. One of the two Sandy Bridge has an Infiniband card connected to a PCI-E x8. Finally, Mellanox provides a virtual interface to each Xeon Phi, allowing a fast and transparent interconnection between all the 84 accelerators in MNIII. Alya is compiled using the last version of the Intel Fortran Compiler and the Intel MPI Library.

In both of the cases shown here, Xeon Phi performance is assessed taking into account the followin aspects:

- Each Xeon Phi has 60 cores, each of them allowing up to 4 *hardware* threads. Therefore, each Xeon Phi can run in parallel up to 240 MPI tasks.
- Pure MPI cases are considered, setting the OpenMP environment variable to OMP_NUMTHREADS=1. This is done explicitly to force single *software* threads in regions where Alya has OpenMP'ed loops.
- Running in native mode, with all the MPI tasks running on board the Xeon Phi. In this first test, the host does not provide computing power.
- MPI tasks are shuffled among four accelerators corresponding to two different hosts.
- No special compilation options was used, except for -O1.

2.2   Simulation Examples

We have chosen several cases of increasing complexity, to examine different simulation scenarios and schemes. The common features of all the cases tested are: relatively complex geometries, non-structured meshes, mixed different element types (tetrahedra, hexahedra, prisms and pyramids). Strong scalability is measured by computing the cpu-time required for each cycle of the time steps loop. Both explicit and implicit schemes are tested. In this paper we show the strong scalability for compressible flow and incompressible flow and combustion for a multi-phsyics case.

Fig. 1. Downwind view and pressure contours showing the characteristic lambda structure for the Onera M6 wing (left) and kiln flow temperature contours

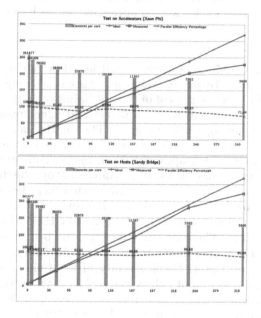

Fig. 2. Onera M6 wing: Strong scalability for both the Xeon Phi (left) and the hosts. Ideal and measured scalabilities, parallel efficiency and mean number of elements per core are shown

Onera M6 Wing: Compressible Inviscid Flow, Explicit Scheme. This is compressible flow passing an Onera M6 wing, under the following conditions: Mach 0.8395, Reynolds number 11.72E06, angle of attack 3.06 degrees and angle of side-slip 0.0 degrees [8]. Flow is solved with an explicit scheme, with a Preconditioned Variational Multiscale (P-VMS) scheme, presented in [7]. Figure 1 shows the pressure contour plot on the downstream surface of the wing. Figure 2 shows the strong scalability for the Xeon Phi. The mesh is made of 1.8M tetrahedra, with four degrees of freedom per node (momentum vector, density scalar and energy scalar).

Figure 2 shows the strong scalability of the Onera M6 compressible flow explicit solver, for both the host nodes and the accelerators. This comparison is done to assess whether the communication overhead is similarly penalizing both cases. Efficiency is degraded a bit earlier in the case of the Xeon Phi due to the fact that the accelerators are much slower processors than the hosts, up to 20 times slower. This fact is commented below in the conclusions. As in previous works [10], we define the scalability "sweet spot" for a certain problem by keeping the parallel efficiency higher than, say, 75% - 80%, while increasing the number of MPI tasks. This gives a mean amount of elements per task which is the lower limit for sustained linear scalability. This number depends on the physical problem solved and how it is implemented, the solution scheme, the size and element types, etc: in this case, compressible flow solved explicitly in 1.8M tetrahedra.

Kiln Furnace: Low Mach Incompressible Flow with Combustion a Chemical Reactions, Implicit Scheme. This is a complex multi-physics problem. It is a kiln furnace, typical of cement industry. It is a large cylindrical vessel in slow rotatory motion where concrete and aggregates is cooked, with temperature values rising up to 2000 degrees. The length can go up to 120 meters and the diameter, up to 20 meters. The air is simulated for an incompressible flow regime with a low Mach approximation, temperature transport is solved with a the heat flow equation as it is convected by the fluid and several species are transported, which reacts with each other, both producing and consuming energy. In this case, there are 5 species. The three problems are solved in a seggregated strongly coupled way, all of them through an implicit time integration scheme. The problem is deeply described in [6].

Figure 1 shows a shapshot of the temperature contours in a kiln during the ignition phase. Figure 3 plots the scalability of the fluid phase. In this case, the elements-per-core sweet spot, where the scalability is sustained with no less than 80% efficiency, goes up to around 10K. In this case, the sweet spot is lower, which allows the authors to go no further than 80 MPI tasks withoug a serious lose of parallel performance.

3   Conclusions and Future Lines

This paper is a very preliminary leverage of Alya on Intel Xeon Phi accelerators. Intel Xeon Phi is a valuable option as an accelerator for supercomputing applications on complex geometries with multiphysics. This is specially the case when the simulation code has already being parallelized using MPI. Just by compiling the code using the -mmic option, a running binary is obtained, with very similar scalability properties when compared to the host binary, with no code re-writting or re-engineering. In this paper we tested it in multi-physics examples with both explicit and implicit schemes. However, there are several points to improve:

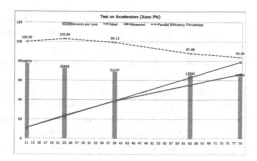

Fig. 3. Strong scalability the Xeon Phi for the flow solution on the kiln furnace simulation. Ideal and measured scalabilities, parallel efficiency and mean number of elements per core are shown.

– A straight comparison with the speed with the Sandy Bridge hosts leaves IXP way behind: the same example with **no MPI** runs around 20 times faster in the Sandy Bridge, which is surprising considering the differences in processors clock (slightly 2x favouring the host). That is to say that, running the same sequential case, one MPI task takes around 20 times longer in the Xeon Phi. Further tracing of the code to analyze its performance is required. Also, it is very likely that a specific IXP compiling option set will make them run much faster. In this paper we have left this optimization aside purposedly.
– The powerful hosts were not used in the runs here, only the IXP. Now that we are sure that the code scales well in the accelerators and once a proper compiling option set is obtained for the IXP, we can establish the true speed ratio between both computing units. Taking into account these figures, we can shuffle the MPI tasks among the host and the accelerator, giving METIS a weight to do a balanced partition.
– Software threading is still to be analyzed, specially for the hybrid MPI-OpenMP mode.

References

1. Metis, family of multilevel partitioning algorithms, `http://glaros.dtc.umn.edu/gkhome/views/metis`
2. Casoni, E., Jérusalem, A., Samaniego, C., Eguzkitza, B., Lafortune, P., Tjahjanto, D., Sáez, X., Houzeaux, G., Vazquez, M.: Alya: computational solid mechanics for supercomputers. Archives of Computational Methods in Engineering (in press, 2014)
3. Houzeaux, G., Vázquez, M., Aubry, R., Cela, J.: A massively parallel fractional step solver for incompressible flows. J. Comput. Phys. 228(17), 6316–6332 (2009)
4. Houzeaux, G., Vázquez, M., Saez, X., Cela, J.: Hybrid mpi-openmp performance in massively parallel computational fluid dynamics. Presented at PARCFD 2008 Internacional Conference on Parallel Computacional Fluid Dynamics, Lyon, France (2008)

5. Marras, S., Moragues, M., Vázquez, M., Jorba, O., Houzeaux, G.: A variational multiscale stabilized finite element method for the solution of the euler equations of nonhydrostatic stratified flows. Journal of Computational Physics 236(0), 380–407 (2013), http://www.sciencedirect.com/science/article/pii/S0021999112006626

6. Mira, D., Ávila, M., Owen, H., Cucchietti, F.M., Vázquez, M., Houzeaux, G.: Large-eddy simulation of the mixing and combustion of the gas phase of a cement kiln using a massive parallel code. Computers and Fluids (submitted, 2014)

7. Moragues, M., Vázquez, M., Houzeaux, G.: Preconditioned vms for compressible flows. In: XI World Congress on Computational Mechanics. CIMNE, Barcelona (2014)

8. Schmitt, V., Charpin, F.: Pressure distributions on the onera-m6-wing at transonic mach numbers. experimental data base for computer program assessment. Tech. Rep. AR 138, AGARD (1979)

9. Vázquez, M., Rubio, F., Houzeaux, G., González, J., Giménez, J., Beltran, V., de la Cruz, R., Folch, A.: Xeon phi performance for hpc-based computational mechanics codes. Tech. rep., PRACE-RI (2014), http://www.prace-ri.eu/IMG/pdf/wp130.pdf

10. Vázquez, M., Houzeaux, G., Koric, S., Artigues, A., Aguado-Sierra, J., Aris, R., Mira, D., Calmet, H., Cucchietti, F., Owen, H., Taha, A., Cela, J.M.: Alya: Towards exascale for engineering simulation codes. arxiv.org (2014), http://arxiv.org/abs/1404.4881

Author Index